The Daley Show

The Daley Show

Inside the Transformative Reign of Chicago's Richard M. Daley

FORREST CLAYPOOL

Foreword by David Axelrod

3 FIELDS BOOKS
An imprint of the University of Illinois Press

Library of Congress Cataloging-in-Publication Data
Names: Claypool, Forrest, 1957– author.
Title: The Daley show : inside the transformative reign of
    Chicago's Richard M. Daley / Forrest Claypool.
Other titles: Inside the transformative reign of Chicago's Richard
    M. Daley
Description: Champaign, IL : 3 Fields Books, an imprint of the
    University of Illinois Press, [2024] | Includes bibliographical
    references and index.
Identifiers: LCCN 2024012433 (print) | LCCN 2024012434
    (ebook) | ISBN 9780252046193 (cloth) | ISBN 9780252047466
    (ebook)
Subjects: LCSH: Daley, Richard M. (Richard Michael), 1942– |
    Mayors—Illinois—Chicago—Biography. | Chicago (Ill.)—
    Politics and government—1951– | Chicago (Ill.)—Biography. |
    Claypool, Forrest, 1957–
Classification: LCC F548.54.D35 C63 2024 (print) | LCC F548.54.
    D35 (ebook) | DDC 977.3/11043092 [B]—dc23/eng/20240402
LC record available at https://lccn.loc.gov/2024012433
LC ebook record available at https://lccn.loc.gov/2024012434

To Daina, Lee, Max, and Caitlin
with love, gratitude, and pride.

And to Richard Dennis, who showed me
that contrarian thinking, at least in politics,
is a lonely but virtuous path.

Contents

Photographs and illustrations follow pages 104 and 190.

Foreword

The day I walked into the *Chicago Tribune* newsroom for the first time as a young reporter in 1976, the mayor was Richard J. Daley, who, by then, had ruled Chicago and its politics for a generation and had left an indelible imprint on the city.

The day I left Chicago, thirty-two years later, to become senior adviser to President Barack Obama in January 2009, the mayor was Richard M. Daley—Richard the Second—who had eclipsed his father's record for longevity and shaped the city in ways that would be felt for generations to come.

Remarkably, the Daleys occupied the citadel of power on the fifth floor of city hall for nearly half a century, separated by twelve turbulent years of change.

In many ways, father and son were strikingly similar. They looked alike. They sounded alike. They each wore their passion for the city on their sleeves and spoke in a mangled syntax that only Chicagoans could understand and love. They also understood how to leverage their power to get things done and shared an extraordinary vision that would help transform Chicago from a provincial Midwestern town to a gleaming international city.

Yet the times during which the father and the son governed were very different, and in some important ways, so were they.

Melding the chairmanship of the Cook County Democratic organization with the vast power and patronage vested in the mayor's office, Richard J. Daley built a legendary political machine that gave him control over every aspect of local government and politics. Business and labor leaders courted him. Presidents came calling. Local politicians, who relied on him for jobs and contracts, bowed to his will. And he used that power to advance his governing goals.

First elected in 1955, Daley quickly earned a national reputation as a doer, a builder, a skillful manager of his self-styled City That Works. With a steady flow of federal dollars, he expanded O'Hare International Airport and Chicago's status as a national transportation hub. He engineered the construction of the city's expressway system to ease passage to and from the growing suburbs. He encouraged the construction of world-class skyscrapers and lured major corporations to downtown Chicago.

But as the turbulent 1960s unfolded, the focus shifted from Daley as a visionary leader to Daley as a bulwark against social change.

Chicago's historic practice of housing segregation was highlighted by Rev. Martin Luther King Jr. during the iconic civil rights leader's open-housing marches in the city during the summer of 1966. When riots ensued after King was assassinated two years later, Daley garnered national attention with his "shoot-to-kill" order against arsonists. And when his police pummeled antiwar protesters on the streets of Chicago during the 1968 Democratic National Convention, a red-faced Mayor Daley became, to many liberals and young people, a symbol of intransigence and repression.

By the time Richard M. Daley was elected mayor in 1989, Chicago had changed. Federal court decrees had eroded the patronage system his father had helped build. Years of racial resistance after the election in 1983 of the city's first Black mayor, Harold Washington, and the void that Washington's untimely death in 1987 created, had ground city hall to a halt. Problems were festering, downtown was dying and Chicago's future looked bleak. The *Wall Street Journal* captured the city's futile, fractious politics in a searing headline, describing Chicago as "Beirut on the Lake."

This was the hand Rich Daley was dealt as mayor. He took office with far greater challenges than his father had faced coming in and fewer levers to deal with them. Yet he amassed an extraordinary record of achievement that rivaled or eclipsed his dad's, deploying some of the governing principles he learned at his father's knee while forging his own path forward.

Once a brash and impudent prince of the machine, Daley had been humbled over the previous thirteen years. Without his dad's clout, he had to learn how to navigate in politics by his own lights. The loss of his three-year-old son, Kevin, had deepened his empathy. And the loss of his first mayoral race in 1983 to Washington—a brutal, racially charged contest that included former mayor Jane Byrne—left him determined to be a healing force.

Daley ran in 1989 on the premise that racial reconciliation was a prelude to progress, and once elected, proved as good as his word. He rejected the perverse political calculus that valued division over addition. By reaching out to every community, he immediately lowered the temperature in a city that had been boiling over. He took control of the city council and worked his connections in Springfield, the state capital, to launch an ambitious array of major initiatives. He reinvigorated downtown Chicago and improved the quality of life in neighborhoods. He upgraded Chicago's schools and parks, public transportation, roads, and airports. Over two decades, Daley literally remade the face of the city, bringing a new aesthetic sense to the town and attracting more businesses, tourists, and positive reviews for his city.

Rich Daley wasn't flawless, nor was the city he left when he retired in 2011. While he never sought to emulate his father as a political boss, he still took care of his friends and allies and had his share of scandals. The big visions that transformed

Chicago, and labor peace, also were expensive, leaving due bills for future mayors and taxpayers. He joined in antigang marches in the neighborhoods and wept for children lost but turned a blind eye to police practices he should not have tolerated.

Still, Chicago was a different city at the end of Daley's long tenure, a city in many ways better and stronger because of his leadership.

How he did it, and what we can learn from it, are the subjects of this book, written by a man who not only observed Daley work but helped execute his vision.

I first met Forrest Claypool in the early 1980s on a street corner on Michigan Avenue outside Tribune Tower, where I worked as a political reporter.

We were introduced by Forrest's then boss, Pat Quinn, an irrepressible, rabble-rousing young reformer who had just been elected to the local Board of Tax Appeals. Despite its eye-glazing name, the office was of great value and importance to the local ward bosses—several of whom doubled as property tax appeal lawyers and counted on their clout with the board to score sweetheart deals for their clients. Quinn was determined to clean up the office, which a few years earlier had been hit by a sweeping federal probe that would send dozens to prison. He enlisted Forrest, a newly minted attorney, in that task. (Decades later, Quinn would become the governor of Illinois.)

Tall and slender with a big, toothy grin, Forrest very much looked and sounded like the small-town, downstate kid he was. But over the years in Chicago, he would become a prominent and impactful government reformer in his own right and one of the most important relationships in my life.

The year after that chance meeting on the street, I quit the newspaper business to become the communications director and eventually the campaign manager for Paul Simon, a congressman from downstate Illinois who was running for the US Senate. Forrest was working for the campaign, and I quickly came to understand what a brilliant, incisive mind he had. He became my indispensable, all-purpose lieutenant in that campaign, which we won despite long odds and a national Republican landslide behind President Ronald Reagan.

After the race, Forrest joined me in launching a consulting firm to provide strategy and produce media for political campaigns. But gifted as he was at messaging and strategy, he wouldn't stay long. Forrest's passion was not politics for its own sake. He saw it as a means to bring about needed change, so when one of our early clients, Rich Daley, was elected mayor, Forrest eagerly accepted a post developing and executing policy in the mayor's office. He would serve two stints as Daley's chief of staff and later reprised that role for Mayor Rahm Emanuel.

In 1993, Daley engineered Forrest's appointment as superintendent of the Chicago Park District, a sprawling bureaucracy that has in its province six hundred city parks. The park district had traditionally been a rich source of patronage for the old Democratic machine but rarely a paragon of imagination or efficiency. Now Daley wanted Forrest to clean the agency up and breathe new life into the park system, which the mayor viewed as essential to the city's quality of life.

Forrest seized Daley's mandate and wrote a record of government reform that would be taught at schools of public administration for decades to come. Shrinking the district's bloated headquarters, Forrest decentralized the park district, sending the dollars to local parks, where he encouraged innovative new programs and held local supervisors accountable. He rehabilitated park field houses, including classic old jewels in neighborhoods throughout the city, and helped facilitate the creation of Millennium Park on South Michigan Avenue, which would become a magnet to draw business and tourists and a key to the revitalization of downtown Chicago.

Forrest later brought to bear that same extraordinary talent and focus—and lessons drawn from his years with Daley—when Mayor Emanuel recruited him to rescue the Chicago Transit Authority from a fiscal and administrative morass. Once again, he wrote a new chapter in government reform, improving efficiency and customer experience in an agency that is vital to the city's success.

In all these assignments—and through his eight years as a reform-minded county commissioner and in his last posting as superintendent of the Chicago public schools—Forrest proved himself to be a brilliant, relentless, and impactful force for positive change. His public works and those of the subject of this book recall the words of Robert F. Kennedy:

"Some people see things as they are and ask 'Why?' I dream of things that never were and ask, 'Why not?'"

David Axelrod

Prologue

"All things good of this earth flow into the
City because of the City's greatness."
—Pericles

Cities are the engines of human progress. With density and diversity, they attract talented and ambitious people seeking intimate collaboration, and the scale to leverage it in spectacular ways—producing breakthroughs in business and finance, medicine, the arts, architecture, science, and technology.

In his book *The Wealth of Cities,* the former Milwaukee mayor John Norquist observes that most urban centers formed originally as marketplaces: "With few exceptions, such as Washington, D.C., cities were created by human interaction and market forces, not by government, and would exist regardless of the form of government."[1]

Great cities are bustling centers of creativity and energy, but they are also complex and fragile. They can be advanced or buffeted by technological, demographic, and economic currents. But *leadership,* more than any other factor, determines how a city navigates those currents and if it is viable and vibrant.

In 1989, as Mayor Richard M. Daley assumed office, Chicago was in an advanced state of atrophy. Violent crime was endemic, including a scourge of murders that began in 1970 and didn't reach its peak until the early 1990s.[2] The city's public schools were roiled by nine teacher strikes in eighteen years, historic dropout rates, and bankruptcy. Chicago's industry was in a long secular decline, hemorrhaging jobs. The city faced an unremitting outflow of people.

John McCarron, the *Chicago Tribune*'s urban affairs columnist, said that when he began covering the grim and moldering city in the 1970s, "The question was, 'Would the last person to leave Chicago please turn out the lights?'"[3]

In 1981, the *Tribune* published a seminal four-part series, "City on the Brink," writing that Chicago appeared to be "on the ropes . . . its future uncertain." The series author, R. C. Longworth, called Chicago "an economic invalid," losing businesses, jobs, and tax revenues and failing to replace the industries that were the original reason for its existence.

"The condition may be permanent," Longworth wrote, "unless the people responsible for its economic future can reverse the long, steady, and seemingly endless slide . . . [o]ften, cities stricken in this way become irrelevant. Business moves away. So do the best young people. The population ages. The city becomes a backwater."[4]

One after another, experts told him, "There is no reason to think it will ever turn around."[5]

But it did.

What transpired in the following decades dramatically reversed the city's downward trajectory, catapulting Chicago into the ranks of the most admired and influential international cities.[6] Although a robust economy in the 1990s greased the wheels, strong mayoral leadership was critical to Chicago's rebirth.

The man behind the city's comeback, Richard M. Daley, was a unique leader. He had a rare combination of political acumen, municipal management insights, and urban-planning vision. He shrewdly and methodically amassed enormous power and relentlessly applied it to lift Chicago from a historic morass.

"In an age of media-tested politicians who are better at sound bites than substance, Daley is an anomaly, an inarticulate politician with a homely countenance, a prickly disposition, and an appetite for important but mundane tasks," wrote the *Tribune* columnist Steve Chapman at the height of Daley's long tenure. "Yet he has reigned like a monarch, largely unchallenged and unchallengeable."[7]

Daley ultimately *was* challenged by an unforeseen crisis that shook the city and the world. The Great Recession shrank Chicago's economy and revenues overnight while exposing high debt levels and contributed to social and political changes that have begun to sap the city's vitality. Unless arrested soon, these forces will threaten Chicago's place among the nation's elite cities.[8]

I arrived in Chicago, a downstate native fresh out of the University of Illinois Law School, the year "City on the Brink" was published. Less than eight years later, I was serving as Mayor Daley's chief of staff. As with everyone who worked for him, our relationship was complex. But in the nearly ten years I served under Daley, including two stints as his top aide, I observed up close his distinctive political and managerial talents as well as his undermining weaknesses. I saw the man underneath the public image and the emotions that often drove him.

Having lived through and participated in some of the tumult that preceded his mayoralty, I also witnessed the many competing forces tugging at the city's fabric and came to appreciate the value of sophisticated and energetic executive leadership in creating cohesion and common purpose in a great city.

By the time he left office, Richard M. Daley had eclipsed his legendary father's record as the longest-serving mayor of Chicago. This book examines those twenty-two years as well as the turbulent preceding years, in which he overcame shocks, reversals, betrayals, and personal tragedies to claim city hall's fifth floor.

This book follows Daley from the tempestuous years following his father's 1976 death in office, including his remarkable personal and political transformation as a state legislator, to his election and service as Cook County's chief prosecutor, to his historic tenure as mayor. The book details how—despite setbacks and calamities—through six terms in office, Daley resuscitated Chicago and rebuilt the city toward his vision, leading it to international prominence, before scandals and mistakes finally began to weaken his grip and the devastating aftershocks of the Great Recession compelled his long-shot bid to reverse the negative economic and political tides arrayed against him.

In writing this book, I did not interview Mayor Daley or seek to; it is not intended to be his version of history. It is instead drawn from the public record and from the insights of those who worked for him (including my own perspectives), or against him, or who observed his administration up close as journalists, activists, business-men, or civic leaders. Some of the most valuable anecdotes and perceptions are provided through the recollections of the important players in his decades in office.

I hope this book will be a useful guide for students, teachers, historians, urban planners, city managers, and aspiring or current politicians—or simply to the citizens who, every four years, determine the fates of cities at the ballot box.

Richard M. Daley's mayoralty holds myriad lessons for future leaders. Those who believe in the importance of cities and wish to see them rise and flourish can do no better than to study the man who reigned successfully in the nation's third-largest metropolis for nearly a quarter century.

Today's pace of economic, cultural, and technological change is staggering. We live in a society in which the newsworthy events of last month are often forgotten, let alone the important events of decades past. But that history is a critically important teacher. For Chicago—or any American city—the past is always prologue.

The Daley Show

Ascent
1976–1989

CHAPTER 1

Tumult

I first met a slightly disheveled and surprisingly demure Richard M. Daley in the fall of 1988. He wasn't what I expected.

The son of the late Mayor Richard J. Daley, who ruled Chicago and its vaunted Democratic Party machine with iron-handed bravado for decades, Rich Daley was as shy and shambling as his famous father was outgoing and natty.

Sitting in a swivel chair in an anteroom of the state's attorney's office, wearing a wrinkled blue shirt, his hair askew, the incumbent Cook County prosecutor greeted me with a weak handshake and an awkward smile.

I was there, along with Daley's longtime consigliere Frank Kruesi, to put the state's attorney through his paces in advance of an important television interview. Back then, before social media reduced adult attention spans to those of toddlers, stations aired political interviews for as long as an hour. That was a challenge for anyone, but particularly for Daley, who was known for his mangled syntax—a habit he came by naturally. Daley's father, the iconic Chicago columnist Mike Royko once wrote, could never "exit from the same paragraph he entered."[1] So when Rich Daley appeared before cameras, which was as infrequently as possible, his handlers were perpetually seated on pins and needles.

Now Daley was running for reelection as state's attorney—with the prospect of a race for mayor around the corner—and confronting the cameras, however unwelcome, was an unavoidable challenge.

I was representing the media company I formed with David Axelrod, a onetime political writer for the *Chicago Tribune*. Axelrod had left journalism in 1984 to help lead Congressman Paul Simon to an upset victory over Senator Charles Percy, a powerful, three-term incumbent who lost in what would otherwise be a strong Republican year. (Axelrod is better known for his later role as senior strategist for another noted Illinois politician: Barack Obama.) I was Axelrod's lieutenant in the Simon campaign, and we launched a firm after that race to provide campaign media consulting. In 1987, our firm handled Mayor Harold Washington's reelection strategy and advertising. As a congressman, Washington had been elected the city's first Black mayor in 1983, defeating the incumbent, Jane Byrne, and State's Attorney Daley.

In 1982, while still at the *Tribune*, Axelrod wrote a lengthy profile of Daley as the rookie prosecutor geared up for a first attempt at the mayor's office. It was headlined "The Son Also Rises,"[2] an allusion to Daley's status as heir to the most famous name in Chicago political history.

When answering questions from a reporter, Axelrod wrote, Daley "behaves a bit like a man in a dentist chair."[3]

Irving Rein, a clever Northwestern University communications professor and speech coach whose help Daley grudgingly accepted, wrote later that his client had a "tendency to misstate the obvious, invent words never imagined by linguistic researchers, introduce irrelevant material, and demonstrate anger at seemingly uneventful moments."[4]

But pundits and pols would learn over time that despite Daley's often nervous public demeanor and uneasy relationship with the English language, he had strengths that would more than compensate for these limitations. He had learned municipal government and politics at the knee of the master and had an innate and nearly unerring sense of the everyman, with whom he authentically connected, in a language all his own.

Still, there was plenty of work to be done.

After losing the three-way Democratic mayoral primary in 1983 to Harold Washington, Daley wanted a modern media adviser and ad maker for his second run. Before then, Daley had relied on the duo of Kruesi, who was more of a policy guru, and the elderly Earl Bush, a chain-smoking ex-newsman who for nearly two decades had served as Mayor Richard J. Daley's press secretary. (Bush once admonished the city hall press corps after one of Richard J.'s labyrinthine rhetorical flights, "Don't print what he *said*! Print what he *meant*!"[5])

Bush followed a set of old-school principles. Among them was avoiding commenting on an adverse or embarrassing news story because that would only extend its shelf life. "Don't say nothin'!" he would commonly thunder.

In our strategy sessions, Bush would flop in a chair, forgetful of the burning cigarette balanced between his fingers. As he spoke, he would raise his hands for emphasis, ignoring the growing protrusion of cigarette ashes. Inevitably, the room would be drawn to his seemingly mystical ability to keep the ashes suspended, hanging flaccidly but not giving way, until finally crumbling onto his rumbled, ash-strewn pants.

Daley appreciated Bush's old-school tradecraft and loyalty, if not the ashes. And "sayin' nothin'" was his preferred tactic. But Kruesi and Daley's youngest brother, Bill, who was his chief strategist, realized that he needed more and hired our firm to modernize the messaging operation and take advantage of Axelrod's ad-writing skills and media connections. Despite no serious opposition for a third term, Daley wanted an advertising blitz that would reintroduce him to Chicago's electorate as he prepared for another race for mayor early the following year.

Washington's sudden and tragic death from a heart attack just seven months into his second term had set up a special election in early 1989. More than a million people lined up to pay tribute, standing in line for hours to file past his casket at city hall. The lines became so long, stretching a half dozen blocks and six people deep, that city officials eventually asked mourners to stay home. Zettie Richardson, an African American nurse from Chicago's South Side, summed up the feelings of many: "I never thought I'd see the day when Chicago would have a black mayor. I waited in line for an hour and a half . . . and among everybody in line there is a sense of unity and brotherly love."[6]

But Washington's historic election in 1983 was hardly an exercise in "unity and brotherly love."

A product of Chicago's Democratic machine, Washington emerged in the 1970s as one of its most passionate and eloquent critics. Then a state legislator, he chafed under Mayor Richard J. Daley's iron-fisted control and affronts to the Black community on issues ranging from policing to housing and public education.

After Daley died in 1976, Washington ran in a special election the following year, carrying five predominantly Black wards on the city's South Side in a Democratic primary challenge to Acting Mayor Michael Bilandic, a Daley protégé appointed by the city council to replace him. A year later, he swamped a machine-backed candidate for a seat in Congress.

Washington's victory was a harbinger of more consequential convulsions soon to upend the Democratic machine.

In 1979, Bilandic, a stolid, nose-to-the-grindstone lawyer with little instinct for politics, sought reelection. So cocky about his chances were the Democratic ward bosses that they paid little attention to an underfunded apostate from their own camp—a woman, no less—who had set her sights on beating Bilandic and winning the Upset of the Century.

Jane Byrne had been one of Richard J. Daley's favorites. A single mother, widowed when her husband, a marine, was killed in a plane crash, Byrne caught Daley's eye as a young organizer for John F. Kennedy's presidential campaign in Chicago. Recognizing changing times, Daley elevated Byrne during the sixties and seventies from party volunteer toiling in the political vineyards to vice chair of the Democratic Party and Commissioner of Consumer Sales, making her the only woman in the mayor's cabinet. Her loyalty to Daley was manifest. But with his death, Byrne lost her sponsor.

Soon stripped of her political title by the surviving party bosses and marginalized at city hall, Byrne exacted her revenge, accusing Mayor Bilandic of ceding power to a "cabal of evil men" in the city council, whom she alleged had "greased" a corrupt deal to raise taxi fares. It was an explosive charge in a city where the odiferous relationship between the taxicab industry and politicians at city hall had long been an issue. Bilandic promptly fired her, unwittingly casting Byrne in the role of reformer and setting up her insurgent bid to replace him.

Byrne was guided by her new husband, Jay McMullen, a wise-cracking rapscallion and longtime city hall reporter for the *Chicago Daily News*; and Don Rose, a brilliant writer and political strategist who had been the communications director for Dr. Martin Luther King's Chicago antidiscrimination marches in 1966 and for the Chicago Seven, who led the convulsive antiwar protests at the Democratic National Convention in 1968.

In the 1970s, Rose had turned to more direct political action, engineering a series of successful insurgent, antimachine candidacies, none more stunning than the election of Bernard Carey, a retired FBI agent, to the prized and sensitive position of Cook County state's attorney. Carey, a Republican, defeated the Democratic incumbent, Edward Hanrahan, by riding a wave of outrage among African American voters and white liberals after Hanrahan orchestrated a controversial police raid on the apartment of the Black Panther leader Fred Hampton in which Hampton and another Panther leader were killed.

Rose hoped to galvanize the same base for Byrne.

But even his finest strategy couldn't help David defeat Goliath without the intervention of fate, which arrived in the form of the infamous Blizzard of '79. After ten days of temperatures below zero that created a base of ice, Chicago was hit with twenty inches of snow. Residents needing to drive found their cars buried in impassable streets.

It was an epic—and seemingly endless—storm, ensnarling the streets and paralyzing the city. The conditions would have challenged any mayor, but Bilandic's response seemed feckless and detached from reality. Despite his pledge to plow and then tow marooned cars to free up streets for traffic, his promises went mostly unfulfilled as city workers struggled to keep up with the steady deluge of snow. The City That Works, as Daley was fond of calling Chicago, worked no longer, and while the city was frozen, frustrations were boiling over.

No one understood this more than Rich Daley, the son who inherited his old man's street sense and could see Bilandic's political troubles mounting with each layer of falling snow. Before he became mayor, Bilandic was not only Daley's hand-picked Eleventh Ward alderman but chair of the all-important Finance Committee, where he meticulously tended to the mayor's agenda. The younger Daley's power base relied on Bilandic's political survival in the position that so many other politicians coveted.

More than a decade later, reminiscing with me on a slow day in the mayor's office, Daley recounted his exasperated attempts during the storms of 1979 to move Bilandic to more aggressive action. Seeing the lack of progress in clearing transportation arteries and sensing political doom, Daley told me he implored Bilandic to call in the national guard. But Bilandic demurred. As they rode together through some of the barely passable streets, surveying the disaster, Bilandic pointed to residents helping each other dig out cars or trudging to their destinations on foot. "See, it's not so bad," Bilandic said. "Everyone's getting along."

Daley turned to Bilandic, incredulous. "Mike, Mike, you don't understand! They hate you! They *hate* you!"

Worse than the roads were the rail lines. The Chicago Transit Authority (CTA) went into meltdown, with so few engines capable of handling the snowy conditions that the agency began shutting stations. When it did, it prioritized keeping open stations with larger ridership in the suburbs, where riders were mostly white, while closing or skipping smaller stations in mostly Black neighborhoods.

If Rose and Team Byrne were looking to ignite a rebellion among Black voters, they could not have asked for better fuel. Local TV news stations captured images of African American residents watching in fury as trains filled with suburbanites whisked past inner-city stations, leaving Black residents standing on the platform in the blowing snow and freezing cold. So when election day rolled in, Black voters, once a reliable bank of votes for the Democratic machine, left Bilandic at the station, carrying Byrne to victory with their overwhelming support.

It was ironic, then, that Byrne's greatest mistake was later to neglect and insult the Black community that had vaulted her to victory. Worried about a challenge from Daley, she moved to shore up her white ethnic base. African American leaders watched with incredulity as the mayor they helped elect sowed the seeds of her own political demise by replacing Black appointees on the Board of Education, the Chicago Housing Authority (CHA), and other agencies with politically connected whites. That betrayal fueled an unprecedented effort to draft a reluctant Harold Washington to jump into the fray.

Comfortable in his House seat, and unconvinced he could win, the congressman stiff-armed community leaders who demanded he run by setting seemingly impossible conditions—raising $500,000 and registering fifty thousand new Black voters. When the fundraising goals were met and *eighty* thousand new African Americans were added to the voting rolls, Washington ceded his agency.

Once in the race, Washington showed no reluctance, campaigning vigorously. The turning point was a series of three-way debates, simulcast for maximum viewership by the city's major television stations. Witty and playful, with soaring oratorical gifts, Washington was a made-for-TV politician in comparison to the taciturn Daley and the brooding and humorless Byrne. With Washington looking and acting mayoral in contrast to both the incumbent and the heir to a famous political franchise, Black voters began to sense that Washington could win.

Although improbable, Washington's victory was not a complete shock to those of us who commuted on trains and buses each day and walked the streets Downtown. As primary day approached, virtually every Black person (and many younger whites) sported the now iconic "Washington for Mayor" button with its blue background and white sunrise. The ubiquity of these buttons should have served as a seismic indicator. Just under the crust of the political world, the tectonic plates were shifting, heralding a powerful earthquake.

Byrne's seismograph picked up the tremors late. Sensing Washington's momentum among Black voters and Daley's continuing strength among white ones, her advisors knew the mayor's only hope was to knock down Daley's support. Heading Byrne's effort was Alderman Edward "Fast Eddie" Vrdolyak, who earned his moniker through years of successful grifting. Vrdolyak was part of the "evil cabal" that Byrne had attacked in her campaign. But the new mayor had barely taken her hand off the Bible at the swearing-in when she invited Vrdolyak to become a top advisor. Later, she would engineer his election as chairman of the Cook County Democratic Organization, the very political machine Daley's father once led.

The son of Croatian immigrants, Vrdolyak fought his way up from the city's Southeast Side, a white ethnic enclave in the shadow of belching steel mills where racist attitudes were right out in the open. Thus he knew better than most how to stir those fires, and his message was crystal clear: every white vote that went to Daley, and not Byrne, was a vote for the Black guy.

"It's a racial thing, don't kid yourself. I'm calling on you to save your city, to save your precinct. We're fighting to keep the city the way it is," Vrdolyak told a gathering of party precinct workers as the election neared.[7]

Less crafty operatives might have sent Byrne campaigning frenetically through white wards to increase support. But Byrne's calculating cadre instead sent her door-to-door in the infamous, nearly all-Black public-housing high-rises. With TV cameras in tow, Byrne pleaded with African American residents for their votes, only to be met with stony silence, passionate support for Washington, or in some cases physical jostling and confrontation—the made-for-TV moments her handlers were seeking. To ensure the most dramatic footage, her advisors arranged for Byrne's bodyguards to disappear.

For white voters watching the evening news, the message was inescapable: The mayoral race was now a two-person affair. A vote for Daley was the equivalent of a vote to elect Washington, a point that party precinct captains working for Byrne stressed in the city's white ethnic wards.

The unvarnished racial appeals did their job. Daley's support dropped. But unfortunately for Byrne, not enough.

Buoyed by a record turnout and overwhelming Black support, Harold Washington won the Democratic primary with 36.3 percent of the vote. Byrne finished second with 33.7 percent to Daley's 29.7 percent.

But Vrdolyak wasn't wrong. Race *was* the issue. Washington's victory was built almost entirely on the votes of Black and Hispanic voters, with just a sliver of white liberal support, while Byrne and Daley divided the remaining two-thirds. So despite being the Democratic nominee in a one-party town, Washington found himself in jeopardy of losing to a Republican in the general election as white Democrats fled in droves.

Washington's opponent, Bernard Epton, was the unlikely vehicle for an overtly racist campaign. A bearded, Jewish Republican state legislator from the city's integrated and liberal Hyde Park community, Epton looked and sounded more like a rabbi than a rabble-rouser. But he was white, and that was good enough for national and state GOP operatives. Sensing a chance, they swept in to rebrand the campaign with a cynical, not very subtle new tagline: "Epton: Before It's Too Late."

Chicago's ugly racial divisions entered national consciousness on Palm Sunday, during a campaign visit by Vice President Walter Mondale in support of the Democratic nominee. As Mondale and Washington attempted to attend services at St. Pascal Catholic Church on the city's Northwest Side, they were greeted by a crowd of furious white demonstrators hurling racial epithets and booing loudly. The ruckus forced them to abandon the services. Photos of the angry confrontation were splashed on the cover of *Newsweek*.

Washington narrowly survived, but the war didn't end.

The 1983 general election set the tone for the coming term. Shortly after the city's first Black mayor was sworn in, a group of twenty-eight white and one Latino aldermen seized the reins of power in the fifty-member city council. The coalition became known as the "Vrdolyak 29" after its combative leader. In 1960, Vrdolyak was employed as an ironworker when he and six others were charged with attempted murder for an attack on the owner of a boiler company who refused to hire union labor, an incident dubbed "union terrorism" by the newspapers.[8] He was acquitted but maintained his taste for battle. Clever with a line and always eager for a fight, Vrdolyak seized on the historic change at city hall to claim control of a city council that had, for decades, been docile supplicants of Chicago mayors.

The Vrdolyak coalition's ostensible purpose was to protect white neighborhoods from the frightening Black interloper now occupying city hall. Behind the scenes, its purpose was to ensure that control of contracts and jobs stayed where it belonged. Despite chants of "Our turn now" by Washington's exuberant African American supporters on election night, most of the spoils belonged not to the victor but to the still-powerful agents of the defeated regime.

For more than three years, Vrdolyak and his allies obstructed Washington and clung to power, always using the prospect of disaster if full control fell into the mayor's hands. Washington, for his part, used Vrdolyak as a foil to ensure that his own base remained fiercely united behind him, despite any disappointment in the slow progress toward racial equity.

By charter Chicago has a "weak mayor" system, in which most of the power is vested in the city council. Normally the natural advantages of the chief executive make this irrelevant, but this was no normal time.

Outside the economically advantaged lakefront, white aldermen were elected from wards occupied by conservative, working-class whites of mostly Polish, Irish, German, and Italian ancestry, many first or second generation. In these "bungalow belt" wards on the city's Northwest and Southwest sides, support for the white candidates matched the ferocity of support that Black wards gave Washington. Notions of racial equity and fairness played poorly here, and lending support to the city's first Black mayor was a quick ticket out of the council.

Thus began a long struggle for control of city government, a struggle that became known as the "Council Wars."

Daley was in an awkward position. Many whites blamed him for Washington's ascent, claiming that he had siphoned off the deciding votes from Byrne. That resentment took a violent turn shortly after the election when an angry white man shouting racial epithets tackled Daley while he was visiting a toy store with his son. In an only-in-Chicago moment, the man wrestled with Daley on the ground in front of aisles of toys and horrified children before bystanders restored comity.

Still the state's attorney, Daley had no interest in taking sides. His belief that a prosecutor should be above partisan politics, at least between elections, provided a rationale for disengagement. But his distance was also dictated by a desire to avoid the undertow of Chicago's boiling racial politics. Daley endorsed Washington as the party's nominee and did nothing to impede the mayor by taking a side in his battle with the council. This ultimately proved critical to Daley's future.

Although Washington declared machine politics dead on his arrival at City Hall, it would take three years for the new mayor to wrest control of the council and city government from Vrdolyak's grip.

Washington was himself a product of the Democratic organization, having risen through the party ranks before declaring his independence later in his career. On his election as mayor, he struck a hammer blow against the traditional patronage system that was the lifeblood of the machine. He ended years of litigation and signed the Shakman decree, named for the attorney Michael Shakman, who had brought the suit. It claimed that Chicago's hiring practices—in which job holders were required to work and financially support the Democratic Party and its candidates as an unwritten condition of employment—violated the free speech and free association protections of the US Constitution. Under the terms of the decree Washington signed, only nine hundred city positions—out of roughly forty thousand—were exempted from the new ban on patronage hiring.

Despite Washington's action, a significant number of "sister agencies"—technically independent government organizations such as the parks, the transit authority, and community colleges—were not covered by the decree. Governed by appointees of past mayors serving staggered terms, these agencies were long a treasure trove for machine hiring and remained in the hands of the opposition.

Within those agencies, the resistance was led by Chicago Park District Superintendent Ed Kelly. For years, the parks were his personal domain. A former boxer, he had an equally pugnacious political style. He was appointed at the direction of Mayor Richard J. Daley but solidified power on the mayor's death, strategically awarding new park facilities to key wards and leveraging a vast well of jobs and contracts to ensure fealty. Kelly's vision of the parks hewed white, with disproportionate spending on his North Side base. A 1982 lawsuit ultimately led to a consent decree, requiring years of disproportionate spending in minority areas to make up for past discrimination.

Kelly joined the anti-Washington forces and hung on until June 1986, more than three years into Washington's term, when the mayor finally wrested control of the board and appointed the district's first African American leader, Jesse Madison.

Even then, Kelly resisted. When Madison showed up for his first day of work, he found that he had been locked out of administrative headquarters.

Two months later, Washington took full control of the Chicago Transit Authority and its vast bus and rail services. After filling expired terms on the seven-member board with four loyalists, Washington eased out the executive chairman, Michael Cardilli, but this time with less drama. Cardilli fought to hold on, but unlike Kelly had no independent power base. Cardilli was a creature of the powerful Illinois House speaker, Michael Madigan. Rather than poison the well in an all-out public fight with the city's African American mayor, Madigan quietly let Cardilli know he was done.

A cunning and inscrutable political tactician, Madigan had seized the speaker's gavel in 1983. Apart from a single term following the national Republican wave in the 1994 elections, Madigan would hold on to it until 2021, becoming the longest-serving leader of any state or federal legislative body.[9]

The sister agency wins were made possible by Washington's capture of city council control, because aldermen confirm agency appointees. That opportunity arrived when a court ordered the remapping of wards and special elections to account for increased Latino populations. In 1986, Washington and Vrdolyak faced off in proxy races. In the decisive contest, Washington backed the activist and mayoral aide Luis Gutiérrez. Vrdolyak's candidate was Cook County Commissioner Manuel Torres.

After a brutal campaign characterized by accusations of treason, drug use, and child-support delinquency, and with streets flooded by armies of door-knocking troops from the old machine and Washington's emerging new one, voters went to the polls to determine who would control city government. The stakes were so high and the chances of shenanigans so certain that State's Attorney Daley and US Attorney Anton Valukas sent in two hundred assistant prosecutors to monitor the voting.

In the end, control of the city council may have come down to a single political miscalculation. Vrdolyak had chosen a candidate who did not speak Spanish. When Spanish television broadcast the final debates between the candidates, Gutiérrez moved back and forth seamlessly between languages, whereas Torres spoke only in English to a largely Spanish-speaking audience. In a close election, it proved decisive.

Vrdolyak had one more card to play—an independent candidacy against Washington in the 1987 mayoral race. But after defeating Byrne in a primary rematch with nearly 54 percent of the vote, Washington handily vanquished Vrdolyak in the general election.

At last, Mayor Washington had secured complete political and governmental dominance.

Seven months later, he was dead.

• • •

In life, Washington had united the Black community, suppressing the conflicts and political rivalries that erupted from below the surface. In death, those fissures reemerged.

After Washington was laid to rest, his allies rallied behind the mayor's city council floor leader, Alderman Tim Evans. But the Evans coalition of progressive Blacks and white "lakefront liberals" was outflanked in a political blitzkrieg launched almost from the moment of Washington's death. It brought to life the old political maxim: there are no permanent alliances, only permanent interests.

The winning coalition was a mix of whites, Latinos, and Blacks more comfortable with transactional politics than ideology, more at home with dealmaking than the vague notions of reform animating Washington's agenda.

Their choice was a veteran African American alderman, Eugene Sawyer, who would be mayor for at least the next sixteen months until a formal election could be held to fill the last two years of Washington's term. The winning group's racial unity, albeit born of a cynical calculus, was in sharp contrast to Council Wars, in which racial animus among aldermen was so profound that the *Wall Street Journal* dubbed Chicago "Beirut on the Lake," a reference to the capital of the Middle Eastern nation experiencing perpetual civil war and strife.

Instead of being divided by Black and white, the new council rulers were united by green, as in the color of money. Sensing Sawyer could be more easily persuadable in giving out lucrative contracts and patronage jobs, they put their money where they thought the money could be made. White alderman also cynically calculated that Sawyer, a dignified and quiet man, was politically too weak to be elected in his own right, giving them a chance to elect one of their own next time.

For many African American aldermen, as for their like-minded white counter-parts, it was a chance to return to the normal patterns of commerce. Washington was as skilled a practitioner as any at passing out the spoils of office to friends and favorites. But for the most part he viewed African American councilmen as mere serfs in his kingdom. They chafed as Washington stiff-armed their requests to place family and friends on the city payroll or steer contracts to campaign contributors or relatives. But they seethed in silence and voted lockstep with the mayor out of fear of their own constituents.

For the entirety of his mayoralty, Washington maintained an iron grip on the imagination of the African American community. For Black politicians, crossing him was political death. Conversely, a mayoral endorsement virtually assured reelection. Even aldermen who routinely voted with the mayor were at risk if they displayed anything but unquestioning allegiance. In the 1987 election, four Black incumbents deemed insufficiently loyal were ousted from the city coun-cil—Aldermen Perry Hutchinson, Niles Sherman, Marian Humes, and Wallace Davis.

According to Gary Rivlin of the *Chicago Reader*, it started with remarks from a sometime spokesman for Operation PUSH, the lawyer Tom Todd. PUSH was founded by the civil rights leader Rev. Jesse Jackson, who for years held come-all Saturday morning gatherings where would-be politicians and favor-seekers came to mingle with rank-and-file activists and seek Jackson's blessing.

By the time of Washington's mayoralty, Jackson was focused on the national and international stage, having run for president in 1984. But he kept PUSH as a local power base. Its Saturday meetings often produced political intrigue.

Normally, warnings about loyalty to Washington would have been general in nature. But Todd named names, Rivlin wrote:

> It was from then on that they . . . were branded the folks interested in jumping to the other side, one well-connected black activist explained. You're talking about a fairly sophisticated electorate in the black community. We've gone through a real education about government and politics in the last few years. You've got people discussing the budget and bond initiatives at bars, and in barbershops, and at parties. Folks would be talking about it hanging out on the corner.
>
> You'd be out in the community when someone would say, "Hey, I heard someone's flirting with the other side. I heard someone's going to jump." People would say, "Yeah—who? Hutchison? Humes? Niles?"
>
> They could never shake it.[10]

But that was then, and this was now.

Some previously constrained Black aldermen began to conspire, even while the mayor was fighting for his life. The Westside Alderman William Henry, an old-style pol who struggled to contain his disdain for Washington's reforms, summoned other aldermen to his office to plot, while keeping an eye on the television's increasingly dire reports from the hospital where Washington lay dying.

"There was an appropriate sadness," said one alderman. "On the other hand, it seemed like 'Hallelujah, we're free.'"[11]

On December 1, 1987, I joined the crowd assembled on the streets outside city hall, a combination of activists, wary citizens, and curiosity-seekers. Inside, the city council was debating who would be the next mayor of Chicago. This was before Twitter feeds provided blow-by-blow updates as dramatic news events unfolded. Standing behind police barricades in the cold, we knew nothing of what was happening inside. Hours rolled by without word. The scene was reminiscent of the vigil for a new pope, except that no whiff of white smoke would herald the selection of the next leader.

Finally, word broke. Late in the night, in a 31–17 vote following a raucous meeting, Sawyer was appointed interim mayor. The aldermen had made their choice.

In less than fifteen months, the voters would make theirs.

CHAPTER 2

Alone

Richard M. Daley's rise to power abounds with irony.

His father, Richard J. Daley, methodically worked his way up the ranks of the Democratic organization, serving loyally as precinct captain, county and state bureaucrat, member of the Illinois House and Senate, county clerk, and as Cook County party chair, a position he leveraged to remove Mayor Martin Kennelly when the incumbent fell out of favor with the machine.

Early in his career, the mayor's son seemed poised to follow a similar path, taking his father's former seat in the Illinois legislature and dutifully following orders in Springfield, a prince in waiting.

But fate broke the stately and predictable order. Before he could claim the family throne, the son of the king was cast into the wilderness alone, forced to reinvent himself—first to survive, and then to lead an assault on the castle his father built, to claim power for himself.

Richard J. Daley played the inside game and played it brilliantly. His son was forced to play the outside game or die and, to the surprise of many, also played it brilliantly, successfully leading an unlikely insurgency.

• • •

In 1972, at age thirty, Daley took his seat in the Illinois Senate. He was a loyal enforcer for his father's political regime. Mean and merciless in imposing party discipline, he took delight in tanking reform legislation offered by the smattering of independent-minded Democrats who dared to defy him. One of their leaders, Sen. Dawn Clark Netsch, derisively labeled him "Dirty Little Richie."

In a preview of future battles, Daley tangled with another independent senator, Harold Washington, who reportedly disdained the entitled scion. During a contentious floor debate, he turned angrily to Daley, decrying "certain spoon-fed senators . . . those of you who didn't even have to work to get here, just walked in or looked across the dinner table and said Daddy I want to be a senator."[1]

Daley made *Chicago* magazine's list of the ten worst state legislators "for arrogance, for sharklike qualities, for living off his father's name, and for pulling puppet strings attached to some of the worst members of the Senate." The writers grudgingly acknowledged his political skills, however, calling him "too shrewd to be one of the worst, but he controls so many of the worst senators that he belongs on the list to represent all of them."[2]

But events soon would humble and mature the sullen prince.

Shortly before Christmas in 1976, during a typical day of meetings and public dedications, Mayor Richard J. Daley collapsed and died of a massive heart attack. The Boss was gone and, instantly, everything changed for his son and namesake. No longer could he rely on his father's power and protection. Vulnerable as never before, Rich Daley was on his own.

But if the loss of his father trimmed Daley's power, it also forced him to reevaluate his life and approach. He was compelled to consider who he wanted to be—and needed to be—to survive and prosper in a political world that was changing.

During this period, Daley faced a second personal trauma. He and his wife, Maggie, had a son, Kevin, who was born with spina bifida, a life-threatening and debilitating birth defect. Kevin lived for less than three years, during which Daley would fly home from Springfield nightly to sit by his bedside.

As Daley coped with these challenges and trauma, his public persona changed. No longer petulant and entitled political royalty, he became a thoughtful legislator and collaborative colleague.

Even former bitter rivals, including Netsch, drew closer. Daley became more open and interested in the details of issues long on the wish list of reformers. With the help of his cerebral legislative aide, Frank Kruesi, Daley authored and passed groundbreaking legislation in alliance with Netsch and her liberal allies: mental-health and nursing-home reforms, and repeal of the sales tax on food and medicine. The latter pitted him against Mayor Byrne and Gov. Jim Thompson, both of whom fought hard to keep the revenue.

Kruesi remembers the sales tax fight as "an incredible battle." Daley's bill passed, but the governor vetoed it, setting up an epic override struggle against the combined forces of the governor of Illinois and the mayor of Chicago.

"The override failed," Kruesi said. "It was close, but it failed. . . . Rich got an amazing amount of attention for his willingness to stand up for senior citizens and for the poor, for basic necessities."[3]

Daley's turn as a reformer was not entirely a product of personal transformation. It was also a way to survive radically changing political circumstances.

In becoming the first woman ever to capture the mayor's office, Jane Byrne had run as a full-throated reformer. But her roots and proclivities were in Democratic machine politics and, almost immediately after winning the election, she began cutting power and patronage-sharing deals with the "cabal of evil men"—the very city council operators she had vilified as a candidate. Obsessed with an almost Shakespearean fear that Richard the Second would reclaim the throne for the Daley clan and their Eleventh Ward allies, Byrne moved to cut off their patronage jobs and contracts and wrest the father's allies from the son.

Daley would always retain the loyalty of a handful of ward leaders, but, for the most part, Byrne ensured that the old machine abandoned him. He needed new allies.

Not long after her election in 1979, Mayor Byrne began systematically dismantling Daley's power base, confident she was isolating him. Instead, she was forcing his hand. Seeking refuge from the mayor's political fusillade, Daley made the audacious move of running against the party for a powerful and sensitive office no one could have predicted—Cook County State's Attorney. The decision was stunning. Not only would Daley be taking on the very machine his father had built to claim the Democratic nomination but he would then have to beat a popular two-term incumbent Republican, Bernard Carey, in the general election.

Byrne immediately settled on Ald. Ed Burke, from the Southwest Side's Fourteenth Ward, as Daley's primary challenger. Although a member of the "evil cabal," he, like other members, was now a loyal member of her inner circle.

After his father's death, State Senator Daley had remade himself from hack to reformer. Now he cleverly navigated his excommunication from his father's machine to his own advantage. Boss Byrne's opposition provided him the mantle of independence. Combined with his successful Springfield crusades, Daley suddenly presented as a reform-minded insurgent battling the regular Democratic organization, boosting his standing in the suburbs, the liberal lakefront, and the African American community.

With Byrne and an oily cast of insiders lining up behind Burke, including the slumlord and power broker Charlie Swibel, Ald. "Fast Eddie" Vrdolyak, and First Ward Committeeman John D'Arco, Daley went on the attack. He dismissed Burke as a tool of the power-hungry mayor, ridiculed Byrne for surrounding herself with the same "evil cabal" she once railed against, and went after her association with D'Arco, who helped manage the mob's interests in the notorious river precincts. The mayor, he said, had become "cozy with the front men for the crime syndicate." Citing *Tribune* reports from police sources, he accused Byrne of shielding D'Arco's First Ward gambling dens from police raids.[4]

In contrast to Byrne's cast of characters, Daley won the endorsements of Netsch and other independent reformers and embraced their good-government planks. Among them was merit selection of judges to replace the system of electing jurists, which traditionally had given the Democratic ward bosses the power to put their pals on the bench on the basis of loyalty rather than legal bona fides. (At slating sessions, testifiers for candidates would often reassure the assembled that "he'll be an alderman's judge.") Daley pledged to run a professional office, free of patronage hiring. "I will not take a letter from any ward committeeman," he said.[5]

• • •

Even before the race began, Byrne had unwittingly helped Daley strengthen his political position. In October 1979, five months before the pivotal Illinois presidential primary and a month before Daley made his surprise announcement for state's attorney, the mayor invited President Jimmy Carter to headline her fundraiser at McCormick Place, which more than ten thousand supplicants paid to attend. Byrne praised the incumbent president for his leadership and his support for cities, uttering a near endorsement.

"If the convention were tonight," Byrne proclaimed, "I would vote in our party caucus without hesitancy to renominate our present leader for another four years."[6]

Two weeks later, the mercurial mayor endorsed Carter's primary rival, Sen. Edward Kennedy. Byrne then orchestrated an unprecedented early endorsement of Kennedy by the Cook County Democratic Central Committee. When Daley's Eleventh Ward and Cook County Assessor Tom Hynes's Nineteenth Ward objected, she rebuked them and began firing payrollers from their organizations.

Byrne's strong-arming for Kennedy was likely born of nostalgia (she began her career as a John F. Kennedy volunteer) and a misplaced sense of the senator's appeal to ethnic voters, particularly the Irish. (The mayor invited Kennedy to the St. Patrick's Day parade and snubbed President Carter, explaining "it would be foolish to have an Englishman lead it."[7]).

Daley understood that despite Byrne's ethnic and nostalgia play for Kennedy, President Carter was more culturally akin to conservative white voters on the Northwest and Southwest Sides. Edward Kennedy's brand of liberalism and his ethical and legal troubles following Chappaquiddick—where years before a young woman had drowned in his car when he drove it off a bridge and then fled the scene of the accident—were anathema to most ethnic voters.

Daley began aligning his allies and political organization closely with Carter's, along with other estranged groups such as the firefighters union, whose more than four thousand members were in a bitter strike against Byrne's administration that coincided with the primary election battle.

Daley's astute political positioning and Byrne's repeated missteps helped Daley crush Burke, while Carter swamped Kennedy. In yet another irony, after the elder Daley had played kingmaker for one Kennedy in the famously close 1960 Illinois presidential election, the younger Daleys effectively ended the presidential aspirations of another.

In Cook County, the tallies showed the near lockstep voting of Carter and Daley supporters, with 63.3 percent for Carter and 62.6 percent for Daley.

Although the Democratic primary turned into a rout, the general election was much tougher. The Republican Bernard Carey was a popular incumbent riding on the coattails of the former California governor Ronald Reagan at the top of the national ticket. Reagan would win the November election over President Jimmy Carter in a landslide.

But in a close election between Carey and Daley, Mayor Byrne proved decisive again.

Although publicly "endorsing" Daley as the Democratic nominee, she worked behind the scenes to muscle more than half of the ward committeemen into backing

Carey. Hundreds of precinct workers for the Democratic machine, most with government jobs to protect, were dispatched to solicit votes for a Republican against a Democrat named Daley. When the son of the Boss announced he was sending in teams of poll watchers to guard against fraud, the irony was too much for the columnist Mike Royko, who called Daley's predicament "the most bizarre happening in Chicago political history," except for the upset mayoral victory of Byrne the year before. Royko noted an additional irony—Carey was the law-enforcement officer in charge of policing election fraud.

"Nailing the precinct captains is Carey's job," Royko penned. "So we have a fascinating drama developing: Will Carey's investigators cry 'stop thief!' when the thief is stealing a vote for Carey? Will Carey haul a first ward cigar-chomper before a grand jury and say: 'This vile fellow was caught voting a graveyard in my behalf'?"[8]

Carey had used opposition to the machine as the basis for successful candidacies in 1972 and 1976, persuading voters that the chief prosecutor should be a check on its power. But with Byrne and most of the ward bosses working for Carey, he struggled to maintain his foundational appeal.

Following the adage "Who needs enemies when you have friends like this," Byrne sealed Carey's fate two weeks before election day, announcing she was "withdrawing" her endorsement of Daley after discovering his complicity in a multiyear scheme by the city's building department to prevent Blacks and Hispanics from moving into Daley's Bridgeport community, as well as the heavily Irish Beverly neighborhood of Daley's top political ally, Assessor Tom Hynes. When Byrne's claims proved false, even Carey had to publicly disassociate himself from her accusations.[9]

Despite carrying Byrne's baggage, Carey almost prevailed by hanging onto the long coattails of Reagan, who ran up big suburban numbers in winning Illinois and forty-eight other states. But Daley had wisely and methodically constructed a strong suburban ground organization to peel away parts of Carey's base and ultimately prevailed by the slimmest of margins, sixteen thousand votes out of 2.1 million cast.

• • •

Byrne and her machine allies expected—and feared—that State's Attorney Daley would punish his enemies with political prosecutions and fill the office with patronage hires. But instead of political reprisals, Daley focused on drugs and violent crime. Instead of awarding jobs to the connected, he became the first county official to sign a federal court decree banning political hiring. He surprised the staff by keeping almost all professional prosecutors and career service administrators. The most shocked was William Kunkel, chief deputy state's attorney. A big man with an imposing presence, Kunkel was a lifelong Republican who had prosecuted the serial killer John Wayne Gacy. He remained a top deputy to Daley for five years.

Daley entered office in December 1980, in the middle of a sprawling undercover FBI investigation of Cook County judges, Operation Greylord. The feds had clued in Carey but now wondered if they could trust Daley, who had so many political friends in high places, including the bench. Ultimately, the FBI concluded it had no choice. Daley was briefed, and never said a word during the subsequent four years of the investigation.

Operation Greylord investigated a web of corrupt lawyers, police officers, sheriff's deputies, court officials, and judges who conspired to fix cases in the Cook County Circuit Courts and share in the flow of bribes. The feds determined that cases were rigged on everything from traffic tickets to murder. One judge, Thomas Maloney, had fixed at least three murder cases in exchange for more than $100,000 in bribes. Ultimately, ninety-three individuals were indicted, including Supervising Judge Richard LeFevour, a close Daley friend who had administered his oath as state's attorney. LeFevour kept a photo of Daley in his judicial office. He took it down the day he was indicted.

Daley brought to the office a clear set of convictions. He declared narcotics dealers public enemy number one, a view that dovetailed with increasingly aggressive federal prosecutions of drug cartels. With Reagan announcing a "war on drugs," the combined federal, state, and local apparatus was in lockstep about getting tough.

"To me, a narcotics dealer is the most dangerous person out there. He makes your murderers, your rapists, your home invaders, destroys your kids," Daley said.[10]

While Daley's focus on gangs and drugs would prove popular, his obvious passion for it was personal. He saw the impact of drugs on young people, and it touched him deeply. More than once, when we were alone in the mayor's fifth-floor office, he brought up the subject. Daley also kept a Mass card on his desk from the memorial service for his son Kevin. He looked at it often, his emotions still raw.

"I don't understand why all these kids want to kill themselves with drugs," Daley said. "Kevin fought so hard to live. All he wanted was to live."

By the end of his first term, Daley was filing five times as many drug-related indictments as his predecessor. Restricting plea bargaining by his prosecutors, Daley insisted on taking even marginal cases to trial, a practice that strained the resources of county courts. He openly attacked judges he felt were soft on crime.

Daley passed new laws in Springfield, one lowering the amount of cocaine possession needed for a class X indictment (minimum six years in prison) from 30 grams to 15, an amount that according to state's attorneys will get five people high. Another Daley law required the automatic transfer to adult court of fifteen- or sixteen-year-old juveniles in possession of more than 15 grams of a hard drug.

Even many Daley prosecutors thought his moves were extreme. Irv Miller was Daley's first-term chief of felony review. He argued that lowering the possession amounts introduced a new type of criminal into the system: the mope.

"You're not getting the hard-core dealers," Miller said. "You're getting the kid who has never been in trouble before. The narcotics officer buys a little bit from the kid and keeps buying until finally he talks the kid into distributing a 'class X' amount. Now the kid who has never been in trouble before is facing six years in jail. The dealer is still sitting in his house. He's never had one contact with the narc officer. He just finds another mope to peddle for him."[11]

But Daley's focus on drug dealers burnished his electoral profile as a tough, no-nonsense prosecutor. With concerns about drug use rising, he fit the country's growing "law and order" mood.

In Chicago, waging war on narcotics dealers meant taking on violent, organized gangs. Unlike New York, Chicago suffers from a deeply embedded "gangs and guns" culture, a result of its concentrated poverty and easy access to firearms from bordering states with few restrictions. In 1989, the University of Chicago sociologist and gangs expert Irving Spergel estimated that Chicago's gang problem was second only to that of Los Angeles, with 125 different gangs controlling twelve thousand members, almost all involved in the narcotics trade.[12]

The turf wars to control lucrative territory contributed to the soaring murder rate, mostly in poor areas, especially the city's high-rise public housing. If gangbangers were killing each other, most Chicagoans took little notice, even as more innocent bystanders became victims. That changed in 1984, when a sixteen-year-old gangbanger shot and killed the high school senior Ben Wilson in a lunchtime altercation outside a grocery store a block from Simeon High School. Wilson was its star basketball player and the number one national prospect, heralded as a future NBA star.

The shooting of a young local celebrity with such a promising future, who had assiduously avoided gangs and drugs, produced an outpouring of rage and sorrow. More than ten thousand mourners spilled out of funeral services at Operation PUSH headquarters at Fiftieth Street and Drexel Boulevard. The Reverend Jesse Jackson, in eulogizing Wilson, said that "this act has gotten our nation's attention and awakened us. If it could happen to Ben Wilson, it could happen to anybody. . . . We are living not by the law of God but by the lottery of the outlaws, unless we collectively resist."[13]

Backed by growing public outrage, Daley kept pushing the envelope in his war on gangs, seeking wiretapping powers and other tools reserved for federal law enforcement. His gang unit had an 84 percent conviction rate, and he asked for higher sentences for gang members. Whether cowed by the threat of Daley calling them out or simply in agreement, criminal court judges meted out sentences in gang-related murders that were on average eight years longer than those for other crimes.

In his nearly nine years as prosecutor, Daley honed his image as one of the nation's toughest law-enforcement officers. But as we shall see, his no-holds-barred approach to crime fighting opened the door to egregious abuses that would take decades to unravel.

CHAPTER 3

Torture

While he was state's attorney—and later mayor—Daley's compulsion to be tough on crime may have led him to look the other way on one of the most heinous examples of civil rights abuses by Chicago police. The brutal interrogation tactics of Detective Jon Burge and a unit he commanded produced confessions and convictions—some of them false—in major cases on Daley's watch as chief county prosecutor. But Burge's abuses, which he continued after being promoted to commander and for which he later served time on a related federal charge, were not merely the isolated acts of a rogue police unit. They were an insidious outgrowth of the underlying racial tension at the heart of big-city law enforcement in one of the nation's most segregated cities. Chicago's racial conflicts are a seemingly indelible stain on the city and a specter that haunted Richard M. Daley throughout his public career.

At the beginning of the twentieth century, the first waves of Black migrants from the South began settling in the city, doubling Chicago's African American population between 1915 and 1920. Invisible lines dictated where Blacks could live and even play. One was along a sandy beach on Lake Michigan, at Twenty-Ninth Street, where in July 1919 an African American boy swimming with friends floated off course into the white area. A group of whites pelted him with stones, and he drowned. The incident triggered a race riot that lasted a week, until the state militia joined local police to quell it. Hundreds were injured; fifteen whites and twenty-three Blacks died. More than a thousand Black families were left homeless after white mobs torched their homes.

President Woodrow Wilson blamed whites for stirring the violence, and a subsequent investigation identified the Hamburg Athletic Club, a white street gang, as a major instigator. Richard J. Daley, a seventeen-year-old member, never admitted or denied participating in the violence.

Mayor Daley's home, the Bridgeport neighborhood on Chicago's near Southwest Side, was the site of numerous violent incidents when Black newcomers tried to move in, or sometimes when they were merely passing through. The Reverend Martin Luther King Jr. brought his "freedom campaign" to Chicago in 1966, seeking open housing in the most segregated city in America. He was greeted by Southwest Side whites waving Confederate flags and hurling rocks and racial slurs.

As mayor, Richard J. Daley viewed integration as a trigger for white flight at a time when the city was rapidly losing middle-class whites to the suburbs. With the support of African American allies on the city council who saw integration as a threat to the captive audiences of their political bases, Daley blocked King's designs for an open-housing ordinance. He also segregated poor Blacks into high-rise public housing projects, including the South Side's twenty-eight-tower Robert Taylor Homes, separated from his Bridgeport community by a fourteen-lane expressway.

Richard M. Daley both embraced elements of his father's legacy and plainly and consciously repudiated others, including the worst of Richard J. Daley's segregation policies. Among the younger Daley's greatest accomplishments, for example, was the razing of the Chicago public-housing high rises his father had built to contain the African American community.[1]

In 1983, in Rich Daley's first run for mayor, he ran as a candidate of restoration, following the chaotic mayoralty of Jane Byrne. But restoration gave way to revolution as Congressman Harold Washington's historic candidacy awakened the Black community. Daley was caught in the crosscurrents between a Black insurgency and a white mayor cynically leveraging white fear in an attempt to remain in power.[2] It was a chilling experience for Daley, who became a target of white backlash after the election, accused of facilitating the election of Chicago's first Black mayor. The scars from that campaign endured through the rest of his career and left him determined to become a force for racial reconciliation.

When Daley ran for mayor the second time in 1989, after Mayor Harold Washington's death, he was determined to avoid the racial strife that engulfed the 1983 campaign. Healing the city's yawning racial divide, which only grew after Washington's passing, became a central theme of his candidacy. But Daley's tough-on-crime tactics as state's attorney ran counter to this narrative, raising some troubling issues of racial disparities in prosecutions and sentencing. And no story posed a greater threat than the appalling tale of Commander Jon Burge. It was a huge scandal with enormous civil rights implications, bubbling beneath the surface throughout Daley's tenure as prosecutor.

• • •

In February 1982, Mayor Byrne's police superintendent, Richard Brzeczek, took the unusual and formal step of delivering a letter to State's Attorney Daley.

Referring correspondence from Dr. John Raba, the medical director for the Cook County Jail, Brzeczek stipulated that a criminal defendant sustained serious injuries while in police custody. The police chief said he would not authorize an investigation until receiving guidance from Daley, because he did not wish to jeopardize the prosecution's case.

"I will forbear from taking any steps . . . in connection with these allegations until I hear from you or one of your assistants," Brzeczek wrote.[3]

The defendant was Andrew Wilson, convicted of murdering two Chicago police officers. In the aftermath of those killings, on February 9, 1982, city police went on a rampage—indiscriminately stopping, frisking, and interrogating African American citizens; verbally and physically abusing both possible suspects and mere bystanders; and torturing suspects. Civil rights organizations received more than 130 complaints of police brutality and urged Daley to investigate. Wilson was identified as the killer, but not because of the aggressive police sweep. An eyewitness led police to a neighbor of Wilson's, who provided enough information to warrant the arrest. Following questioning by police, he confessed.

Wilson was convicted at two different trials and locked away for life. But he filed a civil suit years later, alleging his confession was a result of torture at the hands of Commander Jon Burge and officers of the infamous Area Two police headquarters, later dubbed the "Midnight Crew." The suit resurrected the significance of the Brzeczek letter.

Wilson claimed he was beaten, electrocuted, burned, and suffocated following his arrest. The physical evidence at the civil trial, the same evidence referred to in Brzeczek's letter to Daley, supported his contentions. The jury issued the odd official finding that Area Two had a longstanding practice of torturing suspects accused of shooting police officers but nonetheless exonerated Burge and his codefendants, apparently justifying Wilson's injuries as the result of an understandable emotional outburst by officers.

Wilson was a despicable and unsympathetic plaintiff, but his suit led lawyers and investigators to numerous other defendants who told similar tales of torture at the hands of the Area 2 police, defendants who had no connection to each other and no opportunity to collude. They told nearly identical tales of torture more common in the third world, including suffocation with plastic bags and mock executions. Their testimony suggested that Burge and his crew inflicted excruciating pain by burning and electrocuting both the guilty and innocent, to induce confessions.

State's Attorney Daley never responded to Brzeczek's 1982 letter. He never initiated any investigation of the police misconduct, even after the Illinois Supreme Court cited "extensive medical testimony and photographic evidence corroborating the defendant's injuries" as the basis for overturning Wilson's conviction and death sentence. (Wilson was convicted at a second trial but avoided the death penalty).

Daley's explanations for his inaction varied. In 1990 he told the *Chicago Reader*, a well-read alternative newspaper, that he initiated an investigation through his special prosecution's unit but that Wilson's attorney, the public defender Dale Coventry, declined to cooperate. Coventry responded that he would never have allowed prosecutors access to his client.

"The only thing I would expect from any such investigation they did would be a total whitewash," he said, "and anything they learned would be used by the prosecution against my client. . . . The judges get up there and pretend to believe the police, and they don't, and the police get up there and tell their stories and nothing is ever done on these things."[4]

In a later legal deposition, under oath, Mayor Daley provided a less specific response than his 1990 defense to the *Chicago Reader*. He said he delegated the handling of the letter to his staff but had few recollections of what was done afterward.

The civil jury's exoneration of Burge in the Wilson civil suit, despite its finding on other incidents of torture at Area Two, damped any danger that the Midnight Crew's interrogation practices would see daylight, at least any time soon. As the 1989 mayor's race loomed, they remained hidden from public view, concealing not only hideous crimes but a giant political liability for Daley—one that, had it been known at the time, would have made his ascendency to the mayoralty virtually impossible.

First Term

1989–1991

CHAPTER 4

Campaign

When Richard M. Daley lost his bid for mayor in 1983, his dream of occupying city hall's coveted fifth floor seemed lost. Finishing last in the three-way contest, he was cast as a spoiler who made possible the election of the African American Congressman Harold Washington, alienating parts of his white ethnic base. And with a growing and emboldened Black community led by the charismatic new mayor, few observers would have predicted his ascendency a mere six years later.

But Mayor Harold Washington's untimely death and the languid leadership of his appointed successor Eugene Sawyer reopened the door to city hall. In a city desperate for leadership, Daley carried a name synonymous with strong mayoral governance, and he had spent eight years as state's attorney forging a strong record in his own right. In 1989, the African American community was also divided, as factions supporting Mayor Sawyer battled a progressive camp rallying around Ald. Tim Evans, the torchbearer of the Harold Washington legacy.

By the summer of 1988, Bill Daley, the mayor's wily brother, and other Daley intimates were already sketching a potential race for mayor. But Rich Daley remained introspective; after the last contest devolved into a painful racial maelstrom, he was not anxious to begin planning a second run. As the months passed and he remained noncommittal, Bill Daley became increasingly frustrated, at one point angrily blurting out to his brother, "Well, if you don't run, I will!" But nothing seemed to move Daley from his perplexing complacency.

Daley's hesitancy may have stemmed less from his own concerns than those of his wife Maggie, who was still nursing scars seared by the ugly racial dynamics of the previous race. In fact, when the time finally came to throw his hat in the ring, Daley hadn't yet broached his possible candidacy with her. In his bestselling memoir, *Believer*, David Axelrod—then Daley's media consultant—describes the scene at Daley's home when he and Bill Daley met the state's attorney and his wife for a preliminary strategy session.

> "Here, Rich, is a draft of a script I've written for a kickoff ad," I said, shoving a piece of paper across the coffee table. . . .
> "Script? What script?" Maggie asked. "What are you talking about?"
> "Uh, Mag," Rich said, a little sheepishly, with his face flushing. "There's something I've been meaning to tell you."
> "Okay, then," Bill said nervously, gathering up his papers. "David, why don't you and I go out for a little walk? I'll show you around the neighborhood. . . ."
> When they returned, Maggie made one thing clear.
> "I don't want to have any part of a racial thing," she said.[1]

Assured that her husband's campaign would carry a message of racial healing, Maggie gave her tepid support.

• • •

Although Daley's second mayoral campaign may have benefited from his famous name and his father's reputation for strong leadership, one thing was clear—he was not going to benefit from his father's old machine.

After Bilandic's defeat, State Sen. Daley had watched Mayor Byrne turn the ward committeemen against him. As the 1989 mayoral race loomed, Daley knew the white Northwest and Southwest Side ward chieftains had no choice but to line up against Sawyer, but their loyalties were not necessarily transferable to him. Vrdolyak was a candidate again, running this time as a Republican, and he still had his thumb on many of the ward leaders; others were benefiting from Sawyer's patronage, diminishing their incentive to work hard for Daley. Behind the scenes, the mob-controlled First Ward, which included Chinatown, had cast its lot with Sawyer.

The state's attorney could rely on a few ward bosses, such as Southwest Side Congressman Bill Lipinski, whom Daley had backed in a bitter primary ousting the incumbent Democratic Congressman John Fary; Daley's longtime ally, the Southwest Side committeeman and County Assessor Tom Hynes; and the Northwest Side committeeman Tom Lyons, a former state legislator. In addition, Daley counted on a handful of fraternal relationships with brilliant political organizers who, like him, had learned their craft toiling in Richard J. Daley's political vineyards. At the top of the list was his younger brother Bill, the chief strategist in his 1980 victory in the state's attorney contest. Bill had ventured into national politics as well, building early relationships with Georgia Governor Jimmy Carter when his presidential campaign was a long shot and with his perceptive young pollster, Pat Caddell. Using Caddell's analysis, Bill had warned Rich in 1979 that Mayor Bilandic was going to lose.

Ed Bedore, budget director under Richard J. Daley, was a key advisor with a strong sense of Chicago's neighborhoods. Despite having only a high school education, he rose through the ranks by mastering complex municipal finances and demonstrating shrewd negotiating skills with unions, legislators, and corporations alike. Through trial and error, Bedore and State Sen. Jeremiah Joyce had developed the art of straw polling at neighborhood shopping centers; although not scientific, they proved remarkably accurate.

Joyce had defeated the powerful Nineteenth Ward organization representing the Southwest Side's Beverly community and led by Tom Hynes, to win a seat on the city council. Hynes then embraced him, and Joyce succeeded Hynes in the state senate on his election as assessor. A former cop and prosecutor, Joyce was a member of the Mensa Society, reserved for geniuses scoring in the top 2 percent on standardized intelligence tests. It was unsurprising that the police department assigned him to its intelligence unit, which under Richard J. Daley spied on alleged subversives, earning it the moniker the Red Squad. Joyce worked in the more traditional gang intelligence unit, keeping tabs on actual criminals.

Joyce was a talented political organizer with a penchant for mischief. At the height of her purge of Daley's allies in city government, Mayor Byrne addressed a crowd of Democratic precinct captains at the old Bismarck Hotel. As she spoke, Joyce released a helium balloon carrying a tape recording of the late Mayor Daley's voice booming above their heads, warning that either they would "hang together or hang separately."[2]

It was Joyce's friend and colleague in the state senate, however, representing Daley's Bridgeport community, that the state's attorney entrusted with his campaign's precinct operations. Tim Degnan was assigned the task of building a grassroots neighborhood organization independent of the regular Democrats. Degnan played a key role in Daley's victory over Burke and his razor-thin win over the incumbent Bernard Carey in the 1980 general election.

With so few politicians Daley could trust, Degnan's loyalty was unquestioned. The Degnan and Daley families went back decades together in Bridgeport. Tim's father, Francis "Bud" Degnan, held the critical post of superintendent of streets and sanitation under Richard J. Daley. Bud Degnan enjoyed a unique relationship with Old Man Daley; their blunt and acerbic exchanges were a break from the usual staff obsequiousness. Degnan ensured that garbage pickup, street cleaning and snow removal were handled with competence and urgency. But he was also a street-smart political sounding board and advisor.

Many years after Bud Degnan's retirement, Tim's brother Robert (who later ran the city's fleets department) told me how he brought the entire family together to lobby their father on what he and his siblings thought would be an interesting project. "Dad, you've lived an exciting life and been part of so much history," Robert said. "You've got so many great stories. We think you should write a book."

The laconic elder Degnan listened, paused for a moment, took a puff on his cigar, then said, "There's only one problem with that." Robert looked at his siblings. "What's that?" he asked. His father replied: "We don't write books."[3]

Like Bud, Tim Degnan was as frugal with words as Ebenezer Scrooge with shillings and pence. Degnan intuitively understood Lyndon Johnson's observation: "You ain't learnin' nothin' when you're talkin.'"[4] He was a keen observer of politics and human nature and an invaluable source of unbiased information for Daley and had an eye for raw political talent. Degnan recruited a core of crack organizers, each carrying an insurgent's mentality but with a machine pedigree.

One of Degnan's first recruits was Tom Manion, a suburban chemicals salesman who stumbled into political organizing in 1979 when an Eleventh Ward friend asked for help in Bilandic's campaign. In 1989, Degnan assigned him the white ethnic Northwest Side wards, where Daley would need to roll up big margins. With one exception, Tom Lyons, the Northwest Side committeemen had all fallen in line with Byrne to oppose Daley in 1980. Manion built a powerful alternative field organization, drawing from young enthusiastic volunteers and displaced veterans of previous campaigns. Manion was contemptuous of the committeemen, whom he called "ward comedians," a phrase that became popular among Daley staffers. Even years later, Manion continued to vent his enmity toward the former Byrne-aligned Northwest Side ward bosses.[5]

Chicago's business community was the one place of united establishment support for Daley. Panicked by the city's long downward spiral and the perpetual racial and political divisions helping fuel it, leading businessmen contributed as much as $100,000 each (a quarter million in today's dollars) to jump-start the campaign, including the real estate developer Paul Beitler, the insurance magnate Pat Ryan, the cosmetics kingpin Irving Harris, the industrialist William Farley, and Richard Dennis, a commodities trader known as the "Prince of the Pits" for his dominance of the open-outcry Board of Trade. Dennis's southside Irish roots were closest to Daley's. His father was a streets and sanitation worker who would often punch into work, then play hooky with his school-age sons to watch afternoon White Sox games at Comiskey Park in Bridgeport. Dennis later became a part owner of the team.

Daley built a fundraising machine to match the robustness of his field operation. Led by his longtime finance chair, the real estate developer and restauranteur Paul Stepan, and the thirty-year-old campaign fundraising whiz Rahm Emanuel, a future congressman and mayor, Daley built a substantial lead in campaign cash. Among Stepan's many ventures was Harry Caray's Restaurant, now in its fourth decade in Chicago, celebrating the iconic and colorful broadcaster who, with his unique style, enthusiasm, and humor (and his trademark "Holy cow!"), announced Chicago Cubs games for nearly two decades.

I had met Emanuel in a 1980 campaign in central Illinois, a long-shot bid by Springfield State Rep. David Robinson against the veteran US Representative Paul Findley, the leading congressional advocate for the Palestine Liberation Organization (PLO) at the height of its enmity with Israel. Rahm shrewdly tapped into a vein of wealthy supporters of Israel, and an avalanche of money from the national Jewish community turned this sleepy rural race into a hot contest. Although Robinson fell short, Dick Durbin used the same fundraising base two years later to oust Findley before later succeeding Paul Simon in the US Senate.

Rahm Israel Emanuel went by the less Jewish-sounding alias Ron Madison when interacting with the local rustics and making fundraising cold calls.[6] He would join me most evenings at Springfield's Midway Pub for a beer and a horseshoe, the local delicacy, consisting of either turkey or hamburger buried in fries and smothered in melted Velveeta cheese.

The Stepan-Emanuel fundraising apparatus was so robust that the campaign struggled to find uses for all its cash, even splurging on a Super Bowl TV ad. In a sign of the times and the city, half of the budget went to field operations—paying for the targeted registration of eighty thousand new voters and for foot soldiers to canvass neighborhoods, documenting likely supporters. Casting early ballots was not an option in 1989; everything came down to delivering the vote on election day.

Daley's campaign manager, David Wilhelm, was also an alumnus of the Robinson campaign who had reunited with Rahm and me four years later in Paul Simon's 1984 US Senate race. He then joined US Sen. Joe Biden's 1988 presidential campaign, where he met Bill Daley. Wilhelm oversaw the Iowa caucuses and built a formidable ground operation in the first-in-the-country contest. But before he could put his troops to the test, Biden dropped out following a plagiarism controversy.[7] Taking advantage of Biden's misfortune, Bill Daley snatched this talented political operative for his brother's campaign. (Wilhelm got a second chance at presidential politics four years later, managing Arkansas Gov. Bill Clinton's successful presidential campaign and then serving as chairman of the Democratic National Committee.)

Wilhelm, a native of Athens, Ohio, reminisced with me about some of his first Chicago experiences, remembering them as culture shocks.

In my first voter focus groups, when people were asked where they lived, they didn't say their street name or even their neighborhood. They said they lived in the Tenth Ward or the Thirty-Sixth Ward or Seventeenth Ward. Who talks like that? I found out—Chicago voters do.[8]

On his first day, he received a call from Ald. Eugene Schulter of the heavily German American Forty-Seventh Ward. "We are so proud of you," Schulter told Wilhelm, who had no idea what the alderman was talking about. "Who is 'we,' Mr. Alderman?" Wilhelm asked.

"Why, we are the German people of Chicago," Schulter responded. "We never thought the Daleys would hire a German to run one of their campaigns!"[9]

With all the money he needed, Daley saturated the airwaves with commercials. David Axelrod decided to inoculate against the Sawyer attack everyone knew was coming. Daley's struggles with the Queen's English caused many to question his intelligence, and he was often reminded it took him three tries to pass the bar exam. The belief that Daley was somehow daft became a fixture even in the national press.

"Many voters here wonder whether Mr. Daley is competent enough to run Chicago," the *Washington Post* wrote as Daley prepared for his second mayoral campaign. "He is maligned as, among other things, a lousy lawyer and none too bright."[10]

Axelrod filmed Daley talking directly to the camera, making fun of his own impediments. The concluding line was, "I may not be the best speaker in town, but

I know how to run a government and bring people together." When Sawyer ran the inevitable "dumb-dumb Daley" ads, they had little impact.

Daley's advertising reflected his overarching theme of racial reconciliation. After years of the Council Wars, the city wanted a uniter, not a divider. But in 1989, news coverage was even more important than advertising.

It is difficult to describe how radically different Chicago's political scene was in 1989. Politics was still a spectator sport. The city had been roiled by years of drama and turmoil, from the capricious and revolving-door government of Calamity Jane to the racial power struggle of the Council Wars. In a period before the internet and around-the-clock cable TV, news of the mayoral campaign came in the morning and evening print editions of the *Tribune* and the *Sun-Times*, delivered to your door or for sale on street corners for a quarter; from the oligopoly of TV stations—ABC, NBC, CBS, and WGN; and through a robust band of radio outlets, including influential Latino- and Black-owned stations.

Average Chicagoans had a high degree of political awareness and were hungry for information on what was shaping up to be a historic election. Reporters aggressively sought a fresh angle for the top of each broadcast or edition. For TV stations, it meant breaking fresh news at noon, 4:30, 6:00, and 10:00. Driving this frenzy of coverage were some big media personalities. Each TV station had its own political reporter with deep knowledge of the city's history and politics: Dick Kay and Carol Marin at NBC news, Mike Flannery at CBS, and Hugh Hill and Andy Shaw at ABC. The TV networks' affiliated radio stations had their own veteran political reporters—Bill Cameron, Bob Crawford, and Craig Dellimore—competing against the newspapers and their sister television stations for scoops.

All day, reporters combed their sources, dug through research, and quizzed political operatives. At each campaign stop, Daley would be confronted by a gaggle of journalists shouting questions. Usually the questions were negative, often asking for his response to the latest accusation launched from Sawyer headquarters.

As Daley's message began resonating, his lead climbed. Seeking to protect it, he increasingly tried to shrug off the latest accusations from Sawyer. As he emerged at campaign stops from his chauffeur-driven campaign car, he fell into the habit of sneering at reporters as he dismissed criticism, usually with the disdainful brush-off, "Ah, that's just politics!"

Watching the TV coverage, Bill Daley grew increasingly alarmed. He felt the campaign's momentum was in jeopardy from the constant images of a glowering Daley avoiding legitimate questions and frantically rushing past pursuing reporters.

As the campaign turned in to the home stretch, Bill asked me to his corner office, where he showed me tapes of recent disastrous reporter interactions. "I want you to ride with Rich the rest of the campaign," he told me. My new assignment was to be at Daley's side from early morning until late at night, ensuring a prepared and calm candidate emerged between stops to debunk the latest attacks while staying on message.

The campaign communications chief Avis LaVelle, a former top radio reporter for WGN, set up a tag-team operation. LaVelle monitored breaking news feeds and kibbitzed with reporters to get wind of what Daley would encounter and when. Armed with this often just-in-time intelligence, I engaged Daley in the car with rapid-fire Q and A rehearsals, letting him know what was coming and suggesting language to parry the assaults. Despite the short and sometimes frantic nature of the prep sessions, Daley absorbed the information quickly and gratefully, emerging as a calmer, more confident candidate. Back on offense, Daley's lead stabilized.

In fact, everything was going smoothly again—until I received a strange and disturbing phone call.

I was riding in the backseat of the Daley campaign car, the candidate up front for a change to accommodate a new addition to our traveling team, Deputy Press Secretary Marj Halperin. As the campaign grew even more intense, Marj was another talented and experienced press hand, having been a formidable radio journalist at WBEZ.

As Marj and I compared notes for the coming stop, the car phone rang. Avis informed me that Daley was being accused by the Sawyer campaign of making an overt racial appeal to an audience of predominantly Polish voters on the city's Southwest Side, telling them they needed a "white mayor."

I found the idea of Daley making such a statement absurd, but stranger slipups had occurred in heated campaigns. Had he been fatigued and said something taken out of context? I felt a chill down my spine, knowing the implications. If true, it would blow up the entire premise of Daley's candidacy, put us on the defensive for the rest of the race, and give Sawyer's campaign new life.

I had to deliver the bad news. I tapped Daley on the shoulder and told him what was being reported. His face turned red, and his eyes seemed to recede into his skull. "No, no," he said. "I don't understand."

We didn't have time for staff to gather more information. We were late for a stop in the Northwest Side's Forty-Seventh Ward, hosted by Ald. Eugene Schulter. The local business and neighborhood groups were honoring Daley with a German-themed celebration.

What followed was one of the most painful (yet retrospectively comedic) scenes I've ever witnessed in politics. There, in the middle of the stage, stood candidate Daley, surrounded by fat old men in Lederhosen and buxom women in dirndl dresses with traditional bodices, skirts, and aprons. They were dancing around Daley to alpine folk music. It was a surreal moment. Daley was motionless, reddened eyes fixed straight ahead despite the colorful revelry all around him, his life flashing before his eyes, trying to make sense of what he had just learned.

It seemed like an eternity but somehow Daley managed to thank the audience before quickly departing through the back. By the time we got to the car, the campaign had acquired a tape. Although it was hardly definitive, a casual listener might certainly believe Daley had said "you want a white mayor." As we listened, however, Marj noticed something. "It's the stump speech," she said. "What?" I asked. "It's the stump speech. He turned it around," she said.

Marj and I had heard the speech a thousand times. One line was, "What you want is a mayor who can sit down with everybody." Daley, with his propensity to maul the English language, had stumbled and instead said, "You want a *what mayor* who can sit down with everybody."

Marj and I presented the theory to reporters in what became known as the "what mayor" or "wet mayor" controversy. The traveling press corps was aware of Daley's tendency to mangle speech, had similarly heard the stump speech ad nauseam, and knew his candidacy was premised on racial healing. But in a city riven by racial politics for a decade, the story was irresistible. For Sawyer, whose campaign was flagging, it was a chance to go on the attack and claim the moral high ground.

Daley had spent an inordinate amount of time campaigning in the Black community, primarily to reassure the swing-vote, liberal, white lakefront voters that he would be a mayor for the entire city. The "white mayor" dustup threatened to upend that strategy and shift the race's dynamics in Sawyer's favor.

With white lakefront liberals in mind, the Sawyer camp turned to a group of self-appointed do-gooders called CONDUCT, purportedly a watchdog against inflammatory racial rhetoric. The group had already censured three different Black Sawyer supporters for kindling racial flames. Its leadership was mostly white, and Sawyer's camp wasted no time exploiting their liberal white guilt. After rebuking Sawyer's Black supporters three times, how could they now look aside as Daley made a naked appeal to white voters to elect one of their own?

It was a perfect example of why truth is so often a casualty of politics. Under pressure to look even handed, CONDUCT censured Daley, giving credibility to a risible accusation.

A further irony was the timing of the charges. Daley was in the middle of a multiweek close to the campaign in which he traveled to every ward and participated in themed celebrations of the unique character of each community.

"We challenged each neighborhood to outdo the other in a celebration of their culture, history and pride," Wilhelm remembers. "Those three weeks constitute one of my proudest memories because by the end of it Rich Daley had somehow sewn together a quilt out of individual patches of Chicago, which had seemingly been at war with each other just months ago."[11]

Daley had also spent an inordinate amount of time courting pastors on the Black South and West Sides. He was under no illusions that he would win significant African American votes, but it was a concerted effort to reach out to all communities. To the astonishment of the media and local pols, Daley pulled off a press conference close to the election, flanked by dozens of endorsing Black ministers.

At least in high-profile races, voters are often surprisingly discerning. They had watched Daley long enough to filter the noise and conclude that a brazen racial appeal was not consistent with his personality or character. The "what mayor" gaffe did not turn out to be a game-changing moment.

As election day dawned, Wilhelm experienced more Chicago culture shock. He was presented with a roomful of briefcases containing rolls of quarters. Before ubiquitous cell phones, election workers in the field relied on pay phones to check in, make reminder calls to voters, and report precinct results to headquarters on election night. Next to the briefcases were envelopes filled with tens of thousands of dollars—street cash to be distributed by Degnan's field staff, ostensibly to buy lunches for campaign workers.

An army of Daley operatives, battle hardened from the monthslong campaign, began their most important duties on election day. Before dawn, each precinct leader placed a door hanger at the residence of every known Daley supporter, then headed to the polls, jawboning entering voters. Around two in the afternoon, each worker checked the list of those voting and cross-referenced them to their known supporters, then dispatched "runners" to knock on the doors of those who had not yet voted. If they didn't answer, the runner was instructed to leave a preprinted slip of paper that read simply, "You have not voted."

Wilhelm interpreted the admonition as slightly threatening, or at least cold and unhelpful. He asked Tim Degnan to change it.

"Why don't we warm that up a bit," Wilhelm said. "Perhaps ask people to be sure and vote and add 'please.'"

"It's fine," Degnan replied tersely. "This is the way we've always done it. It's effective."[12]

It was. On primary election day, Daley defeated Mayor Sawyer with 55.6 percent of the vote.

In Chicago, one might think winning the Democratic primary ended the campaign. But in the 1980s, race often trumped party affiliation. Daley had toppled the incumbent mayor but now faced Sawyer's African American rival, Ald. Tim Evans, in the general election, running under the Harold Washington banner, and white former Ald. Ed Vrdolyak, running as a Republican. Both had filed as general election candidates to avoid splitting their respective racial bases.

In the April general election, however, Evans performed no better than Sawyer, and Vrdolyak set a record for fewest votes by a Republican nominee, 3 percent. Richard M. Daley was elected the fifty-fourth mayor of Chicago.

Throughout the campaign, Wilhelm had only limited interactions with the candidate. They spoke mostly through Bill Daley, the campaign chairman. So Wilhelm's last surprise came around four in the afternoon on election day. The phone rang. It was Rich Daley.

"I'd like you to introduce me tonight," he said.

Wilhelm was stunned. "I had close to no relationship with him. I often wondered if he appreciated what I did, or respected me in any way," Wilhelm said. "Of all the people he might have had bring him up to the podium, all the people who played much larger roles in his life, he turned to me. I guess that was his way of saying thanks."[13]

After Wilhelm's introduction and Daley's victory speech, confetti rained down on the packed crowd of cheering supporters and on the stage where Daley stood with his wife Maggie and their children, Nora, Patrick, and Elizabeth. In his second try, just turning forty-seven, he had won the same office as his legendary father. It was a dire time for the city, and he was ready to get to work.

CHAPTER 5

Wins

The new mayor entered office with a sense of urgency. Because Daley was serving the unexpired portion of Mayor Harold Washington's term, he would face voters again in less than twenty-two months, and he would be running on his record as the incumbent. Daley moved swiftly to assemble his leadership team, including his longtime kitchen cabinet advisor, John Schmidt, who agreed to serve as chief of staff, but only for the critical first ninety days. Schmidt had worked closely with State Sen. Daley on his numerous Springfield reforms. He was a wealthy and brilliant lawyer for a nationally renowned law firm. A few years later he would become President Bill Clinton's associate attorney general, the third-highest ranking post in the Justice Department.

Schmidt asked me to join the administration as his deputy, a suggestion from the mayor, who had grown to trust my judgment on the campaign trail.

On Daley's first day in office, the senior team gathered around the chief of staff's conference room table for the first of the daily 7:30 a.m. meetings. The mayor stopped by for a few minutes, lounging against the hallway door with a glint in his eye, chewing on an unlit cigar.

Around the table was a combination of Daley veterans and newbies—Schmidt; the longtime policy aide Frank Kruesi, who had been Daley's senior advisor in the Illinois Senate and state's attorney's office; the new intergovernmental affairs chief Tim Degnan, who had resigned his state senate seat to take the post after successfully running the campaign's precinct operations; Budget Director Ed Bedore, an experienced municipal finance expert and budget director under Richard J. Daley's administration; Press Secretary Avis LaVelle, reprising her campaign role; Kelly Welsh, the corporation counsel; Barbara Grochala, the mayoral scheduler; and Paul Toback, the mayor's new executive assistant who served as one of Degnan's deputies in the campaign.

It was an assertive group, but the most outspoken voice was LaVelle, a veteran reporter for WGN radio who led the campaign's communications and was appointed the mayor's first press secretary. Her appointment was a recruiting coup. Daley meaningfully had chosen a seasoned journalist to be his spokesperson; equally significant, he had appointed an African American. LaValle had the respect of the press corps and valuable relationships. She channeled the media's thinking effectively, warning of what was to come, but she also was a strong voice for the Black community at a time when Daley was still distrusted there.

The morning meeting presented an interesting mix. Bedore and Kruesi resented sharing the table with Daley rookies, given the two operatives' long history in the trenches with the family. But the mayor wanted new blood and old, as a check on groupthink and to ensure a competitive mix of skill sets and ideas.[1] To ensure that competition didn't turn into turf wars and backstabbing (as in the first-term Clinton White House), Daley held the team accountable for the actions of each member. Daley would yell at me for mistakes Frank made and yell at Frank for mistakes I made. He wouldn't hear of any blame shifting. He expected us to work as a team.

Having worked with Kruesi since his time in the state senate, Daley was aware of his proclivity for secrecy. Kruesi was naturally suspicious and would have made a fine secret agent, complete with cloak and dagger. As time passed, perhaps out of necessity or because of Daley's mandate, he opened up more to the outsiders on the team. But his reputation remained intact. When years later he left city hall to accept a top position with the US Department of Transportation, Kruesi was feted at a going-away party. Peter Cunningham, a mayoral advisor and professional musician, wrote a song for the occasion. The chorus was, "How can we be frank with Frank when Frank won't be frank with us?"

During every morning meeting for the next two years, I sat between the two chain smokers—Grochala and Degnan—taking years off my life. Degnan was the glue—guileless, impervious to Daley's moods or criticisms, and an astute observer of human nature with a wealth of political and municipal government experience. Degnan said very little but was the most important voice at the table. As a colleague once observed, "Degnan will sit through an entire meeting with nothing to say, just listening, and then ask the only question that matters."

One of Degnan's top priorities was extending mayoral control beyond city government. In his first term, Mayor Daley confronted the same issue as Harold Washington—sister agencies that remained in the hands of appointees left over from previous administrations. These "independent" agencies, such as the transit authority, city colleges, and the park district, were run by mayoral appointees serving staggered terms. Degnan held weekly meetings to review lists of potential appointees to boards and commissions, carefully monitoring term-expiration dates. The moment a term expired, the post was filled with a Daley loyalist.

Daley's first jobs were to reduce racial tensions, stop the chaotic infighting in the city council, and unite the city behind common goals such as safer neighborhoods and better schools.

Building on the Harold Washington legacy, Daley put together a majority-minority cabinet to reflect the city's diversity. But that was a tougher task when it came to the roughly one thousand confidential, managerial, and policy-making positions that were exempt from legal restrictions on patronage hiring. After six years under Black mayors, the exempt workforce was overwhelmingly minority, and especially African American. Most of Daley's campaign workers were white, and they needed homes in the administration. The government immediately below the cabinet level was going to get a lot whiter, which also meant a lot of pink slips for African American employees. Over time, racial balance in hiring would even out; but in the beginning, loyalty to those who fought in the precincts took precedence over racial politics. By the end of Daley's first year, the number of African Americans holding policy-making positions had fallen 25 percent.

But Daley had another lever to mitigate some of that political liability—affirmative action in contracting. By this time, courts were narrowing the ability of governments to apply affirmative action, allowing it only where historical discrimination was evident. So the City of Chicago had to document, as part of the public record, evidence of its past racial discrimination. Daley found it necessary to appear before the city council as part of its fact finding, testifying that Chicago's government had discriminated against Black and Latino citizens for the past thirty years, a period encompassing the administration of his late father.

"He came in, and he testified that yes, there had been discrimination for the past 30 years. . . . He had to show that this was a remedy for past wrong," said the *Tribune* columnist John McCarron, chuckling at the irony.[2]

Understanding that awards of city contracts were at the heart of mayoral power—especially in an age of reduced patronage—Daley had moved quickly to strip the city council of its authority to approve contracts, a privilege that aldermen had enjoyed under the previous two mayors. Now, he deployed his contracting powers with both governance and politics in mind.

Daley's early years as mayor were sometimes marked by stories of lucrative contracts finding their way to friends and family, in the Chicago tradition; but he deflected criticism by using his minority set-aside ordinance to spread the wealth in contracting, awarding a record 40 percent of city contracts to minority and women-owned firms, paying political dividends among voters who had shunned him in his race for mayor.

Behind the scenes, however, the mayor's set-aside program was not all that it seemed. It had no mechanisms to verify the minority status of owners, nor did it have any policing or the normal auditing accompanying programs of such magnitude. In fact, those weaknesses would ultimately create major headaches for Daley, one of which was entirely of his own making, with roots in a mysterious mayoral relationship.

• • •

On the fifth floor of city hall, a large anteroom abuts the cavernous office where the mayor receives visitors. Two executive secretaries sit at large desks, acting as gatekeepers. As chief of staff in the mayor's first term, I would often walk the fifty feet from my office, past the waiting visitors, to share information with the mayor or to get his guidance. Other Daley aides would come in and out, usually summoned by the mayor for quick instructions or to answer a question.

During these early years, as we chatted among ourselves, a common refrain was, "Why are the Duffs in the waiting room?" Usually the question was followed by an incredulous, "Again? Why are the Duffs seeing the mayor *again*?" The commonplace presence of John "Jack" Duff, Jr. and one or more of his sons was something of an inside joke among staffers.

Shortly after the mayor was elected, Jack's wife, using her maiden name, Patricia Green, formed Windy City Maintenance, a janitorial company. Green had no previous experience in the field. The firm was certified as a woman-owned business under the city's preferential contracting system. In 1990, a city ordinance was amended to allow the Department of Special Events to contract directly with vendors without competitive bidding. Not long after, Windy City received a no-bid contract to handle the annual Taste of Chicago festival in the sprawling Grant Park on the city's lakefront; the contract was later expanded to cover most other city events.

In the next decade, Windy City Maintenance would be awarded more than $100 million in city contracts to provide janitorial services for O'Hare Airport and McCormick Place, police headquarters, the 911 center, and Taste of Chicago—all on the premise that it was operated by a woman.

Patricia Green Duff's husband, Jack, was the family patriarch who for years ran Local 3, the union representing liquor warehouse workers. Duff was also a convicted embezzler and mob associate. Among his closest friends was Anthony "Big Tuna" Accardo, the boss of the Chicago Outfit. Years previously, Duff had helped Accardo beat the rap in his trial for income tax evasion. Accardo claimed he was a salesman for a local beer distributor, Fox Head Beer. The feds believed the company was a front to hide income from his racketeering. But Duff assured them that it was legitimate, testifying that he regularly sold beer to Accardo.

Ernest Rocco Infelise was another Duff pal, an underboss of the Chicago mob who allegedly controlled the rackets on the South Side of Chicago and southern Cook County. When Jack's son John (Jack Duff III) fell behind on his gambling debts to a mob bookie, Infelise did his father a favor by paying them off. According to the FBI, which secretly recorded Jack's conversations, he also palled around with Frank "Fifi" Buccieri, who ran the syndicate's West Coast operations during the 1970s and 1980s, and Anthony Spilotro, who managed Las Vegas casinos for the Outfit. Spilotro was famously murdered by higher-ups who disapproved of his handling of their assets. He and his brother were found buried together in an Indiana cornfield. Spilotro was the basis for the character Nicky Santoro in the director Martin Scorsese's 1995 film *Casino*.

John Duff, the oldest son, also had mob ties. He was removed from his position with the Hotel Restaurant Employees Union for having a ghost union job. He was also accused of threatening to kill a Florida police officer and his family following his arrest for blocking traffic while trying to pick up a prostitute. According to the police report, Duff told the policeman, "You better listen" because he had "connections with organized crime in Chicago."[3]

John Duff may have been in Florida overseeing other business interests. The feds alleged that Duff ran an illegal gambling operation in Florida with New York's Gambino crime family. Unfortunately for the FBI, an agent assigned to the investigation had his own mob-related gambling problems and undercut the probe. Duff was not charged, but the wayward FBI agent spent five years in prison.

The Duff's ties to the Cosa Nostra would have proved difficult for Daley to defend, perhaps explaining Mrs. Duff's return to her maiden name in filing city paperwork; and by most accounts, Patricia Green's firm delivered services efficiently and generated no controversies, at least not until years later.[4] In the meantime, it was merely part of a bonanza of city contracts for minority firms that generated goodwill for Mayor Daley.

• • •

With a new election looming soon, Daley sought wins. They came in many forms.

By reaching out to minority aldermen, finding ways to help them in their wards, he showed that racial cooperation was possible. By balancing his first budgets without tax increases, he demonstrated a quiet competence. In Springfield, he passed ambitious public works projects and laid the groundwork for others, taking advantage of a Democratic legislature and a Republican governor, James Thompson, with a penchant for bipartisan dealmaking.

Some wins were symbolic.

When Daley's press secretary, Avis LaVelle, parked her municipal-plated vehicle in the tow zone in front of city hall, following a tradition among senior City Hall aides, the mayor ordered her car towed. She had to fetch it from the city pound and pay the fine like every other citizen. It was the sort of man-bites-dog story that the press ate up and showed that a new sheriff was in town, bent on reforming the old ways.

The ambitious first-term Springfield agenda required the energy and expertise of most of the senior team, led by Schmidt and Degnan, and supported by the policy expert Kruesi and the finance guru Bedore, who negotiated most of the new funding formulas benefiting the city, including an increase in the income tax shared with municipalities and a rare bump in the gas tax that included a dedicated revenue stream for the city. For Chicago, the 1989–91 sessions of the General Assembly were among the most productive in history.

With Gov. James Thompson anxious to enact big job-creating projects before the following year's statewide elections, Daley cut a deal to rebuild the rotting, dilapidated Navy Pier off the downtown shoreline. Within two months of the mayor's swearing-in, the Illinois legislature authorized a new city-state authority incorporating both Navy Pier and the Metropolitan Exposition Authority, which oversees the McCormick Place convention center, along with $150 million in state bonds to finance the pier's reconstruction. The new hybrid authority became known simply as "McPier."

Extending thirty-three hundred feet into Lake Michigan, Navy Pier was the largest pier in the world when it opened in 1916. Built on top of twenty thousand wooden logs, it was designed for recreation—consistent with the famed architect Daniel Burnham's recommendation for two such piers extending from the central city's shore. But with the outbreak of the First World War in Europe, it was converted to military use, housing soldiers and sailors. During the Second World War, fifteen thousand fighter pilots trained at the pier, flying off makeshift aircraft carriers built from Great Lakes passenger steamers. More than one hundred aircraft that failed to get enough lift lie off the pier at the bottom of Lake Michigan.

It was ironic that, eighteen months before his death in office in December of 1976, the mayor's father, Richard J. Daley,and the city council had approved $7.2 million toward a potential $34 million renovation of the pier, one in a long line of false starts toward restoring this city landmark. The *Tribune* editorial board opined at the time that the "alternative would be to see Navy Pier become even more derelict than it is. Either it will be revived somehow, or it will be a big black eye on Chicago's face. . . . Surely some time Chicago will find a means of turning Navy Pier's unused potential into reality."[5]

That time was fifteen years later, when the son succeeded where the father failed.

Navy Pier was rebuilt as a glistening tourist mecca, which today attracts millions of visitors annually. Its features include a children's museum and a Shakespearean theater. Boat tours launch every half hour during summer months. Restaurants and bars run the length of the wharf, and patrons can sit or walk outside to enjoy the glistening blue waters of Lake Michigan and views of the city's architecturally resplendent buildings.

Navy Pier added its own iconic addition to Chicago's skyline, the Centennial Wheel, a Ferris wheel ride rising two hundred feet, with climate-controlled gondolas that remain in operation year-round. The brightly lit cylinder is an homage to a more primitive version that was the star attraction of the 1893 Chicago World's Fair.

Chicago's lakefront protection ordinance sets rigorous standards limiting new construction, particularly of tall buildings that might affect the unblemished sight-lines. Civic groups such as Friends of the Parks have played a historic watchdog role in preserving the lakefront's unique character.

John Schmidt was aware of the civic group's role and its litigious tendencies. After his ninety-day stint as chief of staff, he was appointed by Daley to be the first chairman of the McPier Authority. For meetings and hearings on the new Navy Pier design, he commissioned a table-top rendering at scale. It included all the structures at their proportional heights, except one. Aware of the controversy a giant Ferris wheel might trigger, Schmidt kept two of the miniature versions in his pocket. One, for public hearings, was the same height as the other structures. The second, which he placed on the display for private meetings with key state officials or architects, was at scale, towering over the other building models.

With Navy Pier secured, including its jumbo Ferris wheel, Schmidt could focus on the other part of his new portfolio, McCormick Place, the city's economically critical convention center.

Thanks to the visionary leadership of the former *Chicago Tribune* publisher Robert McCormick, who for decades championed a lakeside convention center, Chicago built and opened its facility in 1960 and named it for McCormick, who had passed away five years earlier. As a result, Chicago captured an early leading share of the national convention business, aided by its central location, easy airport access, and vibrant nightlife. McCormick Place's status in the pantheon of convention destinations was anchored by the renowned Chicago Auto Show, as well as the Housewares Show and the annual exhibition of the National Restaurant Association.

But by 1990, other cities were making a play for Chicago's business—especially Orlando and Las Vegas, with the advantages of year-round warm weather and the entertainment lures of Disney World and casinos.

McCormick Place provided a size and scale few cities could match, but keeping that competitive advantage required continuous investment. So in 1991 Daley championed a $1 billion expansion requiring state legislative approval, financed with new taxes on hotels, restaurants, and rental cars. When Senate President Philip Rock called Daley's bill prematurely, however, it went down to defeat. Rock was outflanked by anti-Chicago forces led by James "Pate" Philip, the Republican senate leader. Embarrassed by Philip, Rock then stunned city hall a second time by declaring the legislation dead.

Accustomed to more disciplined leadership, Daley was caught by surprise. Not only had he not been consulted, as would be normal protocol, but his own brother, State Senator John Daley, was so unaware of Rock's plans that he wasn't on the floor when the vote was called. Daley and Degnan, veterans of the state senate, took matters into their own hands. Their efforts were a tutorial on the value of historic relationships and the astute leveraging of hard mayoral political capital—money, jobs, and political ambition.[6]

With thousands of jobs at stake, Degnan first called Edward Hanley, the head of the hotel and restaurant employees union, whose members depended heavily on McCormick Place's vitality. Hanley was a major fundraiser for Rock. To peel away downstate votes, Daley reminded Sen. Vince Demuzio (D-Carlinville) that he had supported his successful candidacy for state party chair years previously. He enlisted his close ally, Sen. Jeremiah Joyce, to lean on his friendship with an influential downstate senator, Richard Luft (D-Pekin), who in turn arranged additional downstate support. Daley personally called Sen. Tom Dunn (D-Joliet) to solicit his vote, a big IOU Dunn knew he could keep in his drawer for future use. Closer to home, he peeled away two members of Philip's Republican caucus from Chicago who not coincidentally held city jobs they wanted to protect, including city paramedic Robert Raica and Walter Dudycz, a former police officer seeking reinstatement. Dudycz had resigned his police post on his election but then sought part-time duties like other double-dipping legislators allowed to hold two government jobs.

Daley's flurry of activity raised the legislation from the dead. The resurrected bill passed the General Assembly and was signed into law by newly elected Republican Governor Jim Edgar, setting in motion a massive six-year construction project that would double the size of Chicago's convention center, ensuring that the city would remain among the nation's convention-business leaders.[7]

Daley's legislative successes, including McPier, were an impressive beginning to his mayoralty. But he was just getting started.

CHAPTER 6

Quality of Life

After Chief of Staff John Schmidt took on the new role of McPier chairman and also returned to his law practice in the summer of 1989, Daley facilitated a reshuffling that blended the old and new while navigating potential rivalries. He named me chief administrative officer and Frank Kruesi chief policy officer, announcing us together.

As he turned his office over to me, Schmidt had only one piece of advice—keep Pam Jackson, the executive assistant he inherited from Mayor Sawyer's chief of staff. Given the general distrust of Sawyer officials, it was astonishing that Schmidt kept Jackson to begin with, but she showed her discretion as well as outstanding administrative skills.

"I could keep up with him, and I think that impressed him," Jackson told me, laughing.

As a single mom, Jackson raised two sons in the rough Rockwell Gardens public housing projects but relocated after her community college classes led to a stenographer's job. When her younger son, Jaton, struggled in public school, she scraped together the money for a Catholic education and barely managed to finance college for her older son, Jamal. She caught a break when Jaton won a college football scholarship through a bit of serendipity. After he was expelled from his private school for repeated insubordination, an exasperated Jackson walked him into CVS High School, where he caught the eye of the football coach. Because Jamal stood 6 feet, 4 inches with plenty of girth, the coach asked if he wanted to play football. Before he could answer, his mother interjected.

"Yes, he does," she said, taking the decision away from her son and ensuring another source of tough discipline. He eventually became a fearsome collegiate defensive tackle and, more important, a college graduate.

Jackson worked for me for years, at city hall and the park district, always running the office like clockwork. She later became Mayor Daley's first African American executive assistant.

Happily ceding city policy to Frank, I focused on the mayor's less glamorous housekeeping, or "quality of life," agenda, working closely with Streets and Sanitation, the Department of Transportation, and other core operating departments. A new intelligence-gathering unit provided the information on where to start, an example of how the new mayor used his knowledge of city government's past to improve its future.

Daley installed Eileen Carey as head of a new agency of Inquiry and Information (I&I), a hotline for citizens to report problems or request services. Traditionally, service requests came from aldermen, whom residents would call when they needed anything, from a new garbage can to replacement of a streetlight. I&I didn't end that tradition, but it began to shift it inexorably to city hall.

Carey was a workaholic Daley loyalist from the Nineteenth Ward, an Irish bastion bordering the suburbs on the city's far Southwest Side, and home to many police officers and firefighters. Her brother Tom was a key operative in Daley's close 1980 state's attorney victory. In the prosecutor's office, Eileen Carey was part of a victims' assistance unit, monitoring progress in cases and providing support services. She would later become the first female and longest-serving superintendent of the sprawling Streets and Sanitation department. During snowstorms and other emergencies, Carey would work around the clock for days, catching a couple of hours sleep on her office couch before taking charge again.

Under Carey, I&I became the eyes and ears of the administration. The data unearthed patterns before they became obvious and allowed the revitalized city government to respond immediately to citizen concerns.

Abandoned automobiles topped the list of citizen complaints. In the summer of 1989, more than twenty thousand littered Chicago streets and vacant lots. The city spent millions each year towing the junkers away without making a dent in the backlog. Many were driven in from the suburbs and dumped—providing havens for rats, prostitution, drug deals, and other criminal activity. The mere presence of so many rusting hulks sent a clear message about the state of the surrounding community and the low level of civic concern.

In 1989, abandoned autos, pervasive graffiti, burned-out streetlights, abandoned buildings, weed-strewn lots, homeless encampments, and commonplace sightings of "super rats" all contributed to a sense that no one cared. By addressing these issues aggressively, the mayor intended to restore order and a sense of equity to neglected neighborhoods.

Sarah Pang, a former legislative aide to US Sen. Alan Dixon, served as Daley's senior deputy for public safety, a role in which she worked closely with both police brass and neighborhood organizations. Pang had a name for the benefits of aggressively attacking these community problems—the reservoir theory.

"Bad things are always going to happen," Pang said. "But if your alley is clean, potholes are filled, streetlights are on and city workers are doing a good job with the basics, it creates a reservoir of goodwill to draw on when things go bad."[1]

Abandoned cars exemplified social disorder; Daley made it my problem to solve. I pulled in Daley's talented executive assistant, Paul Toback, to help. A Stanford and

University of Chicago Law School graduate, Toback left the security of his blue-chip law firm to join Daley's campaign. He was a natural-born manager and had a great instinct for politics. A few years later he would serve as the top White House aide to President Bill Clinton's chief of staff Mack McLarty.

Toback told me that he had barely arrived in his office on the first day when Daley summoned him. As Toback walked in, Daley was standing at the floor-to-ceiling windows overlooking downtown. Daley gestured toward the windows and said, "You see that? Do you see what I see?" Toback said it was a moment he had dreamed about. He was working for the mayor of Chicago, who was asking if he saw the same vision for the city.

"I started to answer," Toback recalled, "and tell the mayor that, yes, I too saw the opportunities awaiting us to remake the city outside those windows. But then he interrupted me."

"These windows are filthy!" Daley said. "Get someone in here to clean them!"[2]

Toback and I followed the logical path, starting with local towing companies to supplement the city's resources. We found lots of mom-and-pop shops, but none with the equipment and scale to rid the city of tens of thousands of junkers.

Eventually we got a tip from a mayoral pal, Jeremiah Joyce. In the Chicago tradition, Joyce knew a guy who knew a guy. Martin McNally was a lawyer who for many years had advised E&R Towing, a national business towing autos for insurance companies. Its fleet of large, mechanized flatbed trucks could haul multiple cars in a single run.

The CEO, Ed Corcoran, and his brother Jerry, were veterans of a rough industry but had disarming, down-to-earth demeanors. After a few weeks of discussions, the Corcorans finally made us an offer we couldn't refuse. If we let E&R keep the junked cars to salvage spare parts, the company wouldn't charge us anything. In fact, it would *pay* the city twenty-five dollars for each car it towed away.

Incentivized to tow as many cars as possible, as fast as possible, E&R became a multimillion-dollar moneymaker for the city. More important, it did what no one else could do—rid the city of abandoned cars. Within months, abandoned autos fell from their perch as the top citizen complaint and within a year were no longer a concern at all.

Following that success, we facilitated one Daley housekeeping project after another—Green Streets, the mayor's extensive tree-planting campaign for city parkways and restoration of routine neighborhood tree trimming; doubling garbage pickup in dense residential areas; an antirat program that eventually wiped out 90 percent of the estimated five million rodents on Chicago streets; an alley-lighting program to improve safety; hot-asphalt crews for potholes; and on and on.[3]

Isaac "Sandy" Goldman, a Chicago money manager, brought the mayor an idea for businesses to "adopt a street" and keep it free of litter. Daley put him in charge.[4] The whirlwind of activity produced an unusual presence of city vehicles and personnel throughout city neighborhoods, sending a positive message that the winds of change were blowing.

Many people found these programs mundane; but for Toback and me, they were exhilarating. Traversing city neighborhoods, building relationships with field supervisors, community leaders, and aldermen, we could see and touch the little things that were helping upgrade a community—items with a larger cumulative impact. We also knew that attentiveness to neighborhood concerns and competence in addressing them would yield rich political dividends in time.

Daley ensured no one would miss the unfolding turnaround, holding press conferences illustrating a neighborhood's decay and providing made-for-TV scenes of city vehicles cleaning and restoring it. In one early event at a "fly" (illegal) dumping site, the alderman heard only that the mayor was visiting and quickly had the area cleaned. When the mayor's advance team arrived, they called city departments in a panic. In the nick of time, city crews returned the used and shredded tires, towed the junked cars back into place, and restored as much of the original garbage as they could.

Daley's fixation on cleanliness and orderliness, while seemingly at odds with the naturally chaotic and messy character of urban living, drove consistent improvements in Chicago's quality of life. That elevated confidence in the city, spurring development.

It wasn't an overnight success. Many initiatives took years to gain traction, such as overcoming the scourge of graffiti. All major cities struggle with graffiti; in the 1970s, New York gave up entirely. Graffiti was omnipresent on New York's urban streets and thoroughfares, and the Big Apple's subway cars were mobile message boards for gangbangers.

Daley first leaned on neighborhood organizations, providing free paint and brushes to encourage swift removal. But to bring antigraffiti efforts to scale, he created Graffiti Blasters, specialized teams running dozens of trucks. City crews removed graffiti from unpainted structures of brick, stone, and cement with high-pressure streams of water and baking soda. In the first year alone, Graffiti Blasters removed gang and vandal markings from more than fifteen thousand buildings.

The timeliness of removal, however, is just as important. Gangbangers want to admire their work and mark their territory. If a city can remove graffiti almost as fast it goes up and keep the structure clean, taggers eventually give up. Under Daley, police monitored newly cleaned sites, waited for taggers to return, then made arrests. To ensure those arrests had meaning, Daley passed a state law requiring that even a tagger given probation must perform a minimum of thirty days of community service. The following year he passed an ordinance banning the sale of spray paint in the city. The National Paint and Coatings Association sued and delayed enforcement for three years, but by 1996 Daley had won in federal courts. Enforcement of the ban added more momentum to the city's increasingly successful efforts.[5]

Like graffiti, homelessness affects the urban quality of life. Some progressive cities such as San Francisco and Seattle have long tolerated the presence of homeless encampments occupying parks, viaducts, and other urban niches. Under Daley, Chicago would not be one of them.

Although sympathetic to the plight of people without housing, the mayor was not about to allow encampments on public property. When he assumed office, O'Hare Airport was a common sleeping zone for the homeless and a target-rich environment for panhandling. (The CTA's Blue Line provided a cheap rail connection.) It presented a less than favorable first impression of Chicago for tourists and business travelers. One of my first assignments was to end this problem.

The challenges were many, including legal obstacles. I was assigned a young lawyer from the Corporation Counsel's office. No matter how many permutations I proposed, he rejected them, finally telling me the city simply could not legally require the removal of homeless individuals and that I could be personally liable. Exasperated, I finally told him, "Look, I am the client. You are my lawyer. I have listened to your advice, and I am rejecting it!"

Our plan required closing the airport from midnight to five in the morning. In the hours before midnight, airport personnel—and police if necessary—escorted anyone without a plane ticket out of the terminals. Vans from social service agencies lined up to transport individuals to overnight shelters with meals and beds, including an expanded facility operated by the Christian Industrial League, financed by a one-cent tax on cigarettes that Daley pushed through the city council. It nearly doubled the number of available shelter beds and funded transition assistance programs. The Haymarket Center offered alcohol and drug counseling and interim housing. Every service the city and its partners offered was available in a one-stop shop. For those who accepted not only the ride but the help, it could be life changing.[6] For the majority who didn't, it at least kept them safe.

As Daley began removing hundreds of individuals from the airport, the Coalition for the Homeless protested with pickets at terminals, carrying six mock coffins symbolizing the deaths of six homeless individuals from exposure the previous week.

"We will not stand for people dying on the street. The airport should be open to all people," said John Donahue, the coalition's director.[7]

But Daley said his program, which included counseling and job referral services, was the only humane solution.

"Most cities are stepping over and stepping around [the homeless] and saying, 'It's all right. Let them ride the L. Let them be on the buses. Let them be on the streets and in public buildings,'" the mayor said. "We're trying to do something about it. It's not callous. Just to say, 'You're out,' would be callous. We're providing an alternative."[8]

Similar strategies eliminated homeless encampments under street viaducts and underground areas such as Lower Wacker Drive, where whole communities set up tents and paraphernalia. Under new Streets and Sanitation procedures, notices were posted, and campers were warned that on a certain date and time, the sidewalks would be cleared of all obstructions, which would be sent to landfills. As with the airport, vans with social services personnel joined at the appointed hour.

Daley ensured that, during his twenty-two years in office, city-supported not-for-profits would always have more beds than people seeking shelter, along with meals and attendant support programs. But he had little use for the notion that city property was a substitute.[9]

• • •

In some neighborhoods, the most complex challenges were the city's nearly ten thousand abandoned buildings, the sites of rapes, robberies, and fires. Daley increased the budget for teardowns, but it wasn't until the horrific murder of a six-year-old boy in 1992, his mutilated body found in an abandoned building in Roseland, that Daley put the effort into overdrive. The mayor nearly tripled the demolition budget, set up an abandoned-buildings task force to cut legal red tape, and partnered with churches to board up buildings and maintain vacant lots. The mayor promised community leaders in Roseland and elsewhere that twelve hundred vacant buildings would fall within the first year.[10]

Mayor Daley's surge of city services required money; he inherited a $122 million budget deficit with no political leeway to raise property taxes. But by rounding up city votes for the governor's income-tax hike, he secured a higher share of state revenues for municipalities, including Chicago. He added tens of millions in new revenue through stepped-up bill collections, cracking down on parking ticket scofflaws by placing immovable boots on cars, and forcing businesses and landlords delinquent on water bills to pay up or have their water lines disconnected.

On the cost side, Daley found efficiencies by applying the lessons of the car towing contract, aggressively outsourcing management of city services—tree trimming and stump removal, janitorial services, sewer engineering, and fleet maintenance. Daley even privatized neighborhood drug-treatment centers, saving money but more important, elevating services to addicts. Wait times fell and the number of treated patients rose.

"Cities have taken over functions we should not be doing, and we've lost sight of our vital responsibilities," Daley said.[11]

Daley was instinctively reorganizing city government to focus on its core responsibilities—a concept popularized in the business world by the consultants Tom Peters and Robert Waterman in their best seller *In Search of Excellence*. One of the authors' most important principles is "sticking to the knitting." Successful companies focus on their core competency and mission, rather than trying to do too many disparate things at once. The oil giant Exxon, for example, entered the electronic office systems market in the 1970s, only to exit it with a billion-dollar loss in 1984, continuing "a company pattern of disappointing results when it tried to do something other than drill for and refine oil."[12]

Government was no different. It was an important lesson from Daley that I would later apply relentlessly at the Chicago Park District.[13]

In his first term, the mayor had yet to assume control of the troubled Chicago Public Schools (CPS). But he began investing city dollars in them. With so many schools in declining neighborhoods beset by violence, Daley charged me with beefing up security. Our plan placed two police officers at each high school and metal detectors at entrances to ensure weapons could not enter. Daley ordered the police department to patrol outside schools during the opening and closing hours. The visible police presence ensured students could enter and exit safely each day, with secure classroom environments.

Daley's energetic services expansion and strong fiscal management earned him a wave of favorable news coverage that bordered on the reverential. The Pulitzer Prize-winning cartoonist Jack Higgins published a satiric sketch of the mayor at dawn in front of a group of applauding reporters giving him credit for the sun rising over the city skyline. "Another glorious summer day—Thank you, Rich Daley!" a reporter shouts.

For the first time in a long time, the City that Works—the moniker Daley's father had popularized—was living up to its reputation.

But two events soon threatened to upend the sunny narrative, one struggling to emerge, the other quite visible.

In 1990, Gayle Shines, the mayor's handpicked director of the Office of Professional Standards, the police department's civilian-staffed unit for investigations of officer brutality, forwarded to Police Superintendent Leroy Martin what appeared to be an explosive 160-page investigative report, saying its "conclusions are compelling." The report, by the investigator Michael Goldston, examined fifty allegations of police brutality at Area Two from 1974 to 1986.

The report described cases in which police attached alligator clips to prisoners' various body parts, including genitalia, to administer electrical shocks from a hand-cranked telephone box. In a practice known as "bagging," officers would tie plastic bags over the heads of suspects, leading prisoners to believe they were about to suffocate.

"The type of abuse described was not limited to the usual beating but went into such esoteric areas as psychological techniques and planned torture," Goldston wrote. "The evidence presented by some individuals convinced juries and appellate courts that personnel assigned to Area Two engaged in methodical abuse. Command members were aware of the systemic abuse and perpetuated it either by actively participating in same or failing to take any action to bring it to an end."[14]

In addition to the Goldston report alleging systemic torture, Shines also gave Superintendent Martin a narrower analysis by the investigator Francine Sanders that was confined to the torture of Andrew Wilson. Martin used the Sanders report to fire Commander Burge and two of his detectives the following year but ignored the second report with its detailed accounts of dozens of similar cases. It sat for months until a federal judge ordered it released in February 1992, threatening to blow the lid off the barely contained secrets of Area Two. Both Superintendent Martin and Mayor Daley immediately moved to undermine its credibility, calling it poorly researched. Daley said the report's conclusions were "too broad" and based partially on ongoing investigations, implying that official reviews into police brutality were underway.[15] Despite the sensational findings in the report, the public spotlight quickly waned. A handful of voices would continue to raise the alarm, but for the moment the incendiary charges were defused.[16]

Ten months into the mayor's tenure, a more ordinary political storm accompanied a real one, a February 14 blizzard that the media dubbed the "St. Valentine's Day

Massacre." Although Streets and Sanitation launched its own blizzard of salt trucks and snowplows, it did so at the peak of rush hour, just as the storm was hitting. Icy conditions and blinding snow created traffic jams on all major arteries, stranding the department's vehicles in the same tied-up traffic as everyone else, rendering them useless.

The city was paralyzed.

My deputy, Carol Rubin, and I caught a ride north that evening with Paul Toback. Carol was heading home for a Valentine's Day dinner with her husband. She never made it. Only ten blocks from city hall, we came to a standstill on LaSalle Street, eventually abandoning the car in a snowdrift and making our way on foot to Toback's near-North apartment. From there, we stayed in touch with Streets and Sanitation Commissioner Ray Cachares.

As the evening wore on, it became evident that a slow-motion disaster was playing out. Along Lake Shore Drive, some of the cars ran out of gas while waiting; some commuters simply left their cars and made their way on foot. Thousands of travelers didn't make it through their doorways until midnight. Cachares increasingly engaged in gallows humor, knowing what awaited him in Daley's office the next day.

In Chicago, a failed response to a blizzard inevitably brings up comparisons to 1979, when Mayor Bilandic lost to the insurgent Jane Byrne because of a mishandled snowstorm.[17] Daley's critics were quick to pounce. The city was paralyzed because Cachares "got caught with his pants down," Ald. Robert Shaw said. He said "one more situation like this" would result in Daley suffering Bilandic's fate.[18]

But Daley challenged Alderman Shaw's idiom. "There is nobody in this administration walking around here without any pants," he fumed.[19]

Daley was not amused by the failure of his snow-removal department, but Cachares survived a private and public flogging. He and Daley initiated new procedures. Since that day, Chicago salt trucks and plows have been "forward positioned" when forecasts contemplate even a snowflake. With equipment and drivers throughout the city, roads can be attacked everywhere at once with no danger of bringing up the rear of a parade of rush-hour cars and buses.

The blizzard was a blip, overwhelmed by Daley's blitz of services underscoring his father's maxim: good government is good politics. Every neighborhood and every group benefited from more and better services.

• • •

But Daley also understood political benefits were derived from the gratitude of passionate *slivers* of the electorate, groups sensing through his actions that he was one of them or at least *sympathized* with them. And if those groups were not in his corner previously, all the better. They could now become part of his base, or at least temper the ferocity of the opposition. In politics, drawing in previously suspicious voters through policies or patronage is called "playing to the margins." It's risky if it inflames your core base of supporters, but handled delicately, it can make an elected official increasingly formidable.

Daley was secure enough in his conservative ethnic base to openly embrace the gay community, becoming the first mayor to serve as grand marshal of Chicago's Gay Pride Parade.

Daley's decision caused consternation among his more cautious advisors. Others were exuberant, perhaps displaying a tad too much enthusiasm. The city health department worked closely with gay leaders on HIV education; sensing an opportunity, staffers rushed to purchase thousands of customized condoms displaying a cartoon character in boots advising, "Wear Your Rubbers." On the flip side was printed the official city branding: "Richard M. Daley, mayor." But before they could be distributed at the parade, press chief Avis LaVelle caught wind, and confiscated the colorful mayoral prophylactics.

The absence of mayoral condoms, however, did not diminish the enthusiasm of Daley's reception at the parade. The *Tribune* reported:

> There was Mayor Richard Daley in a bright blue T-bird convertible leading the Gay and Lesbian Pride Parade through the streets of Lakeview . . .
>
> As Daley passed, thousands of onlookers cheered along the 1½ mile parade route. . . .
>
> "Thank you, thank you," one man said to Daley as he shook the mayor's hand. . . .
>
> "It's really something, really something to see the police in the parade and the mayor," said Jon Legris, 37, a jeweler.
>
> For many of the people in their 30's or older, the parade . . . brought back memories of uncomfortable times.
>
> In those days, another Daley was in charge of Chicago and the police were not exactly communing with the people.
>
> "I came out the same year as Stonewall," said Legris, recalling the 1969 New York City riot named for the bar where gays for the first time fought back against a police raid, igniting the gay rights movement.
>
> "Twenty years," he said with wonder. "We've made a lot of progress."
>
> To many, seeing the first Chicago mayor in the parade symbolized a new era of local political clout.[20]

Daley later became one of the first elected officials in the nation—and the first major politician in Illinois—to call for the legalization of gay marriage. In 2006, he was inducted into the Chicago LGBTQ+ Hall of Fame.

An even bigger surprise came early in his mayoralty, following a Supreme Court decision making it easier to restrict abortion access. Two conservative aldermen representing ethnic Catholic communities introduced zoning restrictions eliminating abortion clinics. When the proposed ordinances hit the news, Daley was out of the office and unreachable. But he was scheduled to appear at an evening reception where reporters would seek his reaction.

Marj Halperin, deputy press secretary, told me the mayor's office had moved to Defcon One, scrambling to prepare the mayor for a tricky interchange. Daley was a devout Catholic like his father, who had attended Mass daily, and with a largely religious and conservative base, so his opposition to abortion was a given. Halperin, LaVelle, and Kruesi hurriedly assembled talking points, including the common refrain of Catholic politicians that their personal faith left them no other choice. Grabbing taxis, a handful of aides sped to the reception and intercepted the mayor as he was about to enter. They told Daley the news and warned he would be ambushed by reporters. Halperin pulled out the talking points and tried to hand them to Daley, but he waved her off, scrunching up his face in annoyance.

"Ahh, that's between a woman and her doctor," he said, marching into the building and leaving his slack-jawed staff in his wake.[21] Inside, Daley repeated his view to the assembled reporters, noting that the targeted clinics provided important services beyond abortion, such as health services and counseling.

"Does that mean when there are other issues that are controversial, you're going to start restricting those [through zoning changes]?" Daley asked.[22]

Three years later, when the Cook County Board president, Dick Phelan, offered abortion services at the county hospital, the even more controversial issue of tax-payer-funded abortions was put before the mayor. Daley's idiosyncratic responses were legendary; often, they had the advantage of preventing reporters from pinning him down. In this illustrative exchange, the *Sun-Times* reporter Fran Spielman tries in vain to get Daley to say he supports taxpayer-funded abortions:

Q: President Phelan is going to move today to restore abortions at Cook County Hospital. I'm wondering what your thoughts are.

A: Well, I have said I think it's a decision between a doctor and a patient dealing with the health of an individual. And I think that is held in confidence dealing with the health. And that's how I view that issue.

Q: So you have no problem with what he's doing then?

A: Well, I think it's between a doctor and a patient when it comes to health issues, and I think it should be just like the attorney-client privilege. You know, that's the highest privilege in the world.

Q: But what about the use of public funds for abortion?

A: I think it's—remember, when we talk about health issues, it directly affects the patient. And the patient, when we talk about health issues, the federal and state governments dealing with health issues, and I think it should be on a confidential basis between the patient.

Q: It may cost more money.

A: Right. But I think when we get back to health issues, I keep reiterating between the patient and the doctor. I think that's vitally important.

Q: But what about the use of public funds?

A: Public funds, private funds—whatever it is. It's between the doctor and the patient.

Q: Doesn't it open the door for the use of abortion as birth control at public expense?

A: Well, you know, basically, we're talking about safe sex.[23]

It was in some ways stunning to see a Daley, in a city accustomed to his socially conservative dad, blaze a different political trail that embraced liberal causes. But hot-button social issues were not the only place Daley focused to gain supporters at the margins.

In another first, Daley created a city department on disabilities, appointing a disability activist, Larry Gorski, as its leader. Gorski used a wheelchair after a spinal-cord injury twenty years earlier. Daley was passionate about rights for the disabled but also sensed a political opportunity. A growing number of Americans suffered disabilities, and an aging population was full of potentially disabled citizens.

"We refer to people without disabilities as 'temporarily able-bodied,'" Gorski joked.[24]

Even before Gorski's appointment, Daley charged me with ensuring that city streets, especially downtown, were modified with curb cuts to accommodate wheelchairs. Nearly one thousand new asphalt ramps were added in Daley's first term, and 2 percent of parking spaces in the densest portions of the city were set aside for disabled parking. Shortly after, the CTA began adding wheelchair lifts on key routes.

Daley believed a high quality of life was what sustained cities and that even small amenities could keep people in the city while paying political dividends. He launched "Bike 2000" for cycling advocates with the goal of getting everyone commuting on bikes by the millennium (without ever giving up his own daily commute by chauffeured limousine). He created the city's first Department of the Environment, headed by the erudite Henry Henderson.[25] He also assiduously courted environmentalists, fishermen, and bird-watchers. Daley made full use of the park system, creating bike paths, expanding nature preserves and bird-watching enclaves, sponsoring angler competitions at park lagoons, and opening new lakefront fishing spots.

Daley's steady efforts to reach out to minority and liberal constituencies and his frenetic efforts to boost neighborhood services cemented a growing popularity. The racial discord that had paralyzed the city gave way to visible cooperation across racial and ethnic lines. The *Sun-Times* announced that Chicago "has shed its reputation as Beirut on the Lake," led by "a feel-good administration marked by glitzy projects and crackdowns on everything from tax cheats to City Hall filth."[26]

After two years in office, Daley rode a wave of popularity to 63 percent of the vote in the 1991 three-way Democratic primary featuring the African American West Side Congressman Danny Davis and former mayor Jane Byrne, whose attempt at a comeback garnered less than 6 percent of the vote. The turnout was the lowest in fifty years, primarily because of Daley's huge lead in polling and the shadow of the first Gulf War, which dominated news coverage. Progress among African American voters was small, but Daley broke double digits, an upward trend that would continue in each subsequent election.

With a voter mandate and a full four-year term, Daley was ready to take on even bigger challenges—and take greater risks.

Second Term

1991–1995

CHAPTER 7

Downtown

When he took office, Mayor Richard M. Daley inherited a city in crisis—"on the brink," in the words of the *Tribune*'s R. C. Longworth.[1] During the 1980s he wrote extensively on Chicago's dire economic plight:

> Drive west on the Eisenhower Expressway, out past the hospital complex, and look south. What you'll see is block after block of abandoned, gaping old factories. Or walk under the "L" along 63d Street in Woodlawn, down what used to be, after State Street, the second-busiest shopping street in Chicago. It's as much a ghost town as a Wild West set. . . . In all these places, and hundreds more throughout Chicago, the overwhelming sensation is emptiness. Not so many years ago, these factories and stores throbbed with people, jobs, money, goods, life. Now, all are gone. What's left is, literally, nothing.[2]

The intersection of 26th and California on the city's Near Southwest Side, not far from the county jail and courthouse, was a typical scene. Once the site of a sprawling, fifty-three-acre site of an International Harvester tractor factory that employed fourteen thousand workers, it now produced nothing but weeds. Abandoned warehouses dotted the city landscape in every direction, victims of the decline of manufacturing in the upper Midwest.

The Chicago Loop, the city's downtown core named for its encirclement by the elevated rail tracks (the L) of the CTA, was a ghost town after business hours. Its seedy edges were most striking to the south and west, entry points to impoverished communities.

Despite the city's vast economic challenges, Chicago remained a city of resilient neighborhoods, more than two hundred unique communities with their own histories, races, ethnicities, incomes, and cultures. A street grid system connects them, making navigation easy. Sidewalks run along continuous streets, not through cul de sacs.

"Chicago has the world's most consistent, orderly grid layout," wrote the *Economist*. "Passengers on planes landing at night at O'Hare International Airport . . . see a city that looks like a giant circuit board, with regimented streets going exactly north-south or east-west. At the spring and autumn equinoxes . . . the sun rises and sets in line with the street grid. On those days, Chicagoans flock downtown to see the streets lit up at sunset as though by a perfectly positioned spotlight."[3]

Like its counterparts in the Northeast—New York, Philadelphia, and Boston—the city is dense and compact, with homes and businesses in close proximity. Such cities tend to have stronger urban identities—and more rough and tumble politics—than the big cities of the South and West, where rapid and unplanned growth produced far-flung, disconnected pockets of housing and strip malls strung together by freeways.

Daley knew Chicago's neighborhoods intimately. As a youngster, he traversed them with his father; as a politician, he whisked through them, seeking votes. Daley's drivers would sometimes feel the flick of his finger on the back of their ears, signaling his annoyance as he corrected their navigational errors. He knew every street and alley, even in the most obscure parts of Chicago. Whatever neighborhood he traveled, he knew its history, its racial or ethnic character, and its most important residents.

Daley understood that the Loop was the economic engine making vibrant neighborhoods possible. The jobs and tax revenues from Downtown helped keep property taxes stable and disproportionately funded the costs of schools, parks, and economic development. To turn around Chicago's fortunes, he would have to revive it.

The new mayor had a clear vision for Downtown as a twenty-four-hour-a-day place to live, work, and play. It would attract new residents and tourists, and the accompanying restaurants and retail and entertainment businesses to serve them. A strong central Loop would then provide the resources and momentum to push south and west.

But now, as he began his second term, he had to figure out a way to pay for it.

Desperate for ways to rejuvenate Downtown, and with a national recession hammering Chicago and other cities in the early 1990s, the mayor began to reconsider his long-standing opposition to casino gambling. As the state's attorney and during his mayoral campaigns, Daley had adamantly opposed legalized gambling.

"I am convinced that gambling casinos are not in the public interest and that a majority of Cook County residents do not want them. Such places might be acceptable in resort areas like Las Vegas or Atlantic City, but not in the midst of a community like our own," Daley said as a candidate for chief prosecutor in 1979.[4]

In 1989, while mayor, Daley could have dealt the city in on Springfield deals ushering in legal gambling but stayed on the sidelines. His opposition was less about gambling than about the way the state legalized it. To reap the rewards of gaming while containing its negative impact, Gov. Jim Edgar and the legislature limited gambling to the confines of a small number of riverboats—mostly in depressed river towns downstate. A boat could turn around the fortunes of a small city like Joliet, a sixty-minute drive southwest of Chicago along the Des Plaines River, but what Daley dismissed as "putt-putts" would have only a marginal effect on Chicago's economy.

After the state-awarded franchises had become entrenched, Daley realized the city was losing both revenue and jobs to the suburbs and neighboring Indiana and decided Chicago had to make a play for a casino. To be worthwhile, however, the Chicago casino couldn't be a "putt-putt" moored on the Chicago River; it would have to be a huge, multifaceted, land-based casino capable of generating tens of thousands of jobs and hundreds of millions in tax revenue. Only a return of that magnitude would justify the risk that gambling might negatively alter the fundamental character of Chicago.

So in March 1992, on Daley's signal, three of the largest casino developers in America unveiled a $2 billion Chicago gambling and entertainment complex that would "combine the fantasy of Disneyland with the glitz of Las Vegas." To expand its impact and protect against a casino-only atmosphere, Daley insisted the wagering dens be incorporated into a much larger complex featuring shopping malls, hotels, restaurants, a theme park, and a sports and performing arts center. In all, the development would consume three million square feet in or near downtown.

On paper, Daley's plan made sense. Only Chicago had the size and sophistication to leverage legal casinos for much larger real estate and commercial investments. Only Chicago had a leading national position in conventions and trade shows, which could only be enhanced by adjacent entertainment options. The revenue, jobs, and ancillary economic development would spill over to the benefit of the entire Chicago region.

But politics isn't about logic. It's about power. By 1992, power had shifted south to Republican suburbs and downstate communities desperate to protect their golden geese. The previous GOP governor, Jim Thompson, had been from Chicago; the new one, Jim Edgar, was from downstate Charleston. The owner of an estimated $20 million stake in the Joliet Empress Casino, which had the most to lose from a Chicago casino, was the political insider and later DuPage County Board President Gayle Franzen, a close ally of the anti-Chicago GOP State Senate leader, "Pate" Philip.

Governor Edgar immediately rejected the proposal, saying he opposed making Chicago and Illinois "another Las Vegas." That stopped Daley's mega project in its tracks.

But Daley kept working. Two years later, he tried a less ambitious plan, restricting gambling to the Chicago River. But given Chicago's size, he proposed five riverboats anchoring an $800 million development on the adjacent shores. Edgar was comfortable with the more limited scope and argued that fundamental fairness dictated Chicago be allowed riverboats too.

Edgar's support was a huge step forward but didn't guarantee success. Daley was accustomed to striking deals with former governor Thompson, knowing Thompson's penchant for delivering the Republican votes required to pass legislation. Edgar was different. He would shake hands with Daley but do far less arm-twisting of legislators; for the most part, he deferred to the political needs of the Republican Senate president, Pate Philip.

Philip was not opposed to Chicago getting into the game, but he wanted some things in return. These included long-sought GOP reforms in the state's workers compensation, medical malpractice, and product liability laws—all items at the top of the wish list of business but antithetical to the Democratic constituencies of labor unions and trial lawyers. House Speaker Michael Madigan had law clients seeking casino licenses, so he officially recused himself. Unofficially, however, Madigan ensured no deal could move forward that was attached to the Philip reforms.

After the legislature shot down the Daley-Edgar casino deal in July 1994, the mayor threw in the towel.[5]

• • •

Daley's failure to bring casinos to downtown Chicago may have been a blessing in disguise. He instead turned his focus to more sustainable and impactful economic strategies that would energize—and expand—the economic power of the Loop.

Daley couldn't count on help from the federal government, as his father had decades earlier. The Great Society's free flow of aid for municipalities was long gone, and Republican presidents Ronald Reagan and George Bush limited what was left to addressing extreme poverty. Daley also had faced a property tax revolt during his first term, tying his hands further.

The mayor's toolbox was empty. To rebuild Downtown, he needed a self-help plan.

Daley found it in the one instrument within his control—tax-increment financing districts (TIFs). Mayors Washington and Sawyer had deployed TIFs on a limited basis. In increasingly controversial moves, Daley would eventually blanket more than a quarter of the city with TIFs, stretching—and then breaking through—all previous restrictions on their use, in a relentless effort to bend development to his vision.

To create a TIF, the city draws a line around a geographic area and devotes incremental increases in property taxes to fund redevelopment, from subsidized private construction to new infrastructure such as roads, sewers, and water mains. State law authorizes TIFs for areas of "blight." The definitional criteria—obsolescence, deterioration, and declining property values—are sufficiently broad to bless many projects. The idea of a TIF, however, is to facilitate investments that otherwise would not materialize. In Illinois, a TIF is limited to twenty-three years, although it can be extended another twelve. The mayor and city council can disband a TIF at any time, returning revenue to taxing bodies, with the exception of TIF income streams already dedicated to debt service on municipal bonds.

TIFs provide long-term funding to issue those bonds, so projects can move forward quickly, including the acquisition of commercial properties. The US Constitution prevents the government from seizing private property unless it is for a "public purpose," a right known as eminent domain. But courts have interpreted the restriction broadly to allow for economic development that includes a combination of private and public interests. One example is the interest of cities in redeveloping blighted areas, which requires a partnership with private businesses. This was the justification underlying the broad powers conveyed to municipalities in Illinois's TIF statute.

As Daley expanded the scope and purpose of TIFs, critics attacked them as the mayor's personal slush fund, allowing him to arbitrarily decide what developments went where while shifting tax dollars from schools and social services to the pockets of wealthy developers, often donors to his campaign fund.

In truth, the effect of TIFs is complicated. TIFs can sometimes deny new revenue to tax-capped districts such as schools, but generally do not.[6] Rather, they more often raise property taxes across the board. That's because the overall city assessment base is reduced, requiring higher tax rates to achieve the amount levied. Thus, TIFs usually amount to stealth property tax increases. But if TIF funding makes possible developments unlikely to occur without it, it can produce lasting positive impacts on the city's economy, expanding the retail base and building longer-term real estate values. In those instances, not only does the TIF not raise property taxes but it generates growth, leading to new tax revenue.

An example in the south Loop, at Michigan Avenue and Roosevelt Road, was the boarded-up Avenue Motel, a 1950s structure that was a magnet for vagrants. Police reports documented a pattern of crime in its vicinity. Daley could have invoked municipal powers of eminent domain to acquire it, but legally would have been limited to a public purpose, such as a police station or park. Under the state law authorizing TIFs, however, Daley could acquire property for public or private uses as long as it met certain criteria, including blight, long-standing vacancy, or dilapidated conditions. By creating a TIF district to acquire the Avenue Motel and improve its environs, Daley was able to underwrite private developers constructing a modern thirty-nine-story condominium building.

In time, Daley would use TIFs with sweeping breadth, as tools powerful enough to manipulate markets and allow him personally to affect—and even direct—the path and purpose of billions of dollars in private as well as public investments in Chicago. With legal creativity and arcane authorizing legislation from Springfield, Daley later began to port dollars between TIFs, so that even geography was no longer a barrier to his increasingly expansive vision.

To ensure that the genie never left the bottle—that he need share as little authority as possible—Daley arranged for TIFs to be created and approved by a special board of his own appointees before reaching the city council. Given the historic deference to aldermen concerning matters within their own wards, Daley needed only to gain the support of councilmen touched by the new boundaries, a relatively easy task since a litany of new ward investments would follow.

Many of the mayor's TIF projects were funded with invisible property tax increases (or more accurately, disguised as increases by other city and county taxing bodies);

these were the political equivalent of magic beans, growing stalks of ribbon-cutting projects that Daley and his aldermanic allies could tout without ever revealing the source of the pain inflicted on those financing them.

As the years passed, the growth of TIFs underwrote Daley's exponentially expanding political power. Each new TIF account represented what the *Chicago Reader*'s Ben Joravsky called a "shadow budget," a secret off-the-books kitty of taxpayer money, available for the mayor to spend with little oversight. Projects and expenditures in these accounts weren't subject to official budget proceedings, public review, or city council approval. The mayor found it more convenient to avoid the often annoying scrutiny accompanying such transparency.

The city council could have put on the brakes at any time, but aldermen anxious for their share of dollars were generally compliant. Most lobbied the mayor for projects in their wards. Daley's staffers clued in aldermen on details of TIF spending in their own wards but withheld citywide data. That didn't change until late in the mayor's tenure, when a dogged Joravsky finally obtained documents revealing proposed citywide projects. Some seemed reasonable, such as relocation assistance for United Airlines to move its headquarters into the city; others, such as $28 million for rehab work on Willis Tower (owned by the private suburban company American Landmark Properties) were of questionable value. American Landmark was represented by Jack George of the law firm of Daley & George. George's partner was Michael Daley, the mayor's brother.[7]

Mayor Daley eventually pushed through the city council more than 160 TIF districts, redirecting hundreds of millions of dollars each year with little public transparency.[8] Although a significant portion of project spending was paid for by property taxpayers, the source of the tax increases never appeared on tax bills. To critics such as Joravsky, however, that was less important than the implications for democratic governance.

"To be clear, the fundamental issue here isn't the inaccuracy of our tax bills. It's how much unregulated power we've granted to one man," Joravsky wrote."[9]

• • •

The mayor began to leverage his TIF powers slowly at first, beginning in the downtown area. He targeted blighted Loop properties such as dilapidated or abandoned theaters, office buildings, hotels, and retail stores.

Sarah Pang, the first deputy chief of staff to the mayor, told me she was initially a skeptic of TIFs and relayed a story of the mayor's early efforts to convince her of their potential curative powers. It was 1993, and Pang had just recently joined the administration. The mayor asked her to accompany him on a walk from city hall to parts of the adjacent downtown. It was shortly after work, and Daley pointed to crowds of people leaving the Loop instead of going out for dinner or catching a show.

"He's walking really fast and I'm trying to keep up in high heels," Pang recalls. "Finally, he stops. Even though it's the heart of the Loop, it's seedy. There are theaters all around us and he says, 'TIFs can fix this.' He turns and says, 'What does that say up there?' pointing to the marquee sign on a theater. I'm reading it slowly and realize I can't say it out loud because it's advertising a porn show."

Pang returned to city hall.

"I ran into my colleague Meghan Harte," Pang recalled. "And she said 'You're blushing red. What happened?' I said, 'The mayor took me to a porn theater!'"[10]

Daley used his condemnation powers liberally. Whether leveraging his statutory TIF powers to acquire an unsavory theater or exercising his inherent municipal powers of eminent domain to facilitate a new public project, Daley often pushed the edge of the envelope. If he needed to condemn a building for a new police station, for example, he would acquire as much run-down adjacent property as possible, ostensibly for parking. But usually the need for parking was wildly overestimated. Once buildings were under city control, Daley would raze them or prepare them for retrofits. Often, the city would work with developers to combine parcels to accommodate a more ambitious effort.

An example in the heart of the Loop, at State and Randolph not far from city hall, was an unsightly Walgreens store, two storefront mattress outlets and an all-night ribs joint. The Walgreens store leased its roof, which contained a giant billboard reading, "Get Out of the Loop. Come to Las Vegas." Daley condemned all the buildings. The location was ideal for what he had in mind—student housing for the School of the Art Institute, which was among the early developments bringing 24/7 occupants to the heart of downtown.

Building on the momentum, Daley pressed other universities to convert buildings into downtown dorms. One of the many impressive results is 525 South State, a modern high-rise for student housing serving 1,700 students from Columbia College and DePaul and Roosevelt Universities. The consortium marketed the center as a "one-of-a-kind community in downtown Chicago for combining living, learning, and a collegial spirit in a way never done before."[11]

At the same time, the mayor pushed through the city council sweeping changes to the zoning code encouraging a residential tilt in the Loop, enabling conversion of office buildings into residential lofts, dormitories, and boutique hotels. By clearing out old buildings, writing down loan costs, waiving onerous zoning restrictions and fees, and investing in supportive city infrastructure, Daley convinced skeptical investors and developers to build downtown.

State Street, whose dominant retail businesses struggled early in Daley's tenure, was revitalized in part by the spending of new Downtown residents. The mayor also reversed a poor planning decision by the Byrne administration that blocked car traffic from the street, on the assumption that pedestrians would treat the strip like a suburban mall, enhancing business. Instead, it isolated State Street and drained it of energy.

To make the Loop more appealing, the mayor removed the asphalt and concrete barriers between streets, replacing them with lavishly landscaped medians and planters. He personally selected throwback ornamental street lighting to replace industrial-style illumination; insisted that ugly trash cans be replaced with attractive receptacles; and replaced staffed, ramshackle wooden newsstands, long a fixture downtown, with sleek, dark metal vending machines. This put him in conflict with both the newsstand owners and the city's newspapers, which felt Daley was interfering with the prerogatives of a free press. Many reporters, such as the *Tribune* columnist Mike Royko, also felt the wooden newsstands were part of the colorful flavor of Chicago and objected to Daley's efforts to sanitize the Loop. As chief of staff at the time, I found it amusing that the newsstand operators cloaked themselves in the Constitution's First Amendment. Besides copies of the *Tribune* and *Sun-Times*, they sold only racing forms and pornography and had for years been squatting on prime public property for free, without leases or permits.

Daley's beautification efforts extended beyond the city's Loop to its boulevards, streets, and even busy Lake Shore Drive, eventually building seventy-three linear miles of attractive medians separating traffic, filled with flowers and towering shade trees.

Beyond State Street, the other two main retail corridors were Wabash Avenue, running under the L tracks, and Michigan Avenue. Michigan Avenue north of the Chicago River, known as the "Magnificent Mile," was relatively strong. It was anchored on the northern end by Water Tower Place, opened in 1975. It provided a shopping experience modeled after suburban malls, but with floors of stores connected vertically by escalators. All-glass elevators moved up and down the center, affording shoppers a bird's-eye view of people and shops.

But the vibrancy of commerce on North Michigan Avenue came to a halt south of the majestic Wrigley Building, where it met the Chicago River, which acted as a sort of demarcation line between the upscale north and the tatty south.

With a concentration of historic, architecturally significant, but obsolete office buildings, South Michigan Avenue was ripe for TIF-supported conversions to both modern office spaces and new residential apartments. At the time, both the location and concept were considered risky, and bank financing was difficult to acquire.[12] Daley extended an existing TIF to encompass part of South Michigan Avenue, creating the Historic Michigan Boulevard District. This allowed much of the expense of exterior renovation to be absorbed by the city, freeing capital for extensive interior rehabs. The mayor's plan yielded vibrant mixed-use properties, with restored commercial space below high-end residential housing that advertised unobstructed views of Grant Park and Lake Michigan.

To complement the strong cultural anchors along South Michigan Avenue, the illustrious Art Institute and the Chicago Symphony Orchestra, Daley supported improvements and programs for the Chicago Cultural Center, a nineteenth-century landmark building that once housed the city's main library. It is a restored gem with marble walls and luminous mosaics inspired by Venetian landmarks. Its crowning glory is the enormous Tiffany dome—the largest in the world—shining with a milky iridescence.

The building, with its Beaux-Arts exterior, had barely survived Mayor Richard J. Daley's wrecking ball in 1972, meant to clear the site for a modern office tower. The mayor's wife, Sis Daley, gave a rare interview to the *Tribune*, in which she commented on the planned demolition.

"I don't think that would be nice," Mrs. Daley said. "That's a beautiful site where it is. I'm for keeping and restoring all these beautiful buildings in Chicago."[13]

Mysteriously, the city's plans for the site were scuttled.

Under the leadership of the mayor's irrepressible cultural affairs director, Lois Weisberg, the cultural center became a beehive of activity, hosting weddings, tours, and other private and public events.[14] Among Weisberg's many eclectic contributions as Daley's cultural maven was "Cows on Parade," fiberglass bovines painted by local artists and installed on downtown Chicago streets. It was a shockingly successful tourist draw.

Weisberg and the first lady, Maggie Daley, founded another Chicago cultural beacon to energize downtown, but this one had accidental beginnings.

Starting with its designation as the "North Loop Blighted Commercial District" in 1979 and culminating as the city's first TIF under Mayor Washington, the area of the Loop bounded by State, Randolph, Dearborn, and Washington was slowly cleared of buildings.

The *Tribune* urban affairs columnist John McCarron described the city effort as a "billion-dollar campaign against raunch and honky-tonk. Gone will be the pulse of discount stereo shops; the smell of caramel corn; the complete steak dinner for $3.69. Enter the mixed-use development; the elevator lobby; the 'information and security' desk. Gone too will be some of the Loop's walking-around fun."[15]

By the time the city had demolished the last of the area's "walking-around fun," in 1990, it discovered it had no uses for the site. The "urban renewal" project produced a massive city block emptied of buildings, people, and energy. A victim of the enormity of the empty square footage and a deep recession, the city had no viable developer or tenants. The vacant square block at the center of downtown was an embarrassment and a drag on other retailers. In the winter, Daley set up an outdoor ice-skating rink with concessions, but had no answer for the rest of the year.

If Daley had no answer, his wife, Maggie, did.

Maggie envisioned a place where young people of different incomes, races, and backgrounds could share a common passion for the arts, learn from experienced artists, and even find commercial applications for their talents. When an aide to the mayor informed him of the idea to fill the empty block, he said it was "the worst idea he'd ever heard."[16] Informed it was Maggie's brainchild, he reportedly replied it was the finest idea.

It started out small, a way to fill space productively, but grew from the First Lady's passion for both the arts and children. Gallery 37 was a summer jobs-training program for artists aged fourteen to twenty-one, subsidized by private companies sponsoring work tents on the site. Maggie believed the arts could be a vehicle for teenagers to build confidence, improve their school performance, and find positive creative outlets. Within two months, Lois Weisberg and Maggie Daley knew they had founded a special program.

"There was something magical about it," Maggie recalled. "We would have youngsters from the Robert Taylor Homes and youngsters from Lincoln Park, all over the city. They learned to work together as a team."[17]

In a matter of years, as she threw herself into the task of nurturing and growing her creation, Maggie Daley's Block 37 became an arts mecca for teenagers, overwhelmingly poor and minority. More than four thousand young people were hired and trained as artist apprentices, along with more than four hundred adult professionals.

The success of Gallery 37 provided another cultural anchor for Downtown and a constant infusion of people and energy augmenting other developments in the Loop.

Mayor Daley's vision of a 24/7 downtown was taking hold, rooted deeply in culture and entertainment. He began to capitalize on Chicago's rich theater history to enliven its future, including its many architectural gems. Today's Cadillac Palace Theater, for example, was built in 1926, inspired by the palace of Versailles. The Chicago Theater, opened in 1921, has a façade shaped to mimic the Arc de Triomphe in Paris. Once glamorous, by the 1990s most of these theaters had fallen into disrepair.

Daley began a decade-long effort to restore Chicago's great theaters, expand their capacities, and encourage new entrants. The city helped build a new downtown home for the Tony-award-winning Goodman Theatre, beginning a multiyear partnership that expanded to include the League of Chicago Theaters and Broadway in Chicago. The result was the Chicago Theater District, a concentrated collection of playhouses in the heart of downtown. With $86 million in tax dollars from the downtown TIF, Daley leveraged $233 million in private investments to remake a large portion of the Loop into a vibrant entertainment sector. Other major restored theaters include the Majestic (1906), now the CIBC Theater; the Oriental (1926), now the James M. Nederlander Theater; and the Louis Sullivan–designed Auditorium Theater a few blocks south, known for its size and acoustics and hosting the Joffrey Ballet for nearly two decades. Restoration of Sullivan's masterpiece was privately funded and led by the not-for-profit Auditorium Theater Council and its leading director and advocate, businessman and philanthropist Fred Eychaner.[18]

Daley's theater district brought new life to Downtown, hosting more than eight hundred stage shows a year, attracting five million theatergoers. From 1997 to 2008, the Loop experienced a 53 percent increase in the number of hotel rooms and a 20 percent jump in meeting space. After its first ten years, the theater district was estimated to support nearly ten thousand jobs and bring an annual economic impact to the city of $750 million.

By the mid-1990s, Daley had made sufficient progress in the city core to push development aggressively into the southern and western reaches of the Loop. The edges of Downtown were populated by vacant warehouses and factories—large, complex, often polluted structures. The cost to demolish them, clean up the surrounding domains, and build new infrastructure was enormous. But these investments paved the way for Daley to deploy the same tools that worked in the Loop, jump-starting new commercial and residential development.

A more attractive central Loop began to attract younger professionals and empty nesters. Although the busy expressways bisecting the near West Side blocked development there, a new south Loop began to emerge, with restaurants, condominiums, townhomes, and numerous retail businesses.

With an expanding and thriving downtown, Daley had found his economic engine.

CHAPTER 8

Black Swans

Mayor Daley's efforts to rebuild Downtown hit an unexpected setback early in his second term.

On April 13, 1992, a maintenance worker arrived early at his workplace Downtown, a large department store, to discover that the basement was flooded. Wading through the turbid waters looking for a cause, he was startled by strange movements around him—swimming fish.

In the Great Chicago Flood, 250 million gallons of murky water leaked from the Chicago River into the basements of the city's business district. Lights and power went out over twelve square blocks; the city began evacuating the entire hundred-block Downtown. Thousands of office workers were left without a place to go, and damage to retail merchandise and other assets eventually exceeded $800 million.

A whirlpool near the Kinzie Street Bridge provided the first clue of the floodwater's source. Like bathwater swirling down a drain, the Chicago River poured into the miles of tunnel leading to Loop basements, which were roughly on the same level as the river. Electrical power equipment was threatened, requiring the electrical utility, Commonwealth Edison, to black out the business district. Commerce was suspended. Even the vast trading markets ruled by Chicago's Board of Trade came to a halt.

• • •

In late 1991, the Great Lakes Dredge and Dock Company, operating under a routine city contract, installed wooden pilings in the Chicago River near the Kinzie Street Bridge to act as bumpers protecting the adjacent bridge and bridge tender's house from errant boats. However, the company was unwittingly driving the pilings through a layer of clay above an unmarked freight tunnel.

The drilling ruptured the tunnel, at first with a small hole. In the months that followed, the tunnel gradually weakened at the point of breach until it convulsed into a depression the size of an automobile. The tunnel contained electrical and fiber optic cables that powered Downtown. The forty miles of crisscrossing tunnels were built beginning in 1899, originally to distribute coal throughout the Loop. Some believe Al Capone took advantage of the underground passages to transport his booze around the city.

The extraordinary situation was without precedent; the city had no blueprints or engineering plans to guide them. The closest thing was an obscure 1982 book written by Bruce Moffat, a CTA employee. It was a history of the tunnels and a documentation of their intricacies. Although Moffat's book never threatened to make the *New York Times* bestseller list, it quickly sold 3,500 copies. Marked-up, dog-eared versions could be seen lying near copying machines all over city hall.

To deal with the emergency, Mayor Daley turned to Kenny Construction. John Kenny Jr.'s company held numerous contracts for its expertise in underground work, particularly in the seemingly endless, multidecade-long construction of the area's Deep Tunnel Project, designed to relieve residential flooding by diverting storm and sewage water overflow into giant reservoirs. The project is under the auspices of the Metropolitan Water Reclamation District (MWRD) and ultimately will end the district's practice of discharging raw sewage into Lake Michigan when powerful rainstorms overwhelm sewage systems.

MWRD engineers were first out of the gate with a solution. The district's president, Nicholas Melas, advocated connecting the flooded freight tunnels with the Deep Tunnel, which could hold about a billion gallons of water. His engineers began drilling and blasting holes through drop shafts near the Loop's tunnels. But after only two days, Mayor Daley issued a stop-work order. In consultations with Kenny and the US Army Corps of Engineers, Daley became convinced that the MWRD scheme of removing water quickly would increase water pressure and damage century-old building foundations, as well as the antique tunnel system itself.

Instead of a quick drain, the Loop's basements would remain flooded for weeks.

With Daley and Kenny permanent fixtures along the walls of the Chicago River, engineers began a series of improvisations. The Sewer Department commissioned a giant barge with sandbags and two truckloads of three-inch gravel, dumping it into the whirlpool. The Fire Department even brought a truckload of mattresses to force into the hole.

The makeshift plugging materials slowed the water's flow so that a base could form, allowing the use of quick-setting concrete. These Band-Aids seemed to retard the river's inexorable flow inward. As Kenny poured dye into the river near the site of the leak, it floated downstream rather than being sucked into the vortex.

To prevent continuous leakage into the city's basements, however, Kenny drilled shafts into the tunnels east and west of the river, filling them with cement and stone. Once hardened, these plugs sealed off the leaking part of the tunnel under the river, bringing an end to the flood. To ensure against a future deluge, the firm poured concrete bulkheads at twenty-six places where the tunnels crossed the river.

As the city's efforts to contain the flood became a daily soap opera for TV stations, the handsome Kenny's layman-friendly explanations of the engineering challenges made him a popular local figure, earning him a nickname—the "Flood Stud." With his ruddy Irish complexion, trademark green hardhat and parka, and mud- and paint-stained rubber boots, Kenny became the face of the disaster and the hero of the saga.

Every heroic story, however, must have villains. The city's investigation pointed fingers in multiple directions, starting with the dredging company that had punctured the tunnel. The Great Lakes contract required the company to install new pilings in the same location as the old ones, but it discovered that the existing pilings were too close to the bridge tender's house to be completely removed. With the oral approval of the resident city engineer, Frank Ociepka, the company moved the locations of the new pilings by three to five feet, spots directly above the freight tunnel.

In its defense, the Great Lakes company said the schematic drawing provided by the city showed no underground tunnels, but the city pointed to the contract requiring the company to "inform itself" of underground obstacles. Had the company done so, it would have checked with the Board of Underground and the Map Department, both of which had sketches of the tunnel system. The city sued to recover damages.

Although the initial focus was on the dredging company, Daley soon announced that multiple city employees were to blame as well, having known of the leak but failing to do anything about it in time.

"Individuals did drop the ball. The city didn't," Daley said, presaging a series of firings.[1]

• • •

Professor Scott Sagan of Stanford University observed, "Things that have never happened before happen all the time."[2] But few of us have the imagination to project the unlikely or unfathomable, whether it's the 2008 collapse of the housing market, 9/11, or a catastrophic urban flood.

In his influential book on probabilities and uncertainties, the mathematician Nassim Nicholas Taleb describes such events as "black swans," examples of our blindness to the possibility of random events that deviate dramatically from our experience.[3] The nonchalance of city workers in responding to evidence of a tunnel leak is not excusable, but it is understandable. A chain of city employees was aware of a problem, but none seemed to grasp the need for urgency in resolving it. None could imagine the subsequent flood of a great city's downtown.

The chief bridge engineer, Louis Koncza, knew about the damage in March (a month before the flood) but waited a week to call a meeting about it and another week before soliciting repair estimates from contractors. Following rules on competitive bidding, he was asking for more estimates when the tunnel ruptured. Daley later pegged the cost of fixing the tunnel leak at $10,000.

An assistant project director charged with inspecting the completed pilings failed to do so, because he could not find a parking space near the river. He became aware of the leak in mid-March but didn't alert his supervisor, Koncza, for a week.

A General Services employee charged with assisting cable companies in the tunnels, Jim McTigue, was warned about tunnel damage in late February but waited until March 13 to inspect it. Five days later, he returned to photograph the damage and took the film to a drugstore to be processed. He waited a week to pick it up.

Even the head of the department overseeing the tunnels, acting Transportation Commissioner John LaPlante, who received a memo from Koncza about the leak, failed to understand the potentially disastrous ramifications of an untended breach. Daley fired LaPlante and the other employees who were too slow to act.[4]

Great Lakes Dredge and Dock Company fought the city's lawsuit all the way to the US Supreme Court, where it won a victory limiting damages. The arcane issue was whether its boats were afloat on "navigable waters" and therefore subject to the jurisdiction of federal admiralty law, which strictly limits liability. Ultimately, the most significant damages were to the company's reputation.

In contrast, the Flood Stud was celebrated, with awards from civic groups and free dinners at posh restaurants. Even citizens who normally paid little attention to city news stopped Kenny on the street to offer congratulations or solicit an autograph. For a time, the Museum of Science and Industry displayed his signature jade green mountain parka.

A *Sun-Times* profile a year after the flood described Kenny and his son struggling to hail a cab on a busy Chicago street not long after completing his successful mission. After they spent ten fruitless minutes hand waving, a cab screeched to a halt in front of them. A gentleman in a suit jumped out and said, "Mr. Kenny, you can have my cab because you saved Chicago!"[5]

Some of the Flood Stud's glory was reflected on Daley as well. A ubiquitous presence by the river, coordinating city agencies operating in concert with Kenny, the mayor effectively managed the crisis and looked firm and decisive in holding accountable the dredging company and city employees whose errors had brought to life Chicago's own black swan. He had passed an early test of his administration.

A few years later, however, Daley would face a second black swan, but this time he would be the one who failed to recognize signs of a pending disaster.

• • •

On July 12, 1995, Tom McNamee of the *Sun-Times* wrote: "By Saturday, we could be talking heat wave. . . . The temperature . . . is expected to top 90 degrees, and ozone levels are expected to creep dangerously high. If that happens, Chicago's weather could be more than sticky. It could prove deadly."[6]

In retrospect, McNamee's page 3 story looks like a prescient warning, but on that day it was merely a routine weather article with helpful public-safety reminders. Certainly no one at city hall was ringing alarm bells. After all, it gets hot in the summer in Chicago.

Jerry Taft, the chief meteorologist at ABC News, recalls, "We put out the standard advisory: 'Heat can kill. . . . [If] you're caring for the elderly, they need to have air conditioning.' We basically said the right things. But it's almost like when there's a severe thunderstorm watch. Nobody really changes what they do."[7]

As predicted, on July 12 the mercury climbed to a high of 97; it was hot, but nothing Chicagoans hadn't seen before. Quickly, however, temperatures soared, remaining above 100 for several days, reaching 106 degrees on July 13, with unusually high humidity. The relative heat index—how the temperature feels to the human body when combined with humidity—hit 124 degrees.

Mayor Daley made the usual pro forma announcements encouraging wellness checks for older residents.

"We're really appealing to family members of seniors that are living alone. We appeal to them to go over and see their mother or father or aunt or uncle or loved one," Daley said.[8]

Sarah Pang, the mayor's first deputy for public safety, recalls the lack of awareness of what was beginning to happen.

"I can remember . . . watching a TV while they were picking up dead farm animals in Iowa with bulldozers, because it was so hot in Iowa. And the heat's coming at us, and you could feel it, and we're all talking about it. And it's on the news. But we didn't understand extreme heat. So we didn't mobilize like we would have for a snowstorm that was coming in from Iowa."[9]

These weather conditions ordinarily produce thunderstorms, nature's way of cooling the air when temperature and humidity ascend together. But that didn't happen. It was a "perfect storm" because it never became a storm.

Meteorologists often refer to the dew point as a measure of the "mugginess" of the weather. The higher the dew point, the more moisture is in the air; but the level of discomfort accelerates with a combination of high temperatures and high dew points. The National Weather Service defines any dew point at 65 or higher as "becoming oppressive." In Chicago, dew points reached the low 80s with temperatures averaging 104.

Worse, the fluke weather patterns created a dome effect with no winds or breeze to provide cooling relief. Even sunset didn't help.

"Cities are made of concrete, asphalt, metal, and glass," explained Eric Snodgrass, a University of Illinois atmospheric sciences professor. "The sun beats down during the day and tall buildings act like a canyon, focusing the heat downward where it's absorbed and stored. At night, all of this heat gets released into the lowest atmosphere. This is when the urban heat island effect is greatest, causing the inner city to be as much as 15 degrees warmer than surrounding suburbs and open land."[10]

Those who could sought relief in the waters of Lake Michigan or Park District swimming pools. More than three thousand fire hydrants were opened illegally, creating gushing water but also posing risks to water pressure if firefighters had to extinguish a blaze. Calls to 911 for emergency aid nearly doubled; ten overrun hospital emergency rooms went on "bypass," diverting ambulances to more distant hospitals.

At a press conference, Mayor Daley still didn't grasp the magnitude of what was unfolding.

"It's hot. It's very hot. Yesterday we broke records," Daley said. "We all have our little problems, but let's not blow it out of proportion."[11]

On Saturday, July 15, Mayor Daley was at his summer house in Michigan. Mayoral adviser Terry Teele was in a fifth-floor office at city hall when the police officer staffing the outside foyer came in. "Terry, the coroner is on the phone. I told him the mayor is not here. Will you take the call?"

Teele picked up the line. It was the Cook County Medical Examiner, Edmund Donoghue.

"This is Mr. Donoghue. I'm looking for refrigerated trucks," the coroner said. "And I was calling to ask if maybe y'all had some way to get some. You know you've got Taste of Chicago going on, and a lot of refrigerated trucks were being used."

Teele said, "What an odd question. Let me call around. Well, by the way, why do you need refrigerated trucks?" Donoghue replied: "We have quite a catastrophe on our hands. We've had a high number of deceased over the last couple of days."

As the coroner's words sank in, Teele realized the refrigerated trucks were for bodies.

"I remember hanging up the telephone . . . and I said, 'We've got a big problem. We've got a very big problem.'"[12]

At almost the same time, Pang received a call from Jack Townsend, the first deputy police chief. It was never good news when he phoned on weekends. "We're getting calls from police squads all over the city that people are passing away in their apartments," Townsend told Pang. She called the newly appointed chief of staff, Roger Kiley.

"We need to go meet at city hall and figure out what's going on," she said.[13]

Daley returned from Michigan to take charge. His fifth floor office became a de facto triage station, with top brass from Police and Fire, Health, Streets and Sanitation, and Water all present.

By Sunday, with the media now pummeling city hall with inquiries and tons of second-guessing, Mayor Daley declared an official emergency, opening city cooling centers and dispatching police and other city officials to check on senior citizens.

Overwhelmingly, those dying were older citizens living in impoverished, high-crime neighborhoods. Fear of crime kept many from opening windows, and window air conditioners were thought to encourage break-ins. Others who had installed air conditioners failed to keep them on during the sustained heat for fear of running up utility bills they couldn't pay.

Commonwealth Edison contributed to the crisis. Years of inadequate maintenance led to more than thirteen hundred equipment failures under the stress of power demands, leaving 150,000 residences without cooling or light for up to twenty-seven hours.

Meanwhile, the county coroner was releasing data about the number of fatalities, with several hundred bodies at the morgue. The nightly TV news broadcast powerful images of crowded funeral homes and lines of refrigerated trucks in front of the county's mortuary.

Daley reacted defensively, still struggling to believe that the heat could be causing such a spike in deaths.

"Every day people die of natural causes," Daley said. "You can't put everything as heat related."[14]

Black swans can be difficult to see even when they become increasingly visible.

Federal officials from the Centers for Disease Control and Prevention validated Donoghue's methods. The unprecedented conditions had triggered heat strokes, heart attacks, and respiratory inflammations that ravaged poor communities.

Eventually, reality set in as the mayor led a furious effort to catch up to the unfolding disaster.

"When he heard about the emergency rooms, the number of victims, and realized that heat is cumulative and there would be more deaths, he was frustrated and emotional," Pang said. "It was a humanitarian crisis in his city that could never have been imagined. He was upset that it had happened, that we had not been able to foresee it."[15]

The city's frantic efforts were too little, too late. Across Chicago, 739 citizens were dead, victims of the freakish heat wave.

In the aftermath of the tragedy, Daley appointed a task force to recommend changes to city procedures. He did not have to wait long to put them into action.

On July 28, another wave of high temperatures rolled into the city, reaching the upper 90s. The combination of heat and humidity was oppressive, but it topped out well below the earlier readings. More important, a cooling breeze provided relief to those who could get outdoors. But Daley was taking no chances. He ordered the city's first "heat emergency" and mobilized operating departments at his new $217 million 911 emergency center. A dozen top leaders of the fire and police departments joined Daley on the main floor, while hordes of deputies worked on the second floor, evaluating incoming information and dispatching resources.

Seventy air-conditioned cooling centers opened, mainly in at-risk neighborhoods. The city shipped ice to shut-ins, delivered more than a thousand electric fans to elderly poor, set up regular broadcast alerts for TV and radio, and opened cavernous telephone banks to call senior citizens with wellness checks and offers of assistance. Police officers conducted door-to-door sweeps with health officials, checking on the elderly.

Despite the unusual and dangerous conditions, the medical examiner reported only two heat-related deaths. The city's emergency heat plan became a permanent fixture of city government, in the same way that mobilizing for snow and cold weather emergencies had been the norm for decades.

Shaken by the massive loss of life, Daley was determined that Chicago would never be caught unprepared again. The mayor's revamped emergency procedures, a quarter-billion-dollar state-of-the-art emergency communications center, and politically attuned vigilance helped forestall similar disasters.

But years later, the Daley administration's failure to do the basics, the fundamental blocking and tackling of government, would lead to a series of unimaginable tragedies.

CHAPTER 9

Airport Wars

Although Mayor Daley worked assiduously to revive Downtown, searching for a potent economic engine to ignite development and job creation, he was also aware that Chicago's most powerful economic propellants sat at its northwest and southwest edges—its airports.

Chicago's history and growth are tied inexorably to its status as a transportation hub—first through waterways, then railways, and finally through its airports, especially the crown jewel of O'Hare. The world's busiest airport during much of Daley's mayoralty, it still leads most years in takeoffs and landings, despite having ceded the "world's busiest" title to Atlanta with its higher numbers of boarding passengers.[1]

Chicago's central location and vast aviation infrastructure provide the ideal core of the hub-and-spoke system of major airlines such as United and American. Better than any other US airport, O'Hare provides business travelers direct, nonstop flights to any significant city in the world. For that reason, numerous companies locate their headquarters in Chicago. Cargo and freight operations also rely on both O'Hare and Midway airports and invest heavily in their surrounding rings, fueling jobs and economic activity.

For those reasons, enhancing Chicago's airports and protecting them from outside threats was top of mind in the early years of Daley's administration. But in Chicago's airport wars, Mayor Daley's first flight was poorly planned and wobbly, crashing not long after takeoff.

• • •

In the mid-1980s, with air travel growing rapidly and O'Hare Airport's capacity increasingly strained, suburban airport advocates began lobbying for a third major airfield to supplement O'Hare as well as Midway, a smaller airport operating flights on Chicago's Southwest Side.

The south suburban Republican state Sen. Aldo DeAngelis kicked off a long-running battle in 1985 with legislation funding a study of airport issues by the South Suburban Mayors and Managers Association. In 1987, the Federal Aviation Administration (FAA) funded a tristate study by Illinois, Wisconsin, and Indiana. The all-Republican policy committee of Senator DeAngelis, Lt. Gov. George Ryan, and Illinois Department of Transportation (IDOT) Commissioner Greg Baise supported the report's conclusion that a new airport would be needed by 2000 and that it should be in the southern portion of Cook County.

By 1989, a newly formed Illinois-Indiana Regional Airport Study hired a consultant to select the location of a third major airport. Meanwhile, the FAA continued to issue statements on the "requirement of regional consensus," code for Chicago's participation. Mayors Washington and Sawyer had ignored the various commissions for that reason, because any new airport would come at the expense of Chicago's two aviation hubs.

By 1992, however, early in his second term, Mayor Daley had introduced sweeping legislation in Springfield to build a third airport on Chicago soil, to complement O'Hare and Midway. Designed to retain Chicago's monopoly on regional commercial aviation, the mayor's plan was audacious—and much riskier than he realized at its beginning.

Two years before, as chief of staff in the mayor's first term, I was monitoring the activities of suburban airport activists. I also knew that Daley's policy chief Frank Kruesi was leading a confidential working group examining the possibility of a third airport in the economically distressed Lake Calumet region on the city's Southeast Side. But I didn't consider that a big deal. The research, planning, and due diligence on projects of that magnitude typically take years, and often lead nowhere.

But the mayor surprised me—and everyone else on his staff—with a sudden announcement in February 1990, taking Chicago off the sidelines of the third-airport debate.

At the center of Kruesi's working group was the Chicago aviation firm Ricondo, which had first pitched the mayor on the idea of a third city airport. Ricondo's proposed site contained a large industrial area pummeled by the collapse of the steel industry, running from 103rd Street south to the Indiana state line and including the polluted Lake Calumet. In addition to protecting Chicago's regional monopoly, it would bring major economic development to a distressed part of the city.

The mayor and his team had been working up plans as part of a carefully orchestrated rollout, including lengthy technical studies and political consultations. However, the media caught wind of a meeting between Daley and the Ricondo consultants, taking place just prior to an already scheduled, unrelated mayoral press conference. According to the mayor's press secretary, Avis LaVelle, Daley was supposed to deflect inquiries from reporters by stating that a third Chicago airport was an interesting concept but required lots of study. Instead, when questioned, an exuberant mayor simply announced the $5 billion project.

"It was like, 'What?! Did he just say that?!'" LaVelle said. "And so it didn't give us a chance to do what we needed to do. There was so much . . . political groundwork and there was a lot of feasibilities. I was stunned. And when we went back in the room, I'm like what happened to 'We're going to take this under consideration' and 'We're going to do the homework'?" And he's like, 'I just got excited. . . . I didn't mean to do that, but I think it's a really great idea.'"[2]

To make the plan work, the entire neighborhood of Hegewisch would have to be razed. After the press conference, the *Sun-Times*' Fran Spielman called Marlene Schichner of the Hegewisch Community Committee to ask what she thought of the airport that would wipe out her home. "What airport?" Schichner asked.[3]

When Daley made his announcement, the Illinois-Indiana task force had recommended four potential locations for a third major airport—Gary, Indiana; another site overlapping the Illinois-Indiana state line; and Peotone and Kankakee in northeastern Illinois. The two-state committee had no choice but to add a fifth—Lake Calumet. The mayor's brother Bill was the city's point man on the two-state task force and assembled a 7–5 coalition in favor of building at Lake Calumet. The original suburban architects of the study, including Aldo DeAngelis, were enraged.

Daley's proposal upended the longtime city strategy of stiff-arming regional airport planning, which required power sharing with the state. In 1992, with Republican Gov. Jim Edgar's support, Daley introduced authorizing legislation for a regional airport authority encompassing all three Chicago airports. It included both partial financing for the Lake Calumet airport and the authority to condemn and clear businesses and homes in southeast Chicago.

The detailed plan followed two years of technical feasibility studies, the kind that normally *preceded* formal announcements of giant public-works projects. Because Daley had flipped the script, his plan hit an unexpected problem. The feasibility studies demonstrated that, once fully operational, a third major airport so near Midway, also on the south side of Chicago, would pose insuperable obstacles to air flight scheduling and safety. Due to the realities of air-traffic patterns and commercial growth, Midway eventually would need to close, collateral damage from the mayor's Lake Calumet foray. Daley's impetuosity in making the premature announcement two years earlier now came back to haunt him.

Daley's plan depended on the assistance of two powerful but reluctant Chicago Democrats—US Rep. Bill Lipinski, the top Democrat on the House subcommittee on aviation; and Illinois House Speaker Michael Madigan. Both represented southwest city areas encompassing Midway Airport.

Lipinski owed his seat in Congress to Daley.[4] So despite misgivings, the congressman used his considerable transportation clout to push through federal legislation authorizing a $3 per passenger ticket tax designed to fund Lake Calumet, whose price tag had grown to $10.8 billion.

Madigan was cool to state funding for Lake Calumet but didn't stand in the way of the House passing Daley's authorizing legislation. But it took four tries to get it through and over to the Senate, and realizing Daley's plan would require a series of additional bills.

Legislation approving the acquisition and destruction of factories and homes and relocation of residents met fierce opposition from environmentalists and homeowners. Their opposition, however, had less political significance than the objections of the Republican state senate leader James "Pate" Philip, who was more attuned to suburban colleagues such as DeAngelis than he was to the downstate governor and leader of his party. Philip, always wary of doing anything that would help Chicago, opposed the $2 billion in state funding for Lake Calumet. The bill went down to defeat.

To Governor Edgar, this was a temporary setback; with the proper political logrolling, it would eventually pass. But behind the scenes, Daley had been under increasing pressure from Lipinski and Madigan. Their constituents depended on the jobs and economic benefits of Midway.

Lipinski had pulled off an ironic miracle years earlier that elevated the value and importance of Midway. Among a dwindling cadre of conservative Democrats, Lipinski cast one of a handful of Democratic votes for President Ronald Reagan's aid to the Nicaraguan right-wing contras who were fighting the Marxist Sandinista government. Reagan called Lipinski to thank him for breaking party ranks. Almost as an afterthought, he said, "Is there anything I can do for you?"

Lipinski paused, then said, "Have you ever heard of the Southwest Side rapid-transit system?"[5]

Less than a year later, the federal government had fully funded what is now the CTA's Orange Line, linking downtown Chicago with Midway Airport and the Southwest Side neighborhoods Lipinski represented. The Orange Line was the first expansion of the transit system in a quarter century. It was scheduled to open the following year.

With the Philip-led defeat as his excuse, Daley shocked Edgar by pulling the plug on Lake Calumet. Instead, he announced the city would focus on improving O'Hare and Midway.

All was not lost from Daley's wayward maiden flight. With Lipinski's help, the mayor had secured a long-term cash cow through the airport ticket surcharge. He wasted no time using it, announcing a new nine-hundred-thousand-square-foot Midway terminal and pedestrian bridge connecting to a modern sixty-three-hundred-space covered garage. The spacious new terminal included a fifty-thousand-square-foot food court to showcase local restaurants. The expanded airport also accommodated fourteen additional gates, a nearly 50 percent increase in capacity.

By 1999, Midway was the fastest growing airport in the country, handling larger volumes of cargo but also exploiting the growing popularity of economy fares by its dominant airline, Southwest. By 2019, Midway was serving nearly 21 million passengers a year.

Stung by Daley's abrupt turnaround, Edgar focused on a third airport outside Chicago, with Peotone emerging as the most likely site. Leaning on his fellow

Republican, President H. W. George Bush, who had succeeded Reagan, Edgar secured a starter $2 million FAA grant to begin the Peotone planning process.

Beyond regional arguments for Peotone, some key Republicans had a less visible incentive to promote it as the site for a new airport. Poring through local land records and untangling a web of blind trusts designed to keep secret the names of owners, *Crain's Chicago Business* reported that State Senator DeAngelis had been selling limited real estate partnerships around Peotone for years. Some of his activity came to light in a lawsuit by his investment partners, including Cook County's Republican party leader, Manny Hoffman, who accused DeAngelis of squandering more than $2 million of their money.

It turned out that a considerable number of political insiders had acquired Peotone farmland not to grow corn but to capture potentially huge profits if the state began buying up the land for a new airport.

But their hopes for a windfall were dashed with the 1992 election, when Arkansas Gov. Bill Clinton ousted Bush as president. Not only was Clinton a Democrat but his campaign's leadership team was top-heavy with Chicagoans tied to Daley. The mayor's campaign manager, David Wilhelm, also managed Clinton's victorious campaign. Daley's finance director, Rahm Emanuel, was Clinton's chief fundraiser. Bill Daley assisted as a campaign advisor and helped Clinton secure Mayor Daley's endorsement prior to the critical Illinois primary. Daley's first chief of staff, the attorney John Schmidt, raised hefty campaign sums early in Clinton's long-shot campaign and went on to become a high-ranking member of the Justice Department.

Given the number of Chicago stars in Clinton's political galaxy, it wasn't surprising to see several Chicagoans show up in influential positions in Clinton's US Department of Transportation—an agency that exercised extraordinary influence over Daley's airport plans. Daley's policy chief, Frank Kruesi, became Assistant Secretary of Transportation. Catherine Lang, an assistant Chicago Aviation commissioner, was appointed director of the FAA's Office of Airport Planning, which oversees the passenger ticket tax and approvals for new airport projects. Daley's chief aviation counsel, Susan Kurland, joined the US DOT in 1996 as associate administrator of airports.

Most important, Clinton's first FAA director was David Hinson, a CEO of Midway Airlines. Daley and Lipinski lobbied furiously for his selection. Within months of his appointment, Hinson pulled the Peotone planning funds. Four years later, after Kurland took charge of the program, the FAA quietly removed Peotone from the list of airport projects eligible for federal funding. Peotone had been on the list for more than a decade.

At last, Peotone was dead, as was any threat of suburban encroachment on Chicago's aviation turf.

Or so it seemed.

• • •

In life, what one hand delivers, another sometimes takes away. Daley's airport ambitions had benefited mightily from the election of President Bill Clinton and the appointment of key Daley aides to top positions governing national airport matters. By the midterm elections in 1994, however, Clinton had badly overreached with his national health care plan and was reeling politically. Republicans, led by Congressman Newt Gingrich and his Contract with America, swept into power. The national wave ushered in Republican control of all three branches of the Illinois government. GOP leaders wasted no time using their new influence to expand suburban power at the expense of Chicago.

At the center of their power play was O'Hare Airport. Northwest suburban residents had grown weary of escalating noise from O'Hare as the volume of commercial and freight air traffic continued to grow. The seemingly endless demand for air travel pushed O'Hare's capacity to its limits and fueled talk of expansion. But Republicans wanted any new airport to be on their turf. They also wanted in on the action at Chicago's two existing airports.

In early February 1995, within weeks of assuming control, state Republicans introduced legislation for a regional airport authority to supplant municipal oversight of Midway and O'Hare. The prize was control of lucrative aviation contracts and jobs and the three-dollar fee levied on each passenger moving through either Chicago airport. The income stream from passenger fees could underwrite bonds financing a Peotone airport.

A swaggering Sen. Aldo DeAngelis, the leading proponent of a third airport and suburban control, explained the flurry of Republican legislative activity.

"We're trying to squeeze Mayor Daley's testicles," he said.[6]

Feeling the pressure, Daley was in Springfield the following month, offering caps on nighttime flights to appease suburban Republican legislators. But Philip, whose own home in Wood Dale was a mere fifteen minutes from O'Hare, was feeling his oats and not interested in compromising with Daley. Philip went on a Chicago radio show and announced that it didn't matter if Daley capped flights, nixed new runways, or supported Peotone as a third regional airport. The Republicans were going to create a suburban airport authority to take over O'Hare and Midway—no matter what.

"Its time is due," he said.[7]

Back in Chicago, Daley's corporation counsel, Susan Sher, assembled her top lawyers in a desperate attempt to block the state's plans. It seemed a futile exercise, the challenge insurmountable. Municipalities are creations of state government. Local powers in Illinois are granted at the discretion of Springfield.

With the clock ticking, Daley summoned Sher to his office nearly every day for an update on the legal research.

"It was a very nerve-racking period," Sher told me. "We were aware of how high the stakes were, because these airports were literally the most important economic engine of the city, and our failure would result in a major political defeat for Mayor Daley."[8]

Finally, with Daley increasingly despondent, one of Sher's deputy corporation counsels advanced an unusual idea. Larry Rosenthal was a former federal prosecutor and US Supreme Court clerk. He argued that Chicago could use the US Constitution as a shield against the state takeover. Pursuant to the Constitution's Compact Clause, which provides for interstate compacts, in 1959 Congress gave standing permission for states to operate regional airports jointly. In the ensuing years, both Illinois and Indiana delegated power under this statute to their governmental units, including municipalities.

Rosenthal proposed that Mayor Daley create his *own* regional airport authority with a partner from another contiguous state. The obvious choice sat just across the Chicago border, less than forty-five minutes from downtown: Gary. This Indiana municipality operated its own tiny airport on the outskirts of town.

Once formed, the Chicago-Gary Airport Authority would legally stymie the state of Illinois. Under the Compact Clause, a two-state compact between Gary and Chicago would supersede any entity created by a single state legislature. Although Indiana's legislature was Republican, its governor, Evan Bayh, was a Democrat, obviating concerns of any partisan cross-state conspiracy to undo a deal. Bayh provided state lawyers to assist Gary.

"It was a novel idea, which at first we thought might be far-fetched, but the more we researched it, the more we believed it was a viable solution," Sher told me.[9]

Daley was ecstatic but knew the idea would only work if the process of securing the compact could be kept secret. If the governor or Republican legislative leaders got wind of it, they could move the airports takeover bill immediately. To prevent a leak, Daley confided in only a handful of trusted aides who were necessary to plan the maneuver.

Secrecy was so critical that it sometimes bred paranoia. When it was time to line up financing, the aviation attorney, Susan Kurland, brought Chicago's chief financial officer, Walter Knorr, into the conspiracy. Knorr's office shared a wall with the Budget Office, so Kurland insisted that Knorr meet with her in his office's adjoining private bathroom. The perplexed Knorr, a large man, squeezed into the tiny space on one side of the toilet while Kurland sat on its edge, carefully briefing Knorr on what was happening.

When everything was ready, Daley looked for an opening. Gov. Jim Edgar was scheduled to be on a trip to Israel during Passover and Easter, when the legislature would also be on break. It would be the perfect time. With Sher standing by his side, Daley placed a phone call to Gary's mayor, Tom Barnes.

Sher told me Daley's call went something like this: "We have something important to talk to you about. I'm sending my lawyer to see you—right now. She'll explain everything when she gets there." Sher headed toward the door, intent on avoiding rush-hour traffic. Before she passed the doorway, however, Daley called her back. "Wait!" Calling out to his longtime assistant, Roseanne Bonoma, Daley said, "Get me Earl Neal!"[10]

Earl Neal was among the city's legal elites and its most influential African American attorney. In his first two terms, Daley had leaned on Neal for counsel and trusted him as a city emissary. By chance, Earl was sitting in his office. Daley asked him to accompany Sher, who was white, to Gary, an overwhelmingly African American city. "She'll fill you in as you go," Daley said. Neal volunteered his car and driver.

When the duo arrived, they were greeted by Mayor Barnes and two members of his city council. Neal discovered that both councilmen were from his college fraternity, a bit of serendipity that lent itself to easy conversation. The ice broken, Neal and Sher explained the benefits of an interstate airport authority for Gary. Chicago would provide $1.5 million a year for airport operations and improvements, doubling the Gary Airport's budget. It wasn't a hard sell.

With Gary on board, the final piece was joint approval. Gary's city council needed to pass the agreement, as did Chicago's aldermen. Both cities needed to comply with Open Meetings Act statutes requiring prior public notice, including the posting of an agenda at least forty-eight hours in advance. Gary went first, on the theory it was less likely to attract press attention; lawyers crafted the vaguest agenda possible while allowing it was for an airport agreement. Gary's meeting was scheduled for a Thursday evening. Chicago scheduled its special meeting on Saturday morning—the day before Easter and during the overlapping Passover celebration.

To throw reporters off the scent and take further advantage of the unique situation, Daley made the top agenda item a 36 percent pay raise for the mayor and aldermen. The odd timing of the special meeting appeared to make sense. Of course the cynical politicians would use the religious holidays as cover for their self-dealing! Taxpayers would be busy with their celebrations, and stories of the aldermen lining their pockets would be buried on the Saturday night news.

It worked. The press reported the special meeting's purpose as a stealthy power play for pay raises.

As word of the Gary city council meeting began to leak the Thursday night before Chicago's Saturday session, Daley's team finally dropped the pretense. The story of the interstate pact broke with Friday morning's newspapers—too late for any counteraction by the legislature or the governor, who was stranded in the Holy Land without a prayer of stopping it.

At the Saturday council meeting, Daley presided like the proverbial cat that had swallowed the canary. As one alderman after another stood to applaud the agreement while taking potshots at Philip and the Republicans, Daley stood at the podium with a sardonic smile. In a matter of weeks, he had turned the tables on the cocksure Republican leadership that had so arrogantly and blithely announced their imminent theft of Chicago's crown jewels.

The airports remained firmly in Chicago's grasp.

Republicans would soon seek revenge, targeting another prominent Chicago asset. But this was a glorious moment—and the most brilliant political coup of Daley's mayoralty.

CHAPTER 10

Neighborhoods

Despite momentum from Downtown's renewal, Mayor Daley initially struggled to make an impact outside the Loop and its environs. Many declining parts of the city qualified neither as "blighted," eligible for TIFs; nor "poor," eligible for federal development dollars from the US Department of Housing and Urban Development (HUD). The city's Department of Planning and Development followed traditional guidelines and strategies—carefully circumscribed "spot TIFs" in the worst neighborhoods, and targeted use of HUD funds for the poorest of the poor. The efforts yielded *de minimis* returns.

Frustrated, the mayor began to refer to his bureaucracy as the "Department of No Planning and No Development."

A turning point came in 1994, prompted by the decay of a once-vibrant retail corridor on the city's Northwest Side. The diagonal intersection of Belmont, Ashland, and Lincoln Avenues anchored the strip, and was home to once-iconic stores such as Goldblatt's, Wieboldt's, and Woolworth. But those large traditional retailers were losing ground to more nimble discounters and suburban malls. Retail was changing; consumers were mobile and more dispersed. Prospective customers increasingly required parking spaces, which were lacking in old-fashioned urban domains.

One by one, the big retailers closed their doors en route to bankruptcy. Their large and shabby buildings sat empty.

At the time, the city planning department had a narrow mission of assisting developers with zoning changes. It had no significant financial tools and adhered to a policy of not subsidizing middle-class areas. But the momentum of decay in Lincoln-Belmont had shifted so much that no independent private investment could reverse the trend. Programs such as spot TIFs or HUD funds would be available if the area collapsed entirely, but not in its zombie state.

A talented young developer, Bruce Abrams, approached city hall. He had acquired the empty Wieboldt's building in order to convert it to residential lofts, but the cost of conversion exceeded any potential profits. He needed city assistance.

The city's planning department rejected the idea under the long-standing criteria that the area was insufficiently blighted or impoverished. But Terry Teele, a young aide from downstate Illinois and the mayor's point man for development, felt the city was missing an opportunity. By acting now, the city could take defensive action, preventing further decay.

Teele had caught Daley's attention as an aggressive coordinator of city services at the Office of Inquiry and Information, Chicago's nonemergency hotline. In the mayor's office, Teele was a kinetic force, combining punctilious management with political acumen and an enthusiasm for urban revival that nearly matched his boss's. He accompanied the mayor throughout the city, and the two developed a close bond. In time, Teele could channel Daley's thoughts with eerie precision.

In this instance, Teele was confident of where Daley would land. He decided to force the action. With unfettered access to the mayor's schedule, Teele set up a meeting with the mayor, planning chief Valerie Jarrett, and Comptroller Walter Knorr.

"I felt the mayor needed to see and hear the types of obstacles that were being placed in his way by his own staff," Teele told me. "I thought the best way was just to fight it out in front of him."[1]

When Daley walked in, he asked what the meeting was about. The city had a unique proposal from a developer, Teele told him, and he believed it should get behind it. Knorr and Jarrett expressed sympathy but objected because the surrounding area was middle class and the project met none of the traditional qualifications for a TIF or a city loan. Resources should be reserved for the most distressed areas, they argued, and this was the type of commercial area that funded police, fire, and other key city services. Freezing revenues through a TIF would take those dollars away.

Teele, increasingly animated, argued the project would be preventive, ensuring the surrounding area didn't decay further and undercut the very revenues necessary for public safety.

"In ten years, this area will qualify for HUD funding," Teele told them. "But it's going to get a lot worse before it gets better."[2]

As he so often did during his twenty-two years in office, the mayor indicted his own government for being too timid. He changed city policy on the spot, interpreting "blight" in the state statute more broadly than his own planners and lawyers. The project went forward.

The Abrams project included fewer than one hundred units, but other developers and retailers took notice, igniting a series of private and public investments. Younger professionals moved in, followed by restaurants and boutique stores. Two years later, Whole Foods opened a store at the diagonal, eventually building a mega store across the street, complete with its own trendy wine and coffee bars.

The Abrams development was a game changer that stimulated more aggressive efforts to convert loft buildings and other structures into residential housing.

The combination of TIF subsidies and eminent domain to acquire other dilapidated or vacant buildings became a powerful one-two punch. Working with aldermen and community groups, Daley targeted neighborhood eyesores or businesses, from liquor stores to flophouses, that attracted loitering, prostitution, and other crimes.

Along Lincoln Avenue, running northwest, the city began condemning the rent-by-the-hour "hot-sheet" motels that had dominated the area for decades, building in their place new police stations and libraries and extending nearby parks to fill the remainder. Daley coordinated all city governments in the process. By this time, I had left city hall, having been appointed Daley's parks superintendent in 1993. Daley enlisted me to expand Senn Park on the city's far North Side, absorbing an area left by the demolition of a shabby chicken and hot dog restaurant at the corner of Peterson and Lincoln Avenues. Students from Senn High School now walk by a statue of Abraham Lincoln marking a new western entrance to the campus.

Daley used the city capital budget as a powerful strategic tool. New police and fire stations, city warehouses and maintenance facilities, libraries, even parks and schools, were built on the edges between established and struggling neighborhoods, inside distressed communities but not far from the strong commercial and residential blocks nearby. By bringing in stabilizing influences—the daily presence of police officers or city employees going to work, along with their accompanying economic activity—neighborhoods moved ever closer together, until a tipping point of private investment lured by the new order erased the boundaries between good and bad.

But Mayor Daley's strategy of investing in weak neighborhoods abutting strong ones could work only if sufficient infrastructure was already in place, such as quality housing, the core of any strong neighborhood. Dilapidated or abandoned buildings are harbingers of doom. Once deterioration reaches a point of no return, only demolition is feasible, and the resultant vacant lots send a powerful message of abandonment, choking off further investment. At that point, economic development becomes the proverbial boulder pushed up a hill, rarely with success. Detroit's moonscapes provided a vivid example of urban decline past that point of return.

Unpaid taxes often accompany deteriorating housing, a sign that the owner can no longer take care of the property or simply refuses to. Cook County carries out annual tax scavenger sales, allowing real estate investors and speculators to bid for the tax liens on these delinquent properties. Daley saw the system as part of the problem, because it tied up parcels in an uncoordinated web. He pushed through county ordinances giving him the power to acquire delinquent properties with no-cash bids, preempting speculators.

Most urban leaders have no interest in taking control of troubled properties; besides the headaches and expense of maintenance, city ownership means the political blame from residents for the collateral problems of vacant and unsafe buildings falls squarely on their shoulders. But Daley was willing to assume responsibility. He surprised the county ordinance's sponsors by scooping up properties by the thousands, moving those unclaimed into large enough combinations to attract industrial, commercial, or residential developers, and investing in supportive infrastructure.

One powerful tool, however, simply fell into his lap. In the first few years of his mayoralty, a group of housing activists promoting a temporary federal tax credit began inviting Daley to events around restored housing made possible by the new law.

"We took Rich to a couple of groundbreakings, the first one in Rogers Park, where he saw this former slum transformed into affordable housing that didn't cost the city any money, lowered rents by hundreds of dollars, made it feasible, and allowed for buildings to be reclaimed, and he fell in love with it," recalls Marilyn Katz, a longtime city public relations executive and liberal political activist.

The tax credit was experimental, a vehicle for corporations to invest in affordable housing. It was scheduled for expiration, its fate in the hands of the US House Ways and Means Committee chaired by the powerful Chicago congressman Dan Rostenkowski, a close mayoral ally. When Katz found herself on the same Washington-to-Chicago flight as Rostenkowski, she approached him with trepidation.

"I really need you to pass the low-income housing tax credit. There is no other way for the nation to do housing, and Mayor Daley really likes it," Katz said.

The gruff and physically imposing Rostenkowski retorted, in his booming baritone voice: "If Mayor Daley likes it so much, let him give me a call!"[3]

Katz relayed the message, and Daley made the call.

When Rostenkowski succeeded in making the tax credit permanent in 1992, he said the mayor never failed to bring up the law's fate in their many conversations. The result was impactful not only for Chicago but also for the country. Today, the tax credit generates billions annually for affordable housing. Thanks to Rostenkowski's clout, Chicago has its own allocation.

The new funding stream helped preserve, restore, and rehab properties in struggling neighborhoods such as Woodlawn, Bronzeville, Rogers Park, and Washington Park, and then became part of the mayor's toolbox for redevelopments throughout the city.

Eventually, Daley incorporated all his strategies and tools into Strategic Neighborhood Action Plans (SNAPs), identifying areas in need and coordinating the bureaucracy to channel resources there. His marketing team later rebranded SNAP as "Neighborhoods Alive." The key was for city agencies to coordinate tightly, so that development was holistic, with maximum effect.

Occasionally, though, a department wouldn't "get the memo."

Terry Teele recalls when the city housing department launched its "New Homes for Chicago" program, which wrote down developer costs to reclaim vacant lots and attract working families. On the day of the ribbon cutting for the first two homes in a declining West Side neighborhood, the department's senior staff waited excitedly for the mayor to arrive.

Teele arrived first, about forty-five minutes ahead of the mayor.

"I look around and start to panic," Teele said, "because I'm not seeing two New Homes for Chicago. I'm seeing six vacant lots with garbage on them, four abandoned buildings, and an abandoned gas station. I remember asking the housing staff, 'Who owns these lots? What's the legal status of these abandoned buildings?' They tell me, 'Well, we're the department of housing; that's the building department's responsibility.' I thought to myself, this is not going to go well."[4]

Sure enough, when Daley arrived, he was furious, asking the same questions.

"It bothered him a lot when departments put blinders on and only saw their little part of the world, not taking into account the mayor's vision as a whole," Teele told me. "Putting two new homes on a block doesn't begin to change the community unless it's part of something bigger."[5]

Changing communities was increasingly Daley's focus. But to succeed, he would need to control more than his city government.

CHAPTER 11

Ghost Towns

After winning his first four-year term in 1991, Mayor Daley had city government firmly in his control. But he was only beginning to exert his will on legally independent sister agencies directed by mayoral appointees, entities that could help him revive entire neighborhoods.

His first target was the Chicago Park District, a vast network of more than 550 parks; hundreds of recreational centers with year-round cultural and sports programming, encompassing gyms, auditoriums, swimming pools, fields, and ball diamonds; and more than eight thousand acres of land, including botanic gardens, boat docks, beaches, conservatories, museums, and a zoo. Its expansive regional parks were designed by such legendary nineteenth-century landscape architects as Fredrick Law Olmsted Sr. and Jens Jensen. The park district had its own authority to levy property taxes, employed more than four thousand full-time employees (seven thousand in the summer), and spent hundreds of millions annually.

In 1990, the *Tribune*'s William Recktenwald and Sharman Stein made unannounced visits to Chicago parks and concluded that the district "runs a string of ghost towns," with more employees than patrons. The newspaper's editorial board said the parks were well preserved "because many of the parks and fieldhouses and gyms are rarely used, and the staffers are rarely subjected to the physical strains of work," citing as an example the Fuller Park supervisor who banned kids from the auditorium because their sneakers scuffed the floor.[1]

When recreational facilities were needed the most, on holidays and weekends, they were closed.

In response, Daley appointed the former Buffalo parks chief Robert Penn as the new parks superintendent with a mandate to fix the system. After three years on the job, however, Penn failed to root out the deadwood and invigorate the parks with new programming. Worse, the district continued to levy heavy annual property tax increases, despite little to show for it.

The lack of progress was not lost on neighborhood organizations and civic groups. Friends of the Parks issued a report card with a failing grade, concluding the district was running a jobs program for employees rather than services to citizens. The Civic Federation weighed in with a report calling the district dysfunctional. The city council parks chairwoman, Mary Ann Smith, held hearings to keep a focus on the neglect.

Daley's board chair, the attorney Richard Devine, made progress in areas within his control—cracking down on rampant expense account padding and overtime abuses. Devine, who would later be elected to three terms as Cook County state's attorney, also outsourced the park district's money-losing golf courses.

After Kemper Golf had taken over management, the iconic public television host John Callaway, an avid golfer, described the difference to me. "Before, when we went to play golf at the Waveland course," he recalled, "a surly, cigar-chomping manager would come out and declare, 'What do *you* want?' and we would meekly reply, 'We would like to play a little golf, sir.' 'Well, all right,' the manager would reply before waddling back to his office. Now, as we play on the newly pristine grounds, we're greeted by a freshly scrubbed young Kemper employee who lies, 'Nice shot sir!'"[2]

Despite those victories, Daley increasingly had a political crisis on his hands.

By this time, I was serving as deputy state treasurer under Patrick Quinn, a friend who was positioning a run for governor in the next election. (Quinn eventually succeeded, but not for another fifteen years.) In early 1993, I got an invitation from Tim Degnan to have breakfast at the Bismarck Hotel, a dining hangout for the political class near city hall. Degnan wanted to test my interest in taking over the parks. Daley needed a proven manager he could trust; he couldn't afford to get it wrong a second time.

I didn't need any persuasion.

In a racially divided city, Daley made a practice of separating the leadership of sister agencies by race. In this case, the board chair was white (Dick Devine) and the CEO Black (Robert Penn). That meant Devine needed to move on. He was replaced in the spring, ahead of my summer appointment, by the African American financial whiz John Rogers, founder of the giant money-management firm Ariel Capital. Rogers was an inspired choice—a fitness and sports advocate as well as a former Princeton basketball team captain for the legendary coach Pete Carril. Rogers helped run Carril's unique "Princeton Offense," a disciplined fundamentals-first attack that often allowed less gifted players to triumph over more athletic hoopsters.

Rogers was the type of smart player Carril recruited but also a talented athlete. At an Air Jordan camp for adults years later, Rogers became the first and only camper to defeat the NBA legend Michael Jordan in the camp's obligatory one-on-one game. The winner was the first to score two baskets. Each camper got a video of their matchup with Jordan to take home.

The thin, bespectacled Rogers didn't look the part of giant slayer. He surprised Jordan with a lightning move to the basket to score. Chastened, Jordan took control, drove to the hoop, and tied it. With the game on the line, Jordan now locked in on

Rogers with his fabled competitive intensity. Rogers parried right and then went left. Rising in the air with Jordan literally draped over him, Rogers leaned sideways and launched a left-handed hook shot inches over Jordan's outstretched fingertips.

As Jordan watched in horror, the ball banked in.

For years afterward, to Jordan's irritation, Rogers gleefully mailed hundreds of videotapes of the game to friends, clients, and acquaintances around the country. At one point Jordan approached a couple he knew were friends of Rogers while dining at a Chicago restaurant. "You better tell your friend to stop mouthing off," Jordan said. "I *let* him win that game!"

With Rogers settling in as board chairman, I finally got the call in July. At a press conference in the West Side's Garfield Park, Daley and Rogers announced my appointment as the new superintendent.

I was inheriting a mess that would take time to fix. I needed some quick wins. As a symbolic gesture, I got rid of the superintendent's chauffeur. I also donated the superintendent's luxury skybox at Soldier Field to children's charities. In the past, the skybox had been a perk for entertaining friends and big shots at Bears games. When I mentioned it to my former partner David Axelrod, a veteran of the Chicago press corps, he suggested I hold a press conference.

"Anything to do with Soldier Field and the Bears is a big story in this town," Axelrod said.

I was skeptical, but I held a press briefing with John Rogers, a representative of the Bears, and children from the Cabrini-Green public housing project who would attend the first game (with all the hot dogs, hamburgers, and ice cream they could eat). To my astonishment, every news organization in the city—print, radio, TV—showed up. It was lead news, and the editorial boards voiced approval.

Daley was thrilled, and I had bought some time.

Parks safety was my immediate priority. Gangs were fixtures in too many places—loitering, dealing drugs, and otherwise menacing passersby. In the remaining days of that summer, I raced to meet police at multiple gang-related shootings in the parks.

In my first week, I invited the Chicago police's chief of patrols to visit my office adjacent to Soldier Field. I asked him, "How many policemen do I need to hire to restore safety to the parks?" His reply startled me. "None," he said. I looked at him blankly for a second, then said, "What did you say?" He replied, "None. You just have to get people back in the parks. The drug dealers and gangbangers don't want to be around people."

His simple wisdom was refreshing. I didn't need an expensive occupying police force. I just needed to do what the park advocates were clamoring for and what the mayor desperately wanted—vibrant new programming to lure children and families back into the parks.

It would take time to change the park district from a patronage-centric system to one of customer service. In the meantime, we needed to manufacture exciting new programming out of thin air.

Half of good management is recruiting talented people. I had persuaded Marj Halperin, my colleague in the "what mayor" affair, to head a new department of marketing.[3] She in turn recruited Helen Doria, a protégée of Daley's eclectic-minded Commissioner of Cultural Affairs, Lois Weisberg.

Weisberg was a remarkable civic treasure, as unusual a municipal bureaucrat as you will ever find. In 1999, Malcolm Gladwell, the author of such bestsellers as *The Tipping Point* and *Outliers,* wrote a feature on her called "Six Degrees of Lois Weisberg" in the *New Yorker* magazine. "She's a grandmother," Gladwell wrote as a tease, "she lives in a big house in Chicago, and you've never heard of her. Does she run the world?"[4]

Gladwell described Weisberg as a "connector," someone who seems to know everyone, with tentacles into such disparate worlds as music, acting, parks, medicine, lawyering—even the subcultures of railroad buffs and flea market mavens. Her North Side home was the Grand Central Station of intellectual get-togethers, the site of endless salons. "People like Art Farmer and Thelonious Monk and Dizzy Gillespie and Lenny Bruce would stop by when they were in town," Gladwell writes. For a time, Bruce lived in Weisberg's home.

"My mother was hysterical about it, especially one day when she rang the doorbell and he answered in his bath towel," she told Gladwell.[5]

Weisberg had founded Friends of the Parks, the now influential group that acted as a watchdog and advocate. So Weisberg imparted to Doria a deep passion for the parks.

Like Weisberg, Doria was a creative connector, loquacious and joyful, and a passionate lover of both the city and its cultural assets. In our desperate situation, she was just what we needed. Together, Doria and Halperin devised Parks Partners, a program to connect more than fifty city cultural, artistic, and athletic institutions to the people of Chicago through their local parks. All agreed to donate their services.

In the summer of 1994, the "ghost towns" began to fill up. The Raven Theater taught acting to teenagers. The Chicago Power soccer team put on clinics. The DuSable Black History Museum presented on the Black cowboy tradition. The Shedd Aquarium ported around a giant inflatable whale so kids could enter its belly and learn about marine biology. The Chicago Bulls supplied coaches and scouts to teach basketball. The Field Museum of Natural History ran day camps on pigeon physiology and behavior, taking advantage of the omnipresent cooing urban creatures. Columbia College's Dance Center presented "Dancing in the Parks" to two thousand Chicago teens, teaching the art of dance from ballet to jazz to tap.

Mayor Daley lent a hand with a city grant for sports camps, which paid for high school and college coaches out of work between spring and fall semesters. Not surprisingly, we called them "Mayor Daley's Sports Camps"; every child went home with a T-shirt bearing the logo. For older youth, we partnered with the Bulls again for Late Night Basketball leagues. The areas near lagoons and lakes became homes for urban campers and anglers competing in fishing contests.

My press chief, Nora Moreno, was a whirlwind of energy, working tirelessly to promote the new park district. Her father was a pioneer in Spanish broadcasting; like his, Moreno's career had started in radio. She was passionate about her parks mission, often emotional, which she blamed on her "Mexi-rican" heritage. Her father was Mexican, her mother Puerto Rican, and their relationship was stormy. Moreno produced a radio show for *This American Life* on NPR, using old clips from family recordings, to tell the story of her parents' tempestuous romance. It hit its nadir when her mother shot her father in the mouth when she discovered his infidelity. He survived. The relationship continued.

Moreno saw the potential of the nascent internet in 1993 and created one of the first government websites to let parents schedule sports and cultural programs for their kids. (She wisely ignored my advice not to bother; I explained to her that the internet was a fad.)

The whirlwind of summer programming had begun to revitalize the parks, but as kids headed back to school, we needed other answers. Another of my recruits, Ray Vazquez, came up with one. Vazquez was a veteran YMCA executive who used sports to keep young people off the streets. But he also went out *onto* the streets to establish relationships with gang members, cooling tensions that might boil over into violence. He ensured that his kids could move freely across gang lines. Vazquez believed a neutral rec facility would be a sanctuary.

Vazquez also knew an after-school haven was the best anti-gang program. His brainchild was Park Kids. Every school day, starting in the fall, students were bused from their school to the nearest park, where they got an hour of sports, an hour of arts, and an hour of homework assistance. The program eliminated the latchkey problem for working parents.

When I first explained Park Kids to Mayor Daley, however, I was surprised at his reaction. Rather than expressing his usual enthusiasm for new programs, he slumped in his chair when I told him about the busing and hired tutors. "I guess it's come to that now," he said. "We have to do everything." Daley was lamenting societal changes that left parents with less time to be involved, perhaps because there were so many one-parent households. This reality affected every aspect of city governance, from parks to schools to policing.

Park Kids was a big success and continued to expand each year, part of a plethora of new sports and cultural programming. To ensure professional instruction, I hired an accomplished Boys & Girls Club executive and former coach, Sally Csontos. She developed a rigorous professional development curriculum that eventually became Chicago Park District University. Key instructors and managers were required to pass a series of courses. For the first time—to the consternation of the entrenched old-boy network—a woman was in charge of all sports program delivery at the park district's 259 neighborhood centers.

Because of the vast, underutilized assets of the park district, I knew each day that I had the power to do something meaningful. I could make a kid's life better (or just more fun); give a working mom a sports or arts program to safely occupy and delight her child; or even boost a homeowner's property value with a new or rehabilitated greensward.

To bring change up to scale, however, we needed more programs, and big money to fix long-neglected gyms, fields, auditoriums, and pools. Too many dollars were tied up in unproductive patronage—a vestige of the Ed Kelly years.[6] To make matters worse, the park district ran a series of specialized businesses—and they all bled red ink: Soldier Field, home of the NFL's Bears; the downtown underground parking garages along Michigan Avenue; the lakefront's marinas; Lincoln Park Zoo; and prior to the Kemper takeover, the public golf courses.

All were businesses that should be *making* money—not *losing* it.

Soldier Field was an example.

Although many staffers were hard working, the parks were a haven for connected individuals inclined to conserve energy. So it seemed odd to me that so many employees volunteered to work the Soldier Field parking lots for Chicago Bears football games, breathing in exhaust and freezing their behinds in Bear weather. The park employee's job was to take the ten-dollar payment and direct the car to the next available slot.

For the 1994 football season, I conducted an experiment by hiring Standard Parking Corporation to manage the games. Without "volunteer" park employees collecting cash, our coffers overflowed with ten-dollar bills, generating a record for receipts.

After competitive bidding, Standard began managing the Michigan Avenue parking garages; Spectacor Management Group took over Soldier Field; and Westrec Marinas assumed responsibility for the marinas. In an agreement brokered by the parks counsel, Randy Mehrberg, the Lincoln Park Zoological Society assumed responsibility for day-to-day management of the zoo. In exchange, the group agreed to a twenty-five-year promise to keep zoo admission free.

The park district was soon making money hand over fist—tens of millions in new revenue. The previously dank and dim Michigan Avenue parking garages were dry and brightly lit. Boaters enjoyed repaired docks and new amenities. As demand grew with better service, Westrec and the park district built hundreds of additional boat slips. Soldier Field became more than a place to watch football eight times a year; it became a sought-after venue for other sporting events and concerts, adding additional vitality to the city.

In upsetting the status quo at Soldier Field, however, I made a formidable enemy—the owners of the Bears. As we brought in other events, including mega concerts by the Rolling Stones and the Grateful Dead, the playing field suffered damage requiring repairs. Sometimes the entire field would have to be replaced with new sod. At the same time, the McCaskey family, controlling shareholders of the Bears, complained loudly about the unfairness of the park district lease.

Soldier Field was one of the smallest stadiums in the National Football League, with a limited number of high-margin luxury skyboxes. The Bears also wanted control over concessions, as other teams had. The team demanded either a new stadium or a completely rebuilt Soldier Field; they wanted the city to pay for most of it. If not, they said the suburbs would beckon. Multiple northwest suburbs made noises about combining to build a new stadium near the Kennedy Expressway.

Mayor Daley went back and forth, gravitating between wanting to tell the McCaskeys to pound sand to soliciting ideas to ensure that the Bears remained in the city.

Against this backdrop, the Bears saw a way to keep pressure on Daley. The team's PR office began working the beat reporters, selling a narrative that all the resodding was making the field "unplayable" and "unsafe." The Bears even trotted out their player representative, defensive end Trace Armstrong, to bemoan the poor turf conditions and issue warnings that player safety was threatened.

Although nothing suggested the new turf performed any better or worse, beat reporters took their cues from the team on which they depended for scoops. For weeks the narrative dominated print sports sections and radio and television sports news. In a Bears town, we were the greedy bureaucrats risking the safety of the city's beloved warriors.

Getting in on the fun, the *Sun-Times* cartoonist Jack Higgins published a sketch of a reporter interviewing a parks bureaucrat explaining that the district would resod the field after the Monster Trucks Rally and Demolition Derby. The scoreboard advertised the upcoming Tractor Pull contest. In the background, goats grazed on the Soldier Field turf.

In any public debate, if you're explaining, you're losing. We were never going to explain our way out of the pummeling, especially to sports reporters. So I applied an important principle I'd learned in political campaigns: if you can't win an argument, change the subject.

The Bears president, Michael McCaskey, worked hard to keep the turf controversy going and scheduled an appearance on the city's top-rated morning radio show. Nora Moreno, who had developed a strong relationship with WGN radio host Bob Collins, set up an ambush. Collins thought an impromptu debate would be great theater, so after McCaskey completed his indictment of the park district, Collins opened the line for listener calls. I was waiting.

I reminded McCaskey that the park district lost millions operating Soldier Field for just eight home games and explained to the radio audience that each year a senior citizen living on a fixed income in a Chicago bungalow wrote a check (figuratively) to the wealthy McCaskey family in tony Lake Forest, Illinois.

The next day, I called the mayor to make sure he would support the next step. He did. The park district sent a formal letter to the Bears offering exclusive rights to the stadium, if the team simply made up the multimillion-dollar deficit. Not surprisingly, the McCaskeys didn't take the offer.

In the following days, the narrative turned. No longer were sports reporters the messengers. Now, general news journalists covered the "taxpayer fairness" issue of whether the Bears should be getting such a big subsidy at the expense of working families. The tables were turned; now the McCaskey family was taking the media drubbing.

At the warm-ups prior to the next Sunday home game, I saw McCaskey at mid-field and walked out to meet him. We shook hands and exchanged pleasantries. He was classy, joking about our public relations wars. We agreed to a truce.

I gave a sigh of relief.

But just when I thought I could relax, we took another embarrassing hit.

For many years, the park district had hosted the Black Classic at Soldier Field, a football game between two historic African American colleges. In addition to being a fundraiser for the schools, it was a big draw in the local Black community. Unfortunately, the 1994 contest would fit on only one weekend—a Saturday evening before a Sunday home Bears game. Under the Soldier Field lease, the Bears could block any event within two days of a home contest. But in a game of chicken, neither the Bears nor Mayor Daley would prevent scheduling of the college game; no one wanted to be the bad guy in a racially sensitive situation.

What happened next was, literally, the perfect storm. Just as the two college teams kicked off on Saturday evening, a monsoon swept over the stadium, unleashing unrelenting torrents of rain. It continued unabated as the teams played, their cleats tearing up the surface and leaving only mud in their wake. Kickoff for the Bears game was fourteen hours away.

The only thing the field crews could do was spread tons of sand and clay across the mud to absorb moisture and provide limited traction. The next afternoon, as I watched the nightmare unfold on national TV, the Bears and the New Orleans Saints slogged and slugged through four quarters on what looked like a giant sand-box leavened with Kitty Litter. The national broadcasters had a field day wondering what yahoos were responsible. The condition of the field got as much attention in the postgame press conference as the Bears victory.

Fortunately, the *Tribune* columnist Mike Royko came to our rescue, in a back-handed sort of way. Previously Royko had written for the *Sun-Times* but jumped ship the day it was acquired by the Australian tabloid publisher (and later Fox News founder) Rupert Murdoch.[7] Royko declared that "no self-respecting fish would want to be wrapped in one of Murdoch's publications."[8] His page 3 *Tribune* column was by far the most influential news source in town. Deploying his trademark humor, Royko went after the Bears' whining. In mock sympathy, he worried about the working conditions of the millionaire members of the rough-and-tumble Monsters of the Midway:

> The imperfect turf has become one of our major civic issues, and may be the most poignant sports story of the year. . . . It seems the playing surface at Soldier Field was a bit moist and, in some places, lacked sufficient grass. This caused some of the players to be less than nimble and quick and made them slip, slide, and get glop on their uniforms. This led to widespread moaning by the players and sports commentators that if the intolerable conditions continue, some player might get hurt. Which is shocking, since nobody has ever heard of a football player being injured before.[9]

With this assist from Royko, we moved past the turf wars. The McCaskeys would eventually get their new stadium but would have to wait a bit longer.[10] Soldier Field began to produce valuable new revenues, as did the parking garages, marinas, and other assets—multiple sources of revenue to fund neighborhood parks.

• • •

The hardest part was yet to come, however—the painful reorganization of the bloated bureaucracy.

A 1993 audit by the new chief financial officer, Ron DeNard, a talented executive recruited from Alcoa Corporation, and two outside municipal finance experts, John Filan and Paul Stepusin, discovered the park district was perilously close to its legal debt limit. Yet it was in the middle of an aggressive and expensive construction campaign.

DeNard assumed leadership of a financial office burdened by the same patronage (and nepotism) practices as the rest of the district. The budget department was led by a husband-and-wife team whose daughter also worked for them. Veteran park employees referred to the budget office as "mommy, daddy, and baby." An indication of the level of financial competence was that park district bills were paid each month in alphabetical order rather than by date of invoice, often leaving in the lurch vendors with names further down the alphabet.

DeNard removed the family in charge as well as other department leaders. Together with Filan and Stepusin, veterans of major national accounting firms, he imposed modern, professional standards. Cleaning up the books and imposing financial order across a sprawling organization was difficult and exhausting, but DeNard leavened the task with humor. During long nights and weekends, he lifted staff morale with his consistent and unique jocularity. Besides being a gifted financial strategist, DeNard was something of a stand-up comic, perfectly mimicking colleagues and putting a satiric spin on the many absurdities they encountered, leaving employees in hysterics.

DeNard and I asked the construction expert Joseph Manzi to audit the building projects. Manzi had been hired by Mayor Daley when the Harold Washington library fell behind schedule and was, ironically, woefully short in meeting the 25 percent goal for awards to minority subcontractors. Under no circumstances was Mayor Daley going to cut the ribbon on a building named for the city's first African American mayor and explain why only white companies built it. Riding herd on the contractors, Manzi ensured the library opened on time and with strong minority representation.

Manzi's audit was revealing. Virtually every project was over budget and behind schedule, usually with substandard construction. In one instance, the district purchased an operating YMCA and gutted it beyond recognition. My predecessor had decided not to outsource this work to professional contractors but to build an internal construction team. Leading the internal construction company were the top precinct captains for the powerful state House speaker, Michael Madigan (Thirteenth

Ward), and Cook County Board Commissioner (soon-to-be-president) John Stroger (Eighth Ward). Neither leader of the team had any construction experience.

Stewardship of tens of millions of dollars in complex construction had been determined on the basis of ward politics.

To avoid hitting the debt ceiling and stop the financial bleeding, I laid off the three hundred tradesmen. That was a problem on two fronts. The politically powerful trades unions had benefitted mightily from the program and now faced displaced and angry members. And, not shocking, given that the ward leaders had done the hiring, the force was full of referrals from politicians.

Like so many before him, Superintendent Penn had become enamored of doing favors for powerful politicians, particularly Madigan, whom he referred to as the "redhead." Before issuing the pink slips, I shared the layoff list with Tim Degnan, the mayor's political chief. As he went through the names, he muttered, "Not ours, not ours, not ours, not ours," until he came to the end. In three years under Daley's control, the park district had been filled with new trades patronage hires. But none were his.

Once the pink slips hit, the calls from politicians poured in—some to me directly, but mostly to Degnan. To the mayor's credit, no one was saved. When the dust settled, only two people remained in the internal construction company—the bosses. With no one left to supervise, I thought both should be fired. But Degnan wasn't willing to go that far, given their Madigan and Stroger pedigrees. They were demoted to other roles.

The construction unit was just the tip of the iceberg. The parks were larded with unnecessary positions created with only politics in mind. To hire the qualified personnel we would need to make the parks thrive, we would have to remove a lot of others without disrupting operations.

It was a massive undertaking; once again, recruiting was key. In 1993, my city hall deputy, Carol Rubin, had moved on to the Illinois Facilities Fund, where she was overseeing a statewide construction campaign building day-care centers for low-income families. Under her leadership, the projects came in on time and under budget. Rubin was an incisive expert on organizations and a skilled and unrelenting manager. She didn't suffer fools gladly and only surrounded herself with those she described as "A-plus people." I tapped her to be the district's chief operating officer and to lead the park district's restructuring.

One of the other recruits was Randy Mehrberg, the general counsel, who took a leave from his lucrative post as a partner at the prestigious Jenner & Block law firm. Mehrberg had a soft spot for kids; the opportunity to contribute to the parks' turnaround was a big lure. Along with his colleague, the former US attorney Anton "Tony" Valukas, Mehrberg tutored children in an after-school program at the notorious Cabrini-Green public housing projects. Each also served as a "big brother" and mentor for one of the projects' fatherless kids from grade school through college.[11] After graduating, Mehrberg's mentee went to work for Jenner & Block and stayed for twenty-five years. I hired Mehrberg for his legal mind, but once I grasped the magnitude of his managerial talents, I gave him responsibility for overseeing the lakefront and all its revenue-producing assets.

Over the next eighteen months, our team streamlined and reorganized the park district into a modern professional organization. No longer were there assistants to assistants or deputies to deputies. The infamous central bureaucracy was dismantled; hiring, budgeting, and programming were devolved to the neighborhood level, increasing responsiveness.

With expenses down and revenue up, I could now rebuild the parks without new taxes. In each of my five budgets, property taxes remained flat or declined. For Daley, that was almost as much of a relief as the whirlwind of new programming. In his first term, Daley had faced a tax revolt by his white ethnic base, partly fueled by park-district tax hikes.

Issuing bonds, we began aggressive improvements to neighborhood parks, including three new beach houses along the south lakefront, eighty acres of new parkland, a water park for the South Side's Washington Park, and renovation of all nine hundred city baseball diamonds. We put out an ambitious $230 million five-year capital plan.

I soon learned it wasn't nearly enough.

Having battled through two years of painful cuts and restructuring, I was too protective of our hard-won financial stability. Daley would later pay a painful political price for my conservatism.

CHAPTER 12

Broken Windows

As a prosecutor, Rich Daley made the war on drugs his trademark; as mayor, he was immediately haunted by its accelerating carnage. Lucrative precisely because of their illegality, narcotics spawned endless, violent urban warfare. A parade of drug warlords battled for city turf; when one went down by bullet or indictment, another ambitious hoodlum stepped in.

In the late 1980s, a glut of Colombian cocaine caused prices to plummet. Drug cartels innovated, converting the excess powder into a solid, smokeable form of cocaine dubbed "crack." It was easy to use, cheap to make and packed a powerful high. Its concentrated form made it easy to carry, conceal, and market. It also fostered a more retail-friendly form of street distribution—one that escalated violent gang clashes.

Fueled by the crack epidemic, Chicago street-gang murders hit an all-time high in 1990, and the overall homicide rate reached a ten-year peak. Daley faced increasing pressure as the violence and murder rates continued to climb, reaching a symbolic zenith in October 1992, when seven-year-old Dantrell Davis was killed by a sniper bullet as he walked with his mother to school in the Cabrini-Green public housing complex. A thirty-three-year-old gang leader, Anthony Garrett, fired from a tenth-floor apartment, aiming for a rival gangbanger but striking Dantrell in the head.

"His death became a symbol of a sort of urban hell," the *Tribune* wrote, "a world so violent and out of control that even a little kid walking a short distance to school wasn't safe."[1]

The *Sun-Times* took the mayor to task in a scathing analysis:

For nearly three years, Mayor Daley has dodged responsibility for the city's soaring homicide rate. . . . On the day after Dantrell Davis was murdered only steps from his home at Cabrini-Green, the mayor was true to form. He blamed the federal government for the drug scourge, declared CHA high-rises a failure and plugged Democratic presidential nominee Bill Clinton's plan to put another 100,000 police officers on the streets of the nation's big cities. . . . When a 7-year-old boy accompanied by his mother is gunned down on the way to school, the politics of blame doesn't work anymore.[2]

Responding to the crime wave, Daley beefed up the police force with hundreds of additional officers. Using a Booz Allen consulting report as cover, he also replaced expensive officers holding administrative positions with cheaper civilians, freeing hundreds of desk-bound cops for street duty.

More important, Daley began listening to two key deputies to Police Superintendent Matt Rodriquez—Barbara McDonald and Charles Ramsey, who were developing the experimental new strategy of community policing, in which officers work consistently in the same areas to win the confidence and cooperation of residents. Rather than an "incident-driven" approach, with patrols responding to 911 calls, community policing is intended to solve neighborhood problems before they blossom into serious crime.

The mayor was particularly receptive because this strategy dovetailed with his own philosophy of neighborhood service delivery.

Daley intuitively followed the "broken windows" theory of policing, a doctrine advanced in 1982 by the social scientists James Q. Wilson and George Kelling. The idea was that decay, disorder, and incivility spawn crime. When a city focuses only on violent crime and downplays minor offenses such as public drunkenness and urination, graffiti, panhandling, and street prostitution, an aura of disorder and fear prevails. Convinced that an area is unsafe, people withdraw along with the social controls previously deterring criminals. Over time, disorder and decay feed on each other in a vicious downward cycle.

"Broken windows" refers to physical decay such as vacant buildings, graffiti, and trash-strewn vacant lots; but it also means social disorder such as homeless encampments, aggressive beggars, and street-corner loitering.

The theory came to national prominence in the 1990s in New York City under Mayor Rudy Giuliani and Police Superintendent William Bratton. In Bratton's previous role leading the city's transit police, he put hundreds of officers in plainclothes to arrest turnstile jumpers; and as his misdemeanor arrests increased, crime decreased. As chief of police, he focused on "quality of life" offenses. The most reported example was a crackdown on "squeegee men" who would emerge at red lights to clean the windshields of startled motorists, and then hit them up for cash. Crime rates plummeted.

But the first major city to practice broken windows theory wasn't New York. It was Chicago.

Daley didn't need a sociologist to tell him that cleaning up the streets and imposing a sense of order was important. In fact, it was his obsession. As he drove about the city, Daley famously took copious notes of everything he saw, then sent furious waves of orders to department heads to address everything from graffiti to missing alley lights to potholes. He ordered sweeps of homeless encampments, combined with offers of help for those willing to take it; cleaned up the widespread scourge of junked automobiles in poor neighborhoods; and began tearing down abandoned buildings by the thousands. Weedy, littered vacant lots were condemned and acquired, then cleaned, mowed, and fenced, and made available in combined parcels for business development or new affordable housing.

Although both New York and Chicago were practitioners of broken windows theory, they went about it differently.

"An important feature of Chicago's approach to solving (crime) problems is it does not just involve arresting people," said Professor Wesley Skogan of Northwestern University. "Unlike New York's 'zero tolerance' approach to addressing community problems by making tens of thousands of arrests for minor offenses, Chicago's solution for broken windows is to fix the windows."[3]

Community policing is a kissing cousin of broken windows theory because it focuses on winning the trust and cooperation of a neighborhood to keep it safe. Daley viewed city services as glue to further cement the police and community partnership.

Mayor Daley created the Community Alternative Policing Strategy (CAPS), 280 police beats overlying neighborhoods. Officers held monthly meetings with residents and paid particular attention to community block clubs. The meetings were opportunities for citizens to raise seemingly minor issues (repeated graffiti) or major concerns (a drug house operating in the neighborhood).

"You're getting feedback on crime that's concerning the community," said Rob Huberman, a Chicago police officer who manned a CAPS beat and later headed a series of city agencies, including the Office of Emergency Management. "It was very often different than the crime that you might have been concerned about. You might have cared heavily about a burglary pattern or a robbery pattern, right? But people care about the crimes that they can see. So they care about, you know, the loud tavern on the corner. They would care about the graffiti in the alley. They would care about that drunk homeless guy around the corner."[4]

Under community policing, beat cops became more than law enforcement officers; they became liaisons with the city bureaucracy, ensuring service issues were addressed.

Daley saw enormous value in block clubs because they were organized and led by residents. If a beat had none, the mayor took pains to ensure that one was created. In time, those block clubs joined with police and city agencies in anticrime marches, sending a message of unity in protecting and enhancing neighborhoods.

"Before a CAPS march, there was always a police roll call," recalled Sarah Pang, the mayor's deputy for public safety. "You would see police from the whole district lined up in uniform, with the block club folks, with the neighbors. And the mayor added all the city services to the lineup."[5]

Police cars, Streets and Sanitation trucks, transportation department asphalt machines and assorted other city vehicles lined up as if for a parade. City crews would move through the neighborhood, cutting down dead trees, picking up garbage, towing away abandoned cars, removing graffiti, replacing streetlights, filling potholes—any conceivable city service that could be deployed quickly with scale and force. These exercises helped strengthen bonds between the police, city agencies, and residents.

Jesse Smart was president of the 1100 North Lawndale Block Club on the West Side. A tool and die maker at a General Motors factory in suburban Bedford Park, Smart had moved back to his childhood neighborhood with his wife and two young children in the early 1990s.

"We wanted to own, not rent, so we found this nice house near Chicago Avenue. The Polish lady who owned it fell in love with my wife, so she gave it to us for ten thousand dollars less, so we could afford it," Smart remembered fondly.[6] The neighborhood was primarily African American but contained a smattering of Latinos, as well as older Polish and Italian residents.

Smart told me the origin of his involvement with CAPS was a street confrontation with gangbangers.

"I had just moved on the block and started having conversations with the gangbangers standing on the corner, to try and get them to move on. Some of the other men in the neighborhood got wind of what I was doing and joined me, and we got the drug dealers off the corner," Smart said.[7]

Smart turned this small neighborhood victory into a formal organization and began participating in CAPS meetings. Along with the men who had joined him in confronting the corner drug dealers, he also formed the Eleventh District Men's Club, encompassing the entire police district. It grew to more than three dozen residents who began working directly with city hall staff, including the mayor's infrastructure deputy Terry Teele, Streets and Sanitation assistant Sue Sardo, and Ed Severns from the Buildings Department. Each Saturday, Smart and the city team would travel the CAPS district together and identify problems to attack—illicit drug activity or prostitution, abandoned buildings, weedy and unfenced vacant lots, fly dumping, abandoned cars.

Gradually, with Smart and his block clubs leading the way, the dilapidated buildings fell, lots were cleaned and fenced, community gardens were planted, graffiti removed, and consistent pressure was exerted by police against gangbangers and drug dealers, enforcing loitering laws and conducting stings to make arrests. The combined effort brought residents closer and improved the daily life of people living in Smart's West Side community,

"Back then, the police were very involved," Smart told me. "Mayor Daley demanded that they work with us. Block clubs had a lot of power and they believed in the process. We would hold our meetings on the street, pull up chairs on the corner next to the drug dealers. The police commander, the mayor, the key departments would show up to support us."[8]

Smart said the neighborhood, with CAPS representatives, would pick streets like Division or Pulaski or Chicago Avenue and hold marches in the evenings protesting drug dealing, inevitably leading to confrontations with gangbangers. Pastors from local churches would bring congregants to join other block club members and neighbors. Police would cooperate with residents by shutting down the streets on short notice. Engaging in dialogue with drug dealers and gangbangers, Smart and other CAPS leaders would sometimes establish personal relationships and connect them to job assistance or other support to turn their lives around. They had some success but kept the pressure on the criminals who remained.

Smart, who today coordinates police and community relations for Ald. Walter Burnett of the Twenty-Seventh Ward, said his CAPS experience opened his eyes to the good things that can happen, even in challenged neighborhoods, when residents, police, and City Hall work closely together.

"In those days, CAPS had a deep relationship to the community, and that made the community comfortable because they knew the police would come when we called. Today the community doesn't trust the police anymore, but back then we had trust," Smart said.[9]

Daley's frequent visits and outreach added to the sense that he had the backs of residents fighting for better neighborhoods. The mayor held banquets honoring block club and CAPS leaders. Smart said the mayor would personally ask the awardees to come up to the front, where he would present them with a plaque that expressed the city's gratitude and recognized their role in CAPS' successes.

"Daley empowered block clubs, and the big dinners made people feel like they were wanted," Smart said. "They didn't mind going out to try and take their blocks back from the drug dealers and gangbangers because they knew they could get help in doing these things."[10]

As Daley's community policing initiative grew, so did the number and size of block clubs and their clout. The names of block club leaders filled the Rolodexes of top mayoral aides, and those leaders had a direct hotline to the fifth floor. Eventually, Mayor Daley filled the McCormick Place Convention Center with an annual block club jamboree, at which neighborhood activists celebrated their successes and heard from the police department, the mayor, and keynote speakers. One year the special guest was General Colin Powell.

As the mayor's second term ended, he had turned the corner. Crime was receding under the combined assault of mayoral initiatives. By 1997, Police Superintendent Matt Rodriguez announced the lowest crime rate in a decade, exceeding the national urban trend. The combination of more police on the streets, an increasing emphasis on community policing, and enhanced "quality of life" service delivery was paying off.

After more than five years at the helm, Superintendent Rodriguez had presided over a major reversal of crime trends and won plaudits for his department's pioneering work in community policing. But as the year ended, the *Tribune* reported that Rodriguez had for many years associated closely with a known felon, a violation of department rules. Under normal circumstances, the superintendent could have apologized, severed the tie, and remained in office, but the disclosure came on the heels of a long list of police brutality and corruption cases, including an officer being outed as a member of a Chicago street gang; three policemen charged in drug cases; and multiple allegations of police beatings, including that of a Black officer at the hands of eleven white cops, even as he was waving his badge.

Hours after the *Tribune* story, Rodriguez gave Mayor Daley his resignation.

Mayor Richard J. Daley heads down a city hall corridor, accompanied
by his son, Richard M. Daley, and a bodyguard. April 5, 1972.
Credit: James Quinn/*Chicago Tribune*.

State's Attorney Richard M. Daley, with his wife, Maggie, during the 1983 mayoral campaign. Credit: Richard J. Daley Library, Special Collections, University of Illinois-Chicago.

Harold Washington, Richard Daley, and Jane Byrne at the conclusion of the fourth and final mayoral debate, January 31, 1983. Credit: Anne Cusack/*Chicago Tribune*.

Ald. Luis Gutierrez introduces the mayoral candidate Richard M. Daley to a cheering crowd of Latino supporters in the final days of the 1989 election. Credit: *Chicago Tribune* archive photo.

Richard M. Daley celebrates with supporters on the night of his election as mayor, April 4, 1989. Credit: Chris Walker/*Chicago Tribune*.

Mayor Richard M. Daley, the grand marshal of Chicago's Gay Pride Parade, June 25, 1989. Credit: Richard J. Daley Library, Special Collections, University of Illinois-Chicago.

Mayor Daley shares a laugh with Gov. James "Big Jim" Thompson (standing at podium); left to right, the new McPier Chairman John Schmidt and the new McPier CEO Jim Reilly, announcing the rebuild of Navy Pier, July 17, 1989. Credit: Richard J. Daley Library, Special Collections, University of Illinois-Chicago.

The *Sun-Times* cartoonist Jack Higgins's satiric take on Mayor Daley's reverential press coverage following his early successes, 1989.
Credit: Jack Higgins, *Chicago Sun-Times*.

Third Term

1995–1999

CHAPTER 13

Go West

As Mayor Daley entered his third term, Downtown development accelerated, pushing at the edges of the Loop's traditional boundaries. A new "south Loop" began to emerge, a combination of modern condos and townhomes, restaurants, and retail stores. But the near West Side remained isolated, separated from the bustling Downtown by the busy Dan Ryan Expressway.

In the mid-1990s, however, two unrelated events gave Daley a unique opportunity to remake the impoverished near West Side of Chicago, part of the larger West Side still reeling from the devastation of the 1968 riots following Martin Luther King's assassination.

The first was presaged in 1984; no one could have predicted its remarkable impact.

The Chicago Bulls had just completed a dismal season of twenty-seven wins and fifty-five losses, qualifying the team for the third pick in the NBA draft. At the time, the league was dominated by big men, and the Bulls coveted one of the two available seven-foot centers. With two teams picking ahead of them, however, they had to settle for a twenty-one-year-old guard from North Carolina, Michael Jordan.

The Jordan selection underscores the old saying, "It's better to be lucky than good." Although Houston's number-one pick, Hakeem Olajuwon, went on to a Hall of Fame career (a small consolation for the Rockets), Portland's selection of the injury-plagued Sam Bowie was retrospectively named the worst draft pick in the history of North American professional sports.[1]

As the years passed, it became clear that Michael Jordan would change not only the narrative of Chicago basketball but that of the entire NBA. The Babe Ruth of basketball—the greatest player of all time—was wearing a Chicago Bulls jersey. With international interest in basketball exploding, Jordan became a worldwide figure and the new face of Chicago, a happy replacement for Al Capone.

Attendance at Bulls games soared and tickets became hot commodities.[2] Local businesses wanted to entertain clients anxious to see Jordan and were happy to pay handsomely. But the rickety old Chicago Stadium could seat only 17,300 fans and had no luxury suites for the hoity-toity. So the Bulls owner, Jerry Reinsdorf, partnered with Bill Wirtz, the owner of the hockey Blackhawks, to build a new $175 million stadium, the United Center, with a capacity of 20,917 seats, ringed by two rows of private skyboxes. To their credit, Reinsdorf and Wirtz built the new stadium without taxpayer subsidies.

Although financed with bank loans and the owners' money, the new United Center was the House that Jordan Built. As the Bulls improved year after year on their march to six championships in the 1990s, real estate near the United Center boomed, adding new restaurants, retail businesses, and condominiums. By the time Daley left office, fans coming to and from the games were spending more than half a billion dollars a year, supporting more than twenty thousand jobs, and generating close to $2 billion in economic activity.[3]

The rise of Michael Jordan became the rise of the near West Side of Chicago.

• • •

But the United Center was just the first step, a strategic anchor around which to build.

The second opportunity was the decision of the Democratic National Committee, headed by Daley's former campaign manager, David Wilhelm (who had also guided Clinton's 1992 presidential win), to select Chicago as host of its 1996 national political convention at the United Center. Besides being a vehicle for development, it was an opportunity for Daley to exorcise the ghosts of the 1968 Democratic convention, where his father was famously accused of presiding over a "police riot," with out-of-control officers violently assaulting young people protesting the Vietnam War.[4]

The 1996 convention, where Bill Clinton would be nominated for a second term as president, was a chance to rethink the struggling areas west of Downtown, where perceptions of crime kept significant development from moving past the expressway, at the time acting as a wall separating Daley's new Chicago from the old.

One couple was tired of the wall, and they let the mayor know.

Anne and Lewis Kostiner were pioneering real estate developers in the near West Side. They sensed before anyone else that the area was ripe for residential development because of its proximity to a rebounding Downtown. They began acquiring empty and boarded-up warehouses and converting them into quality loft apartments, replete with amenities, attracting a mix of artists and young professionals. Rents were a quarter of those in posh Lincoln Park.

But it was risky. One of their first developments was 312 North May in the Fulton Market district, today the hottest commercial and residential neighborhood in Chicago. At the time, the abandoned building was next to a Waste Management garbage processing plant and a chicken slaughterhouse.

"We were upfront with prospective tenants," Anne Kostiner told me. "We said, 'There's no park, no dry cleaner, lots of rats, the streets are bloody and the chickens smelly, and noisy trucks back in and out of here starting at three or four in the morning."[5] For urban pioneers willing to put up with all that, the reward was an affordable, roomy, high-ceiling apartment with breathtaking upper-floor views of the Chicago skyline, from the Sears Tower to the Hancock Building. It was also a short commute to work downtown.

The Kostiners' motivation was making a living, but they also had a deep love for the city, and especially a desire to preserve the turn-of-the-twentieth-century architecture that helped define Chicago's international reputation as an industrial metropolis. They were afraid these unique structures would eventually be torn down.

"These old buildings were built to last forever," Anne said. "We thought it was a shame to let them die there. Why not rehab and restore these beautiful, sturdy structures?"[6]

In addition to warehouse-to-residential conversions, the Kostiners began building an indoor ice-skating rink, Johnny's Icehouse, a few blocks from the United Center. It was only the second indoor ice-skating rink in the city and the first privately owned and managed one.

Despite their increasing investments, the Kostiners saw little evidence that the city was concerned about their area or the risks they were taking to improve it. The Fulton Market district had no functional sidewalks, garbage was everywhere, stop signs were missing, and prostitution and panhandling were common. Lewis and Anne made a video of this imagery, placed it in an envelope, addressed it to Mayor Daley, and dropped it in the mail with a note: "Why does the city of Chicago neglect this area, considering its proximity to the Loop? It has so much potential, but first you have to invest in it. We have already invested millions. How about you?"[7]

The video ended up with Chief of Staff Gery Chico, who took it to the mayoral infrastructure deputy, Terry Teele.

"Gery said, 'Some nut jobs sent this video to the mayor' and dropped it on my desk. I popped the tape in and watched. Then I called Lewis Kostiner," Teele said.[8]

"We were surprised to get the call," said Anne, who didn't expect anything to come from their gesture of protest. "Our experience with people at the city had been negative. When we called about problems like missing stop signs, they didn't even recognize the street names."[9]

At about the same time, the incumbent alderman was defeated by Walter Burnett, a protégé of the popular state representative and future Illinois secretary of state Jesse White. Together, Teele and Burnett began showing some long overdue love to Lewis and Anne Kostiner.

"You tell me where you want the stop signs, and we'll put them there," Anne recalls Alderman Burnett telling her.[10]

Teele brought the Kostiners into planning discussions for the convention; they were instrumental in helping guide a city task force on loft conversions. It was the beginning of a long and productive partnership. As the months and years passed, the Kostiners continued to invest in the near West Side as the city finally ramped up its efforts to rebuild the area.

"It was a partnership, but we never got any city funding; it was all our own money. We didn't want the red tape and the delays. Terry and the mayor appreciated that," Kostiner told me.[11]

Daley had been thinking about a new West Side initiative as soon as he won reelection to a third term in the spring of 1995. Planning Commissioner Valerie Jarrett had begun to facilitate new affordable housing west of the expressway, and a few companies were acquiring land there. One of the first was the international giant Walsh Construction, led by longtime Chicago business leaders Dan and Matt Walsh. In 1992, they converted a 1908 warehouse into a modern glass and brick headquarters with 93,000 square feet of wide-open spaces, skylights, and sleek angular designs, with pioneering applications of solar and water-conservation technology.

These nascent developments were welcome, but with the convention coming, Daley wanted a complete makeover and gave Teele an aggressive timeline. To fund all the development, Daley created a special tax district encompassing a large swath of the West Side stretching from Western to Halsted and from Lake to Van Buren. The area covered the city's skid row, still populated by vagrants and alcohol and drug addicts. Social service agencies and flophouses were interspersed among the dispossessed.

Teele determined that an area along Madison from Ogden to Paulina qualified under state law as "blight." He designated twelve buildings for condemnation; some were vacant, and some were marginal businesses such as a liquor store and a pawn shop, which turned out to be owned by the family of a county judge. When the mayor's Eleventh Ward alderman and city council floor leader Pat Huels came across the acquisition ordinance, he angrily complained to Daley's new chief of staff, Roger Kiley. Kiley dutifully notified Daley, who summoned Teele to explain. As Teele entered, Kiley was sitting in a chair across from Daley's desk.

"Terry, Roger is asking about some properties on Madison Street we are acquiring," the mayor said.

"Yes sir, the ones you and I have talked about for a year and half—the ones attracting the homeless, drug dealers, prostitutes, the ones with ten outdoor pay phones up and down the block," Teele said, pulling out a map and handing it to the mayor.

The mayor squinted at the streets and buildings and said, "What about this vacant one in the intersection of Ogden, Madison and Ashland with the big billboards towering over the street?" he asked.

"I didn't have enough budget money to acquire that one," Teele responded.

"Well, put it in the ordinance. I'll find the money," Daley said forcefully. "Anything else, Roger?"

Mystified, Kiley replied, "No, sir."[12]

Daley ordered an intense beautification of Madison Avenue, the main transportation artery linking the United Center and the downtown hotels that would host the conventioneers. Teele told me he had decided to dispense with the usual requirement of a public hearing and didn't notify anyone about the city's plans, including the alderman and local businesses. He started on a Friday morning, ordering the Department of Transportation to work through the weekend, taking out one of the four street lanes and replacing it with a median of trees and flowers. Stop signs were installed to slow traffic, streets were paved, and new antique-style electrolier lights were installed. The gritty adjacent industrial businesses, with trucks moving in and out day and night, were enraged by the constricted streets and emblems of gentrification. But the deed was done.

"You could never get away with that today," Teele said, laughing.[13]

To encourage residential development and entrepreneurs like the Kostiners, Daley changed the zoning codes to make it easier to convert industrial real estate to commercial and residential. It was the first official recognition that the area would be changing, its status as a transportation and industrial hub gradually giving way to a different kind of future.

• • •

In the year leading up to the convention, the near West Side changed dramatically, as Daley's beautification campaign reached its zenith. As parks superintendent at the time, I was working with both city hall and the public schools to convert acres of ugly asphalt surrounding neighborhood schools into new campus parks. Daley tapped this partnership to create a major expansion of Skinner Park that would connect it to Whitney Young High School a few blocks from the United Center, creating a new oasis of trees, flowers, and green pathways for passing conventioneers.

Demolition and construction activity abounded. The US Secret Service, charged with the security of the president and other dignitaries attending the national convention, complained about the pace of changes. The agency was forced to repeat flyovers photographing areas around the United Center because so many buildings were coming down and so many new ones were going up.

When the convention began, the Secret Service was also hard pressed to keep up with a hyperactive President Bill Clinton. He soon brought national attention to Chicago's oddest tourist attraction, Taste of Chicago, a weeklong food fest featuring local vendors occupying Grant Park. The president was famous for his lack of discipline and outsize appetites, both sexual and gastronomical. In a Saturday Night Live (SNL) parody, Clinton interrupts his morning jog with Secret Service agents to enter a McDonald's, where the president schmoozes with a seated diner before asking, "Are you going to finish those fries?" At Taste of Chicago, Clinton worked his way through a half dozen food vendors, downing Polish and Indian food and then a plate of jerk chicken and beans.

An astonished server remarked, "He almost finished the whole thing!"

The *Tribune* was impressed with the display of presidential gluttony:

"Bear in mind all of this was after Clinton's appetizer, a double cheeseburger from the Billy Goat Grill. 'Let's hear it, cheeseboorger, cheeseboorger,' the president yelled to the Billy Goat crew, directing them in the tavern's now famous chant" (also of SNL fame).[14]

Meanwhile, the city police department was planning strategies to ensure a safe convention. Daley was concerned about protesters, given the scars of 1968. Although the country was at peace and the economy booming, protestors still descended on the city, focused on immigration, affordable housing, and a smorgasbord of other liberal issues. They were aware of Chicago's history, and many went out of their way to try and provoke the police.

Deputy Superintendent Jack Townsend trained his troops not to take the bait, which extended to their equine animals. Mounted police formed a protective barrier between protesters and delegates entering the United Center. Sometimes aggressive demonstrators would hit the horses with sticks, throw manure at officers, and even drop firecrackers around the horses' hooves to try and get a reaction. But Townsend's troops—and their horses—remained stoic.

Of course, the tactics did wear on Townsend's good will, which mayoral deputy Sarah Pang told me resulted in a final altercation with demonstrators on the last day of the convention.

The protestors used expensive road bikes to move around, sometimes carrying purloined police radios to monitor the city's communications. They parked their bicycles close to the convention hall. On that last day, Townsend noticed a group of kids from the nearby Henry Horner public housing projects; they were eyeing the bicycles and then eyeing the police, including Townsend, the stout, decorated commander in charge. As the juveniles warily inched toward the untethered bikes, Townsend sent a subtle signal to his officers. The kids gradually moved past the demonstrators and bystanders, and then clearly beyond the demarcation line, but the police didn't push them back. The street-savvy kids had their cue; they made a dash for the bikes, hopped on, and rode off, knowing the police wouldn't follow.

When agitated protest leaders demanded Townsend get their bikes back, he coolly instructed them to go file a complaint.

• • •

Despite minor glitches, the 1996 Democratic National Convention was a huge success and something of a coming-out party for the emerging new Chicago. Referring to Daley's previously dismissive critics, the *Washington Post* wrote:

"They are gone from here in what is more than ever Rich Daley's Chicago. As delegates to the Democratic National Convention, which begins Monday, began streaming into the city, Chicago and its mayor were in the midst of a remarkable renaissance."[15]

The *Wall Street Journal* praised the new Chicago, noting that under Daley more than eighty thousand jobs had shifted from manufacturing to services, and another thirty-five thousand from traditional warehousing and distribution to communications and transportation, the latter increasingly connected to the growing O'Hare airport. Huge new investments were going into the city's housing stock, the paper noted, and the increasing population density downtown was fueling rising tax receipts paying for major infrastructure improvements.

More important, the *Journal* wrote glowingly, Chicago's quality of life was transcendent, becoming an appealing destination for knowledge workers driving the new American economy:

> This is America's urban paradise.
> Don't laugh.
> As Democrats return next week to the scene of their violent 1968 convention, many will be surprised to find that, despite a 1980s manufacturing collapse, the flight of nearly one million residents and a humbling loss of political power, Chicago not only survived but blossomed into an economic, cultural and lifestyle marvel. . . .
> Increasingly, people with job skills or affluence to live anywhere choose Chicago, finding here much that is desirable about Los Angeles and New York and considerably less that is irksome. . . .
> "Getting an executive in New York to move to Chicago is a headhunter's second toughest sell," cracks recruiter Peter D. Crist of Crist Partners, Ltd. "The toughest sell is getting him to move back."[16]

The 1996 convention showcased Chicago's transformation to the world. It provided the impetus to turbocharge redevelopment on the near West Side, taking advantage of the new United Center and its increasing number of commercial offshoots.

And it put to rest, at last, the ghosts of 1968.

Daley now presided over an increasingly prosperous Downtown, extending south from its original borders, and finally leaping over the West Side expressways to connect to the United Center's economic engine.

The mayor now turned his attention increasingly to the city's most troubled neighborhoods.

CHAPTER 14

Anchors

Strong cities have many and varied assets, but they all contain anchors, large and small, that keep their communities stable, especially when the winds of change bring threatening waves.

Daley was concerned about two important institutions in the Auburn Gresham neighborhood near 79th Street that anchored the struggling community—St. Sabina Church, led by the charismatic activist priest Michael Pfleger, and the Catholic Leo High School, offering quality educations for poor, minority children. Unchecked crime was leading Leo to consider an exit, and Pfleger spent most of his time not leading his flock in prayer but marching on the streets protesting lawlessness. St. Sabina regularly offered cash rewards for tips leading to arrests and held marches every Friday night, ending with church congregants knocking on the doors of known drug dealers in order to confront them.

In 1996, Mayor Daley appointed his aide Terry Peterson to represent the South Side's Auburn Gresham and West Chatham neighborhoods in the city council, following corruption charges against his Seventeenth Ward predecessor, Allan Streeter. Peterson would face voters in a special election for alderman, so Daley moved quickly to ensure he would have a strong record.

When Peterson took over, the area was characterized by unkempt fast-food outlets, boarded-up buildings, and low-end retail businesses such as wig stores. Broken sidewalks and streetlights were common, and the area had a general sense of malaise. He began an energetic campaign of revival with the full weight of the mayor's office at his back.

Peterson and Daley first put a new police station at 78th and Halsted Streets, ensuring a consistent law-enforcement presence. With financial assistance, a new Jewel-Osco grocery store went up next door, and a little mayoral arm-twisting convinced the civic-minded LaSalle Bank CEO, Norm Bobins, to open a branch across the street. The mayor's affordable housing program partnered with St. Sabina to operate two senior residential buildings not far from the church. The first neighborhood sit-down restaurant opened.

Peterson targeted long-standing flooding in West Chatham with new sewers and water mains. A wave of city services descended on the area, wiping out graffiti, cleaning and repaving streets, trimming trees, and otherwise acting as a temporary occupying force. In his first four years, Peterson told me, his ward attracted between $200 and $300 million in public and private investment.[1]

Leo stayed. St. Sabina's grew. A tough part of the city retained its anchors, which now had breathing room to carry on their missions.

• • •

As community anchors, perhaps none are more important to cities than universities. In the early 1960s, Richard J. Daley took on part of his own white ethnic base to build a Chicago campus extension of the University of Illinois at Urbana-Champaign. In an epic political and legal fight to preserve their Italian American neighborhood, residents led by Florence Scala protested and filed lawsuits that delayed the project for two years, only ending when the US Supreme Court declined to hear their appeal. The high court's decision cleared the way for Daley to bulldoze one hundred acres in the heart of the city, destroying two hundred businesses and eight hundred homes, and displacing more than five thousand residents.

The destruction of a thriving, tight-knit community in the heart of the city was tragic, a rip in the city fabric, but Richard J. Daley believed it was a price worth paying to bring a major public university to Chicago. Today, thirty-three thousand students attend UI-C's sixteen colleges.

Early in his administration, Richard M. Daley began a practice of periodic one-on-one meetings with the city's major institutions, including the presidents of Chicago's universities, such as Northwestern, DePaul, Loyola, and the University of Chicago. John Schmidt, who served as Daley's chief of staff in the early months of his administration, recalled the parade of leaders.

"Everybody in the city in those first weeks would come by to talk to him. I mean, the CEOs of big companies. The CEOs of big hospitals. The presidents of universities. They all come [sic]. And they all would come in with their kind of wish list of things. But one thing that struck me was first of all, he was very good at talking with them, and genuinely interested in finding out what their problems were."[2]

Daley wanted to send the message that he would personally remove city roadblocks or make important investments to help them. It might be as simple as a stoplight on a busy street to enhance campus safety or as major as acquiring private property to facilitate university expansion.

A critical moment came in the late 1990s, when the Illinois Institute of Technology (IIT) was making plans to move its campus from the city's near South Side to the suburbs. The board's chairman, Craig Duchossois, met with the mayor and staff at city hall to break the news. Duchossois's martial bearing befitted a former Marine Corps officer whose father was a decorated World War II tank commander under

General George Patton. He was the CEO of a billion-dollar family manufacturing concern that employed thousands of workers. As IIT chairman, he led a board of directors increasingly concerned about the safety of the university's students and faculty.

Duchossois told Daley that pervasive crime in the neighborhood surrounding the campus, including recent shootings, was costing the university recruits. With increasing vacancies and gang activity at nearby public housing projects, including Stateway Gardens and the Robert Taylor Homes, the school believed it had no choice but to leave the city.

The decision was especially painful because IIT, under the leadership of its president, Lew Collins, and its external affairs director, David Baker, had been laying the groundwork for a complete makeover of the university, designed in the years following the Second World War by the architect Ludwig Mies van der Rohe. His grandson, Dirk Lohan, who studied and began his architectural career at IIT, created a master plan that included a redesigned campus center. The university planned new modern dorms, attractive housing for faculty near the campus, a commercial and retail corridor, and a partnership with the city to remove old rail lines, city streets, and parking spaces and replace them with a new campus parkway replete with more than a thousand trees.

But the Plan for Transformation that would soon raze the city's public housing high-rises had yet to begin.[3] Despite Daley's assurances that the problematic buildings eventually would be gone, Duchossois held firm. Finally, as the meeting was ending, Daley's aide Terry Teele whispered in the mayor's ear. Turning to the university chairman, Daley made a final appeal.

"What if we put a new police headquarters on 35th Street, by the university? If we put the police there, will you stay?" Daley asked.

Duchossois smiled. "I think that would work," he said.[4]

Armed with Daley's pledge to tear down the nearby public housing projects and build the new police station abutting the university, President Collins persuaded the Chicago industrialist Robert Pritzker and Motorola's CEO and chairman Robert Galvin to commit $60 million each to the university, cementing its future in Chicago. Given as part of a challenge grant, their donations leveraged an additional $150 million. IIT's campus was rebuilt, and the school created a generous scholarship program based solely on merit, siphoning off top students from competing universities.

As with IIT, the mayor wielded his power on behalf of the city's seven community colleges, locating new campuses strategically. Daley realized that the thirty-year bond used to build Wright College was expiring. Rather than retire the debt, the mayor decided to use it to help the poverty- and crime-stricken Englewood Community on the South Side, building the new Kennedy-King College to replace the one farther north.

Examining his options, Daley circled the huge Englewood Mall, largely abandoned except for stores selling sports gear, mostly the baseball caps and team jackets favored by gangbangers. Condemning the site gave the mayor the core for a forty-acre campus with dozens of classrooms, laboratories, and athletic facilities. Opened in 2007, the new college specialized in broadcasting, culinary arts, and applied sciences. The modern Kennedy-King College boasted three broadcast studios and a radio and TV station; four kitchens, a teaching restaurant, and dining hall; and working labs and shops for auto-body work, printing, welding, and HVAC. The mayor ensured that more than half the construction work went to minority firms.

The city's $200 million Englewood investment helped leverage new retail nearby, including a grocery store in what had been a food desert.[5] Working with the non-profit arm of a local church, the mayor added affordable housing to take advantage of demand generated by the college.

Englewood would continue to struggle, but the new campus embedded an educational asset that was also an economic engine and gave hope to the many neighborhood leaders who never gave up on the area and would continue to fight for its revival.[6]

By investing in neighborhood anchors and listening to the voices of institutional leaders, Daley ensured that a community's decline would not be inexorable and that steady, incremental improvements in safety, job opportunities, and local amenities would improve the lives of residents while making possible an eventual recovery.

The mayor's concern for community anchors supplemented his larger "inner-out" strategy of harnessing economically vibrant areas to chip away at declining ones, beginning with a revived downtown.[7] Year after year, more dilapidated and impoverished neighborhoods became middle-class, expanding in a concentric circle from the city core. Urban pioneers were followed by professional renovators who were followed by home builders.

With safer and more stable neighborhoods, and improved housing stock, a wave of new residents began to migrate to the city. Chicago's expanding cultural and culinary offerings attracted more empty nesters and young professionals. A growing services economy convinced companies to reside in the city, accessing the benefits of Chicago's eminent institutions of finance, medicine, and higher education.

The suburban office malls of previous decades were increasingly stressed as companies moved into Chicago. In the battle for talent, more corporations recognized that younger employees were drawn to the excitement of city life. These trends steadily drove up property values and stabilized the city's population after a 23 percent decline during the previous four decades. From 1990 to 2000, Chicago added 112,011 residents; it was the city's first decade of growth since the 1940s.[8]

But to fully reclaim communities, Daley would need to do more. Other institutional anchors, especially those that solidified and enhanced family life in the city, such as good schools and parks, were key to creating cohesive and growing neighborhoods. By his third term, Daley had accumulated the power—and was making the sweeping changes—required to restore those building blocks and fundamentally alter the character of the city.

CHAPTER 15

Takeover

In November 1994, a political earthquake in Washington, DC, set in motion events that would spawn a revolution in Chicago.

After two rocky years of the Clinton presidency, including the collapse of a proposed national health care initiative, Republicans ran the table in national elections. The GOP won control of both the US Senate and the House, which had not been out of Democratic hands in forty years. Republicans picked up ten governor's mansions and control of fifteen additional state legislatures.

Illinois was one of the flips. Republicans now held the governor's mansion and both the state Senate and House, gaining a two-year window of unfettered GOP rule that has not been repeated since.

The Republican Governor Jim Edgar hailed from downstate Charleston and owed his election to suburban and rural voters. Senate President James "Pate" Philip, from suburban DuPage County, was hostile to Chicago, believing it represented a type of decadence and decay antithetical to the conservative values and upward striving of his white, middle-class constituents.

Undercutting Chicago and expanding suburban and downstate power immediately rose to the top of Springfield's agenda. As we saw earlier, this manifested itself in a naked power play for control of Chicago's aviation assets.[1] It also resulted in a surprising and perhaps mischievous education reform bill.

After decades of routine, prolonged teacher strikes; bankruptcy and bailouts; and plummeting student performance, Chicago schools hit rock bottom in the late 1980s. ACT scores ranked among the lowest in the nation; dropout rates were skyrocketing. President Ronald Reagan's education secretary William Bennett came to town and famously labeled Chicago schools "the worst in the nation." Mayor Harold Washington convened an education summit that kicked off a period of experimentation and attempted reforms.

The state legislature, following recommendations from a consortium of local education activists and experts, devolved power to local school councils (LSCs)—consisting of teachers, parents, and community residents—to hire and fire principals, design curricula, and approve budgets. Under the new system, each neighborhood school was under the authority of whoever ran and won in a tiny-turnout LSC election, regardless of capabilities, expertise, or motives.

The board of education was appointed by a strange and unwieldy system guaranteeing a lack of accountability. A 1988 state law created the School Board Nominating Commission, consisting of twenty-three parent and community representatives. The commission's job was to present the mayor with a slate of three nominees for each position on a new fifteen-member board. If the mayor rejected all three nominees for one of the board's slots, the commission had to produce three more. This amateur-run process produced not highly accomplished civic leaders devoted to school improvement but a smorgasbord of mid-level managers, retirees, small-time attorneys, community organizers, and clergy.

In Daley's first term, when we analyzed the names being submitted, our choices often came down to selecting the least offensive candidate or debating the odds that a rejected slate would produce even worse candidates the next time.

Daley was mandated to ensure that a board was legally constituted, so he did the best he could. At one point, the mayor was so frustrated with the mediocre candidates, some with criminal records and others with obvious political agendas, that he rejected the entire slate of submissions by the nominating commission.

This decentralized grassroots model of school governance not surprisingly failed to lift the fortunes of Chicago schools, which remained mired in incompetent, unaccountable management, and dismal educational outcomes.

It was against this backdrop that the new Republican government passed landmark legislation transferring direct appointive power for school governance to the mayor of Chicago; removed a longstanding financial oversight body; freed special-purpose funds for general education; limited teacher tenure and the union's ability to bargain on noneconomic issues; and otherwise swept away most vestiges of the previous regime. Although local school councils remained, their influence was diminished. None of this would have happened if Democrats had maintained even one of the three power centers in Springfield.

To this day, those who were part of the historic transfer of power debate the motives of Republican leaders. Governor Edgar, an educator himself, seemed to believe sincerely that the changes would improve Chicago's schools, as did House Speaker Lee Daniels of suburban Elmhurst. But many felt that Senator Philip, a mayoral antagonist, had a Machiavellian mindset, convinced he was sending Daley a hand grenade with the pin pulled. In his eyes, the school system was in such dire straits—financially crippled, riddled with incompetent teachers, and saddled with decaying buildings—that any effort to turn it around was doomed to failure. When it did, Daley would personally wear the jacket.

It was a view shared by many Democrats opposed to the bill. State Sen. Miguel del Valle asked whether the state was giving Daley "the rope that the mayor of Chicago needs to hang himself" and the school system with him.[2]

If Daley had any doubts, he never showed it. Publicly, he relished the chance to oversee the sprawling school system. He named a diverse and accomplished set of business and civic leaders to govern the system, including LaSalle Bank's CEO, Norm Bobins; Smith Barney's director, Gene Saffold; Mount Sinai Health Center's director, Dr. Tariq Butt; and Harold Washington's former budget director and chief operating officer, Sharon Gist Gilliam.

To underscore his personal commitment to owning the results, in 1995 he appointed his chief of staff, Gery Chico, as chairman of the board, and his budget director, Paul Vallas, as the school's new chief executive officer, setting in motion a drama city hall staffers came to call the "Paul and Gery Show," a dizzying array of reforms and improvements that dominated news cycles for years to come.

The son of a Greek mother and a Mexican American father, Chico grew up in Chicago's working class McKinley Park neighborhood adjacent to Bridgeport, the Daley family's home. As a college student he volunteered for the Daleys' Eleventh Ward organization. The mayor recruited Chico from his law practice at the prestigious Sidley & Austin law firm, where he specialized in real estate and zoning issues that brought him into regular contact with mayoral and city council officials.

Vallas was a longtime financial guru in state and local government, heading the Illinois Economic and Fiscal Commission before taking the reins of the Chicago Department of Revenue. Daley later tapped him to lead the budget office. As a young legislative aide in Springfield, he worked closely with Phil Rock, the senate president, and Dawn Clark Netsch, who had been state Sen. Daley's key ally in pushing through reforms to the state's mental health code and repeal of the sales tax on food and medicine.

The two men moved with alacrity to set a new tone. In his first week, Vallas chastised his own two top aides for redecorating their offices; suspended the practice of providing catered food for meetings; dumped his chauffeur; and held a press conference at a CPS warehouse to display dozens of computers, hundreds of pieces of brand-new furniture, and even nine new pianos—all covered in dust, unused. Vallas ordered everything to be sent to classrooms. Chico and Vallas reeled in hundreds of unnecessary cell phones and pagers that had been handed out to bureaucrats like candy, saving $5 million.

Daley's new school board began routine internal audits, uncovering juicy horror stories of government malfeasance. In one, the Monitoring Commission for Desegregation Implementation, a product of a judicial consent decree, spent thousands of dollars from the general education fund on a suburban retreat complete with steak dinners, fine wine, liquor, and theater tickets. The group also paid more than $200,000 to twenty-five consultants without documentation or work product.

As the Paul and Gery Show closed its first month, the teachers union agreed to a new four-year contract and a 13 percent raise, a quick conclusion to bargaining made possible by the new state law. The union's traditional leverage was temporarily restrained by a ban on strikes for eighteen months and bargaining limited to wages and benefits.

The new regime cut the bureaucracy by a thousand jobs; began squeezing hundreds of millions in savings by renegotiating long-term bus transportation and employee health-care contracts; and repurposed tens of millions previously frozen into specialized accounts under state law. Almost overnight, the $150 million budget deficit for 1996 and the projected $1.4 billion four-year shortfall vanished. Tens of millions of dollars were added to create after-school and summer programs, build an army of tutors for failing students, and fund apprenticeship programs for likely dropouts.

A month later, Chico and Vallas announced a $600 million, five-year school construction program, including twenty new schools, accompanied by more than $200 million in additional education programs. These were the finishing touches on a sixty-day whirlwind of accomplishments that left reporters, politicians, and civic organizations speechless. Having helped run the city, Chico and Vallas didn't need on-the-job training. They knew where to look—and which levers to pull—to quickly reshape the vast and moribund CPS bureaucracy. The new state law gave them unprecedented flexibility and authority, and Daley placed the entirety of his support behind them.

Within seven months, CPS received a bond rating upgrade from Wall Street, its first since 1979, when the state was forced to bail out a bankrupt district; it saved $100 million on the next capital raise. The new rating "was viewed by school officials as the end to a financial crisis that has kept most Chicago schools in a state of neglect and disrepair for the last 20 years or more," the *Tribune* reported.[3]

Daley sent his own "tough love" message in September, personally announcing plans to transfer problem students to six new discipline-focused schools and threatening public aid cuts for parents of the approximately twenty thousand chronic truants—many responsible for more than four thousand crimes during school hours. The truancy also cost the school district close to $50 million annually in lost revenues under the state's education funding formula.

"We will not tolerate illegal activity in the schools that jeopardize the learning environment. You cannot have 25 disrupt 1,000. Then you're spending all your money and time on the 25 and forgetting about the rest," the mayor said.[4]

The focus on troubled students extended to troubled schools. The new state legislation authorized interventions when schools were in an educational crisis. The new school board adopted a policy with sixteen indicators to guide decisions. If a school qualified, the board could remove the principal and local school council.

When protests erupted, Vallas was unmoved.

"We can't just sit around and wait for 20-some groups to reach consensus," Vallas said. "We're not trying to be vindictive or dictatorial. We're not trying to undermine school reform. But we can't sit around fiddling while Rome burns."[5]

By January 1996, Vallas and Chico were ready to act. They leaked news that at least forty academically troubled schools would be placed on remediation, with potential removals of principals, LSCs, and senior staff. By the end of the year, 109 schools were on academic probation, forcing failing leadership and subpar teachers to execute corrective plans successfully or be replaced.

When Chico and Vallas fired Englewood High School's principal, Warner Birts, the local school council refused to meet with his interim replacement, illustrating the often cozy relationships between LSCs and principals. In seven years under Birts, Englewood had the lowest test scores in the state; only two of three students showed up for classes each day; and street gangs were allowed to hold assemblies in the school. At one assembly, awards were presented to the imprisoned Gangster Disciples leader, Larry Hoover, and the Vice Lords chief, Willie Lloyd.

A year later, the reform school board's choice to take over struggling Clemente High School, suburban principal Jerry Anderson, withdrew his acceptance after receiving violent threats via letters and phone calls, including a caller promising to kill Anderson if he became Clemente's leader. The LSC favored the interim principal, Edward Negron, who had close ties to Puerto Rican pro-independence groups and gangs. The school board removed Negron to signal its own independence from threats.

Methodically changing failed leadership at the top was important, but raising standards at the bottom was equally critical. Among the most consequential reforms of the new school board, and one that quickly gained national attention, was putting an end to social promotions. Each year, the school district had promoted and graduated thousands of students who had not met minimum academic standards, eventually producing either dropouts or students with empty diplomas, lacking the skills required to succeed. Under the new plan, students as young as third graders were subject to mandatory summer school and special tutoring to bring them up to grade level before they could advance.

"Social promotion was a disaster," Vallas said. "When you're talking about social promotion, there's not pressure on the child or the schools to reach the standards you must reach before you go to the next level."[6]

But the new policy had a loophole. When nearly a third of the 6,795 eighth graders subjected to mandatory summer school failed but were still promoted to high school, the Board of Education quickly ended the practice. Instead, it announced that six regional transition centers would open the following year, providing intense instruction for those flunking remedial summer classes. The message was clear—Daley's new administration would not give up on even a single child.

To help give struggling kids the discipline to succeed, Vallas and Chico added another idea—military academies. In partnership with each branch of the armed services, CPS opened ROTC programs serving nearly eleven thousand kids. Vallas recalled fondly the annual Veterans Day parade, led by student members of the academies.

"It was like VE day," Vallas chuckled, "because they would march, one after another after another—air force, navy."[7]

A laser focus on at-risk kids was one mission, but Daley had another—reversing the outflow of parents of school-age children from the city to the suburbs.

The key was offering quality choices. A big draw for middle-class parents was new selective enrollment schools—Walter Payton College Prep on the near North Side; Jones College Prep downtown; Lindblom Math and Science Academy in Englewood; Martin Luther King Jr. College Prep in Kenwood; and Gwendolyn Brooks College Prep Academy in the far South Side's Roseland neighborhood. These magnet schools were supplemented by fifteen International Baccalaureate programs in existing high schools, essentially high-performance schools within schools. In IB programs, students must meet rigorous standards in core competencies such as language and literature, mathematics, science, history, philosophy, and the arts. Parents could also choose new language academies or STEM schools, which focused on science, technology, engineering, and mathematics.

In time, these high schools provided high-performing options for parents seeking to remain in the city; in fact, five Chicago high schools rank among the top one hundred in the nation, according to *U.S. News and World Report*.[8]

"The whole idea was to try to find magnet programs that we can put in each of our neighborhood schools to make those schools competitive. And then those magnet programs like the IBs were open enrollment, so even if you didn't live in the neighborhood, you could pursue those programs. . . . [A]nd Daley was very, very supportive of that. . . . He just wanted more expanded school choice," Vallas said.[9]

In the 1994–95 school year, forty-five of the fifty lowest-scoring Illinois high schools on standardized tests were in Chicago. The average Chicago public high school student missed two months of classes each year. The large size of high schools—many with student bodies in the thousands—caused younger students to be lost. The new CPS Chief Education Officer, Lynn St. James, called Chicago's high schools "very close to total failure."[10]

The reform school board began to break up the behemoths, creating segregated freshman-sophomore academies, where students could receive greater support. Fluffy elective classes were eliminated and replaced with a core curriculum focused on reading, math, and science. Mandatory summer school awaited students who failed. Numerous high schools were put on probation, allowing Vallas and Chico's board to micro-manage their operations.

The payoff was swift.

In May of 1997, an exuberant Mayor Daley announced major across-the-board gains in test scores for ninth through 11th grade students, basking in the glow of his first academic win since the legislature gave him control two years earlier. Elementary test scores also rose.

"This is the clearest indication yet that Chicago public schools are getting better," the mayor said.[11]

Vallas argued the results showed the state legislature could now trust Chicago to be a good steward of more education funding.

"There's always the excuse in Springfield that if they gave any money, it's like throwing money down the sewers in Chicago to the public school system. . . . That was the old argument. The argument is gone," he said.[12]

The timing was propitious. With its new credibility, CPS paired with high-poverty downstate schools to push for higher funding for poor districts serving seven hundred thousand low-income students, paid for with tax hikes on cigarettes, riverboat casinos, and telephone bills. A key part of the legislation allowed CPS to divert teacher pension payments to classroom spending for ten years, or until actuarial funding fell below 90 percent. At the time, the pension system was more than fully funded, but the teachers union, strong supporters of House Speaker Mike Madigan, was opposed.

When the $485 million package came up for a vote, it sailed through the Senate but failed in the House. With a mere two-seat majority, Madigan was looking to the following year's elections. In his calculus, the pension provision would reduce teachers union campaign contributions. The tax increase would hurt swing Democratic suburban representatives, who gained little from the additional school poverty funds. He allowed the tally to be close but ensured its failure.

But Gov. Jim Edgar, who made increased education funding one of his gubernatorial legacies, called the General Assembly back into session to reconsider the bill. Daley supported Edgar's efforts with a "children's lobby" to pressure legislators, shaming them for standing with casinos and cigarette companies instead of kids. The second time, the bill passed easily.

The *Tribune* called the episode "a rare political miscalculation by House Speaker Michael Madigan," saying the speaker "never believed that Mayor Richard Daley and the Chicago City Council would publicly pillory Chicago Democrats who voted against the plan."[13]

With more state funding and continuing success in the classroom, Daley began looking toward his next reelection campaign. The mayor pushed his CPS team to lock up a new labor agreement well ahead of the election and ten months before the expiration of the existing contract. The terms were generous—nearly 22 percent raises for most teachers over four years, depending on seniority—but it gave the mayor another powerful campaign plank and guaranteed labor peace for his next term.[14]

The city's newspapers continued to praise his CPS turnaround.

"There has been no more stunning development on Daley's watch than the transformation of the Chicago Public Schools. . . . Under school board President Gery Chico and CEO Paul Vallas, student attendance and achievement are on the rise. There is unprecedented cooperation between teachers and management. The number of schools on the state's academic watch list has plummeted from 148 in 1994 to 58 today," the *Tribune*'s editorial board opined.[15]

After nearly four years of success, the accolades for Daley poured in.

Linda Lenz, editor of the school reform journal *Catalyst*, gave Vallas an A+.

"He just wowed everyone," Lenz said. "And this is the first administration—and you can throw the mayor in here—where the people say and act as though they really believe all children can learn."[16]

Daley's education successes even brought the president of the United States to Chicago. As Daley sat beaming on the stage behind him, Bill Clinton addressed a crowd at the North Side's Oscar Mayer Elementary School, saying "I want what is happening in Chicago to happen all over America."[17]

It was heady praise. With their energy and skill, Chico and Vallas had catalyzed a major urban school transformation. But with success also came competition for credit, power grabs, and growing tensions behind the scenes, threatening the longevity of the Paul and Gery Show.

CHAPTER 16

Northerly Island

Reforming a dysfunctional public school system was not the only long-term challenge Mayor Daley launched in his third term. For years, Daley had dreamed of converting Meigs Field, a tiny airport on Chicago's downtown lakefront, into a great urban park. The airstrip serviced politicians flying back and forth to the state capitol and business executives flying in from nearby states for day meetings.

The airport was situated on Northerly Island, an artificial island built in 1925. It was to be the first and northernmost of five islands envisioned by the legendary architect Daniel Burnham. ("Make no little plans, they have no magic to stir men's souls.") In his 1909 Plan of Chicago, the islands would float off Chicago's shoreline, connected by bridges and pedestrian walkways. The islands would protect a majestic lagoon more than five miles long, a park he argued would attract wealthy tourists from Europe, who at the time spent their dollars in Vienna and on the French Riviera. After completion of the first island, however, the city's obsession with building the historic 1933 Chicago World's Fair and the onset of the Great Depression ended further progress.

Daley understood the remarkable, untapped value of an island outside Chicago's thriving Loop. For a major city, it was an incredibly unique asset. With the city's fifty-year lease to operate the airport expiring at the end of 1996, the mayor decided to pull back the curtain on his vision. As Daley's parks superintendent, on July 2, 1996, I held a press conference announcing a $27 million plan to build something unparalleled in the world: Northerly Island Park. It would feature a vastly expanded beachfront and playgrounds for recreation, but also a nature lover's dream—lagoons, a botanic garden, prairie, wetlands, and an educational nature center, among other assets.

The announcement turned out to be merely the opening salvo in a long and complicated battle, pitting Daley against business leaders, lawyers, political opponents, and the Republican political establishment. But despite the predictable protests at the time, Daley was thrilled. He saw Northerly Island as a legacy-burnishing achievement where Chicago families and tourists would enjoy the quiet and wonder of a nature preserve on the edge of a sea of skyscrapers.

The glow from the announcement, however, was short lived.

So much of politics is about symbolism. The details of policy and governance are often lost on the average citizen. But a single powerful symbol can convey a transcendent message. Congressman Bobby Rush, the mayor's next election rival, found one.

A few weeks after Daley's Northerly Island announcement, Rush stood before the dilapidated and shuttered 63rd Street pavilion on Chicago's Black South Side. Despite being a historic and architecturally significant building once providing changing rooms, showers, toilets, and food concessions for a thriving beach scene, in the summer of 1996 it was a decrepit shell closed long ago by safety concerns. Standing before reporters, Rush shook the padlock and chains on the building's entrance. The congressman asked how Daley could build a $27 million park downtown but couldn't afford to restore a major recreational asset for his working-class constituents.

In the previous year's capital budget, I had not included a rebuild of the 63rd Street structure, due to the complexity and cost of restoring the enormous facility from its degraded condition. Having just navigated the district through a financial maelstrom, I was too conservative in issuing new debt. But in truth, all the reforms we had so painstakingly carried out gave us much more financial leeway, and now Daley was paying the price because I failed to use it aggressively.

Rush hit two nerves. The first was race. Daley was making inroads in the Black community, and Rush needed to stop that in its tracks. The second was the age-old political bugaboo of downtown investments coming at the expense of neighborhoods. From Rush's perspective, it was two home runs with a single swing.

His point was also powerful.

When I was at city hall the next day, the mayor's CFO, Ed Bedore, grabbed me in a hallway. "You better go see him," Bedore said. "He's fuming about the Bobby Rush thing."

I walked to the mayor's office and tapped on the open entrance before entering. Daley was sitting alone at his desk. I could see his rage spark. His face flushed bright red, and he chomped hard on his trademark unlit cigar; he said nothing, but his rising ire neared incandescence. Astutely sensing danger, I withdrew, but not before timorously offering, "Mayor, we're going to have a lot more flexibility in our next capital budget."

A few months later, I condensed the five-year capital plan into two. Mayor Daley announced an expansive set of neighborhood park improvements—new gyms, playgrounds, pools and water parks, ice skating rinks, bike paths, soccer fields, ball diamonds and acres of open green space.

First on the list was restoration of the 63rd Street pavilion.

• • •

Daley's neighborhood park investments parried political attacks from Rush and other community activists, but it still didn't clear the air of powerful detractors. The business community, and many influential politicians, were adamantly opposed to the closing of Meigs Airport.

Daley's most powerful opponent was the Republican governor, Jim Edgar. He liked the convenience of flying from the capitol in downstate Springfield to an airport blocks from his Chicago office. He also believed Meigs had value to the businesses that used it for regional flights. Edgar was joined by Republican leaders who were agnostic regarding Meigs but looking for revenge following Daley's victory in the battle for control of Chicago airports the previous year.[1]

Republican bills to assume authority over Meigs began moving swiftly through the General Assembly, and Daley dispatched me to Springfield to testify. With the GOP in control of all three branches of government, the result was preordained, so I didn't feel a need to be particularly respectful. I began my testimony by quoting the former newspaper editor and judge Gideon Tucker, who insightfully wrote, "No man's life, liberty or property is safe while the legislature is in session."[2] As I glanced at the assembled lawmakers, I could see my sarcasm went unappreciated.

The Republicans pushed the takeover bill to passage, and it was signed by Governor Edgar. It could not become official until the following June, however, under the technical rules of the state Constitution. Instead, the General Assembly would reconvene after the first of the year and redo their work, so that the law could become effective in January.

In the months leading up to the state takeover, political aides for both Daley and Edgar sought a compromise. The controversy over a tiny airstrip was poisoning mayoral-gubernatorial relations, and an ambitious agenda awaited the new General Assembly, including education funding and a modern stadium for the Chicago Bears. Edgar and Daley needed a modicum of cooperation to achieve their own political goals.

The mayor and governor never talked during the negotiations, with Daley acknowledging that relations were "sour." When a deal was finally reached, it was announced at separate news conferences two hundred miles apart—Daley in Chicago and Edgar in Springfield. Under its terms, Daley would keep Meigs operating as an airport for five years, after which he would be free to convert it to a park.

It seemed to be the end of the story. It wasn't.

Of the many memories Chicagoans have of Mayor Richard M. Daley, one of the most indelible is what came a few years later, when the deal expired. Facing continued political opposition and threats of lawsuits to keep the tiny airport open, Daley decided to end the tug of war—once and for all. Using the potential of terrorist threats to downtown buildings as his pretext, Daley sent bulldozers to Meigs Field in the middle of the night and gouged X-shaped trenches in the runway.

The preemptive strike was likened to the actions of a banana-republic dictator. The raid violated a host of Federal Aviation Administration (FAA) regulations.

Sixteen aircraft and their pilots and crew were stranded. Planes in the air were required to reroute. Daley held a press conference later that day to defend his order.

"The reason we closed the airport now is a fear . . . about all those airplanes coming so close to so many people in the downtown area," Daley said. "I am not willing to wait for a tragedy."[3]

But Steve Whitney, president of Friends of Meigs Field, said that Daley's midnight raid resulted in "the only U.S. infrastructure destroyed by terrorism since September 11, 2001."[4]

The *Tribune* columnist Eric Zorn later called it the "signature act" of Daley's mayoralty.

> I woke to the news . . . with a roiling brew of emotions that encapsulates my overall attitude toward his reign: admiration, outrage, and amusement.
>
> Admiration because he gets the job done. . . . Outrage because he didn't go through the motions of democracy, as he usually did, to get his way. And amusement because he offered a ludicrous excuse for his autocratic pre-emption—terrorists might take advantage of it to attack downtown![5]

The audacious move proved once again that Daley was willing to expend vast political capital—even risking ridicule, retribution, and federal penalties and reprobation—to advance his idea for Northerly Island Park. The "green mayor" stubbornly clung to his vision of an extraordinary island park at the edge of Chicago's vibrant Downtown.

In the end, Daley's plan never came to fruition. A decade after he left office, *Chicago Magazine* described Northerly Island as "a ratty island stuck in development purgatory" and "Chicago's most cursed public park," part of a century of unfulfilled promises.[6] Given the ambition and scope of Daley's later construction of Millennium Park, which required every public financing trick and every dollar that could be squeezed from private philanthropy, it's not surprising the Northerly Island project stumbled.[7] Not long after the completion of the giant Grant Park venture, the economy collapsed under the weight of the national housing crisis, indefinitely postponing any projects on such a grand scale.[8]

Although Daley's vision for Northerly Island remains unfulfilled, he succeeded in creating a different lakefront oasis next to it, perhaps of greater significance. In one of the great engineering feats in the 1990s, financed with portions of a bond issue for the McCormick Place expansion, the city moved the five northbound lanes of busy Lake Shore Drive that had bisected the sites of three of Chicago's premier museums—the Adler Planetarium, the Shedd Aquarium, and the Field Museum of Natural History. By shifting the expressway to the west of Soldier Field, along the same route as the southbound lanes, Daley freed fifty-seven acres to become a united Museum Campus, as well as a lakefront park complete with flora and fauna, rolling green terraces, walkways and jogging paths, and breathtaking views of Lake Michigan and the downtown skyline. A pedestrian tunnel runs underneath the reconstructed Lake Shore Drive. An isthmus connects the mainland to Northerly Island. Soldier Field, modernized in the following decade, sits at the western edge of the campus.

Daley's $110 million project required the removal of 120,000 cubic yards of dirt and the lowering of sections of the ground by twenty-two feet. The *Chicago Tribune*'s architecture critic, Blair Kamin, described it as "a heroic urban-planning undertaking," one that "rids the shoreline of cars and returns it to the people, just as Daniel Burnham envisioned in his 1909 Plan of Chicago."[9]

The unified campus brought hundreds of thousands of new visitors to the three resident museums, helping to fuel their expansions, and became a lively destination where both city residents and tourists could explore the lakefront's beaches and marinas against the backdrop of the downtown skyline.[10]

The impressive new museum campus removed some of the sting from Daley's struggles with Northerly Island, whose failure at least had the advantage of freeing capital for other park projects. Sustaining the wave of neighborhood park investments was expensive. Fortunately, under the supervision of my general counsel and lakefront director, Randy Mehrberg, and his talented deputy Bridget Reidy, our commercial assets continued to generate millions in new revenue.

Mehrberg's skills and energy made him our team's most impactful member. In fact, he would be the catalyst for the single greatest achievement of Mayor Daley's two-decade mayoralty.

But not before he almost cost me my job.

• • •

For nine years, an advocacy group for marijuana legalization held an annual gathering in Lincoln Park, in fields near the lakefront. Every year, no one paid much attention. Organizers called it "Weedfest." Its leaders used the event to educate and lobby for marijuana reform. But not surprisingly, it attracted a lot of young people who liked to smoke illegal pot.

As a hands-on manager, Randy Mehrberg would regularly bike the lakefront to check operations. The previous year he had passed by Weedfest. What he saw appalled him—joint-smoking kids mixing and mingling with children and parents in the lakefront fields. So for the group's 1996 festival the following year, Mehrberg decided he would shield children from the event. Unencumbered in his thinking by political experience, Mehrberg decided the solution was to move the event to a Soldier Field parking lot, where participants would be contained.

Suddenly a group holding an annual get-together with virtually no attention and limited parking had the marquee address of Soldier Field and its vast parking lots off Lake Shore Drive, near the expressway. An event that had brought hundreds would morph to thousands, with vendors hawking wares and serving food at booths. Over the two days of the festival, an estimated twenty-five thousand people attended.

When news leaked that the park district had issued a permit for Weedfest at Soldier Field, St. Sabina's activist priest, Michael Pfleger, began staging protests and holding news conferences denouncing the parks and city for encouraging drug use.

"Here it is the city hosting a pot party," Pfleger said. "You've got all this talk about how drugs do so much damage, and then the city is allowing, on public property, a Weedfest where you can openly smoke. It's a stamp of approval for smoking an illegal product. I think the city owes an apology to the people of Chicago."[11]

Members of the city council piled on as well. "This will be Claypool's Waterloo," thundered Ald. Eugene Schulter of the Forty-Seventh Ward.

Mayor Daley called an emergency meeting at city hall with parks and police personnel. It was too late to undo the damage, with the permit issued and the festival imminent. The meeting became a what-went-wrong discussion, along with some not so subtle finger pointing. I realized I could be a sacrificial lamb despite all the good work we had done. That's always a possibility when serving in an appointed leadership position under an elected official. But after a long and emotional discussion Daley said, "Maybe it will blow over," not appreciating the humor.

The day the festival began was a nervous one around park district headquarters. But contrary to the media hype and Pfleger's portrait of drug use run amok, the event turned out to be tame. As the *Tribune* reported, "Talk was earnest inside the nerve center at Weedfest. . . . Advocates of decriminalizing the plant were discussing its many respectable uses: helping terminally ill patients . . . being the raw material in blue jeans, petroleum projects and even cheese substitutes. . . . "[12]

But reporters also noted that, despite discouragement from event leaders, dozens of attendees were enjoying the "recreational use" of marijuana: "'I am pretty stoned, that's for sure,'" said one 18-year-old from suburban Lemont, passing a pipe among friends. "'Everyone is just chilling.'"[13]

Plainclothes police officers went undercover at the event, arresting a dozen of the most brazen pot smokers. Our spin was that we had protected both free speech and the law, but it was weak public relations. Nonetheless, the arrests showed no one was condoning illegal drug use. Daley's prediction proved right. Like the marijuana smoke wafting above Soldier Field, the scandal blew over.

When the Weedfest organizers applied for their Soldier Field permit the next year, we used the evidence of illicit drug use as legal grounds to deny it. Never again would we make such a colossal public-relations blunder.

Meanwhile, Mehrberg was continuing to stir up trouble. The next time he did, however, it would be with an extraordinary result.

CHAPTER 17

Legend

Urban legend, repeated often in writings about Chicago's iconic Millennium Park, is that Mayor Daley was sitting in his dentist's office in the upper floors of a building overlooking Grant Park. Seeing the eyesore of the sunken railroad tracks and dirt pits below, he decided to build a new park over the blight.[1]

The legend is preposterous.

Daley didn't need the elevated perch of his dentist's office to know about the 150-year-old railroad acreage in the middle of Grant Park and how it detracted mightily from what was otherwise a beautiful downtown oasis. As Chicago's "green mayor," known for his fixation with planting acres of trees and flowers, Daley didn't require a high-rise epiphany to understand the space would be better used as an addition to scarce city parkland. Had he been able to, Daley would have jumped at the chance. But like generations of mayors and civic activists before him, he couldn't. The Illinois Central Railroad owned the land.

Or so everyone believed.

In 1995, Mayor Daley asked me and John Rogers, the park district board president, to pay a visit to the Sara Lee chairman and CEO, John Bryan. Bryan had helped build Sara Lee into an international conglomerate and Fortune 200 company. He was also a major force in Chicago's arts community, leading the $100 million campaign for an addition to Symphony Hall and to provide a new home for the Chicago Lyric Opera. A longtime chair of the Art Institute, Bryan launched the $350 million effort for the Art Institute's Modern Wing.

Bryan believed Chicago should celebrate the coming millennium (2000) by creating an inspiring monument that would be instantly recognizable as the symbol of Chicago, in the same manner as the Statue of Liberty in New York, the Gateway Arch in St. Louis, or the Golden Gate Bridge in San Francisco. Standing in his upper-floor offices overlooking Lake Michigan and Grant Park, Bryan described his idea to build an obelisk in the lake and asked us to determine the engineering challenges and costs. Rogers and I secured the engineering studies, which concluded that it was impractical. Bryan was disappointed but accepted the verdict.

Bryan's idea was off base, but his vision of a mega project that would define Chicago for the next century was not. When the time came, he would leave his mark on Chicago as few before him have ever done.

• • •

A year after my meeting with John Bryan, the park district's general counsel and lakefront director, Randy Mehrberg, was once again riding his bike, on the lookout for problems. He noticed a vandalized fence separating part of Grant Park from a ravine leading down to the inactive Illinois Central Railroad tracks below. At the bottom of the ravine was a gravel parking lot operated under a lease from the railroad. The hole in the fence, big enough for people to step through, was being used by parking commuters as a shortcut to offices on Randolph Street. Their treks through the park had left an ugly, muddy path. Furious, Mehrberg ordered immediate repairs to the fence and landscaping.

Some weeks later, Mehrberg again happened by and noticed a fresh hole, and with it a new path through the park. Once again, he had it fixed.

Now checking regularly, he realized that as soon as the fence was repaired, a new hole would appear. Mehrberg confronted the parking lot operator, believing he was likely behind the vandalism. Not only didn't the operator deny it, but he said he would continue to tear open the fence every time the park district fixed it. Days later, Mehrberg returned, questioning the operator about his lease and the condition of the grounds. After this second confrontation, the operator declined to answer more questions and filed an ethics complaint against Mehrberg, the grounds for which puzzled the park district's law office.

The unsightly new path simply extended the blight of the muddy, rock-strewn parking lot, which was just one piece of a vast eyesore—an ugly hole of more than twenty acres in the middle of what was otherwise one of the most beautiful parts of the city. The contrast was striking, as was the suboptimal use of one of the most valuable pieces of real estate in any American metropolis. The Illinois Central's freight railroad was no longer active, having ceased operations decades before, but the company maintained a single rail line running north to south and curving in the direction of the Chicago Yacht Club on Lake Shore Drive. The railroad placed a single, stationary boxcar on the tracks as if to signify to the casual passer-by that something was being transported.

• • •

In his Plan of Chicago, Daniel Burnham wrote that "the landscaped setting of the Grant Park Group offers opportunities of the highest order," arguing for a fully verdant setting.[2] But he had built his plans around the Illinois Central Railroad, which had been granted its land in 1852 in exchange for building a breakwall into the lake to protect the shoreline.

In 1977, a group of civic and business activists targeted the same underused and blemished railroad land to complete Burnham's vision. The coalition announced plans for a Lakefront Garden for the Performing Arts. Led by the civic leaders George and Vicky Ranney, the group created blueprints and drawings, selling the vision to raise money for purchase and development of the site. The costs, however, were prohibitive, even if the railroad had been willing to sell. The Bilandic administration was interested but lacked the ability to make it happen.

Not long after I was appointed parks superintendent in 1993, I stood on upper Michigan Avenue directly above the same Illinois Central property. The occasion was a press conference by Friends of the Parks, led by the resolute Erma Tranter,[3] dedicating a memorial to A. Montgomery Ward, the hero of the fight to preserve the lakefront from development in the late nineteenth century.

As in other US cities at that time, Chicago's waterfront was occupied by commerce and slums. The waterfronts of most cities are still dominated by commerce, such as Boston, Cleveland, and New York. But Ward had a different vision for Chicago.

At the onset of his crusade, Chicago's shoreline was muddy and muddled, with buildings abutting what is now the west side of Michigan Avenue. At one point, the Illinois Central Railroad tracks hugged the shore, but gradually the city dumped landfill—including most of the debris from the Great Chicago Fire of 1871—into the lake, east of the tracks. Lois Wille, a former *Sun-Times* editor and the author of the definitive book about how Chicago's lakefront was preserved, describes Ward's view from his offices above Michigan Avenue:

"The view . . . turned his stomach: stables, squatters' shacks, mountains of ashes and garbage, the ruins of a monstrous old exposition hall, railroad sheds, a firehouse, the litter of one of the circuses that continually moved in and out, prize fights, wrestling matches and the masquerade balls thrown by Aldermen [Michael] Hinky Dink Kenna and Bathhouse John Coughlin for the ladies of the Levee"—women from Carrie Watson's famed brothel, who arrived with police escorts.[4]

Kenna is remembered for his pithy observation that "Chicago ain't no sissy town."[5]

Ward filed suit to enforce the restrictions from the Chicago Canal Commissioners' plat of 1836, which designated the eastern lakefront as "Public Ground—Forever Open, Clear and Free of any buildings, or Other Obstruction Whatever."[6] It was the beginning of a twenty-year battle, culminating in a ruling by the Illinois Supreme Court that the city's acceptance of the Canal Commissioners' actions had created an enforceable right to an open, unobstructed lakefront.

By the time he won, Ward was a reviled figure, following years of personal attacks from bitterly resistant businesses, landlords, politicians, newspapers, and even ordinary citizens, all of whom wanted to develop the lakefront. He later commented: "Had I known in 1890 how long it would take me to preserve a park for the people against their will I doubt I would have undertaken it."[7]

Friends of the Parks insisted on a public memorial, because unlike Daniel Burnham and other epic figures of Chicago's unique and historical parks system, Ward and his valiant role in almost singlehandedly preserving Chicago's greatest asset had largely faded from memory.

One of the speakers that day was Ald. Ed Burke, an amateur Chicago historian. At the end of his speech he turned and swept his arms backward to point to the blighted indentation to the east and declared, "And someday—someday!—we will fulfill Daniel Burnham's and A. Montgomery Ward's vision and reclaim and restore this land behind us for the people of Chicago!"

• • •

Three years after the A. Montgomery Ward dedication, Randy Mehrberg stared down into the same unsightly canyon, fuming over the rogue parking-lot operator and his arrogant enablement of landscape damage. As the weeks passed, he continued to stew, frustrated by his limited options. Then one day, as he was again walking along Grant Park above the railroad, he had an epiphany.

At Jenner & Block, Mehrberg had represented creditors in three railroad bankruptcies, in one case suing the Illinois Central for fraudulent transfer of assets. He became familiar with the intricacies of railroad operations as well as their sometimes unusual land-acquisition strategies. In thinking about ways to constrain the railroad's parking-lot operator, he decided to pursue a hunch.

Mehrberg dug deep into the nineteenth-century land records until he discovered the original deed for the Illinois Central land.

What he found would change Chicago history.

In property law, ownership can take many forms. The most common is "fee simple." Fee simple means the acquirer owns the property outright—free and clear of any liens or encumbrances. In examining the records, however, Mehrberg could see that the Illinois Central land below Randolph and Michigan Avenues was not owned in fee simple. Instead, a restrictive covenant had been attached to the deed. The covenant said that if the land should ever cease to be used for railroad purposes, it would revert to the City of Chicago.

On the day the Illinois Central ceased railroad operations, title had shifted to the city. But no one knew.

Mehrberg and I presented the evidence to the mayor and Susan Sher, the city's corporation counsel. Daley didn't waste time. Within weeks, Sher had filed a lawsuit against the Illinois Central to secure the land. After six months of litigation, in which the company asserted farcical arguments, including that railroad employees parking at the site constituted "railroad purposes," the company threw in the towel.

The future site of Chicago's Millennium Park was in the city's hands.

History is so often the confluence of unlikely events and serendipity. I had hired a railroad expert as the parks general counsel. In an unusual twist, that lawyer demonstrated exceptional management skills, leading to his assignment to oversee the lakefront and all its assets. Then, oddest of all, the same lawyer stumbled into a battle with a parking-lot operator to protect parkland from abuse. Somehow, all of this led to Chicago's reclaiming of its most valuable land, a goal that had frustrated civic and political leaders for 150 years, making possible the construction of the epochal Millennium Park.

CHAPTER 18

Gangs and Guns

In 1997, after five years overseeing a pioneering effort to build community policing in Chicago, with success in driving down previously intractable violent crime, Superintendent Matt Rodriguez had resigned. Under city rules, the Chicago Police Board, with appointees serving staggered terms by mayoral appointment, was required to present three candidates for the police superintendency. The board nominated Charles Ramsey, deputy superintendent of the Bureau of Staff Services; Terry Hillard, chief of detectives; and Raymond Risley, chief of the organized crime unit. Both Ramsey and Hillard were African American.

Risley was white, which made his candidacy moot from the outset. Daley's previous appointment of a white fire chief virtually ensured that a minority member would succeed Rodriguez. More important, the Black community was increasingly enraged by incidents of police brutality involving white officers and African American citizens. The most visible was the case of Jeremiah Mearday, a Black teen. White officers used flashlights to beat him, fracturing his upper jaw and knocking out most of his front teeth. He was then collared for resisting arrest. (The officers were eventually fired.)

Ramsey was the heavy favorite. He was the architect of the city's successful community policing program, so his appointment was viewed as a foregone conclusion. Daley admired and appreciated Ramsey's leadership and had a good working relationship with him.

"Barring any unforeseen development in interviews that Daley is conducting with the candidates, Ramsey will be Chicago's next police superintendent," a mayor's office source told the *Sun-Times*.[1]

The mayor knew Hillard less well but had seen his work up close when Hillard managed city security during Chicago's 1996 Democratic National Convention. As chief of detectives, Hillard was also a regular participant in mayoral meetings.

Ramsey and Hillard had contrasting styles. Ramsey was comfortable in front of people and microphones, confident in his strategies and abilities. Hillard was more reserved, talking only when needed but with an inner toughness that commanded the respect of his troops. He was widely considered to be a "policemen's policeman."

Both Ramsey and Hillard sat for hours of interviews with Mayor Daley, discussing in detail their personal lives, their police experiences, and their visions for the office. Sarah Pang, the mayor's deputy for public safety, worked closely with police department leadership. She told me that the mayor appreciated Hillard's humility; if he didn't have an immediate answer, he wasn't afraid to say, "I'll get back to you." In contrast, the confident Ramsey, used to basking in local and national attention for his leadership in community policing, startled Daley when asked about his long-term goals. "I'd like to be a mayor sometime," Ramsey told Daley.[2]

As the weeks progressed, Daley began to establish a personal affinity with Hillard but still felt Ramsey was the leader more likely to take community policing to the next level.

I had just begun my second stint as chief of staff, having returned after nearly five years running the Chicago Park District. As decision day neared, I noticed that Jack Townsend, the first deputy police superintendent, had entered Daley's fifth-floor office in an unscheduled, unannounced visit. Curious, I checked in periodically; the meeting was long, and the mayor's anteroom became crowded as the delay backed up his calendar.

Daley had placed Townsend in the number-two spot for his skills but also because of his long relationship with the Daley family, having served as a bodyguard for Richard J. Daley. He still lived in the family's original home of Bridgeport. Townsend was a trusted source of information and prized for his tactical police skills, moving forces nimbly to combat outbreaks of crime.

I suspect Townsend knew which way Daley was leaning and was concerned about Ramsey's elevation. As keeper of the mayor's back in the department, Townsend may have been more concerned with politics than policing.

Only Daley knows what was said, but when the meeting finally ended, the mayor came out troubled. The conversation seemed to have thrown the superintendency up for grabs again.

"He would definitely have gone in there during that period," Pang told me. "He used to use phrases from older decades. I could see him saying 'Ramsey may be getting too big for his britches.'"[3]

In fact, months before, the city hall veteran *Sun-Times* reporter Fran Spielman had speculated on the same thing.

"There's a concern in some mayoral circles that Ramsey may be 'too' practiced and independent, and therefore harder for the mayor to control. Whereas Hillard may be more guarded—the kind of guy who's not going to go off and say stuff Daley doesn't want him to say," Spielman wrote.[4]

In mid-February, Hillard was meeting with detectives about a pattern of North Side armed robberies when a call came from the mayor's office. Hillard recalled the conversation.

"Good morning, Mr. Superintendent," Daley said when Hillard answered. The mayor said he had tossed and turned in a sleepless night but had made his decision. He wanted Hillard to join him for a city hall press conference later that morning. There the superintendent-designate was bombarded with questions, but one seemed to reflect suspicions he had been selected over Ramsey because he would be Daley's yes-man.

"I'm 54 years old, a former Marine," Hillard began. "I've been through colon cancer. I've been shot. I've survived Vietnam. At this stage of my life, I figure I've earned the right to say what I want to say. I'm not a yes-man. I speak my mind and if I have something to say, I say it."[5]

Hillard began his leadership of seventeen thousand police officers facing the same challenges as his predecessors—guns, gangs, and drugs. Only Los Angeles rivaled Chicago in the severity of this toxic combination.

According to the US Justice Department, Chicago's status as a middle-of-the-country transportation hub makes it a staging ground for the national flow of drugs. Just as Amazon uses regional warehouses as part of its hub-and-spoke delivery system, so do Mexican drug cartels use Chicago's extensive logistical assets.

Surrounded by states with lax gun laws, Chicago street gangs have no problem acquiring firepower. Only about 40 percent of recovered guns illegally used in Chicago are from Illinois dealers. The rest come from loosely regulated surrounding states (Indiana, Wisconsin) and the deep south (Mississippi, ranked number two). Gangs often recruit "straw buyers," those without criminal records that would be red flags in background checks, to buy caches of guns. Not surprisingly, straw purchasers migrate to places that don't ask a lot of questions. For convenience, many gangbangers choose Chuck's Gun Shop, a notorious weapons store in suburban Riverdale that sells one in five traceable guns recovered at Chicago crime scenes.[6]

While on a drug-surveillance assignment, Chicago police officer Michael Ceriale was fatally shot with a .357-caliber Magnum revolver. It was one of a batch of nine guns purchased at Chuck's Gun Shop by the straw buyer Ezra Evans while a Gangster Disciples gang leader, James Jackson, strutted about the store, picking out the weapons for Evans to buy. Another straw buyer purchased a gun at Chuck's that was found by police, along with a bulletproof vest, on a man sitting outside the home of Illinois Senator and presidential candidate Barack Obama in 2008.[7]

Westforth Sports, a small store in Gary, Indiana, was the third-largest supplier of guns recovered by Chicago police—more than 850 between 2009 and 2016.[8] A steady stream of straw purchasers drove the few miles from Chicago across the state line and then resold the guns to felons otherwise ineligible to purchase firearms. The guns were used in a series of violent crimes.

One straw buyer was Darryl Ivery Jr., an Indiana resident who purchased nineteen guns from Westforth over six months, paying more than $10,000, all in cash.

In a legal deposition, the store's owner, Earl Westforth, was asked why he ignored all the red flags that Ivery, later convicted of falsifying federal background check forms, was a straw buyer funneling guns to criminals.

"Maybe the guy just loves guns," Westforth said.[9]

The see-nothing, hear-nothing, ask-nothing policy of irresponsible gun dealers selling to straw purchasers, and lax laws that make it possible, exponentially increase the odds of violence.[10] Chicago police collect guns at a 50 percent higher rate than the larger Los Angeles and a remarkable six times more guns than New York.[11]

Gangs perpetually have been a more prominent component of Chicago's violence than in other cities. Estimates range from sixty thousand to more than one hundred thousand active gang members in the Chicago metro region. Despite a population three times larger, New York City has less than a third the number of gangbangers.[12] Most experts attribute Chicago's gang problem to its historically concentrated poverty. The city's high-rise public housing projects were breeding grounds for gangs and natural venues for drug sales and distribution. Even when they were razed, many residents migrated to nearby low-income neighborhoods. Some were gang members.

Although federal prosecutors decapitated major gangs operating in Chicago in the 1990s, the resulting fragmentation and undisciplined, leaderless factions produced even more violence.

Years after he had left the superintendency, Hillard remarked on the situation he faced.

"The city streets you are responsible for are full of guns and drugs. Your enemy is a massive countercultural organization of gang members that is at least triple the size of your police force, and it is better armed. Your enemy has embraced violence as a way of life."[13]

For Hillard, the upside was that crime had been declining for six years under the success of community policing, as well as a strong economy. But he felt it had not reached its full potential. As an African American with a strong rank-and-file following and a guileless persona, he was well suited to expand the initiative. Hillard made community outreach a hallmark of his administration, building a reservoir of goodwill that he would have to tap later, when tensions over police shootings threatened to roil the city.

While the new superintendent stayed the course on community policing, his actions elsewhere may have had a bigger and longer-lasting impact. Hillard was impressed with the potential game-changing impact of technology. In a public-private partnership increasingly common under Daley's leadership, the software giant Oracle partnered with Chicago police to build a data retrieval and analytics platform christened Citizen Law Enforcement Analysis and Reporting (CLEAR).

Ron Huberman, the young beat officer whose diverse skills had caught the attention of supervisors, was assigned to help. Recruiting eighteen of his fellow officers to assist, he worked closely with Barbara McDonald, the same deputy superintendent who originally helped launch community policing. Eventually, thousands of police cars were outfitted with computer terminals that could tap complex relational databases. With a few entries and a retrieval time of seconds rather than days, a police officer had access to nearly 10 million police and crime reports, including such minute details as a suspect's identifying tattoo, reported by a witness. Under CLEAR, that single data point could lead to many others instantly—a name, mug shot, gang affiliation, accomplices, likely hangouts.

Layering information such as shootings on the system's mapping technology also allowed for more predictive policing, revealing patterns that could be acted on preemptively.

"They're using CLEAR data to anticipate where crime may occur so we can have the resources there before it happens," McDonald said.[14] In fact, the power of CLEAR was so vast, the problem wasn't its utility but rather the ability of police officers to master the tool and integrate it in everyday police work.

"Chicago was dramatically ahead of the country in tech," Huberman told me. "We built the infrastructure to tell us where crime was occurring. Computer dispatch showed us where all the cops are. I talked to NYPD. They would have died for it."[15]

Huberman believes Chicago failed to capture the full potential of the CLEAR system, never integrating it in a way that fundamentally altered and drove policing strategies. But Hillard's first deputy, Phil Cline, did begin to use it to effect.

"Phil was the first person to seize the power of all that data," Huberman said.[16]

Cline broadcast the data on screens at police headquarters as a real-time tracker of crime, and worked it into his questioning of street officers. Detecting patterns and eliciting granular detail on likely perpetrators, Cline began using a more tactical approach to policing that emphasized mobility. Later, as superintendent, he would expand this strategy.

Hillard was wedded not to an ideology but to what worked. He saw Cline's pivot as necessary flexibility, balancing some of the inherent limitations of community policing. But strong community relations were a critical part of his strategy and for more reasons than fighting crime. The relationship between police and poor residents in minority communities has always been fragile, and when aggressive police conduct appears to cross over into brutality or lawlessness, it can be the equivalent of a match on dry tinder.

That match was lit on the evening of June 4, 1999, enflaming the Black community. In separate incidents hours apart, Chicago police officers stopped and killed two promising young African Americans, LaTanya Haggerty, twenty-six, a computer analyst for Encyclopedia Britannica; and Robert Russ, twenty-two, an expectant father and defensive tackle on the Northwestern University football team. Both were unarmed.

Hillard was traveling to Sun Valley, Idaho, for the national Major City Chiefs Association meeting. When he landed for his connecting flight in Colorado, two uniformed Denver police officers were waiting, carrying a faxed photograph to identify him. They escorted Hillard to a phone to call his office; he was informed of the shootings, the surging unrest in the Black community, and the mayor's order to return to Chicago immediately. Denver police had already intercepted his luggage and arranged for him to return on the next flight.

When he arrived back at police headquarters, he learned that Haggerty had caught a ride with a friend, Raymond Smith. Traveling to a South Side neighborhood, Smith pulled the car onto the wrong side of the road to talk to an acquaintance. Police approached, asking for a driver's license. Smith was driving on a suspended license, was on court supervision from a previous arrest, and had marijuana in the car. He took off, leading officers on a thirty-block chase before another squad car blocked his escape. Smith maneuvered the car and escaped again, as the officers fired four shots, targeting his tires. Although dispatch instructed the officers to break off the pursuit, they continued.

After another long chase, Smith was stopped and pulled from the vehicle by two officers, following a short struggle. Another officer, Serena Daniels, ordered Haggerty, who was talking on a cell phone and looking straight ahead, to drop the phone and put her hands up. Positioned on the driver's side between the front and back windows, Daniels testified later that she saw Haggerty turn in her direction and raise her right hand, containing a silver object. Concluding it was the barrel of a handgun, she fired, killing Haggerty.

Hours after the Haggerty shooting, police officers noticed Robert Russ driving erratically on South Lake Shore Drive. After an initial stop, Russ similarly sped off, triggering a long street chase that included other responding units and ended on the Dan Ryan Expressway. After a police vehicle with flashing lights pulled alongside him, Russ attempted to escape by ramming it three times; instead, his car spun out of control and came to a stop. But Russ wasn't done. Although boxed in by four police cars, he accelerated into one of the vehicles but could not break through. His car surrounded, officers ordered Russ to show his hands and exit. Because the car had tinted windows, Officer Van Watts used a tire iron to break the glass and pointed his weapon at Russ, who was motionless but without hands in view. Officer Watts testified that Russ turned suddenly and grabbed his weapon, and as he pulled back and struggled, his firearm discharged, killing Russ.

Following the shootings, Black ministers, community activists, and aldermen framed the incidents as wanton police brutality. As protests grew, the Reverend Jesse Jackson called the shootings part of "a new wave of terrorism sweeping across America."[17] The city council held multiple hearings; Hillard was placed on the defensive.

Partly obscured by the higher profile Haggerty-Russ shootings, a third killing added to the pressure on the department. In an incident eerily paralleled by the murder of George Floyd by Minneapolis police in 2020, but in an age without camera-wielding bystanders, Chicago police struggled to arrest a three-time convict, George Riley, on drug charges. He died after police put so much pressure on his neck and chest that he could not breathe. When at a public meeting Hillard attempted to frame the spate of police killings as exceptional and not reflective of the police force, he was met by loud jeers from an angry room of protestors.

Although rank-and-file officers had become accustomed to Hillard's unequivocal backing, here he broke with pattern. After an unusually quick five-week investigation, Hillard called for firing all four officers in the Haggerty shooting, noting they had failed to heed directions to cut off the pursuit, fired at a vehicle without sufficient justification, and engaged in the improper use of deadly force. In the Russ case, Hillard recommended only a fifteen-day suspension for Watts and additional training on handling weapons and pursuing fleeing vehicles. Although civilian witnesses testified they did not see a struggle for the weapon, casting doubt on Watt's account, Hillard emphasized the veteran officer's exemplary record.

As he had throughout his superintendency, Hillard reached out to community leaders, clergy, and activists who might help restore calm, providing as much transparency as possible. His long work of building goodwill in the Black community might have been the saving grace in an otherwise volatile situation. Had cell-phone cameras or police body cams been available in 1999, however, it's possible that no amount of goodwill would have prevented peaceful protests from turning violent.

In a wrongful death lawsuit, a Cook County jury awarded the estate of Robert Russ $9.6 million, accepting plaintiff arguments that Officer Watts fabricated his account of a struggle and accidental discharge of his weapon. The city settled with the family of LaTanya Haggerty for an unprecedented $18 million award.

"This is an expensive lesson for the city," said Haggerty's attorney, Johnnie Cochran, of O. J. Simpson fame. "Police have to treat people with respect. They can't be profiling. They can't be shooting at cars."[18]

On appeal, Circuit Court Judge Aaron Jaffe upheld the termination of Serena Daniels, the Haggerty shooter, writing, "Serena Daniels was a police officer who should not have been in control of a deadly weapon."[19]

In the wake of the shootings, Hillard ordered multiple high-level reviews by outside experts, resulting in changes to police procedures on traffic stops, high-speed pursuits, and other high-risk responses, as well as significant new training on the growing issue of racial profiling. He put video cameras in patrol cars and ordered the videotaping of murder confessions.

Suddenly, the "policemen's policeman" was under attack by the police union and fellow officers.

"If a guy has a gun, we're supposed to say, 'Sir, please put that gun down,'" said a commander, speaking to reporters on condition of anonymity. "It's a joke. I think he's forgotten what it's like out here."[20]

Like many urban leaders, Superintendent Hillard and Mayor Daley walked a tightrope between effective policing and the potential for brutality and misconduct. As subsequent mayors learned, not just in Chicago, a demoralized police force—in which officers believe they may be second-guessed and ostracized for aggressive action—is a prescription for chaos. Conversely, impunity from penalties for misconduct leads to more misconduct.

When police actions threatened the peace in Chicago, Daley was able to reach into his painstakingly built well of community relationships. Even then, the city came close to combusting more than once. Terry Hillard told me the night of the Russ-Haggerty shootings was one of those times.

"We were this far from having a full-blown riot in this city," Hillard said, holding up his thumb and finger to show a gap of inches. "And by the grace of God, with all the relationships we had built, we got through it."[21]

After the shootings, Hillard, his command staff, and the senior officers responsible for community policing visited all the major churches and explained the facts as they knew them. They briefed advocates and activists, the same ones with whom they had proactively consulted in quarterly listening forums, hearing their often angry accusations about police misconduct.

"We routinely talked to the people who didn't like us, didn't even respect us," Hillard told me, "because we needed to hear what they had to say about our cops messing up, and do something. When you mess up, you fess up, and straighten up. That was our approach. I think that helped us big time."[22]

In the years following what Hillard called the "night from Hell," he continued to advance community outreach and policing, improved technology and training, and green-lighted the beginning of a more tactical approach to policing, one that would supercharge already successful efforts to drive down violent crime.

Fourth Term

1999–2003

CHAPTER 19

Revolution Stalled

Despite enormous progress at Chicago's public schools under Daley's reform team, the first signs of trouble surfaced not long after Daley's reelection to a fourth term in early 1999. Previously hidden conflicts between the board chairman, Gery Chico, and the CEO, Paul Vallas, burst into the open. The Board of Education was forced to referee a power struggle over the newly appointed CPS inspector general, Maribeth Vander Weele. Aware of the political danger of a powerful investigator independently rummaging through his bureaucracy, Vallas objected to Chico's plan for Weele to work for him. In a Solomonic move, the board directed the IG to report to both men.

Meanwhile, test scores were beginning to stagnate. Scores for reading and math rose for a fifth consecutive year for elementary students and for a third consecutive year for high schools. But the gains were small, and third and sixth graders—considered in their "benchmark" years—posted troubling declines. Despite all the advances in the first four years of reform, two-thirds of the system's 436,000 students still could not read at grade level. Math performance was higher, with 40 percent at national norms.

Then, in fall 1999, the district received bad news about the Illinois Standards Achievement Tests, whose measurements are somewhat different than the nationally normed Iowa Tests of Basic Skills used by CPS. In the Illinois tests, Chicago students were below the statewide averages for students meeting state standards; a larger percentage of students were in the worst category.

In another crack in the edifice in 2000, reporters began probing the law business of the board president, Gery Chico. His law firm, Altheimer & Gray, had eighteen clients who lobbied city hall in 1995, when Chico became the CPS board chairman, but had nearly two hundred four years later. Prominent developers and utilities such as Commonwealth Edison and Ameritech were among his stable of clients. Chico abstained 359 times on official votes involving clients; the Board of Education awarded $577 million to his firm's clients or affiliated companies. Chico's aggressive leveraging of his status as a city power broker was not lost on Daley, who increasingly chafed at what he considered overreach by his former chief of staff. He began telling aides to ask companies not to steer further business to Chico.

Mayor Daley's annoyance at Chico extended to Vallas as well. Heady with success, Vallas behaved increasingly as if he were the *elected* chief of the schools, failing to consult city hall in the dispensation of jobs and contracts, building up personal chits with politicians, labor leaders, and clergy.

As long as test scores kept rising, the mayor looked the other way.

Test scores, however, were flattening, especially in reading among elementary students, a trend highlighted in a report by Alfred Hess Jr., an influential professor of education at Northwestern University. Daley became increasingly vocal about the need for urgency and renewed momentum. To underscore his limited patience, the mayor held his own national conference on the importance of reading and announced that a new mayoral aide would be devoted exclusively to reading strategies. Feeling the pressure, in the spring of 2001 Chico vowed to shake up the CPS team.

A month later, CPS announced a 1.6 percent gain in third- and eighth-grade reading levels, continuing the gradual trend upward. However, reversals in high school reading and elementary school math wiped out two years of improvements.

That was all Daley needed to make his move.

Until then, Vallas had been politically untouchable, so successful and popular that his removal would have ignited a firestorm. Late in the previous year, Daley had tried to ease Vallas out by encouraging him to run for governor in the 2002 election and pledging his support. Vallas considered it but concluded he loved the CPS job too much and was constitutionally more a manager than a politician.

Vallas's decision demonstrated a blind spot and a lack of understanding of Daley's psyche. If the mayor felt Vallas was critical to his continuing rebuild of the schools, he would not have encouraged Vallas's political ambitions. The backroom conversations led to rumors that Vallas finally quashed in a public statement in February 2001, in which he ruled out a gubernatorial run.

Months later, however, Chico announced his resignation following a meeting with the mayor. Daley had no personal conversation with Vallas, who was slow to pick up on the mayor's intentions. So city hall aides began leaking hints to the media that Vallas would soon be gone. After playing Whac-A-Mole trying to eliminate the various rumors, Vallas finally threw in the towel. In a meeting of the *Tribune* editorial board, he announced his resignation.

"Am I going? Yeah, I'm going, OK? Simple as that," Vallas said. "I don't want to play these games for another year."[1]

At a going-away press conference, Vallas graciously thanked the mayor for the opportunity and Daley heaped praise on his departing CPS chief.

"To say that Paul has been an outstanding CEO is an understatement," Daley said. In fact, he "has been quite simply the best chief executive in the history of the Chicago Public Schools."[2]

After six remarkable years, the curtain fell on the Paul and Gery Show.

After departing CPS, Vallas belatedly pivoted to a race for governor in the 2002 Democratic primary. Despite running a poor campaign and raising far fewer dollars than the winner, Congressman Rod Blagojevich, Vallas fell a mere two percentage points shy of victory. Had he accepted Mayor Daley's earlier offer of support, he likely would have won.[3]

• • •

What Daley perceived as hubris in his school leaders was not the primary motivation for his decision to remove them. The mayor was genuinely distressed that the revolution he had started in 1995 seemed to have stalled. Daley did not believe appointed executives became better over time; rather, he felt success often bred complacency, and he wanted fresh perspectives and energy. Throughout his mayoralty, Daley swapped out executives with regularity, sometimes sending them on to the private sector or to Washington, DC, but often simply assigning them to different city posts.[4]

To replace Chico, Daley announced the West Side real estate developer, AT&T executive, and park district board member Michael Scott. Scott had a long history with Daley, dating to when Mayor Jane Byrne removed him from the Board of Education. Byrne had replaced Black board members with whites to solidify white ethnic support prior to the 1983 election. After his removal, the mayor's brother, Bill Daley, solicited Scott to become part of the Daley team. He later served in a variety of appointed governmental roles.

The mayor's choice for CEO was a surprise, an unknown thirty-six-year-old deputy to Vallas who previously ran a small neighborhood school, Ariel Academy, founded by the money manager and former park district board chairman John Rogers. Arne Duncan also led the Rogers "I have a Dream" initiative that paid for the college educations of at-risk sixth graders, provided they graduated from high school. Duncan may also have caught the mayor's eye as lead manager of the district's neighborhood magnet school's initiative, key to Daley's obsession with keeping middle-class families in the city.

Duncan was raised in the South Side's Hyde Park community, home of the University of Chicago. His mother, Susan Goodrich, ran a highly respected after-school program primarily for African American children in adjacent Kenwood, an impoverished community. Duncan grew up with more Black peers than whites, including during thousands of hours on local basketball courts. A six-feet-five guard, Duncan was an unrecruited walk-on to Harvard's basketball program. By his sophomore year, he was a starter, by his senior year the team captain.

"Nobody had a higher work ethic than Arne," Harvard's assistant coach Steve Bzomowski told me. "He was in the gym practicing at ten-thirty at night. He was there so often that he had a key to the building."[5] After graduating, Duncan played professional basketball in Australia, where he met his wife, Karen.

In selecting Duncan, Mayor Daley was betting that a less frenetic, less combative leader was what the system needed in phase two reforms. In personality and approach, Duncan could not have been more different from Vallas. Exuding a preternatural calm, Duncan was a guileless, data-driven, and consensus-building executive, sharply contrasting with his high-octane, intuitive, and decisive predecessor. Where Vallas sought the limelight like a moth drawn to flame, Duncan resisted it.

Scott, too, maintained a steady, low-key, patient persona that helped him defuse conflict, particularly in public meetings and hearings. He maintained great credibility throughout the African American community. The new team, Daley said, can "work with people and groups with different views to find the common ground that puts our children first."[6]

The *Tribune* picked up on the shift in personalities as well as Daley's desire for less confrontation and more reconciliation: "One clear difference under the Duncan and Scott administration is their peacemaking with grassroots reformers, advocacy groups for local control, and foundations that had been shunned or ostracized after Daley took over the system in 1995."[7]

To set the new tone, Duncan immediately ceased the Vallas practice of sweeping "interventions," authorized by the 1995 state law and allowing wholesale dismissal of teachers at failing schools, an anathema to the teachers union.

As school opened in the fall of 2001, Mayor Daley announced a "new culture of literacy"; he built on his personal crusade the following year. With merely one in three students reading at grade level, Duncan mandated that elementary school children spend two hours a day reading; in addition, English and math periods were doubled for high school students. To assist teachers, 125 reading specialists were dispatched to schools, and Duncan outlined a $20 million effort to create a more uniform and effective method of teaching reading. Tim Shanahan, a University of Illinois-Chicago education professor, called the new reading reforms the most ambitious in the nation.

In 2002, a year after shaking up his leadership team, Daley got the results he wanted—the highest test scores since he had taken over the system. Elementary reading and math and high school reading scores jumped 3 to 4 percent. In grade schools, students were approaching national norms in math and reading, at 47 and 43 percent, respectively.

A further sign of progress was a small, 2,400-student increase in enrollment, reaching 440,000. The continued momentum earned Daley another enthusiastic nod for reelection from the newspapers.

"Daley's greatest achievement has been the substantial improvement in the Chicago Public Schools. . . . [T]he progress has been and continues to be remarkable. Daley has earned national recognition on his education efforts, and it has been deserved," the *Tribune* wrote.[8]

The new team's more conciliatory approach, however, had its downsides. The union convinced Duncan to restore teachers' authority to promote students who were failing summer school, provided their scores were close to the cutoff. The result was a 98 percent "graduation" rate from summer classes. Test scores for promoted students fell to their lowest levels since social promotions ended in 1996. Duncan admitted the new policy was too lenient and set minimum test scores for the following summer school, resulting in 13,308 students being held back—the highest number since Daley ended social promotions.

The spirit of cooperation also did little to address one of school reform's most important and pressing issues. Daley's emphasis on labor peace kept it off the bargaining table, and the window to address it effectively closed early in the Vallas-Chico reign, when CTU regained the right to strike. No one took it on until Mayor Rahm Emanuel in 2011.

The issue was Chicago's scandalously short school day. At five and one-half hours, it was the shortest in Illinois and the shortest in the nation among major cities. More typical were Houston, Detroit, and Philadelphia, where children were in class seven hours a day. Chicago's school year was also among the laggards. A *Tribune* investigation found the most disadvantaged students had the least amount of school time.

In response to criticism, Duncan agreed that more instruction time was needed. Despite Chicago's shortest-in-the-nation school day, he called for higher teacher salaries in exchange. He looked to the General Assembly for more money.

"This is the kind of issue that I would love to go hand in hand with Debbie Lynch to Springfield to push," he said, referring to the CTU leader.[9]

Education scholars have long stressed the correlation between instructional time and academic proficiency, a reason most national school reformers have made it a central focus. But not in Chicago, where Daley elevated school labor tranquility over all else.

• • •

Although lengthening the school day was never Daley's priority, what happened after school was always a mayoral focus, from the wave of after-school programs in the initial burst of activity under Vallas and Chico to the work of his wife, Maggie. By 2000, she had merged her successful Gallery 37 program for teenage artists into a much larger, more comprehensive initiative, After School Matters (ASM), in partnership with Chicago Public Schools. ASM provides after-school programs for the arts but also in science, technology, sports, communications, and cuisine.

Describing the reaction of attendees to a fundraiser for After School Matters, at which student artists were showcased, the *Tribune* described some of the significance of Maggie Daley's work:

> A vast sea of the well-connected would reliably appear.... They would mingle and then, a tad reluctantly, head in for a weeknight show. But the chosen student performers would proceed to blow everyone away by singing, dancing, and playing in a huge, dynamic, technically remarkable, unwaveringly beautiful swarm. Maggie Daley made sure of that.
>
> And thus everyone present would simultaneously arrive at the same personal revelation: To offer top-level artistic opportunity only to an elite is to

deny the self-evident truth that raw artistic talent can and does show up in all kinds of economic circumstances.[10]

In 2002, Maggie Daley was diagnosed with breast cancer. At the time, the survival rate for metastasized breast cancer was one to two years. Jackie Heard, the mayor's press secretary, describes the period as Mayor Daley's "lowest point" in his long tenure.

"I remember him coming to me right before the press conference. . . . [H]e was waiting at the door, which I thought was odd. And he said, 'I need to tell you something.' And he took me around the corner somewhere. And he could barely get the words out to tell me that Maggie's sick. And I was like, 'Oh my goodness.' And . . . he was just totally inconsolable."[11]

After he eventually composed himself, Daley went ahead with the scheduled press conference. But midway, a reporter asked about Maggie.

"I'm not really sure how, but someone in the press corps that day asked, because they had heard a rumor," Heard said. "And so he started out—got out probably a couple of words, and then moved away from the podium, because he couldn't go through with it."[12]

Maggie Daley began intensive chemotherapy treatments and continued her work for another decade, despite numerous setbacks, operations, and pain. Hundreds of thousands of young people have benefited from her creations, and After School Matters remains a lasting and powerful legacy of Chicago's exemplary First Lady.

ASM and other after-school programs helped mitigate the loss of classroom time but couldn't make up for all its impacts. After the burst of renewed growth in the first year, Duncan's second-year gains leveled off. Although math scores rose to an all-time high, reading scores dipped 2 percent despite the enormous efforts behind Daley's reading initiative. In the 2003 scores a year later, results were generally flat as well.

In an encouraging sign, however, scores in the critical eighth-grade benchmark soared to new highs and exceeded national averages for the first time. In fact, 57 percent of CPS eighth graders met national norms in math, and nearly 55 percent met them in reading.

Although celebrating the results, Daley again urged a renewed effort to move the needle. "The enemy is complacency," he said. The mayor blamed the more disappointing high school results on a "lack of creativity," fingering a "one size fits all" approach.[13] His comments were revelatory, signaling that his patience was at an end, not merely with underperforming secondary schools but with the persistently troubled elementary classrooms defying reform. Daley was foreshadowing a major change to shake up those intractable schools.

CHAPTER 20

Expansion

Mayor Daley had defeated attempts by Republican state leaders to build a third major airport outside Chicago, as well as their brazen 1995 power play to assume oversight of O'Hare and Midway.[1] But Chicago's success in protecting its airport duopoly from Springfield's predation did nothing to address the issue of aviation capacity. Without the ability to accommodate more air traffic, the economic engine of O'Hare would gradually run down. By the late 1990s, the FAA was already limiting flights into Chicago, and other national airports were taking advantage by building their own new runways.

Under state law, O'Hare's expansion required approval of the Republican governor, now George Ryan, the former secretary of state who had succeeded Jim Edgar. Like all Republican governors, Ryan was attuned to the noise and congestion complaints of GOP voters inhabiting the suburban ring around O'Hare; but his home was in Kankakee, not far from the proposed third airport at Peotone, which he strongly supported.

Daley—and everyone else—knew Ryan's approval for new runways was not forthcoming. In addition to undercutting Peotone and increasing noise levels, it would require annexation of surrounding suburban land, a move bitterly opposed by neighboring communities. So if Chicago's mayor had acknowledged the need for greater capacity, the governor and Republicans in Springfield would have offered a new suburban airport as the only plausible answer.

O'Hare's central role in the nation's hub-and-spoke air-traffic system had national ramifications. By 2000, when O'Hare sneezed, the rest of the country caught cold. Without alternate runways to accommodate additional flights, any significant storms or mechanical problems caused cascading delays throughout the country. Passengers not just at O'Hare but around the world had their flights delayed or canceled as the O'Hare effect rippled through the system.

US Sen. John McCain, chair of the Senate committee with jurisdiction over the nation's transportation network and a frequent national traveler, called out the self-interested local politics that was hurting the country.

"I say pox on all of them," McCain said, referring to both Daley and the Republicans in charge downstate. "Chicago is one of the most gridlocked places in America and a critical transportation hub. We can't get O'Hare expanded, and we can't build another airport. And those are the only two options."[2]

While Daley dithered, paralyzed by the state's Byzantine politics, Chicago's business leaders grew increasingly alarmed at the specter of a declining O'Hare. They believed O'Hare needed another east-west runway to handle the increase in flights. But Daley met them largely with complacency.

Taking matters into their own hands, the major corporate leaders—primarily acting through the Civic Committee of the Commercial Club of Chicago—launched a sophisticated, well-funded campaign to build public support and mobilize CEOs to pressure the administration and legislators. Their efforts brought the issue to the fore, but Daley remained uncharacteristically silent.

"Rich was not really interested in the expansion, or didn't show an interest in the expansion of O'Hare until the business community . . . really went out and got such backing," said Lester Crown, arguably Chicago's most influential business leader. "We went . . . to the newspapers themselves and the other parts of the information world. And we went to many, many companies and really showed the mayor that there was a tremendous amount of pressure because of a need for expanding O'Hare."[3]

A November 1998 report from the consulting firm Booz-Allen & Hamilton, commissioned by the Chicagoland Chamber of Commerce, underscored what was at stake, concluding that Chicago's airports contributed $35 billion annually to the regional economy, generating nearly half a million jobs. With expansion, the report said, Chicago could become "the leading international aviation hub of North America," growing its international air traffic five-fold and adding $26 billion in economic activity to the Chicago metro region.[4] The report warned that Chicago was in a competitive battle, particularly with New York's John F. Kennedy Airport.

"Chicago's opportunity is to become the principal U.S. gateway beyond New York and, in fact, to capture a share of international services from New York. Kennedy is vulnerable because connections to other U.S. cities are weak, while Chicago offers the broadest range of connecting services in the U.S."[5]

As the city's business leaders continued to press their case, summer travel was making vivid the delays at O'Hare, with passengers camped out in the airport's waiting rooms. A report by the US Department of Transportation's inspector general documented nearly ten thousand "chronically delayed" flights—postponements of an hour or more—at O'Hare, by far the nation's worst number. In a single year—from 1999 to 2000—delays increased 26 percent and cancellations by 21 percent.

"The combination of burgeoning demand and limited capacity have resulted in widespread dissatisfaction with air travel," the DOT report concluded.[6]

• • •

In politics, as in life, timing is everything. By the summer of 2001, the stars began to align. The long delays in air service throughout the country, fueled by O'Hare's limitations, began to get the attention of prominent members of Congress. At a summer hearing on regional aviation issues in Chicago, a US Senate committee lambasted local officials for the stalemate. The two senators from neighboring Iowa threatened to pass a law eliminating the Illinois governor's authority to block new runways at O'Hare. Chicago Congressman Bill Lipinski began to move such a bill through the House. The FAA convened the O'Hare Delay Task Force.

In August, the final domino fell. Republican Gov. George Ryan announced he would not seek reelection. No longer concerned with undermining his political base, Ryan dropped his opposition to new runways at O'Hare in exchange for Daley's support of a single runway at Peotone. The agreement provided no funding but kept the state's planning process intact.

Behind the scenes, Daley had been quietly studying the fast-growing Atlanta Airport and recognized its advantages over O'Hare's obsolete design. With state opposition removed, federal pressure building, and the local business community increasingly apoplectic at the lack of progress, Daley finally convened the city's leading corporate actors and presented his plan—*six* runways, all parallel. The new configuration would replace the inefficiencies of crisscrossing runways and ensure the maximum number of simultaneous flights—a visionary design that shocked those who only weeks before believed Daley to be AWOL on the most important issue facing the city.

"We really only were trying to promote one (runway) to begin with," said Lester Crown. "Rich got a plan put together that is the plan that has since been instituted, already instituted on the O'Hare modernization program. And he presented it to us, or presented it to the city, and it was a far, far more visionary plan than anything that we had put together."[7]

The prodigiously ambitious O'Hare Modernization Program (OMP) carried an $8 billion price tag, including the construction of four new runways and the extension of two others. Three runways affected by crosswinds would be decommissioned. By redesigning the airport to have six parallel east-west runways, the new design removed the takeoff and landing contingencies associated with the existing intersecting pathways and measurably enhanced airfield safety. When completed, the OMP would expand O'Hare's capacity by seven hundred thousand flights a year, a 78 percent increase.[8]

When it was time to announce the plan publicly, Mayor Daley held a press conference, surrounded by aviation and planning experts. But he was the one who stepped forward to explain it in intricate detail.

"It was brilliant in how comprehensive it was, and how strategic," recalls Daley's chief of staff, Sheila O'Grady. "He led the discussion of each piece. And the press corps could be jaded at some times, but I . . . remember that that was a day they fully understood how great he was at his job, how well he knew it, and what a strong vision he had for what needed to happen for the city."[9]

From announcement to completion, the plan took twenty years to navigate its way through a labyrinth of federal and state regulatory approvals, as well as negotiations with airlines funding significant portions of the project. Construction was ongoing for more than sixteen years. The US Department of Transportation reported to Congress that "the complexity and magnitude of the O'Hare Modernization Project cannot be overstated, as it is one of the largest and most costly reconfigurations of an airport in the United States. In terms of infrastructure projects, the OMP may be second only to Boston's Central Artery/Ted Williams Tunnel project (the "Big Dig"), which is estimated to cost $14.6 billion when completed."[10]

When a new runway opened in 2020, among the last of the major slated improvements, it made possible the landing of aircraft on four runways at once, lifting O'Hare's capacity by a third from the previous year. The number and length of flight delays fell, and hundreds of additional flights were added daily.

Two decades earlier, Chicago's business and civic leaders had warned Mayor Daley of inaction, as other airports began chipping away at O'Hare's market share. Their findings, presented in granular detail in the Booz-Allen & Hamilton report, also presented a vision of what *could* be—a world in which Chicago became the premier North American international hub. By 2022, Chicago was on its way to fulfilling that vision. It is North America's most connected airport, serving 278 unique destinations worldwide.[11]

The O'Hare Modernization Project salvaged O'Hare's place as a nexus of America's national aviation system and ensured that it would remain the biggest economic engine for Chicago, its surrounding region, and the greater Midwest.

In the airport wars, Mayor Daley had vanquished local enemies and deflected national rivals. It took every ounce of his political skills, legal creativity, brazen power politics, and exploitation of national alliances, plus a bit of dumb luck. But he had triumphed. Today, Chicago remains an epicenter of the aviation world.

CHAPTER 21

Razing Hell

The story of Chicago's public-housing high-rises is a tale of unintended consequences and of the enormous power of the federal government to do great harm in the pursuit of good.

It is also a story bookended by father and son.

In the 1950s and sixties, Mayor Richard J. Daley took federal dollars on the federal government's terms, and erected densely packed public housing towers that quickly evolved into hellish vertical ghettos. In 2001, Mayor Richard M. Daley took federal dollars, on his terms, and began to tear them down.

What replaced them would fundamentally alter the demographic, economic, and political landscape of the City of Chicago.

• • •

A few years after World War II, the federal government adopted a new strategy for the problems of housing in cities—urban renewal. Using expanded powers of eminent domain to condemn and acquire property and swimming in federal largesse, ambitious local politicians and do-gooders began clearing slums, erecting public high-rises in their place, and building new roads and highways replacing or bisecting many of the same neighborhoods.

The impulse to expand housing was driven by shortages after the war as well as a desire to improve health conditions for inner-city residents, where poor sanitation and great density led to disproportionate illness. Rather than promoting better water and sewer infrastructure and widespread immunizations, however, federal and local civic planners advocated "slum clearance" as the path to progress.

Less visible to outsiders, most of these slums were strongly interconnected communities of self-reliant people. Families tended to be intact, and cooperation among residents living in close proximity often formed a strong sense of social cohesion.[1] In the same way careless habitat destruction upsets delicate life-supporting ecosystems, the industrial-scale obliteration of whole neighborhoods by government fiat left in its wake something far more dysfunctional.

John O. Norquist, the former mayor of Milwaukee and retired CEO of the Congress for the New Urbanism, calls the federal urban renewal practices "destroying the village in order to save it." He argues that cities had low-cost, affordable housing long before governments claimed to invent it:

> Tenements, low-rent hotels, flophouses, what are now called single-room occupancy apartments (SROs)—all served people with low incomes . . . seeking to make it in the city. Though much of this housing fell short of today's standards and much of it was filled beyond safe capacity, people were never separated from the weave of urban life by contrived housing arrangements. Not all housing was pretty, and some could be a tight fit, but the options included walk-ups, apartments over stores, triplexes, duplexes, single-family houses, apartments over garages, flats in back, boarding-houses, tenements, and row houses. . . . Efficient, low-income housing techniques grew organically in cities.[2]

In his influential book *Making the Second Ghetto,* the historian Arnold Hirsch demonstrated how Chicago's slum clearance and public-housing projects displaced residents during construction and sent Black residents into white neighborhoods in search of housing.[3] The neighborhoods proximate to the Black ghettos usually housed first-generation white immigrants, who in turn were easily swindled by unscrupulous real-estate speculators spreading fear in "blockbusting" schemes. Financial institutions withdrew support from collapsing neighborhoods. Black families paid inflated prices to buy properties, requiring them to take in more residents to meet mortgage payments.

The result of urban renewal in Chicago—enforced through the combined exercise of federal, state, and municipal power—was not the containing of ghettos but rather the creation of new ones, some in the sky and some sprawling across the South and West Sides of the city.

In one of his first official acts in 1955, the newly elected mayor, Richard J. Daley, dedicated the groundbreaking for the Cabrini-Green public-housing high-rise, made possible by slum clearance on the city's near North Side. A crowd of more than a thousand onlookers swamped police lines to try and shake his hand. The first of the Cabrini buildings was completed in 1959 and occupied by more whites than Blacks, with a mix of families and incomes. By 1962, Cabrini was 100 percent Black and dominated by the poor as housing of the last resort.

The design flaws of Cabrini-Green should have been obvious: people warehoused high in the air; malfunctioning elevators; and stairwells and corridors perfect for predatory criminality. Children had playgrounds, including basketball courts with missing rims, but even these dilapidated areas were inaccessible most of the time to kids living in apartments a dozen floors up or higher.

"We thought we were playing God in those days," the architect Larry Amstadter told the *Tribune* in 1982. "We thought we were doing a great thing, doing a lot of innovative design things, like putting open galleries on each floor so kids could play in front of their apartments. We didn't foresee the kids throwing each other off them."[4]

Rather than waiting to see the results of its early social experiments in housing and transportation, the federal government simply pushed ahead with more money and more programs for urban renewal, even creating a vast federal department to oversee it all.

"In 1965, the federal government did what it often does when it creates suffering. It grew a new bureaucracy named after the problem it created . . . the Department of [Housing and] Urban Development—*urban* as in urban problem, urban dilemma, urban distress, urban decline, urban decay, and, ultimately, urban death," Norquist wrote in his book *The Wealth of Cities.*[5]

Richard J. Daley, a prolific collector of federal funds for Chicago, was aided and abetted by President Lyndon B. Johnson, a fellow Democrat waging a war on poverty through his Great Society program. Johnson opened a spigot of federal money for Daley, who used it to repeat the failure of Cabrini-Green nine more times, including Stateway Gardens, eight ten- and seventeen-story buildings on the near South Side; the infamous Robert Taylor Homes, twenty-eight sixteen-story buildings pressed along the South Side's Dan Ryan Expressway; and the expansion of the Henry Horner Homes, nineteen high-rises with ten stories each, on the city's West Side.

Although the physical problems of the high-rises were evident by the end of the 1950s, Chicago continued building them until 1968, when the federal government ceased its funding. With each year, the CHA buildings deteriorated further, a result of inadequate maintenance and few resources for residents. Working-class tenants began vanishing, penalized by federal regulations that automatically raised rents with pay increases. Drug dealers and other criminals moved in, and only those without options remained.

In 1987, the *New York Times* published Adam Walinsky's "What It's Like to Be in Hell," which described the living conditions in Chicago's housing projects—plastic sheeting filling broken windows; buildings and apartments in a permanent state of disrepair; a neighborhood without grocery stores or banks or currency exchanges and into which delivery services or cabs would not enter; women and children mugged by youth of all ages; fifteen-year old girls recruited into prostitution and eight-year-old boys into drug sales; single mothers moving refrigerators in front of doors broken by intruders, because the authorities took weeks to fix the doors or required bribes simply to do the paperwork.

"Dominant authority is exercised by the gangs. . . . The gangs engage in regular and constant warfare for control of the drug and vice trades," Walinsky wrote. "They are armed with pistols, rifles, automatic weapons, and occasional grenades. Firefights may erupt at any time. Children dodge machine-gun crossfire as they leave the school. Sudden bullets smash through windows into apartment walls. Watch the residents walk; they have the affinity for ground of seasoned infantry soldiers."[6]

Poor, politically powerless, struggling merely to survive from day to day, public-housing residents were in no position to stem the tide of neglect. Those in charge, at least in the early decades of high-rise public housing, felt little need to answer to them. In fact, the CHA became yet another playground for Chicago politicians and power brokers, a rich source of patronage jobs and government contracts.

No one epitomized the CHA's face better than Charlie Swibel. The youngest member of the board at age twenty-nine, he was appointed by Mayor Richard J. Daley in 1956 and became chairman in 1963. Charming and unctuous, Swibel developed a reputation for getting things done for powerful people. He began his career working for one of Chicago's largest slum landlords, Marks & Company, and later assumed control, expanding the empire of neglected housing. Mayor Jane Byrne famously ran against an "evil cabal" controlling the city when she defeated Mayor Bilandic in 1979. Swibel was a charter member, but she made him an important part of her inner circle, deciding that the evil cabal was not so bad after all.

A 1982 U.S. Housing and Urban Development (HUD) report concluded that only a handful of Swibel's CHA managers were "competent or knowledgeable enough to be managing projects," and that because of the political nature of the workforce, the CHA had never fired or even laid off an employee. The level of incompetence and neglect was staggering, manifesting itself in the appalling daily conditions of residents. More than a third of CHA elevators, for example, were not working at any given time, forcing single mothers to haul groceries and escort children up and down dirty, dank, and dangerous stairwells. HUD reported that not only was no one effectively managing the agency but no one seemed to genuinely care.

The federal government threatened to withhold its money—finally forcing the hand of Mayor Jane Byrne. Under pressure, in 1982, she replaced Swibel, bringing an end to his long CHA reign.

Swibel's departure did little to change the trajectory of the CHA. In the next five years, it cycled through eight executive directors, misspending public dollars at a staggering rate. In 1987, as HUD was threatening to seize control of Chicago's public housing, CHA executives acknowledged HUD's characterization of "historic mismanagement . . . and appalling lack of financial controls," but promised to do better. Millions in funds were misappropriated, but the CHA said record-keeping was so poor that it was impossible to know where the money went.[7]

By 1988, interim Mayor Eugene Sawyer, appointed by the city council following the death of Harold Washington, nominated the real estate developer Vincent Lane to be CHA executive director. Lane was charismatic and ambitious. His company, American Community Housing Associates, was one of the largest Black-owned real estate firms in the country. So desperate was Sawyer to stave off a federal takeover that he acceded to Lane's request to serve as both chief executive and chairman of the board—while still operating his private company.

Lane quickly showed he would not be like previous directors. Although living conditions in the high-rises had deteriorated to unprecedented levels, the greatest fear of residents was the dominance of gangbangers and drug dealers. Lane began a series of security sweeps, but with an inauspicious beginning.

At Rockwell Gardens, where rival street gangs were engaged in warfare over control of buildings, Lane deployed sixty police officers enforcing a single entrance and exit. He identified and badged legitimate residents and escorted trespassers out. The surprise raid was designed to confiscate weapons and narcotics, but Lane was disappointed to find only one gun and no drugs, and no arrests were made. So pervasive was the gangs' control that their intelligence networks had unearthed Lane's plans before he could execute them. The drug dealers simply moved their guns and inventory elsewhere.

Undeterred, Lane continued periodic, unannounced sweeps in the coming years over the vociferous odd-couple objections of the American Civil Liberties Union and the National Rifle Association.

Lane was a visionary. He understood the importance of encouraging work among tenants, mostly permanent dependents of the state. With an overwhelming need for maintenance, he incentivized outside contractors to train and hire CHA residents and fostered competition between in-house and private crews. With jobs came dignity, experience, and growing independence for those willing to grab the opportunity.

"If the Ku Klux Klan had set out to destroy black people, they couldn't have done a better, more systematic job of it than this combination we have of welfare and public housing," Lane said. "We need more working people in public housing. We need the right role models to compete with the gangs and drug dealers."[8]

But Lane's greatest contribution was in envisioning a new type of mixed income developments that included public housing. His ideas caught the attention of national leaders, including Presidents George H. W. Bush and Bill Clinton. His name was bandied about as a potential cabinet member.

Lane showcased his idea at Lake Parc Place, a $17 million rehab of CHA housing on the South Side. The concept, which proved successful, was to divide the three hundred apartments among the unemployed poor and working-class families anxious to find better housing at lower rents. The rehabbed complex boasted amenities like ceiling fans, stucco walls, landscaping, a well-tended playground and wading pool for children, and twenty-four-hour lobby security. To protect Lake Parc Place from the type of criminality and deterioration characteristic of CHA high-rises, Lane required background checks for prospective tenants and proof of employment and income from at least half the families.

"The working residents will provide a role model," Lane told the *Tribune*, "at least in the minds of families on welfare, that is achievable: bus drivers, plumbers, medical technicians. They're not doctors and lawyers, but if the goal that's set for you looks so far out that you don't believe you can achieve it, you won't even try."[9]

Lane's energy and ideas changed the debate, but his failures as a manager prevented him from leading a revolution. Lane was more interested in promoting his vision than in tending to the unglamorous day-to-day challenges of a deeply troubled organization. His private business was also a distraction and increasingly a focus of potential conflicts of interest.

By 1995, the CHA had slid back into a place of dysfunction and despair. Lane's grand plans to apply the Lake Parc model to the denser, daunting high-rises, such as Cabrini-Green, were too slow to materialize, and both Mayor Daley and federal officials ran out of patience. Residents of the West Side's Henry Horner Homes filed suit, claiming the Lane administration's lack of maintenance amounted to "de facto demolition." Also troubling was the first whiff of scandal in Lane's seven-year tenure, including the disappearance of $37 million in employee pension funds.

Lane was unrepentant.

"Should I have dealt with the details? No!" he said. "I'd have spent all my time making sure nobody stole from the store. The real problem is that the store is burning down."[10]

President Bill Clinton's regional HUD director, Edwin Eisendrath, a former Chicago alderman and Daley ally, had filed a series of increasingly dire reports during 1995 about conditions in the projects. Federal officials said the "despairing" information became a tipping point. Eisendrath helped work out a federal takeover with Daley's blessing. Joseph Shuldiner, HUD's assistant secretary for Public and Indian Housing, replaced Lane.

The HUD secretary, Henry Cisneros, praised Lane as a visionary but said both he and Mayor Daley had grown angry at his failure to resolve the CHA's myriad problems, from inadequate heating and disabled elevators to the deaths of children falling from high-rise windows.

"You can't leave a major city with the isolation and slow-burning anger that characterizes CHA developments," Cisneros said.[11]

Over the next few years, Shuldiner stabilized the agency by shoring up finances, mitigating the worst of the housing conditions, and creating a planning dialogue with residents. By 1998, HUD had approached Mayor Daley about beginning a transition to city control. Daley welcomed the opportunity but viewed it through the same lens as his takeover of the troubled Chicago Public Schools three years earlier. To succeed, he would need a high degree of autonomy. In the same way the state lifted mandates and loosened strings on how monies could be used in schools, Daley insisted on HUD carve-outs for Chicago—changes that did not sit well with federal bureaucrats.

• • •

Mayor Daley had little interest in tinkering at the margins of public housing, simply bringing more efficiency and improved services. Rather, he envisioned a dramatically scaled version of Vince Lane's mixed-income communities, of which public housing would be merely a part. Integrating public housing with market-rate and subsidized housing could, in his view, curtail the pathologies of concentrated CHA buildings. Those structures, in the mayor's plan, would no longer be isolated, crime-ridden high-rises but instead low-rise housing.

He called it the Plan for Transformation.

However, Daley was convinced that his transformative vision, requiring the razing of dozens of public-housing high-rises and the construction of vast new communities, would fail if HUD's timid, bureaucratic, incremental rules governed Chicago's reforms.

David Brint, whose nationally recognized Brinshore Development later redeveloped both the West Side's Henry Horner Homes and the sprawling South Side Robert Taylor Homes, told me that Daley's plan was far more ambitious than anything contemplated by other cities.

"Daley's idea was to knock down public housing and replace it. No one except Chicago said, 'We're going to knock it all down,'" Brint said.[12]

Under the main federal program for public housing revitalization, Hope 6, cities were eligible for grants of up to $50 million, allocated one at a time at the discretion of HUD. Under the Clinton administration, the HUD Secretary was the notoriously controlling Andrew Cuomo, the son of former New York governor Mario Cuomo and himself a future governor. Cuomo used his position with an eye to promoting his own political future; he also had little use for Mayor Daley or for the mayor's suggestion that Cuomo's agency cede power to Chicago.

Through the following year, city and federal officials engaged in taut negotiations over the transition and operating agreement. In the same way he approached other economic development, Daley sought a comprehensive and strategic blueprint for the entire city, requiring multiple and simultaneous Hope 6 grants. Rather than spending the CHA's average annual federal allotment of $130 to $150 million incrementally, ensuring a glacial pace of redevelopment, Daley asked HUD to guarantee a $1.5 billion income stream for ten years. When combined with Daley's commitment of more than $4 billion in city resources, the plan would attack dilapidated public-housing high-rises across the board while building new neighborhoods simultaneously.

In this way, city initiatives for economic development would be seamlessly integrated, providing critical new infrastructure such as roads, sewers, and water mains, as well as new parks, schools, police and fire stations, and incentives for retail corridors serving the newly created neighborhoods. Nowhere in the country was a city prepared to pour as much of its own resources into improving public and affordable housing.

But Cuomo wouldn't give Daley the time of day.

Undeterred, in October 1999, Daley announced his plan. Decaying CHA highrises, fifty-one in all containing sixteen thousand units, would be razed. Mixed-income communities would replace them, roughly one-third public housing, one-third affordable or subsidized private housing, and one-third market-rate housing. Including senior housing, which would remain but undergo major improvements, the plan called ultimately for twenty-five thousand new or rehabilitated units.

Even while the federal government was in control, Daley had moved to integrate more city services and infrastructure spending to benefit Shuldiner's efforts.

"The untold story is how much the city has contributed" already to the initial public housing redevelopment, Shuldiner said. "I have never seen this amount of local support in terms of real money."[13] Shuldiner had worked previously in public housing in Los Angeles and New York.

Daley's infrastructure investments were not his only early contribution. Julia Stasch was the city housing commissioner, and Daley's point person on the transition planning.[14] She said the mayor "is doing a lot of arm-twisting on behalf of jobs for residents. He realizes that putting somebody in a new house with a pretty bow isn't enough."[15]

However, some of the resident groups, buoyed by public interest lawyers and activists, resisted the city's plans, and argued for continuing federal controls.

"It's like giving a blank check to a thief," said Grant Newberger of the Coalition to Protect Public Housing.[16] Others expressed distrust of the CHA's promise to build new homes and return residents to them.

Cuomo sided with the activists, putting the brakes on Daley's plan and seizing the opportunity to advance his national image as a champion of the poor. HUD officials said replacement housing had to be identified in advance for displaced tenants, and demolition could occur only if HUD's market analysis determined Chicago had sufficient affordable housing for Section 8 private housing vouchers.

"The final determination is to be made by the resident," said Harold Lucas, Cuomo's assistant director. "No one is to be forced from the city." He noted that tenants could reject suitable replacement housing in the suburbs.

Cuomo also said that HUD could only guarantee $545 million of the $1.5 billion requested by the city and questioned the number of regulatory waivers sought by Daley. Conflicts between HUD and Chicago slowed progress and threatened to torpedo Daley's vision.

Although Cuomo's fixation on control and political posturing fueled the extended transition, the city contributed to the ill will.

After being designated by Mayor Daley as the interim CHA executive director, Phillip Jackson held a news conference to highlight alleged waste and mismanagement under Shuldiner, displaying $700,000 of computers and equipment sitting idly in CHA warehouses. It was an odd stunt, considering Shuldiner's support for Daley's plan and the remaining approvals required by the feds. As the deputy to Chicago Public Schools chief Paul Vallas, Jackson had watched Vallas hold a similar press conference shortly after taking control, displaying dust-covered furniture and computers from CPS warehouses and ordering it sent to classrooms. No doubt Jackson hoped to replicate the positive press Vallas had received. Instead, he incurred the wrath of his federal overseers.

"What kind of bullshit is this," the HUD lawyer Howard Glaser faxed in a handwritten text. Minutes later a second fax arrived. "Consider your deal cancelled."[17]

Although Clinton's White House intervened to ensure the plan was not canceled, HUD froze an initial congressional grant of $148 million. The following weekend Cuomo's appointees held a public hearing in Chicago over the mayor's objections and without inviting the CHA or Daley. The hearing showcased opponents of Daley's plan, hand picked to parade a series of grievances against the mayor. At the hearing, HUD Assistant Secretary Harold Lucas took a direct shot at Daley while presenting his boss as the hero.

"The days in which federal officials in Washington work behind closed doors with City Hall to decide what's best for local neighborhoods are over," he declared.[18]

Daley responded furiously, attacking Lucas and other "political appointees" for meddling in local matters, his frustration boiling over after months of behind-the-scenes conflict.

Despite this open warfare, President Clinton's imminent departure from office on January 20, 2001, kept the pressure on to reach an agreement. Daley had tapped South Side alderman Terry Peterson to lead the ten-year Plan for Transformation. Along with his senior team of chief operating officer Bridget Reidy (formerly my deputy at the park district and city hall) and communications director Lisa Schneider, Peterson made enough progress to warrant a final session in Washington. He and his team sat down with HUD officials for four hours. Secretary Cuomo joined for about half the meeting, including the session's conclusion. Peterson said the meeting was exceptionally positive. He spent much of his time with Cuomo outlining the billions the city was contributing.

"I came back thinking it was a great meeting," Peterson recalled to me. "But as the calendar got closer and closer to January twentieth, I couldn't get anything signed. The clock is ticking, and Cuomo is slow walking it. He refuses to sign."[19]

Peterson reported to Mayor Daley that Cuomo had set up a blockade.

In the final week of his eight-year presidency, Clinton was making a "thank-you" tour around the country, including Chicago. Daley arranged for Clinton to attend a Chicago public school to highlight education reforms. Peterson recalls getting a call from the mayor's chief of staff, Sheila O'Grady, telling him he would be riding with the mayor and the president when Clinton's motorcade left the school.

Peterson said that he didn't really believe he would be riding with the president. But as Clinton left the press conference, shaking hands along the pathway to the presidential limousine, the mayor tapped Peterson on the shoulder. "You ready?" he said.

"Sure enough, I follow the mayor," Peterson told me. "The doors swing open, I get in, the doors close. I'm sitting next to the president of the United States. Before I say a word, the mayor has some colorful language to describe the president's HUD director. Then he says, 'Tell him, Terry.' So I explain to the president the meeting in Washington, the hours we spent with the secretary and his staff, and how I thought we had an agreement. Clinton listens, then tells his staffer to get Cuomo on the phone. When he does, Clinton tells him, 'Andrew, get it done. The mayor's team will be in Washington tomorrow to pick it up.'"[20]

Reidy and Schneider got on a plane to Washington, DC the next day.

"They called me from the airport on their way back," Peterson remembers. "They screamed at me on the phone, 'We got it!'"[21]

Daley's Plan for Transformation—not merely of public housing but of much of Chicago—was about to begin.

CHAPTER 22

Betrayal

In 2002, I decided to run for public office. In Chicago. Against the machine. As it turned out, against Mayor Daley.

It was an obscure office, Cook County Commissioner. But that's less important than the politics behind both the election and what came after, and what county government meant to the Daley empire.

In retrospect, the campaign was a near perfect window into a fascinating world of Chicago politics that no longer exists, one populated by colorful characters wielding tribal power when the city's ward politics was still dominant, and neighborhoods had clear ethnic and political boundaries.

In just a few years, the legendary reach of the Chicago machine would begin its decline, the victim of hubris and overreach, and the clear ethnic and ideological lines demarcating neighborhoods would begin to blur. Ironically, the man who dealt the final death blow to the machine was the son of its greatest leader. But first, Mayor Richard M. Daley led it to a new zenith, one uniquely his own.[1]

• • •

After Mayor Daley was reelected to a fourth term in 1999, winning in a landslide over the South Side Congressman Bobby Rush, I left his administration for the private sector. But in 2001, the mayor reached out to discuss a new political opportunity.

Rod Blagojevich, later infamous for attempting to sell President Obama's former US Senate seat, was giving up his Northwest side congressional post to run for governor. The seat was important to Chicago but was threatened by redistricting following city population losses in the 2000 census. The mayor, however, used his considerable political capital to protect the Chicago district when the new congressional district lines were drawn.

Daley, at the peak of his popularity and power, also intended to orchestrate who would be the next congressional representative. By itself, Daley's endorsement swayed considerable votes—and dollars. But with loyal, patronage-rich ward organizations on the Northwest Side, Daley's support also meant that an army of experienced precinct captains would blanket neighborhoods on behalf of his chosen candidate. It meant a nearly insurmountable edge for a rare open congressional seat.

In Daley's mind, there were only two candidates to consider—Rahm Emanuel and me. Emanuel had been Daley's fundraiser in the 1989 campaign. Although Rahm had sought a mayoral appointment, the mayor blocked it, saying he didn't want his fundraiser inside the government. But he later grew to respect Rahm for his service as a senior White House aide to President Clinton.

Although we both had funny names, and neither of us was born and raised in Chicago, I had a better mayoral relationship and had lived on the Northwest Side for more than fifteen years. So the mayor gave me first dibs. Rahm, who was busy mining his national contacts as an investment banker, volunteered to chair my campaign. Rahm was candid that he wanted the seat but figured I would run for another office soon; he sought the incumbent's gratitude. At the time, his ambition was to be the first Jewish Speaker of the House of Representatives.

The prospect of serving in Washington should have been exciting. But working for Daley, operating city government and a sister agency with a visible impact on the quality of life in a great metropolis, had spoiled me. Serving as a freshman member of a 435-member body, with no operational authority over anything, was not terribly appealing. Neither was the prospect of spending four nights a week away from my young family.

My friend and intellectual mentor, Richard Dennis, a Chicago commodities trader and philanthropist, also bluntly warned me of the reality I would face in an environment of ideological litmus tests and rigid control by party leadership. "You might as well just give them your voting card when you walk in the door," he said.

Yet I knew what I would be passing up, and its implications for any political future. As Rahm told me, "When a door opens, you have to walk through it."

I turned down the opportunity. The door closed.

Rahm was a better congressman than I ever could have been, leveraging his Clinton contacts, White House experience, and considerable fundraising skills to vault to senior leadership rapidly, benefiting Chicago. He would later succeed Daley as mayor.

A few months after declining the congressional opportunity, I read about new district boundaries for the Cook County Board, following the census changes. The map was drawn by Commissioner Thaddeus "Ted" Lechowicz, a powerful political insider and the embodiment of a machine politician.

Lechowicz served many years as a state senator but also managed to hold a second job on the county payroll, entitling him to two salaries and two public pensions in the widespread practice known as "double dipping." At one point, he was a "triple dipper." Conspiring with his buddy, Secretary of State George Ryan (who would follow the Illinois tradition of being elected governor and then entering a federal penitentiary), Lechowicz exploited a loophole to boost his annual pension by twenty-thousand dollars for just six weeks on Ryan's payroll.

"For this now-prohibited trick," wrote the *Tribune*, "Lechowicz earned a Pig at the Trough Award from *Chicago* magazine and became the archetype for oily, out-of-touch insiders who clog our system, misuse our money, and call it public service."[2]

While Lechowicz was busy padding his pensions, county government was falling into disarray. Rising property and sales taxes paid for vast bloat. Managerial incompetence and neglect were rampant, victimizing at-risk kids and adults without health insurance who depended on county services.

As I studied the new map, I noticed my home had been drawn into Lechowicz's district. I wondered if this could be another door opening.

County government was local government, where my passion resided. I could also go home every night to my family. Unlike Congress, it was a part-time job, so I could maintain another career. But most important, it could be a stepping stone to an executive job I wanted, president of the Cook County Board.

Outside of mayor and governor, the one big elected job with significant managerial responsibilities was the board's presidency. Although the county board mostly authorized billions in annual appropriations for the offices of other elected officials such as state's attorney and sheriff, its leader held direct operational control of the forest preserves, the Juvenile Detention Center, and the public hospitals and network of health clinics.

The main allure was the county health care system, with its enormous potential to save lives, improve health, and lift the quality of life in city neighborhoods.

It was a fight worth taking on.

In drawing the new map, Lechowicz made the strategic decision to include my Forty-Seventh Ward in his district, banking on his longtime friendship with Committeeman Ed Kelly. Although Kelly no longer controlled his park district empire, he remained head of the "Fighting 47th" regular Democratic organization.[3]

Similarly, Lechowicz folded the Thirty-Second Ward into his new district. The Thirty-Second was led by the veteran alderman and committeeman Terry Gabinski, a protégé of the former congressman Dan Rostenkowski, who had held enormous power for years as chairman of the House Ways and Means Committee. More important, Gabinski was Lechowicz's poker-playing buddy and had provided a political home for the commissioner when he lost his own committeeman's post in the Thirtieth Ward.

Lechowicz distrusted the other Northwest Side committeemen, fearful they might run one of their own against him if given a sufficient share of the vote. So he used a scalpel elsewhere, carving out portions of wards heavy with his fellow Polish Americans but ensuring that no ward heeler had too much control.

Each of these strategic moves by the cunning Lechowicz turned out to be a mistake.

The eastward Forty-Seventh and Thirty-Second Wards were changing, slowly but inexorably gentrifying. "If Teddy ever showed up east of Western Avenue, he might have noticed," one Lechowicz pal told me early in the campaign. And without his park district patronage, Kelly was relying on nostalgia to motivate captains.

Kelly also made his own strategic mistake, instigating a feud with his formerly loyal alderman Eugene Schulter. Schulter was the antithesis of a ward heeler, genteel and businesslike. But he was a ferocious advocate for his ward, and he built his own political organization without the committeeman's title.

Schulter and I were at odds in my park-district days, as I dismantled the parks' patronage empire with all its Forty-Seventh Ward captains. But in yet another illustration of a classic political maxim—*the enemy of my enemy is my friend*—Schulter and I quickly became bosom buddies.

Schulter's new political organization didn't resemble those of legendary status—Mike Madigan's Thirteenth, which Madigan ran with military-style discipline; or John Stroger's Eighth, which overwhelmed foes with waves of organizers pulled from county government; or even Patricia Cullerton's Thirty-Eighth, with her the heir of a long line of Cullertons who controlled Northwest-Side votes and jobs since Patrick "Parky" Cullerton first claimed the ward's aldermanic post in 1935.

But if the somewhat rag-tag crew of Schulter's new army was less experienced, they were no less enthusiastic. They adopted their leader's antipathy for Kelly and his pal Lechowicz. My challenge to Kelly's candidate set up a proxy war between the committeeman and his former protégé. The small but boisterous weekly ward gatherings were energized by the prospect of an all-out fight for Forty-Seventh-Ward supremacy.

When I made my decision to run, I dutifully trekked to city hall to inform the mayor first. Unlike with the congressional opportunity, I wasn't seeking his endorsement. I knew the underlying politics were too complicated. Lechowicz was part of the leadership team in County Board President John Stroger's administration, along with the mayor's brother, County Board Finance Committee Chairman John Daley. Stroger was a strong mayoral ally, the most important African American leader in the state.

The Stroger-Daley alliance was part personal, part practical. Stroger had been among the few African American leaders to support Daley when he ran against Harold Washington, the city's first Black mayor. The powerful Stroger also was important to Daley as a shield against perceptions that the white mayor held too much sway in a majority-minority city.

But I also knew the history between the Daley family and Lechowicz, who had leveraged his array of friendships to wield outsize power in Springfield. Bringing the same approach to the county board, Lechowicz immediately challenged John Daley for the chairmanship of the powerful Finance Committee.

That was a mistake.

John Daley had no trouble winning, and his brother went to work exacting revenge. Mayor Daley combined two Polish wards into one as part of aldermanic redistricting, forcing an election between Lechowicz's alderman Carole Bialczak and Daley's hand-picked candidate, Michael Wojcik. It was ironic that Daley had appointed Bialczak to a vacant council seat at Lechowicz's request. Wojcik defeated Bialczak and went on to dethrone Lechowicz as ward committeeman.

The *Tribune*'s John Kass wrote of the aftermath of the two elections:

A week after the March primary, Lechowicz was walking through City Hall, pale and stiff, looking as if he had spent a month in a meat locker.

But Daley spotted him that morning, and instead of ignoring him, quickened his stride toward the aging Polish war horse. . . . "Hi, Ted," Daley chirped, locking eyes, then speaking without looking back as he passed his victim. "You OK?"

Lechowicz narrowed his eyes, smirked, nodded, and started a salute, as if he were a military casualty and not a tired guy in a loud sport coat with a "Kick Me" sign on his back. Some aides walking with the mayor giggled.

Still striding, some 30 feet farther on, the mayor spoke out of the side of his mouth. "I bet he's just standing there, right?"

And there was Lechowicz, trying to stare a hole in the back of the mayor's balding head, the lobby filling with city workers, the ex-ward boss being left behind, swallowed up by the crowd as the political workers and civilians pushed toward the elevators.[4]

The following year, Wojcik announced he was considering challenging Lechowicz for his county board seat, with Daley's support. Faced with this final existential threat, Lechowicz did the only thing he could do. He offered fealty to the mayor's brother and to his most important African American ally. As someone who enjoyed the genuflections of subordinates and his nightly greeting as "Mr. Commissioner" at the pol-saturated Gibson's Steakhouse near the Loop, Lechowicz was not too proud to bow and scrape to get back on the A list. As an effective politician and legislative tactician, Lechowicz had something real to offer, and he quickly became a useful tool in the Stroger-Daley alliance.

That's why I didn't expect the mayor to endorse me, but I also knew how he really felt about Lechowicz. After all, I had loyally and effectively served the mayor; Lechowicz had tried to topple an important family power base.

So my ask was a simple one: "Mayor, I'm not asking you to endorse me; I'm just asking that you not hurt me," I said.

"Oh, don't worry," Daley replied. "I won't hurt you."

Thinking I had secured the mayor's neutrality, I announced my campaign.

• • •

The county board election was what politicians call a "down-ballot" race, one of the last places you'll find the names of offices and candidates. In my case, it was *literally* the last contest on the ballot.

Voters tend to mark their ballots for the marquee races at the top of the ticket—president, senator, governor—and to a lesser degree Congress and the state legislature. But a lot never make it to the bottom. Many voters don't even know there's a contest down there, especially with endless rows of retention-seeking judicial candidates in between.

The news media also don't cover down ballot races, unless it's part of a newspaper's "wrap-up" story with a token paragraph about each race, so the paper can check the box saying it had informed its readers. It's perfunctory and among the back pages usually valued by subscribers for use in litter boxes and birdcages.

As a result, well-known incumbents, especially those backed by legions of door-knocking precinct captains, maintain a huge advantage in down-ballot contests. Lechowicz had many such advantages—his county power base, a campaign fund flush with hundreds of thousands of dollars, and the backing of every ward committeeman in the district. As a longtime state senator and county commissioner, he was well known on the Northwest Side, with a loyal following among a large contingent of Polish American voters.

I had no money and no organization. Taking on Lechowicz seemed like a suicide mission.

But I was motivated as much by anger as by ambition. It was a chance to challenge everything I hated about abusive government and self-serving politics. Lechowicz, conveniently, personified it all.

But to have a shot at winning, I had to be right on a few assumptions. On one, I was confident: Lechowicz would not spend most of the money in his campaign account.

Lechowicz was obsessed with feathering his own nest. His relentless decades-long quest to squeeze every dollar from state and local pension funds was an example. He also was singlehandedly responsible for the enormous 66 percent pay raise for county commissioners, orchestrating it in a surprise, cover-of-darkness, midnight vote. He was relentless when it came to securing dollars for himself.

And I was aware of something else.

In previous decades, Illinois pols often had accumulated large campaign war chests; on retirement, they converted the money to personal use. Under the law, if politicians paid taxes on it, the money legally was theirs to keep. This loophole put the normal temptations to trade votes for campaign contributions into overdrive. It was a corrupting force in an already corrupt system.

Calling it "legalized bribery," in 1998 a young state senator with the unusual name of Barack Obama decided this practice should end. Using his considerable skills, and an assist from his mentor, state senator Emil Jones, later president of the Senate, Obama put his fellow legislators in the uncomfortable position of voting to defend the indefensible.

Obama's bill passed. The long-standing practice of pocketing campaign cash was history.

Sort of.

This being Illinois, it wasn't quite that simple. The bill was prospective only. Under the new law, all campaign funds at the time of the bill's signing were "grandfathered." No one's retirement kitty would be at risk.

Since then, nearly sixty Illinois elected officials have paid themselves more than $6 million from campaign funds. Former state representative Ralph Capparelli pocketed $583,357 and did so while collecting a pension padded with even more gimmicks than Lechowicz's. At the time, he was garnering more than two hundred thousand dollars a year from local and state pension funds. The former Cook County sheriff Michael Sheahan supplemented his $225,000 annual taxpayer-funded pension with a $392,606 payout to himself.[5]

Among the grandfathered pols was Lechowicz, who had accumulated more than a quarter of a million dollars by the June 30, 1998, cut-off date.

So when I calculated my financial disadvantage, I felt comfortable subtracting several hundred thousand dollars. Of course, Lechowicz would still be able to shake down county contractors and employees for donations to fund his primary contest, but I wasn't looking at an insurmountable disadvantage.

Still, taking on every ward committeeman in the district in a low-profile, down-ballot race was a classic David-versus-Goliath scenario. But I wondered how hard the committeemen would work for Lechowicz with Daley on the sidelines and another big race with much more at stake on the ballot—the contest for governor.

Most Northwest Side committeemen were gearing up for a massive effort on behalf of Congressman Rod Blagojevich. Recruited into politics and elected through the support of his powerful father-in-law, Dick Mell, alderman and Thirty-Third Ward committeeman, Blagojevich was a slight favorite to win. The exuberant Mell was a popular figure in the city council. A self-made millionaire from his manufacturing company, Mell was in politics for the fun of it.

He was also the consummate transactional politician, a model practitioner of the old political adage, "There are no permanent alliances, only permanent interests." With a self-built, well-trained, and loyal organization of precinct captains, most with jobs secured by Mell, the alderman would often negotiate pacts with other candidates and invade far-flung territory with his army. More than one colleague compared Mell to an Afghan warlord.

Many of the traveling mercenaries in his crew were equally colorful. One of Mell's most effective captains was John "Quarters" Boyle, a flamboyant political operative who previously had run an armored car company under contract to the Illinois Tollway Authority. In the days when a trip on the tollway cost twenty-five cents, Boyle went to prison for pilfering $4 million in quarters. Several years later, Boyle was again indicted, this time for taking payoffs in his city job.

Another Mell captain was Dominic Longo, who doubled as treasurer of the dubiously named Coalition for Better Government (CBG). According to an investigation of the Chicago Teamsters Union, members were pressured for years to contribute to the CBG for "job security."[6]

The governor's office had not been in Democratic hands for a quarter of a century, and the incumbent Republican governor, George Ryan, was wounded by scandal. The local ward chieftains smelled blood—and jobs. Lots of them. Putting the governor's office under the control of a fellow committeeman from their backyard meant slicing open vast and previously untouchable veins of patronage jobs and contracts.

With such tantalizing rewards diverting the committeemen's energies, and the mayor uninvolved, I felt Lechowicz's organizational advantage could be mitigated.

By the time I realized I was wrong, it was too late to turn back.

• • •

As the filing date neared, I received a call from John Doerr, the mayor's director of intergovernmental affairs, asking me to meet him at city hall. When I arrived, Doerr told me Daley wanted me to drop out of the race.

"The mayor is taking heat from all the Polish American politicians," Doerr said. "He can't be pissing off the Polish community."

I got emotional hearing this change of heart from Daley. I knew it was B.S. First, the mayor wasn't worried about the wrath of the Polish community; Lechowicz wasn't some iconic ethnic representative. Second, Daley had promised me his neutrality in a face-to-face meeting. Now, after I had publicly committed, he was sending an emissary to ask me to meekly bow out. I refused.

Weeks later, not long after I filed nominating petitions and lost the lottery for top ballot position, the mayor made his perfidy official. The *Sun-Times* political columnist Steve Neal broke the news that Mayor Daley was endorsing Lechowicz. Almost worse, he was hosting Lechowicz's first campaign fundraiser.

When I had announced, Neal's fellow *Sun-Times* columnist Mark Brown had written a favorable column about my candidacy, while ripping Lechowicz's long history of skullduggery. Now, Lechowicz gleefully sent Brown a copy of the mayor's fundraising invitation.

John Daley had twisted his brother's arm—hard enough to get the mayor to swallow his distaste for Lechowicz and shaft a former top aide. Suddenly, all my calculations about the ambivalence of the ward organizations went out the window. Not only would Lechowicz be able to trumpet the popular mayor's support, but he would have each ward boss working hard on his behalf.

As I should have predicted, John saw my candidacy as a personal affront, an embarrassment in front of his county colleagues. Now that the three had made peace, how could John explain to both Lechowicz and Stroger that he couldn't control the actions of his brother's former chief of staff? John made it his mission to rally the Daley troops for Lechowicz and make an example of me.

On hearing the news, I was overcome with an odd, preternatural calm. It was strangely liberating to have no political ties to worry about, no calculations to modify what I said or did. I no longer had to limit my attacks to Lechowicz; I could bring the mayor's friend Stroger into the conversation where it served my purposes. More important, if I did manage to pull off the upset, I would owe nothing to Mayor Daley. I would be independent.

With no experienced campaign managers willing to take my race, I tapped a prelaw student, David Spiegel. What he lacked in experience he made up in enthusiasm. Pete Giangreco, a top national political consultant for Democrats at the

Strategy Group, took on direct-mail responsibilities, producing some of the more humorous and memorable mail pieces in local lore.

I decided to run a single-issue campaign around high property taxes, linking every Lechowicz tax vote, pay raise, and personal enrichment scheme back to homeowners' bills. Pete brilliantly condensed all this into the comic-book figure of "Tax Man," a pudgy antihero dressed in tights and a cape with Lechowicz's head superimposed. Tax Man traveled the city, raising everyone's property taxes, sales taxes, and income taxes while feasting personally on the revenue. In one mailer, Giangreco dredged up an old Lechowicz nickname, "Well-Fed Ted," and showed him dining at a fancy restaurant, his tie splattered with cheesecake.

Giangreco warned me about the difficulty of what we were undertaking. "You can run a perfect campaign, but you still won't win unless they run a bad one," he said. We held up our end with a nearly flawless campaign; luckily, Lechowicz gave us a shot by running a poor one. First, he let me own neighborhood mailboxes in the early weeks. I had started early, gambling I'd raise more money later. I emphasized the array of local park improvements when I was parks chief, and then shifted to the Tax Man attack.

When Lechowicz did fight back, it was with an odd insinuation that I was African American. His mail pieces said I was "not from the Northwest side," but "from down South," technically true since I grew up in Southern Illinois but intended to mean Chicago's Black South Side. His mail vendor darkened my picture to support the innuendo.

On the advice of Tom Manion, a friend and the longtime Daley field general, I had become the first Chicago candidate to put his photograph on campaign yard signs. As more of my signs sprang up, each one earned through hours of door-knocking, it slowly undercut the Lechowicz narrative that I was a Black interloper from the South Side. Lechowicz's racist, cynical strategy also looked increasingly foolish as I flooded the district with photo-filled mailers.

By the midpoint of the campaign, I had Lechowicz on his heels. Residents had begun to look forward to the next installment of Giangreco's Tax Man series, with its humorous and colorful storylines. I was increasingly recognized as I knocked on doors, primarily in the center of Lechowicz country in the vast bungalow belt. I was also collecting large donations from businessmen by framing the race as a referendum on predatory government, even providing enough money to air a TV ad.

To his delight, this gave my old media colleague, David Axelrod, a chance to contribute, producing a humorous ad playing off Lechowicz's "Pigs at the Trough" award from *Chicago* magazine. Even a casual viewer couldn't miss the spot, which abruptly kicked off with the images and loud snorts of dozens of pigs fighting over trough slop. When the first ad hit the airwaves on a Saturday morning, Axelrod grinned and said, "Well, Teddy's home phone is lighting up about now!"

Stroger, the county board president, began telling friends, "Teddy looks like a deer in headlights."

Unfortunately, John Daley and other sophisticated operatives took control and reminded Lechowicz of his biggest asset—Mayor Daley. From that point on, all of Teddy's mailers and door-to-door messaging was some version of "Lechowicz endorsed by Mayor Daley! Mayor Daley says he needs Ted Lechowicz on the county board!" The machine precinct captains responded to pressure from Stroger and Daley and ran hard with the new messaging.

Lechowicz's pals were also treating the race like a political jihad. After being defeated by Daley's candidate for Thirtieth Ward committeeman, Lechowicz had joined the Thirty-Second for protection. From Committeeman Terry Gabinski's standpoint, Lechowicz's seat was now a Thirty-Second ward seat, to be protected at all costs. Gabinski began pushing his captains hard; some crossed the line. Many of my volunteers came back from door-to-door canvassing to report being followed, punched, or shoved. Several had their tires slashed or their car windows broken. Even our Forty-Seventh-Ward-based headquarters had a brick thrown through the front window in the middle of the night, another gift from the Thirty-Second Ward. Yard signs that voters had agreed to display in Gabinski's neighborhoods vanished within minutes.

As election day neared, Kristi Lafleur, a friend and experienced campaign hand approached me. "You know, you can win the race and still lose it on election day," she said. In other words, it doesn't matter if you've won hearts and minds if the opposition ground troops have a monopoly on turning out the vote and on passing out palm cards and jawboning entering voters at the polling stations. I knew she was right, but few of my supporters could take a day off work; those that could had to be deployed strategically. Kristi trained volunteers and armed them with door hangers for known "plus" Claypool voters, palm cards for persuading voters going into vote, and two yard signs to plant on sidewalks near voting sites.

The ward bosses ensured that every precinct had multiple "leather-jacket guys," precinct captains working voters for the endorsed ticket, and especially the down-ballot race for county board, where voters were more likely to be persuaded on the way in. Many would agree to give their neighborhood captain some help, even if they were not willing to change their vote for a top-of-the-ticket race like governor.

I felt good about my home ward, where Schulter's troops would be out in force, and about Kristi's precinct operation, knowing we would have the most vote-rich precincts covered by at least one trained volunteer. But when I walked out my door on election morning, I saw what we were up against.

I lived a block off Ashland Avenue, one of the major north-south corridors in the city. As I turned the corner onto Ashland, my mouth was agape. As far as the eye could see in both directions, down the median of the thoroughfare, were Lechowicz signs—illegally occupying public property but still impressive as hell. As I turned the corner toward my polling place, similar lines of city property were adorned with endless waves of Lechowicz advertising. The polling places themselves seemed hidden behind walls of Lechowicz signs, with machine captains busily working the sidewalks.

Now I knew what Kristi had warned about—winning the race but losing it on election day. With the full weight of the mayor's political machine behind him, Lechowicz made up a lot of ground on the day votes were cast.

That night, I checked the Board of Elections website to see the returns, which showed me with a consistent lead. Lechowicz went ballistic, calling the board's executive director, Lance Gough. "What are you doing?!" he screamed at Gough, as if somehow it was Gough's job to ensure the totals put him in the lead.[7] By the evening's end, I had won 51.5 percent of the vote, just enough to take my seat on the Cook County Board. It had taken an enormous effort to overcome the Daley effect, but I had squeaked in.

That evening, I gathered with volunteers and supporters at a North Side tavern for a raucous celebration. Standing on top of the bar, I delivered my victory speech, then cranked up the loudspeakers to play the Beatles' classic song "Tax Man."

CHAPTER 23

Millennium Park

The road to the remarkable, final incarnation of Millennium Park was long and winding.

After Park District general counsel Randy Mehrberg's astonishing discovery—that the City of Chicago was the rightful owner of the expansive, prime lakefront acreage in Grant Park, not the Illinois Central Railroad, which had occupied it—Mayor Daley sued to gain control of the land and immediately set out to build a new park over the blight.[1]

Daley's initial plan, announced in April 1998, was modest, with a cost of $150 million. The city dubbed it "Lakefront Gardens," perhaps a homage to the unsuccessful civic proposal two decades before. It consisted of a sloping lawn as part of a new music venue with a three-hundred-seat indoor performance center behind an outdoor concert stage. The new green space would lie on a freshly constructed bridge covering the railroad acreage east of the Loop. A parking garage below would provide the revenues to pay for the construction.

On the surface, the plan seemed straightforward. But the engineering complexities of building a giant bridge, supported by hundreds of caissons, was a major challenge. In addition, innumerable risks accompany any underground construction, such as the proposed vast parking lot. But the most daunting challenge was the mayor's impatience. Managers and contractors were charged with completing the entire project in little more than two years, in time to celebrate the imminent millennium.

The frantic beginnings to Millennium Park underscore the aphorism, "Haste makes waste." Unlike most projects, construction on Millennium Park began before plans were complete and without the normal engineering and architectural designs, in part because of Mayor Daley's aggressive timeline. But it was also because the financing depended on completing the underground parking garage. The mayor had promised taxpayers the park would be built without their dollars.

Because of the project's importance and political visibility, Mayor Daley also set aside normal professional processes. He selected his longtime ally Ed Bedore, budget director under both Mayor Daleys, to lead the effort. Now operating as a consultant, Bedore was the mayor's go-to guy for big projects, including the successful construction of a new stadium for the Chicago Bears. In turn, Bedore provided a no-bid contract to the engineering firm of James McDonough for construction designs. McDonough, with deep ties to the Daley family, had been Streets and Sanitation commissioner during Richard J. Daley's administration.

Not until eight months later did the city hire a construction manager to oversee the project. Mayor Daley chose Lakefront Millennium Managers, a recently incorporated entity consisting of Kenny Construction and McDonough's firm, creating a situation in which McDonough would be overseeing its own work. Not only was this at odds with standard industry practice but it was also an extraordinary arrangement given the cost, complexity, and scope of the project.

"It's pretty hard to take a critical, objective view of the design when the design was done by a member of the construction team. If Lakefront tells McDonough there's a screw-up in engineering, well, they are the ones doing the engineering," said Professor Jim Rodger of California Polytechnic State University, who headed the university's construction management department.[2]

I was completing my second tour of duty as Daley's chief of staff during the time leading up to his spring 1999 reelection. Because of the importance of the Millennium Park project, I assigned my deputy chief of staff, Bridget Reidy, to be a watchdog on the construction. Reidy had proven to be a star manager during my park district tenure, overseeing contractors for the Michigan Avenue underground parking garages, the lakefront marinas, and Soldier Field.

Reidy began reporting back to me on emerging problems. The cash flow from the new garage, she believed, would be inadequate to cover debt service on the bonds.[3] She also objected to demolition plans affecting the bridge over the train tracks, which lacked proper designs and competitive bidding—concerns shared by Stan Kaderbek, the chief city engineer in charge of bridges and transit.

Reidy's questions and criticisms, however, began to rile Ed Bedore; behind my back, he complained to Mayor Daley about what he perceived to be her interference with his prerogatives. Without bothering to get the other side of the story, the mayor summoned me to his office to let me know he was removing Reidy from the project.

"I can't be having my deputy chief of staff spending all her time on one project," Daley told me. I was heartened by the mayor's concern for my deputy's time, but I fully understood what he was really saying: I can't have an upstart young woman questioning the decisions of experienced older men who are also longtime political allies.

The 2,500-space parking garage, the financial foundation of the park, proved costly and complex to build. Only two companies bid on the project, which included the bridge over the Metra tracks. The lower bid, by a joint venture of G. M. Harston Construction and Paul Schwendener, Inc., was 20 percent higher than city estimates. To save time, rather than rebidding, the mayor authorized a negotiation slightly lowering the price. But design flaws in the McDonough plans in the parking garage columns and a sprinkler system that proved to have inadequate pressure delayed the project out of the gate.

The city's mistakes and repeated pivots fueled more than a thousand design revisions—a handful at a time. The "project has turned into an expensive public-works debacle that can be traced to haphazard planning, design snafus and cronyism," the *Tribune* wrote, citing the soaring construction costs and multiyear delays.[4]

By the summer of 2000, the originally planned date for the park's opening, the city pulled Harston-Schwendener off the job, and responsibility for oversight was shifted from Lakefront Millennium Managers to Joseph Manzi, the same construction management expert who had assisted me at the park district and rode herd for Mayor Daley on construction of the Harold Washington Library.

With negative publicity mounting and delays and costs escalating, Daley summoned Manzi to his fifth-floor offices. In critical moments, Daley would often zero in on someone he believed could turn the tide against whatever challenge he was facing. He then worked to establish a personal relationship and ensure that no one got between him and his newly designated project leader. In the months that followed, Daley would summon Manzi repeatedly to his office for one-on-one briefings and strategy sessions.

Manzi told me of his first meeting with Daley in his back office, sitting in the easy chair while Daley sat on the couch. Manzi lived and worked in the suburb of Park Ridge, was not in any way part of Chicago's political or business milieu, and was private and circumspect. So he was surprised when Daley leaned forward, paused for a moment, and began the conversation by mentioning the death of Manzi's son from cystic fibrosis.

"How are you doing? I know what happened," Daley said. "I lost a son too. I know how tough it is."

"You're right," Manzi replied. "It's brutal. It's with you every bloody day."

As Manzi talked, he noticed Daley becoming emotional.

"I could see it was affecting him, as it would any father," Manzi recalled, "so I veered off because we were both welling up."[5]

Manzi had helped the mayor manage a politically sensitive construction crisis before; now he faced his biggest challenge yet, with enormous implications. He approached the job first as a herder of cats, organizing all the different entities and companies working for the city into a unified, coherent whole.

"Everyone was working in their own little foxholes," Manzi told me, "and the job looked like a bunch of individual dominos but with no unity to them, no organization—too sporadic."[6] He installed a new system of central control under city leadership. Gradually, Manzi began to restore stability, sequencing construction segments methodically and carefully documenting failures by contractors to meet timelines or specifications.

The biggest challenge was to bring order to the constantly shifting designs as elements of the project were changed or added, due to the evolving nature of Millennium Park. What started as a bridge with grass and flowers on top gradually became something quite different. The designers and engineers scrambling to keep up probably didn't understand it, but they were being buffeted primarily by one man, and it was no longer Mayor Daley.

It was John Bryan.

Daley had asked the Sara Lee CEO to raise $30 million in private donations to complement the park's original design with artwork. But Bryan believed that was too modest a sum.

When Daley had sent John Rogers and me to visit Bryan five years before to discuss his idea for a lakefront millennium monument, his timing was off and his idea impractical. Now, looking at the virgin twenty-four-acre site in the heart of Downtown, Bryan envisioned a series of great works of art organized into an unprecedented urban tableau. With his expansive Rolodex and southern charm, Bryan began to assemble Chicago's elite to paint the mosaic and raise the hundreds of millions of dollars it would take to pull it off.

Bryan's contributions in the rarified world of Chicago art and music were well established, but fewer knew of his long-standing commitment to civil rights. In his native Mississippi, in the 1960s, Bryan joined Black parents in suing the school board in his hometown of West Point for failing to integrate, in violation of the US Supreme Court's landmark decision in *Brown v. Board of Education*. The town of West Point had closed public schools rather than admit Black children. When the Black elementary schools reopened, Bryan enrolled his own children there.

But it was Bryan's ardent love of both art and Chicago that ignited his drive on Millennium Park.

The fabulously rich of America's great cities give to many charities, but donations tend to be concentrated heavily in the arts, education, or medical research. Sitting in his office one day, musing on his career, Bryan explained to me his choice of fundraising causes. Bryan said he had always been passionate about the arts and was amazingly good at raising funds in its advancement; but he made me laugh when he paused for a moment and added, "Besides, I could just never get into diseases."

Bryan's fellow conspirators in the business and philanthropic worlds, including his committee cochair Donna LaPietra, the CEO of Kurtis Productions, and business luminaries such as Marshall Field V, generated ideas and commissioned new works of art. The art dramatically affected the underlying construction already long underway. The foundational work of the park was never meant to support multiton structures, but the creativity and clout of Bryan's committee began slowly to require that it did.

To hit his goals, John Bryan followed the traditional triangle model of fundraising. Many people would contribute to the park's creation, and he would accept no less than $1 million from those capable of it, but he needed very large donations to form the base of his pyramid. These would be the "lead founder" gifts and carry naming opportunities. But one gift would be the largest and most significant—the "lead gift"—meant to inspire others to follow. The obvious naming opportunity for the lead gift was the new band shell that sat at the heart of the initial Lakefront Gardens plan.

In many great endeavors there comes a turning point, a seminal moment that, in retrospect, fundamentally altered the trajectory of a mission. For Millennium Park, it arrived in the form of a blunt-spoken civic leader and philanthropist, Cindy Pritzker. She had been approached by Bryan and LaPietra to underwrite the new music pavilion. But when Pritzker saw the design for the centerpiece structure and the larger park, which included traditional English-style formal gardens, she reacted with disappointment.

"What millennium are you talking about?" LaPietra remembers Pritzker asking rhetorically. "This is so yesterday. You need something forward looking."[7]

"That was a lightbulb moment," LaPietra told me. "That thought of hers not only flipped the *band shell*, but the sense of all the other *rooms* of the park. We almost immediately pivoted to a different strategy that looked only at designers and artists speaking toward the future, the up and comers in worlds of art and sculpture and design."[8]

The renowned Chicago architect Adrian Smith, whose company, Skidmore, Owings & Merrill, had created the park's master design, suggested commissioning Frank Gehry for a sculpture. Gehry was an extraordinary artist and architect who could create a masterpiece of lasting significance, something that would define the park for generations. But Gehry was in high demand, having gained international fame with his unique and spectacular design of the Guggenheim Museum in Bilbao, Spain, which opened in 1997.

Fortunately, the woman who had shifted the committee's focus to modernism was also the key to Gehry's heart and sat on Bryan's art and architecture committees—Cindy Pritzker. The Pritzker family, which among other assets controls the Hyatt Hotel chain, for many years had endowed the Pritzker Prize, considered the highest award in architecture. In 1989, before Gehry was a household name, he had been given the award, which led to a friendship between Cindy Pritzker and the architect. Pritzker was not only the path to Gehry but also the one who first suggested what Gehry should build—the band pavilion that would define the eastern portion of Millennium Park.[9]

The architect Ed Uhlir, the former planning chief for the park district, was lured out of retirement to help coordinate the design efforts. He flew to Los Angeles to meet Gehry. Gehry was overwhelmed with work and wasn't looking for a new commission. It wasn't until Uhlir revealed that Pritzker had suggested he design the music pavilion and would donate an initial $15 million that Gehry set aside his reluctance.

When Mayor Daley announced Gehry's project, the engineers again had to scramble to shore up the park's foundations. Gehry's design was revolutionary—a band shell dominated by a "headdress" of intertwined metal ribbons—seven hundred feet of crisscrossing metal pipes above a great lawn where concertgoers could picnic with views of the city skyline—and an acoustic system of symphony quality. The weight of the structure, combined with the effect of Chicago's winds on the metal ribbons, required seventeen new caissons and a rebuild of the tops of all those already in place.

Gehry cemented his indelible footprint on Millennium Park by also designing the pedestrian bridge connecting Pritzker Pavilion and Millennium Park to the rest of Grant Park and the lakefront. The bridge spans Columbus Drive and doubles as a sound barrier, protecting the musical venue from the noise of passing cars. Gehry chose a snakelike design of curving steel, adding a correlative visual to the undulating elements of his pavilion.

Even more foundational work was required to accommodate the committee's next project, a sixty-foot-long, thirty-foot-high elliptical sculpture resembling a jellybean, weighing 150 tons. The piece was called "Cloud Gate," referring to the sculptor Anish Kapoor's intent that the mirrorlike surfaces would reflect the sun, the sky, and the surrounding skyscrapers. Kapoor's proposal had been selected from several prominent artists. The most influential voice in support was Mayor Daley, who predicted Kapoor's work would rival Picasso's famous sculpture in the plaza of the Richard J. Daley Center.[10]

Cloud Gate, better known by its local moniker, the "Bean," became the most popular tourist draw, with gaggles of visitors snapping pictures of their reflections, surrounded by the city skyline and towering clouds and sun.

Yet another heavyweight addition came by virtue of Chicago's Crown family, led by the civic and business icon Lester Crown. *Crain's Chicago Business* described him as "the most civically engaged Chicago business figure of his generation."[11] Crown had played a critical role in the efforts to modernize and expand O'Hare Airport, among other endeavors.[12] The Crown family owns a significant percentage of the aerospace company General Dynamics, which merged with the family's original company, Material Services Corporation, the world's largest building materials distributor. Lester helped expand the Crown family's holdings into hotels, technology, and sports and entertainment, including a stake in the Chicago Bulls.

The Crown family's project was the only artwork directed independent of Bryan's architecture committee. The family contributed $10 million of the $17 million cost of a unique work of art leveraging advanced technology—an interactive video sculpture designed by the Spanish artist Jaume Plensa. The Crown Fountain consists of two fifty-foot-blocks of black granite facing each other from the opposite ends of a rectangular reflecting pool. LED lighting projects giant digital videos of the faces of more than one thousand Chicagoans in rotation. Water cascades down the sides into the open granite basin. At regular intervals, the mouths of the digital faces pucker and water spouts, appearing to originate from the lips of the faces, an innovation delighting untold numbers of children playing in the reflecting pool underneath, drenching themselves under the watchful eyes of parents arrayed along benches facing the fountain.

These preeminent and innovative works of art were further enhanced by the 1,500-seat Harris Music and Dance Theatre, tucked into the northern edge of Millennium Park and funded primarily with $39 million in donations and loans from the industrialist Irving Harris. Irving Harris was best known for his philanthropy and leadership in early childhood education. Asked why he had contributed such a spectacular sum to a center for the performing arts, he grinned and put his arm around his wife Joan, a longtime Chicago arts activist.

"Because of her," Irving said. "This is something Joan has dreamed of for 20 years."[13]

The Harris Theatre regularly features Chicago's Joffrey Ballet and Hubbard Street Dance Chicago. National and international groups also make stops, including the New York City Ballet.

The philanthropist Ann Lurie, better known for her affiliation with Lurie Children's Hospital, provided $10 million for the park's southern anchor. Lurie Gardens is a 2.5-acre collection of perennial flowers, grasses, and shrubs. Trees provide a canopy protecting the shade-loving plants while an open space allows the sun-loving perennials to flourish in Chicago's summer heat.

Millennium Park's odd man out sits in its northwest corner, abutting Michigan Avenue, a fountain and public plaza in striking contrast to the modernist theme of the rest of the park. Wrigley Square, funded in part by the chewing gum magnate William Wrigley Jr.'s foundation, contains a curving limestone peristyle. On the pedestal are engraved the names of donors of $1 million or more to Millennium Park, a lasting reminder of Chicago's moneyed elite at the turn of the twenty-first century.

Also fronting Michigan Avenue is the McCormick Tribune Plaza and Ice Rink. In the winter, the ice rink attracts more than a hundred thousand skaters and provides a center of energy and crowd watching akin to Rockefeller Center in New York. In the summer, the rink is transformed into a spacious outdoor dining plaza. In Chicago, of course, no large public works can be completed without at least one scandal. The lucrative contract for the site's restaurant was won by a group dominated by investors close to Mayor Daley, and the lease contained a clause exempting it from property taxes.

Mayor Rahm Emanuel, Daley's successor, sued to have the sweetheart terms overturned but was rejected by the courts. Daley blamed the deal on hidden conflicts of interest at the park district; a member of the committee choosing the winner was secretly having an affair with the restaurant's owner, and in fact was pregnant with their baby.

John Bryan's final contribution to Millennium Park came five years later, when the Art Institute completed its Modern Wing and connected its entry to Millennium Park via the Nicholas Bridgeway linking pedestrians to the south end of the park. The Italian architect Renzo Piano, the architect of the Modern Wing, also designed the bridge, inspired by the hull of a boat.

• • •

On July 15, 2004, the *Tribune* wrote:

The sun will rise Friday on an opened Millennium Park . . . above a blighted, sunken site once occupied by railroad tracks and a gravel parking lot. . . . Millennium Park, which cost more than $475 million and spans 24.5 acres, is quintessential Chicago. This city—that makes no small plans, that reversed the flow of its own river, that boasts the nation's tallest building, that forever labors to shed its "second city" status—could never be sated by a run-of-the-mill greensward.[14]

The night before the public opening, Mayor Daley held a private VIP reception. Women in formal dresses and men in tuxedos wandered around the new park, sipping cocktails and marveling at what they saw. I ran into John Callaway, the distinguished local public television host, dining with his wife at one of the many tables scattered throughout the plazas.

Callaway was joyful, expressing amazement at such an incredible civic triumph.

"Yeah," I said. "It was years late and millions over budget, but the park is so beautiful that in fifteen years no one will remember that."

Callaway responded: "Fifteen years? Hell, fifteen minutes!"

Writing in an economics journal not long after the park's completion, Ed Uhlir noted that developers from seven new condominium projects cited Millennium Park as the key to their successful sales. A 2005 commercial study projected that the impact of the park on Chicago's real estate market would exceed $1.4 billion within ten years. By 2006, within two blocks of Millennium Park, five towers, each more than fifty-five stories tall, were in the works, part of a remarkable twenty-one such new towers designed to serve Mayor Daley's burgeoning downtown population.[15] The combination of Millennium Park and Daley's adjacent theater district was predicted to generate from $428.5 million to $586.6 million for hotels, from $672.1 million to $867.1 million for restaurants, and between $529.6 million and $711.1 million for retailers over the following decade.[16]

In the first six months of the park's opening, more than 2 million people visited. The travel company Priceline reported that the most requested destination in the United States for the summer of 2006 was Millennium Park. Visitor spending in the subsequent decade was said to exceed $2 billion.

Millennium Park succeeded at long last in linking the upscale "Magnificent Mile" north of the Chicago River with a new, culturally resplendent cultural mile to the south. The park was the punctuation mark on Daley's long, steady effort to rebuild Downtown and make Chicago an international city and a tourist mecca.

With a deep understanding of his city, Daley served for the most part as his own chief of planning, and he was skilled in using the vast powers of his office to marshal public and private resources in the service of remaking Chicago. With Millennium Park, he had done what even Daniel Burnham could not—remove the Illinois Central railroad tracks, reclaim the land for the people, and not only restore the legendary architect's vision of a unified "verdant setting" but also create a magnificent front lawn for Chicago of priceless treasures and transcendent beauty.

As for John Bryan, without whom Millennium Park could not have happened, he secured his own vision of a monument for the twenty-first century that would define Chicago for generations to come.

Mayor Daley and Democratic National Committee Chairman David Wilhelm hold a street sign signifying Chicago's selection as host of the 1996 Democratic National Convention at the United Center on Madison Avenue, August 4, 1994. Credit: Richard J. Daley Library, Special Collections, University of Illinois-Chicago.

Mayor Daley, proudly sporting his favorite team's baseball cap, with the team owner Jerry Reinsdorf and Park District Superintendent Forrest Claypool, announcing a $1 million donation from the White Sox to rebuild baseball diamonds in city parks, May 24, 1995. Credit: Richard J. Daley Library, Special Collections, University of Illinois-Chicago.

An exuberant Mayor Daley, Grand Marshall of the 1996 Bud Billiken Parade, rides down Martin Luther King Drive on the city's South Side, waving to parade spectators. Credit: *Chicago Tribune* archive photo.

President Bill Clinton watches as Mayor Daley addresses the crowd at the Oscar Mayer School, celebrating school reform successes, October 1997. Credit: Richard J. Daley Library, Special Collections, University of Illinois-Chicago.

Mayor Daley shakes hands with residents of the ABLA public
housing projects, following announcement of rehab plans in 1997.
Credit: Ovie Carter/*Chicago Tribune*.

Mayor Daley with the Millennium Park artists and designers: left to right, Anish
Kapoor (Cloud Gate, a.k.a. The Bean); Frank Gehry (Pritzker Music Pavilion
and BP Bridge); Jaume Plensa (Crown Fountain); Kathryn Gustafson (Lurie
Gardens); and the Millennium Park Committee Chair, John Bryan, July 16, 2004.
Credit: Richard J. Daley Library, Special Collections, University of Illinois-Chicago.

Mayor Daley escorts his wife Maggie out of Northwestern Memorial Hospital in July 2006 after her outpatient breast cancer surgery. Credit: Nancy Stone, *Chicago Tribune*.

President Barack Obama, First Lady Michelle Obama, Mayor Daley, and the Olympian Jackie Joyner Kersee at a 2009 event on the South Lawn of the White House promoting Chicago's bid for the 2016 Summer Olympic Games. Credit: Michael Tercha, *Chicago Tribune*.

"NO, RICHIE...THOSE AREN'T *OLYMPIC* TORCHES!"

Jack Higgins's satiric perspective on the reversal of Mayor Daley's political fortunes, 2009. Credit: Jack Higgins, *Chicago Sun-Times*.

Mayor Daley receives a standing ovation after his final city council meeting, Wednesday, May 4, 2011. Credit: Nancy Stone/*Chicago Tribune*.

Fifth Term

2003–2007

CHAPTER 24

Deadly Silos

A big city mayor is like the CEO of a giant company, overseeing a sprawling and intricate organization. Whether a large government or a multinational corporation, highly scaled and complex institutions depend on specialization for effective management, producing isolation between units known as silos. Human nature tends to exacerbate their isolating impact. Without responsibility for the organization as a whole, employees and managers tend to think only of their areas of expertise or immediate role and objectives, while vigilantly protecting their bureaucratic turf. If not managed properly, silos can impede productivity and accountability.

They can also be deadly.

Two simultaneously unfolding national scandals laid bare the risk of poorly managed silos.

In the early 2000s, scores of military veterans suffered long delays in accessing medical care at Veterans Affairs (VA) hospitals. Many died before they could receive treatment. Employees and supervisors across dozens of VA hospitals were aware that official waiting lists were being manipulated to reflect shorter wait times.

The official VA goal, tied to performance incentives, was to ensure that no patient waited more than fourteen days for an appointment. With doctor shortages, however, hospitals struggled to meet deadlines. Instead, they adopted gaming strategies to make their waiting lists look shorter. Some patients were put on secret waiting lists off the books. The VA's Phoenix, Arizona facility had 1,700 patients on a secret list. In other instances, hospital staff scheduled patients without notifying them, ensuring they would not show up, and then booked new appointments to restart the clock.

These practices were not coordinated; rather, they occurred organically. Harried supervisors issued vague orders to "fix" the scheduling problems. In doing so, clerical staff displayed varying degrees of inventiveness. Knowledge of the deceptions was widespread. Yet up and down the chain, individual employees and managers either did not understand the implications or felt it was not their responsibility to raise an alarm.

In the same decade, numerous General Motors (GM) engineers, managers, and lawyers were aware of a flaw in the Cobalt ignition switch that could accidently turn off the engine while the car was in motion, causing the driver to lose control while simultaneously disabling safety features such as airbags, antilock brakes, and power steering.

By 2014, GM was forced to recall 2.6 million vehicles and acknowledge it had known about the defect, continued to sell the defective cars for years, and concealed the defect from the public and regulators. By then, 124 people had died in accidents caused by the fatal flaw. Hundreds more had been injured or maimed.

In a postmortem analysis by the Chicago law firm of Jenner & Block, commissioned by GM, the lead attorney, Anton Valukas, unsparingly detailed how employees across different departments failed to act, despite a remarkable amount of evidence that lives were at risk.

In a 2012 meeting of GM lawyers reviewing litigation claims, for example, a junior attorney pointed out the overwhelming evidence of the deadly defect and asked why no recall had been ordered. Other lawyers assured him that engineers were aware of the problem.

"The Cobalt ignition switch passed through an astonishing number of committees. But determining the identity of any actual decision-maker was impenetrable," Valukas wrote. "Although everyone had a responsibility to fix the problem, nobody took responsibility."[1]

In the GM and VA scandals, individuals had important information with life-or-death consequences yet did nothing, because they believed it was not within their area of responsibility. Or they believed someone else was dealing with the problem. Similarly, silos sometimes turn deadly because of a failure to connect the dots—resulting from incomplete or flawed procedures, inadequate communication, and unclear managerial roles and responsibilities.

In 2003, a year of tragedy in Chicago, those failures in Mayor Daley's government, now in its fifth term, proved catastrophic.

• • •

It wasn't supposed to be open that night. It wasn't supposed to be open at all.

On the evening of February 16, 2003, up to 1,500 guests crowded into the E2 nightclub, operating on the floor above an upscale restaurant on the near South Side. The revelers were at the club, known for its raucous dance parties, despite a July court order closing it for eleven different building and fire code violations. E2 simply carried on, even advertising heavily.

Shortly after 2 a.m., firefighters responded to a 911 call. Security guards had used pepper spray to break up a fistfight between two women. Reports vary about what happened next. One witness said someone shouted, "Poison gas!" Another heard, "Terrorist attack!" The security detail formed a human chain attempting to stop departures, adding to the panic. But the combination of an eye irritant wafting into the crowd and shouted warnings triggered a stampede.

The club's exit doors were inexplicably locked; others were obstructed by supplies. The main front glass doors were quickly blocked by a crush of bodies. Firefighters, their rescue efforts slowed by the locked doors, arrived at a harrowing scene of bodies piled on top of each other in the single stairwell leading to the ground floor.

"People were being trapped underneath you . . . so we're actually standing on people's heads, and we didn't even know it," Amishoov Blackwell told the *Associated Press*. "It was bodies laying everywhere." Blackwell said one man struggling to breathe asked to hold his hand and said, "If I don't make it, tell my mom that I love her."[2]

Patrons were crushed or suffocated; some suffered cardiac arrest. By the time first responders could rescue and treat all the trapped partygoers, twenty-one were dead. Another fifty-five were injured, many hospitalized. So many people needed medical help that some patrons assisted paramedics by carrying lifeless bodies to waiting ambulances.

For years, neighbors had been petitioning to close the nightclub. Assaults and shootings around the business were common, at least eighty incidents in three years. The city had been in court three times to enforce compliance of the closure order, including the previous month. Nonetheless, the club continued to operate normally.

The Fire Department sent inspectors to the property multiple times, but during the day, when the second floor was empty. Police responded with regularity to calls about altercations at the club but were never made aware of the outstanding code violations and closure orders. Each city department—Buildings, Law, Fire, and Police—operated in the isolation of its own silo. The lack of communication and coordination was deadly.

In a follow-up court enforcement appearance the previous September, a city attorney had told a judge a city inspector had found "exiting issues" and promised to alert the Fire Department. "They should address those issues," he said.[3]

Two months before the tragedy, the neighborhood organization Bringing About Reform (BAR) wrote a letter to E2's lead owner, Dwaine Kyles, warning of protests and an organized boycott if "extreme overcrowding" conditions were not addressed.

"One of the callers indicated that the dance floor was so crowded, she could not move. You should certainly be aware that, should an event such as a fire break out in your establishment, the results could be catastrophic," BAR President Derrick Mosley wrote. Mosley never got a response.

The city announced a criminal investigation and an attorney representing victims secured a court order to photograph and videotape the club before it could be cleaned. The *Sun-Times* reported the scene:

"Clothes, shoes and socks, hair extensions, jewelry and eyeglasses still cover the floors and stairs. Coats still drape the chairs. Upstairs, where paramedics made the floor into a triage center, the latex gloves, syringes, and the empty containers of epinephrine they used to try to revive people still were scattered about. Photos and videos show the front stairwell is long, narrow, and steep."[4]

In the wake of the catastrophe, the most obvious question was how the nightclub could so brazenly ignore community protests and court orders for so long—and get away with it. E2 cleared an estimated $20,000 to $25,000 per night, so its owners had a clear incentive to circumvent the law.

The week following the disaster, Mayor Daley announced a blue-ribbon committee to investigate, headed by two leading African American attorneys—Andrea Zopp, a Sara Lee corporation executive and former prosecutor, and William Cousins, a former appellate court judge.[5]

"Clearly there are some communication issues between city agencies that need to be addressed," Zopp told the media. "It seems to me there was no communication at all between the city and the police." The Zopp-Cousins report, released in early July, confirmed the obvious: better communication between the city departments could have prevented the tragedy. The police and fire departments needed timely information on building-code violation orders to ensure enforcement.

"The corporation counsel's office handles cases in court and then hands off," Zopp said. "The problem is there's no clear authority about what happens after they hand off. You can't point to one person because the system to deal with this isn't there yet."[6]

Two months later, Daley proposed reforms, including a centralized database for court-ordered closings, a requirement of self-inspection by owners, and new rules on safety exit signage and evacuation routes.

The nightclub owners, Dwain Kyles and Calvin Hollins, were cleared of manslaughter charges but convicted of criminal contempt and sentenced to two years in prison. Neither man served time, however, as a series of appeals, reversals, and more appeals worked their way through the system over the following twelve years. In 2013, an Illinois appellate court ruled that the original sentencing had relied on the clubgoers' deaths and injuries, even though the owners' actions were not "the legal proximate cause" of the tragedy.[7] After consulting with the families of victims, the corporation counsel, Steve Patton, negotiated a deal to sentence Kyles and Hollins to two years of probation and five hundred hours of community service.

"If any message comes out of this hearing, it's the importance of building orders," Patton said. "Public health and safety hinges on these orders. If we don't take seriously a violation under these circumstances, when do you?"[8]

• • •

In June 2003, young adults assembled at one of the city's countless apartment get-togethers, celebrating on a beautiful Chicago evening. The partygoers gathered on the third-floor back porch of a building in Lincoln Park, sharing drinks and engaging in small talk. Around midnight, between forty and fifty people were on the porch when, without warning, the deck collapsed. The falling platform, along with the weight of victims, brought down the balconies beneath it and crushed people below. Thirteen people died, most in their twenties.

Mere months after the E2 nightclub disaster, this horrific tragedy again raised questions about the adequacy and enforcement of the city's building codes, and communication between departments, landlords, and contractors. The porch had been constructed without the required permit and was improperly built. The deck jutted out a foot beyond what was permissible and exceeded the allowed square footage by more than 50 percent, likely contributing to the disaster. In addition, the contractor did not use support beams of the required size.

If the building code had been observed, the accident likely would never have happened. But the number of porches and decks in Chicago easily exceeded one hundred thousand, and it would be unrealistic to expect that all of them could be examined. Nonetheless, Daley ordered a blitz of inspections, relying mostly on calls to the city's complaints hotline. By winter, the Buildings Department had surveyed four thousand porches and found four hundred sufficiently dangerous to take the owners to court.

Daley's administration sued the owners and managers of the Lincoln Park building, eventually settling the case with fines and a ban on any further work in Chicago by the contractor. Closing a loophole, Daley also pushed through a new licensing requirement for general contractors.

"When general contractors exhibit poor workmanship, we encourage landlords and tenants to report them to the city of Chicago, so we can follow up and possibly suspend their licenses or prohibit them from obtaining permits," Daley said.[9]

The city council passed a new law requiring leases to contain warnings about overloaded decks and to provide a checklist for owners or renters to determine if a building complied with city code. The Buildings Department listed three approved porch designs on its website, waived design fees, and allowed expedited permits for those using them. Letters were mailed to all city landlords warning of their responsibilities.

"But I want to remind everyone that new laws, improved regulation and stepped-up enforcement will never supplant the day-to-day responsibility of landlords and tenants," Daley said.[10]

• • •

A common superstition is that catastrophes come in threes, and so it was for Chicago in 2003.

On October 17, Cook County State's Attorney Dick Devine was huddled with members of his team on the twenty-second floor of the county's downtown office building. They were interrupted by an intercom announcement instructing them to evacuate because of a fire in the building.

A small blaze had broken out in a supply room on the twelfth floor of the thirty-five-story building. The Fire Department responded with 145 firefighters and paramedics. To extinguish the flames, firefighters opened the door connecting the supply room to the adjacent stairs. This gave them access to the blaze but also allowed smoke to escape into the enclosed stairwell.

As Devine and his staff joined other building tenants in descending, smoke from below was rising in the stairwell, creating a chimney effect. As they neared the twelfth floor, the smoke was so dense that a firefighter told them to go back up. As they ascended, Devine's group tried the door on each floor, trying to get back to safety. Each one was locked—including their own offices on the twenty-second floor. Investigators learned later that stairwell doors in the building locked automatically.

Finally, on the twenty-seventh floor, Devine's group found an open doorway; a staffer had had the presence of mind to place a doorstop before exiting. Other employees were not so lucky. Thirteen people neither made it down to the lobby nor up to the open twenty-seventh-floor door. After the blaze was extinguished, firefighters found them, unconscious. Seven were resuscitated. Six perished.

Once again, Fire Department procedures were in question.

More than ninety minutes passed between 911 calls from victims trapped in the stairwell and the arrival of rescuing firefighters, a delay that Fire Commissioner James Joyce could not explain. An anonymous city official later told the *Sun-Times*, "I don't know why they didn't send someone directly to 21 [after receiving cell phone calls that people were trapped there]. The elevators were in service. The building is not a towering inferno, it's just a floor or two. That's something that has to be addressed."[11]

Fire Department protocol called for first responders to take over a building's public address system. In contained fires in high-rises, tenants are safer if they remain in their offices. The announcement by building personnel to evacuate, however, was never countermanded by firefighters.

Cook County's public guardian, Patrick Murphy, whose office represents abused and neglected children, seniors, and disabled people, lost three employees in the fire.

"Once they were sent into that stairwell, they were in a coffin," he said. "Why would you have a system of doors that sends people into that?"[12]

After six weeks of review, Daley released the city's internal report. In it, the city accepted blame for failing to take command of the building's address system and carry out a top-to-bottom search of the stairwells. It faulted the building's managers for ordering the evacuation in contravention of training in the city's high-rise evacuation procedures.

The disaster was a product of missed opportunities, siloed communication, and a failure to follow procedures across groups, in and outside of the Fire Department's chain of command.

The Fire Department issued a new High-Rise Incident Command Order, with procedures to facilitate more effective communications between 911 dispatch, the incident commander, and the firefighters inside the building. The city building code was amended to require mandatory life-safety reviews by building owners and managers, new mandates for sprinklers, and requirements to prevent stairwell doors from locking in emergencies.

One year later, the reforms were tested when firefighters responded to a major fire on the twenty-ninth floor of the Loop's LaSalle Bank building. This time, the new procedures proved effective; the blaze was extinguished with no casualties.

By the end of 2003, this trio of horrific tragedies had called into question the adequacy of Chicago's building and fire codes, the city's enforcement of those codes, and the ability of the Daley administration to communicate and coordinate competently within its own government. Silos—and the inadequate mechanisms to manage across them effectively—had proved lethal.

Forty people had perished, most of them young, and hundreds more had been injured. Building and fire codes were revised and improved, but the need for simple, better coordination and communication across silos was at the heart of each calamity.

The Daley administration learned hard lessons that improved the city's safety but at a terrible cost.

CHAPTER 25

Scandal

In early 2003, Mayor Daley was at the peak of his power. He had just won a fifth term in office, dispatching his opponent in a landslide. Under his fourteen-year rule, Chicago had changed for the better, and voters across the city gave him a big share of the credit.

But as Daley rode the wave of popularity and consolidated his power, he also changed. The people around him changed. The way he went about his business changed. And those changes had consequences.

In the next few years, Daley would face an existential threat to his mayoralty. The former prosecutor would find himself in need of a criminal defense attorney. The FBI would question him in his fifth-floor office. His administration would be engulfed by major scandals over the distribution of jobs and contracts—levers that since time immemorial had been at the heart of mayoral power in Chicago.

• • •

It might have been Chicago's first mayor, William Ogden (1837–38), who stumbled on the value of a good patronage job or a well-placed municipal contract to secure political loyalty, a practice that generations of future mayors, mostly Irish, would follow. But it was the Bohemian immigrant Anton Cermak, elected mayor in 1931, who recognized that spreading the benefits of power beyond the Irish to all the city's ethnic groups—Italians, Poles, Jews, Germans, and Czechs—could fuel a political machine.

As chairman of the Cook County Board and leader of the local Democratic Party in the 1920s, Cermak made adroit use of patronage and ethnic ticket balancing, helping to create the fabled Chicago machine, which reached its apex under the direction of Mayor Richard J. Daley from 1955 to 1976. (Having perfected the model, Cermak served just two years as mayor. He was slain in 1933 by an assassin's bullet meant for President-Elect Franklin Delano Roosevelt, with whom the unlucky political boss was sharing an open car.)

In this powerful machine's heyday, the Democratic Party and city hall acted as interlocking gears. Anyone wanting a job first had to prove themselves in the precincts, ringing doorbells and helping deliver the vote. The former Mayor Jane Byrne recounted her first meeting with Richard J. Daley. "I could name you to any post," he said. "But if you don't help out, no matter what I try to do, they'll get you down below. So go out and work for your ward organization."

Byrne did. "That's how I got started," she said.[1]

The party also was insular. In 1948, an idealistic University of Chicago law student (and future congressman), Abner Mikva, inspired by Adlai Stevenson's gubernatorial campaign, tried to volunteer at his local Democratic ward office. He was greeted by a cigar-chomping precinct captain who looked at him with great suspicion. "Who sent you?" asked the man at the desk. When Mikva explained that no one had sent him, the captain tersely dispatched him. "We don't want nobody nobody sent!"[2]

In addition to awarding jobs, Richard J. Daley made an artform of "pinstripe patronage," rewarding with lucrative public contracts a web of politicians, donors, and others whose support he needed. To cement his power, Daley was more than willing to tolerate a degree of graft among members of the party. "I let them take so much, but no more," he allegedly once explained to a skittish business supporter.

Leaders of the machine were involved in so many public and private deals that the legendary newspaper columnist Mike Royko suggested that Chicago should change its city motto from *Urbs in Horto*, which means "City in a Garden," to *Ubi est mea,* or "Where's Mine?"[3]

Richard J. Daley leveraged his power to become Daley the Builder, constructing airports and highways, high rises, and parks. His congressmen and state legislators brought home the bacon with new revenue, grants, funding for construction projects, and legal waivers and state permissions to remake his city. Patronage greased the wheels; control of vast quantities of votes ensured that his voice was heard and his wishes for the most part heeded. As municipalities are creatures of the state, and thus legally subservient, Daley's power also protected Chicago against encroachment by hostile politicians in Springfield.

• • •

The mayor's son, Richard M. Daley, was an unlikely reformer. He had served as an enforcer for the machine in Springfield and benefited from pinstripe patronage in his young law practice.

But he had turned to liberal reformers as allies on his father's death and pledged to honor antipatronage decrees as state's attorney and mayor. In 1983, Mayor Harold Washington signed the federal court decree allowing patronage hiring for only nine hundred sensitive or supervisory positions in a city workforce of forty thousand. When Daley assumed the mayoralty, he was legally bound to its terms. He managed to reward supporters with key jobs early in his administration without running afoul of the law while also abiding by state and municipal procurement rules.

Only once in Daley's first four terms did he face a serious scandal.

For years, the mayor had socialized with an ex-felon with close ties to the Chicago mob, John Duff Jr., even facilitating large contracts to Windy City Maintenance, allegedly a woman-owned enterprise under the city's affirmative action program because it was owned by Duff's wife under her maiden name, Patricia Green.[4]

In 1999, the *Tribune* disclosed that Windy City Maintenance's status as a woman-owned firm was a sham. The company was actually run by a younger Duff son, James. In addition to the scheme involving his mother, James had convinced an African American employee to pose as the operating owner of a temporary services company receiving city contracts under the minority set-aside program. Eventually, the federal government charged James Duff with thirty-three counts of fraud, including allegations he avoided $3 million in workers compensation premiums by classifying his blue-collar laborers as white-collar clerical employees.[5] Duff pled guilty and was sentenced to nearly ten years in prison. Charges against his mother were dropped due to her ill health.

When the scandal broke, Daley moved swiftly into damage-control mode. The mayor's outreach to female and minority contractors had been one of his political strengths. If it now appeared that many of those efforts were fake, it could damage him—especially in the African American community, where his support had grown but remained soft. Black aldermen complained loudly about the previous year's numbers—just 9 percent of $1.3 billion in city contracts went to African American firms.

Daley appointed Barbara Lumpkin, the African American city treasurer, to lead a task force on identifying more minority-owned companies. Then he announced that for the first time, the city would do more than take an applicant's word that it was a minority enterprise; it would conduct checks of company sites and interview customers to guard against fraud.

When the *Tribune* first began investigating the Duffs and their illicit scheme, Daley had professed that he knew them, but said they weren't social friends.

"I know them, but I don't know them personally," he said. "I know a lot of people as mayor."[6]

But Daley had been seen dining with the Duffs at their favorite hangout, the Como Inn on Milwaukee Avenue, and socializing with them at the same gym. The Duffs hosted fundraisers for the mayor and even supplied financial support and workers for Daley's favored candidates.

Mayor Daley's close relationship with the Duffs is mysterious. It may have had its origins in social relations between Jack Duff, Jr. and the mayor's father, Richard J. Daley. Sources indicated they may have spent vacation time together at the home of the hotel workers union leader Ed Hanley, a mayoral friend who owned a home in Land O' Lakes, Wisconsin. Duff had a vacation house nearby.

Jack Duff Jr.'s death in 2008 freed the FBI to release his file to the Better Government Association (BGA) pursuant to a Freedom of Information Act request. Although filled with redactions of names and details, the six hundred pages of intelligence mention the younger Daley more than twenty times. Nothing infers wrongdoing by the mayor, but it supports the notion that Daley was close to the Duffs.

One unidentified FBI source reported the following: "Whenever [redacted] would contact [redacted], Jack Duff, Jr., and it was Jack Duff, Jr. who would call city hall. After complaining to [redacted] whatever the problem was, it was corrected, such as the pay problem. [Redacted] said it was common knowledge that Jack Duff, Jr. and Mayor Daley were close friends and that Jack Duff, Jr. had direct access to the mayor."[7]

When members of the Duff family were indicted in the minority-enterprise scam several years after the *Tribune*'s investigation, Daley was only slightly more forthcoming about the nature of his relationship.

"Oh, I know them. Sure," he said. "You know that. They're hard-working people. This is an unfortunate incident." When asked about the family's ties to organized crime, the former prosecutor said, "Geez. I don't know about that."[8]

The Duffs' contracting scandal had been an embarrassment to Daley and a political liability in minority communities, but it was not a threat to his power or his status as mayor. For the most part, Daley ran a clean ship, and his numerous accomplishments earned him plaudits and reelections.

That changed a few years later, following his election to a fifth term, when huge contracting and patronage scandals threatened his mayoralty and even his freedom.

• • •

The seeds of Daley's twin scandals germinated in fertile soil as the mayor's hubris grew and the nature of his city hall team evolved. But its roots actually dated as far back as 1988, when Ald. Ed Vrdolyak's collapsing star ignited the supernova HDO—the Hispanic Democratic Organization, which would eventually grow into the most powerful political arm of Daley's new machine and play an outsized role in the illegalities threatening the mayor's reign.

For four years, Vrdolyak had led white resistance to the city's first Black mayor, assembling a majority coalition on the fifty-member city council. But Mayor Harold Washington eventually won control of the council and crushed Vrdolyak's third-party candidacy for mayor in 1987. Vrdolyak then tried to resuscitate his career as a Republican candidate for Clerk of the Circuit Court. His Tenth Ward Latino precinct captains balked, refusing to serve the party of Ronald Reagan.

As Vrdolyak's most powerful captain, Al Sanchez had leveraged Vrdolyak's clout to find jobs for the ward's blue-collar workers left idle by the decline of the Southeast Side's steel industry. Now he saw which way the winds were blowing and brokered a meeting with Rich Daley's brother, Eleventh Ward Committeeman John Daley. Tim

Degnan and his deputy, Victor Reyes, also attended. The Daleys saw an opportunity both to further diminish Vrdolyak and to strengthen their hand with Latino voters. Vrdolyak's Latino crew pledged fealty, and HDO began its climb to prominence.

Under the direction of Reyes and Sanchez, a nascent version of HDO played a small role in Daley's 1989 election. Its size and influence grew in the mid-1990s, when the political consigliere Tim Degnan, the head of the Office of Intergovernmental Affairs (IGA) and a longtime Daley confidant, retired. He was replaced by Reyes. Degnan was understood to be the most powerful person at city hall not named Daley. As a founder of HDO now occupying Degnan's seat, Reyes moved quickly to cement a similar status.

Waves of HDO political workers soon found homes in city government and in turn worked precincts on the mayor's behalf, whether in his own campaigns or in support of his allies in the city council and state legislature. In time it merged with—or subsumed—the informal political network born under Degnan in the 1989 campaign. Daley election coordinators in all fifty wards forwarded job recommendations for exemplary precinct workers, and less powerful Democratic ward organizations were pushed to the margins of influence.

If there was a coming-out party for HDO, it arrived on a rainy, windswept March day in 1998. The popular independent state senator Jesús "Chuy" García lost renomination in the Democratic primary to an unknown HDO police officer, Antonio "Tony" Muñoz from the Eleventh Ward. The district sprawled across the West and Southwest Side neighborhoods of McKinley Park, Little Village, Back of the Yards, and Brighton Park and into suburban Cicero.

García never saw it coming. The HDO leaders had conspired with white ward bosses to bring an army of workers to campaign for Muñoz. On election day, the rain poured from dawn to dusk; handfuls of soaked García workers could be seen campaigning under awnings and at bus stops. Muñoz workers, however, were everywhere—outfitted with raincoats. They lined up two and three deep in precincts to greet incoming voters and plastered Muñoz signs on every corner, in every commercial business, on every building and fence post.

As part of the same stealth blitz, HDO targeted three other independents and beat all but one.

On election night, García pointedly congratulated Mayor Daley rather than his opponent.

"They had a good day," said García. "This was probably the most effective mobilization of the city-county patronage army in a long time. I don't think I've seen it like this in my fourteen years in elected office."[9]

The word was out. HDO had become a formidable political force. By the early 2000s, HDO was raising nearly three-quarters of a million dollars a year and had elected from its membership three state senators, a state representative, and three aldermen.

By 2003, independent politicians were playing ball with Daley and HDO. By then, HDO had at least a thousand members on city payrolls, according to a *Tribune* analysis, and many more wannabes who could be called on to overwhelm precincts on behalf of HDO-supported candidates. The most visible sign of surrender by independents came in the fall of 2003 at HDO's tenth-anniversary fundraiser at Navy Pier. HDO shrewdly decided to "honor" a half dozen independent Latino state and local elected officials. All but one—Metropolitan Water Reclamation District Commissioner M. Frank Avila—accepted both the invitation and plaques from HDO officials on stage.

When the *Chicago Reader*'s Ben Joravsky caught up with the independent Thirty-Fifth Ward Ald. Rey Colón, Colón was sheepish.

"You're making me feel sort of guilty," Colón said about lending his name to HDO's fundraiser. "I guess it looks like I'm part of the lineup. I won't give you any BS about this—the mayor's been good to me so far. Everybody in City Hall has been bending over backwards."[10]

The one-two punch of stick (HDO) and carrot (regal treatment from the mayor's office) wore down the opposition. Daley's ability to carry out his agenda free from dissent elevated his power and popularity to unparalleled heights.

Ensconced at city hall in Tim Degnan's former role, Victor Reyes had methodically expanded his influence and that of HDO. With the mayor's support, and with Intergovernmental Affairs under Reyes increasingly acting as the nerve center of city government, key departments fell under HDO control. The former HDO treasurer Michi Peña assumed command of the powerful General Services Department. Reyes's ally Bea Reyna-Hickey ran the Revenue Department. Most powerful of all, Reyes's HDO cofounder, Al Sanchez, became the commissioner of Streets and Sanitation.

At the same time, the lines separating governance from politics were blurring or disappearing altogether.

• • •

In the fall of 2003, the fickle finger of fate showed up on a leafy Chicago neighborhood block, where city crews were repairing water pipes. An award-winning investigative reporter for the *Sun-Times*, Tim Novak, lived on that street.

Walking out of his house one morning, Novak noticed a parked red truck. It had a sign affixed saying it was leased to the City of Chicago. Curious, Novak began to watch and eventually spent five days staking out city water crews and their hired trucks. Other than a trip to McDonald's, the hired trucks never moved—never carried any equipment or materials, never hauled any waste debris, and never transported any personnel. Each truck was billed to taxpayers at fifty dollars an hour.

The idle red truck led Novak to many more idle trucks until the fleet was so large—and the spider web of associated corruption so wide and deep, so tangled and enmeshed in the city power structure—that it brought the FBI to the fifth floor of city hall and threatened the mayoralty of Richard M. Daley.

The genesis of the scandal happened much earlier, and I played a part.

I had begun my second stint as Daley's chief of staff in January 1998, following a scandal involving the mayor's Eleventh Ward alderman and city council floor leader, Patrick Huels, and Michael Tadin, a businessman.

Tadin had known Daley since childhood and operated Marina Cartage, a family trucking and hauling business, out of the mayor's Bridgeport neighborhood. Despite his mayoral ties and a series of sweetheart deals leasing property to the city, Tadin was a dependable cartage vendor who could be counted on to deliver a wide range of equipment and trucks with skilled drivers on short notice. It was this intersection of politics and convenience that drove his dominance of fleet business.

It was Tadin's business expansion into a new site in Bridgeport, however, that brought him notoriety.

To accommodate his company's growth, Tadin needed more space; he found it in Bridgeport's Stockyards Industrial Park. With the backing of Huels, the city provided $1.1 million in financing and millions in property tax breaks for Tadin to build a new $4.5 million terminal and headquarters. And when Huels' private security business ran afoul of the IRS, Tadin loaned the alderman $2 million to extinguish tax liens. Huels failed to disclose the loan on city ethics forms, but reporters found out. The firestorm that followed led to Huels' stepping down.

The Bridgeport nexus brought scandal too close to the mayor's office just as the 1999 mayoral election loomed. To send a signal that he was tightening the reins over city operations, Daley asked me to return for a second time as chief of staff. My park district reforms were fresh in the public's mind, and I knew my way around city hall.

I was headed back to my old office when new, embarrassing stories broke that Tadin's Marina Cartage had been collecting the lion's share of the city's truck-rental business. The connection to Tadin was problematic, but more worrisome was that all the business was going to a white-male-owned firm. Daley was supposed to meet the contracting goals of the minority set-aside ordinance. African American and Latino aldermen were furious; although their wards had few companies that could compete for prime work in building a CTA station or water-treatment facility, they had plenty of small trucking companies and mom-and-pop operations using trucks as part of their businesses.

Like the Duffs' contracting scandal, the Tadin cartage controversy threatened to undercut Daley's support among minority politicians and voters.

Daley's direction to me was to shift as much of Tadin's business as possible—as fast as possible—to minority trucking firms. Each week, I collected the data from operating departments and produced a report for the mayor measuring progress. It took a while to whittle down Tadin's business without disrupting city projects, but bit by bit we reduced his numbers and increased minority participation.

When the second Tadin controversy had taken off toward the end of 1997, Daley had shifted control over city cartage contracts from the Fleet Department to the Office of Budget and Management (OMB), ironically to ensure tighter controls.

In the months leading up to Daley's 1999 reelection, however, the HDO operative Angelo Torres, who less than three years earlier had been hired to place boots on the cars of parking ticket scofflaws, began overseeing administration of hired-truck operations. Dollars flowing to the program began increasing with his arrival, expanding 30 percent in 2000 to $40 million annually.

The quiet ascent of Torres was ominous, a sign of HDO's continuing penetration into the bowels of city operations.

When I left city hall after Daley's election to a fourth term in 1999, I didn't give the trucking contracts another thought—until Novak's stories started coming out five years later. In the intervening years, the city had grown the list of trucking vendors to 165, using a no-bid, open-source contract in which firms listed their truck availabilities and rates. The operating departments of Streets and Sanitation, Transportation, Sewers, and Water decided the number of trucks they needed and selected them off the list. The idea was to spread the business widely.

Although created with healthy intentions, the program gradually mutated into a cancer, with tentacles permeating nearly the entire body of city government.

• • •

Tim Novak's exposé of the hired truck fraud, in concert with the work of his *Sun-Times* colleague Steve Warmbir, eventually produced 118 stories over twenty months. Their reporting showed that many of the hired truck firms did no actual work. Dump trucks and their drivers sat idle at worksites while city crews performed work. This naturally led to resentment among the city workers who were laying pipe, repairing water mains, and hauling bulk trash.

"If anybody's going to sit around and do nothing, it ought to be a city worker," groused one sewer department employee.[11]

Given the easy pickings of the no-bid, discretionary allocations, organized-crime figures not surprisingly found their niche. At least one of every ten trucking firms participating in the program was owned by a reputed member of the Chicago Outfit or a family member. A Bridgeport mob bookie who doubled as a city employee, Nick "The Stick" Lococo, managed to run point for the Transportation Department's hired-truck needs. He was later indicted for secretly putting one of his own trucks into the program but died in a horseback-riding accident before his trial. The son of a former burglar with syndicate ties set up his father's sister-in-law in the program as a "disadvantaged" female-owned enterprise. She collected more than $400,000 in 2003 alone. Relatives of the late Ald. Fred Roti, a made member of the mob who looked out for its interests on the city council, were among the most favored recipients of hired truck business.

With so much money flowing so easily, the program became a source of campaign contributions to anyone who might influence the decision makers. Over time, vendors in the program wrote nearly $1 million in checks to Illinois politicians and political organizations. This included Mayor Daley, of course, but also his brother

John, the Cook County commissioner; the state house speaker, Michael Madigan; HDO and numerous Latino politicians; and even the state's attorney Jeff Tomczak in faraway Will County. Tomczak, who received more than $20,000 in donations, was the son of the Water Department operations chief Don Tomczak, a longtime Daley political operative. The elder Tomczak was later convicted of taking more than $500,000 in bribes to put trucks in the program.

Other city employees got in on the friends-and-family plan. Angelo Torres, the HDO-tied budget office overseer, managed to get his father-in-law into the program; he collected nearly $200,000 between 2001 and 2003. Torres later became the first person charged in the scandal, going to prison for extorting a hired-truck firm. The transportation department employees Gerald Wesolowski and John "Quarters" Boyle, an ex-con who earned his nickname for $4 million in tollway coinage theft, similarly entered the penitentiary for extorting truckers. Other city employees facilitated more creative corruption. Patrick Stillo was convicted of taking bribes from a trucking company that didn't idle its trucks; instead, it used them to steal asphalt from city job sites.

In all, forty-nine people were indicted, including thirty-three city employees, and all but the deceased bookie Lococo were convicted.

Returning early from a Florida vacation in late January 2004, following the initial *Sun-Times* series, a shaken Daley apologized and pledged to do better.

"I'm responsible for everything that happens in city government," he said "I am embarrassed. I'm angry, and I'm disappointed because I feel I have let the people down."[12]

The drip-drip of new revelations and federal charges began to chip away at Daley's reputation as a hands-on manager who sweated the details of governance, from potholes to street light outages. It also led many to question his commitment to rooting out the underlying culture of favoritism and corruption that was never too far below the surface.

The hired-truck program was an example of the law of unintended consequences; expanded originally to defuse a minor political problem, it took on a life of its own. Its perversion into a feeding trough for Outfit families and corrupt city employees was facilitated by the mayor's growing hubris and his desire to solidify his ever-growing control of the government and the city. The scandal bloomed while Daley enjoyed his greatest political popularity and when he was riding high and least willing to tolerate criticism of his style of governance or goals.

Mayor Daley was no longer content to simply pass his budgets and initiatives through the city council; he expected them to pass unanimously. His increasingly blunt applications of political power ensured docility, as did his appointive powers when aldermen resigned, usually to trade their pinstripes for orange jumpsuits.[13] At one point, Daley had appointed nearly half the city council.

Lord Acton's maxim that power tends to corrupt and absolute power corrupts absolutely is only partially true. Power by itself does not corrupt, but it takes an extraordinary individual not to succumb to the siren song of near-absolute power.

Daley was no different. The more powerful and popular he became—the more his personal edicts were translated immediately into policy—the more he felt imbued with superior judgment and stature. The senior team around him, while competent, reflected the mayor's changing style of governance. They were not the politically experienced, tough-minded, and uniquely talented crew that had served him loyally and well in the early years of his administration. They would not offer him contrary views. They were individuals content to take orders, their sole job to execute.

Whereas Tim Degnan advanced the mayor's political interests, he did so with a wary eye for booby traps. His successor, Victor Reyes, was single-mindedly focused on the mayor's political hegemony. Reyes ensured that those responsible for HDO's precinct success were rewarded with patronage jobs; with HDO's increasing influence in the hired-truck program, politically connected businesses also benefited and showed their gratitude to the mayor's allies in their own communities.

The 2002 and 2003 state, federal, and municipal elections marked the high-water mark of HDO power and influence, and not coincidentally that of Mayor Daley.

CHAPTER 26

Hiring Fraud

As the feds penetrated deeper into Daley's inner sanctum in investigating the hired-trucks scandal, they followed the breadcrumbs to a new array of illicit activity. The more they looked, the more city workers and managers they interviewed, the more they suspected a pattern of widespread fraud in city hiring. The federal Seventh Circuit Court of Appeals declared that the early questioning of city employees in the hired truck probe "turned out to be the wedge that allowed prosecutors to split the log of fraudulent city hiring."[1]

Many of the same players in hired trucks were also dispensers of patronage and leaders of political armies. The Water Department operations chief, Donald Tomczak, for example, routinely awarded jobs, promotions, raises, and overtime dibs to the best-performing precinct workers. Tomczak even organized his troops by ethnicity—African American, Italian, Polish, Irish—depending on which neighborhood precincts they would work. His army was dispatched on instructions from the Office of Intergovernmental Affairs (IGA), the mayor's internal political arm. In 2002, one of those assignments was to provide the organizational backbone for the congressional candidate Rahm Emanuel, Daley's choice against state Representative Nancy Kaszak.

Although Tomczak was charged with bribery in the hired-truck scandal, he was able to mitigate his sentence by testifying for the government about the operations of city hall's illegal patronage system.

But the first clue for the feds may have come in September 2004, when the *Sun-Times* columnist Carol Marin revealed that the nineteen-year-old son of a carpenters union official had been hired as a $50,000-a-year city building inspector.[2] The youth falsified his application, claiming to have completed a four-year apprenticeship. If that were true, he would have started his career at age fifteen. His shocking hiring to a key safety-enforcement position came just a year after the collapse of an apartment building porch in Lincoln Park that killed thirteen young people.[3]

Marin's scoop turned up more malfeasance. Daley's IGA had sponsored four unqualified men with ties to carpenters union leaders for positions as building safety inspectors. All of them had made bogus claims on their résumés to circumvent the qualifications requirements. The carpenters union was a major contributor to the mayor and a source of campaign workers.

Under the antipatronage Shakman federal court decrees, thirty-seven thousand of the roughly thirty-eight thousand city jobs were supposed to be filled through a rigorous hiring system in which positions were advertised, candidates screened, and hiring decisions made that ensured only qualified individuals were selected.[4]

Seven months after Marin's story, the FBI raided IGA's offices and those of key operating departments, seizing documents, Rolodexes, and computer hard drives. Leading up to the raid, FBI agents interviewed dozens of city workers, who confirmed their jobs were tied to weekend work knocking on doors for political candidates. "Several employees have described the results of the interview process as pre-ordained," FBI Special Agent John Hauser wrote in requesting a search warrant for the IGA offices.[5]

In July 2005, the federal government brought criminal charges against Daley's patronage chief, Robert Sorich; Timothy McCarthy, a former Sorich aide; John Sullivan, an assistant commissioner in Streets and Sanitation; Patrick Slattery, a former Streets and Sanitation official; and former Deputy Streets and Sanitation Commissioner Daniel Katalinic. They were charged with fraud for corrupting the city's hiring and promotion practices. In other words, they were charged with violating the Shakman court decree banning political hiring.

The Shakman decree was the product of a civil case, in which remedies are usually money damages. The theory that Shakman violations were crimes was novel; by itself it would have proved difficult to sustain in criminal court. Fortunately for the government, the defendants made it easy for them by engaging in run-of-the-mill fraud, tampering, and evidence destruction.

According to the government's case, IGA would refer recommended candidates to operating departments such as Streets and Sanitation, Transportation, Sewers, Water, and Aviation. Senior managers such as Slattery and Sullivan would conduct sham job interviews and then falsify forms to ensure selection of the favored candidates. Where merit tests were required, such as physical skills for a tree trimmer, the results were simply ignored. The evidence showed that Sorich even pressured managers to approve applicants with drinking problems for jobs overseeing workplace safety. In fact, one applicant was picked despite protests from staff that he was drunk during the interview.

Sometimes, interviews were dispensed with entirely. One political organizer was selected for a job despite having died before the interview was allegedly held. Another won a perfect score on his interview despite serving in Iraq at the time. When a union official complained after its members did poorly in a batch of job interviews, she asked Slattery for copies of the interview forms justifying the city's decisions. Slattery told the stunned union rep that the interview forms hadn't yet been completed. According to court records, the official testified that she had asked, "Pat, please tell me you had a legitimate business reason for selecting the people you selected. Did you base it on performance, attendance, anything?" Slattery, according to her testimony, simply replied, "No."[6]

The systemic way in which the conspirators operated seemed designed to leave nothing to chance, to ensure that each job went to the politically designated person. It was not enough to wink and nod their way to political appointments in excess of the approximately one thousand Shakman-exempt positions; it was as if they viewed *every* city job as theirs.

Of the initial five defendants, only Daniel Katalinic waived his right to trial and pled guilty, cooperating with authorities. Katalinic provided early, vivid testimony about how performance in precincts dictated eligibility for jobs and promotions. Like other city employees, Katalinic was ensnared in both the hired-truck and illegal patronage hiring scandals, giving him an added incentive to testify for the prosecution. The feds charged him with accepting $15,000 in bribes from "Quarters" Boyle to steer trucking business.

In 2000, Katalinic had approached Sorich about forming a new "white ethnic" organization of city workers to supplement HDO and the smaller African American groups. Another predominately white pro-Daley group, the Coalition for Better Government, had been operating effectively on the city's Northwest Side for years but lately had been the subject of negative news stories, some focusing on its colorful leader, Dominic Longo, who was convicted of stuffing ballot boxes in the 1980s.

Katalinic launched his group with a small team that helped elect the Democrat Bob Ryan over the Republican mayor of Lansing, Bob West, for a suburban seat in the state legislature. Katalinic then quickly assembled a political organization of more than three hundred workers, all on the city payroll or seeking a city job. They were dispatched by IGA to support voter registration drives, key suburban races such as Democrat Susan Garrett's flip of a Republican senate seat in 2002, and Rahm Emanuel's congressional campaign, among others. Katalinic testified that Sorich would ask him to list his job requests "in order of importance as far as political importance in the organization."[7]

As the government's questioning of city employees escalated, Sorich instructed an information-systems technician to delete all the files from Sorich's own computer and that of the former IGA chief Victor Reyes. When told the files were backed up on the city's mainframe computer, Sorich then instructed the aide to erase those records as well; according to court records, Sorich said "I'm giving you an order."[8] Despite these frenzied efforts to cover up the most dramatic evidence of the conspiracy, FBI forensic analysts ultimately retrieved partial files showing 5,700 job seekers and their sponsors.

If the hired-truck scandal hit uncomfortably close to home, with a quarter of all dollars flowing to firms in Daley's Eleventh Ward, the rigged-hiring scandal was even worse. Sorich and his fellow defendant Patrick Slattery were from Daley's home base of Bridgeport. Sorich's father was the official photographer for Richard J. Daley.

Slattery married one of Daley's personal secretaries. Sorich routinely commuted to work with mayoral brother and Eleventh Ward Committeeman John Daley.

"This is the guy who drives down alleys looking for ruts," said the political consultant Don Rose, referring to Mayor Daley, "and he doesn't know what's going on down the hall from him with the guy who's responsible for patronage?" Referring to Sorich, Rose continued, "What we've got is a guy who was directly responsible to Daley, appointed by Daley, Daley knows his family. You can't get any closer, short of one of the Daley brothers."[9]

Sorich was as close as the feds came to Daley himself. He was sentenced to forty-six months. He served his time stoically and returned to a hero's welcome before a small gathering in a Bridgeport banquet hall. Slattery, Sorich's best friend, was sentenced to two years and three months. McCarthy and Sullivan cooperated with prosecutors and received lighter sentences—eighteen months for McCarthy and two months for Sullivan. Katalinic, the original fifth defendant who testified for the government, was sentenced to a year in prison.

Daley's Hispanic Democratic Organization (HDO) was front and center throughout the investigation. In court filings the previous September, the HDO chief and former IGA director Victor Reyes was named as "Individual A" and a "co-schemer" in the illegal patronage operation. Sorich worked under him until 2000, when Reyes left the government. Witnesses said Reyes continued to influence hiring and promotions after he left city hall; however, he was never charged in the case. Reyes's HDO cofounder, Streets and Sanitation Commissioner Al Sanchez, was not so lucky. He was convicted for his role in the conspiracy in 2009 and again at a retrial in 2010 and sentenced to thirty months behind bars.

Before the feds broke the scandal, Daley had been in court trying to remove the restrictions of the twenty-year-old Shakman decree barring patronage hiring, arguing that it was no longer necessary.

"Democrats, Republicans, independents. I don't care who they are," Daley told reporters in January 2004. "We don't hire anyone on a political basis. We have never done that in the city."[10]

A mere nineteen months later, following the Sorich indictments, Daley hired a Washington, DC, white-collar criminal-defense attorney, John Villa, to represent him as FBI agents sat in his fifth-floor office and questioned his knowledge of the illegal patronage scheme that had oozed from every crevice of his government. Daley appeared before the media shortly after the interviews. Reporters who were present described Daley as shaken, his eyes red and brimming with tears.

"Things like this, you get embarrassed," Daley said. "Things like this, you get mad. Things like this, you get disappointed, but then you do something about it. I love this city. Maybe I'm married to it too much. But I love this city."[11]

Rather than an end to the Shakman decree, Daley got a new court-appointed monitor to oversee city hiring practices.

• • •

The dissonance between Daley the manager, sweating the small stuff of governance, and Daley the politician, unaware of ingrained corruption in his administration, is hard to square. But like many skilled politicians, Daley kept a distance from the sometimes squalid details of managing the politics required to stay in power and exercise power effectively.

The executive of a large and complex metropolis cannot rely on moral suasion alone. Elected politicians in the city council and legislature, state executive offices, and Congress are trying to advance their own political standing and power, as are the groups that do business with them or against them. Rarely do truth and righteousness prevail against an ambitious politician's opportunity to play demagogue or exploit weakness in the executive.

A mayor has a powerful toolbox. One instrument is the bully pulpit—the ability to command the spotlight, set the agenda, and position messaging. But this is one of the weakest tools; numerous politicians and special interest groups command the media's attention, especially those who generate interesting news by attacking city hall.

Behind the scenes, successful mayors aggressively build alliances. Sometimes they do this through the support of well-organized interest groups, but most times they do this by helping other politicians advance their careers. That can come in the form of fundraising assistance, the loan of political foot soldiers at election time, and aggressive city support for improvements in an alderman's ward or a state legislator's district.

Especially when ensuring that the state is more helpful than harmful, a mayor must unite representatives from city districts. Otherwise, in the absence of strong mayoral leadership, legislators will fall back on their own narrow political needs and be picked off by opportunistic special interest groups. When the rookie politician and new Chicago mayor Lori Lightfoot relied on mere appeals to conscience to stop additional firefighter pension liabilities from being heaped on Chicago taxpayers and objected to legislation stripping the mayor of authority over public schools, the entire Chicago delegation abandoned her. With nothing to offer, legislators took their cues from powerful public-employee unions, which offer money, ground troops, and air cover in paid local mailers and media: "Senator Martwick supports teachers and firefighters!" Missing are mailers announcing the truth: "Senator Martwick just raised your property taxes and ensured a steady decline in the quality of your schools!"

But the carrot of mayoral help is insufficient. The stick of mayoral retribution is even more important. The Renaissance political theorist Niccolò Machiavelli argued, "It is better to be feared than loved if you cannot be both."[12] Machiavelli asserted that given human nature, fear is a much more powerful motivator than love and thus far more effective as a weapon to be wielded by leaders.

At the end of the day, most politicians simply want to keep their jobs. For most, it's the best job they've ever had, and they know it's the best job they ever *will* have. If the chief executive has access to money, motivated troops, and a sophisticated political and media operation—and demonstrates a willingness to bring its full weight to bear against those who undermine the city's interests—then he will overcome the opportunists who would sell out the city to advance themselves.

As someone who cared genuinely about Chicago and enjoyed working closely with community leaders, Daley was a micromanager when it came to offering the carrots of neighborhood improvements. He relished the opportunity to help promote the careers of aldermen and legislators by helping them make their communities better places to live.

But he was happy to delegate the duties of pinstripe and hiring patronage, knowing it was being handled in the background. When a Wall Street bond house came to me as parks superintendent with a refinancing plan to save the district money, I let city hall know. I was surprised when I received a call from the mayor's CFO, Ed Bedore. Bedore told me to turn it down and ask the representative to call him. The firm was one of the few that had not supported the mayor's requests for financial help in support of city projects and charities.

If a hiring or firing was politically sensitive, it was Tim Degnan who called. Bedore and Degnan were grizzled veterans of virtually all the Daley family's political battles. Along with Daley's policy advisor Frank Kruesi, they provided a sophisticated political cocoon surrounding the mayor. Each knew where lines had to be drawn, what was appropriate for political consideration and what was not, and where the risks of aggressive use of mayoral power outweighed the political benefits.

By the late 1990s, Degnan was retired from politics; Bedore was a lobbyist living in Springfield; and Kruesi was a senior federal official with the US Department of Transportation. The adult supervision had left the building. Daley, feeling his oats as the uber mayor, concluded he no longer needed aides who approximated peers, who tended to be annoyingly forthright in their questioning of his daily deeds and strategies. Those who tried to fill the role of truth teller hit brick walls; many left the administration.

Daley knew that his allies would receive consideration in hiring and contracting. That much is not in doubt. What he never imagined, I am sure, is the ham-handed way in which his more junior troops went about that business. A clumsier, more over-the-top scheme could not have been concocted. If Daley knew that his aides were writing fake personnel records, destroying documents, and ignoring every single legal and procedural guardrail, he would have torn out his hair. If he knew they were also carefully documenting their illegality, he would have been even more astonished and enraged.

When Tim Degnan left city hall, he and his assistant walked out without touching the filing cabinet. That's because there was never anything *in* the filing cabinet. In six years as IGA chief, Degnan never created a single piece of paper. And he certainly didn't keep a hard drive. More important, Degnan never believed that Rich Daley had to restore his father's patronage empire to be successful. Instead, when someone was deserving of consideration, Degnan would write the name on a 3 × 5 card in his trademark green ink, and simply say, "See if you can help this guy." If that sometimes resulted in circumventing the Shakman decree, it was hardly systematic and certainly not the result of a centrally organized conspiracy.

It is ironic that the very tools that a mayor requires to advance his agenda and build a better city, as well as to protect against rearguard actions by the legislature, are the same tools that when mishandled can lead to widespread corruption. Large cities are complex and unwieldy and will not long maintain their viability with weak or meek leadership; but in the end, a powerful leader's honesty and devotion to his city are as important as his managerial and political skills. Citizens demand both a well-run metropolis and one that does not constantly run afoul of the law—particularly when it is at their expense.

• • •

Patronage and contracts fraud were at the center of two other major Illinois scandals during Daley's time as mayor, leading to the imprisonment of two Illinois governors.

When he was secretary of state, George Ryan's patronage workers were put under so much pressure to sell fundraising tickets that many began collecting bribes from drivers who could not qualify for licenses. Rather than pocketing the money, they contributed it to Ryan's campaign fund. One unqualified driver who secured his license through bribery later was responsible for the deaths of six children in a fiery highway accident. The subsequent investigation, which followed Ryan into the governor's office, led to his criminal conviction for taking payoffs in exchange for state contracts.

Ryan's successor, Gov. Rod Blagojevich, aggressively leveraged state contracts for campaign cash. His efforts were so brazen that the US attorney Patrick Fitzgerald charged him with extorting millions from companies awarded state contracts. In one instance, he held up the release of state funds to a children's hospital to secure a fifty-thousand-dollar campaign contribution. His most notorious crime was attempting to sell the appointment to Barack Obama's vacant US Senate seat for paid jobs and appointments for himself and his wife.

In both state scandals, the executives sought personal financial gain. Neither was known for sincerity, and neither displayed any abiding love for his home state.

The contrasts to Daley are obvious. Corruption often swirled around both Mayor Daley and his father, but neither was accused of benefiting financially. Equally important, voters appreciated a mayor who wore his emotions on his sleeve and so obviously cared about the city he governed. The late comedian George Burns could have been referring to most politicians when he said, "If you can fake sincerity, you've got it made." But sincerity is hard to fake for long; voters see through the façade. Daley's sincerity was genuine. That went a long way in shielding him from the full political consequences of his scandals, allowing him to retain the power and influence necessary to complete his transformation of Chicago.

CHAPTER 27

Renaissance 2010

When Mayor Daley sensed that his first wave of reforms at Chicago Public Schools (CPS) had stalled, he swiftly replaced his leadership team, despite their impressive track record. Now, with his second wave of reforms surging but crashing against the shoals of too many stubbornly underperforming neighborhood schools, he escalated his tactics.

In 2004, Daley announced an extraordinarily ambitious plan with the support of corporations and foundations. It was radical, certainly the most sweeping national effort to overturn an existing educational order. Dubbed Renaissance 2010, the plan called for closing the system's sixty worst schools—roughly 10 percent—and replacing them with one hundred new schools by the end of the decade. Importantly, two-thirds would be privately operated either as charters or contract schools. With independence from the CPS bureaucracy, local school councils, and the teachers union, the new schools could develop and apply whatever worked to boost student learning.

"This is the most ambitious educational agenda for any urban area in the country," said Timothy Knowles, director of the University of Chicago Urban Education Institute. "This is an incredible moment for the city. It has enormous challenges but the opportunity for Chicago is once in a generation, maybe once in two or three generations."[1]

As the long process of Renaissance 2010 played out, the CPS chief, Arne Duncan, remained focused on data, increasingly turning to two influential partners. One was a subsidiary of Knowles's organization, the Consortium on Chicago School Research, directed by John Easton. The consortium dug deep into the data underlying Chicago's vast system and its educational outcomes. In a pioneering study with national implications, it concluded that freshman year is the make-or-break year of high school.

In the consortium's findings, ninth-grade attendance and course grades predict which students graduate. Students who miss two or more weeks of semester classes will likely flunk, even if they have high test scores entering high school. Students with a B average or better have a 95 percent chance of graduating; a C-minus or lower means a likely dropout. The research showed that freshman-year data were more significant than all other statistics, including 8th-grade test scores and even family background.

Duncan adopted the consortium's on-track indicator as a classroom tool. Freshmen were tracked for signs of progress or slippage; if they were slipping, interventions were swift. The granular focus on individual freshmen and their month-by-month trek allowed mid-course corrections in a student's trajectory before it was too late.[2]

The consortium also examined the elements that determined a successful school, including teacher training, high expectations, strong ties to parents and community, and a safe and supportive learning environment. But its most important factor was leadership. A strong principal can lift even the most challenged school.[3]

Duncan's second influential partner adopted school leadership as its core mission. In 2000, business and civic leaders founded the Chicago Public Education Fund (The Fund) to support the recruitment, training, support, and retention of talented school principals. The Fund acted much like a venture capital firm, making investments with an expectation of returns. Every four or five years, after measuring results, The Fund would either fold in disappointment or raise a new round of capital to invest, in anticipation of the same or better returns.

In the case of The Fund, the returns were higher qualified, better trained, more effective CPS principals and proof of their outsize impact. The first investment fund was $10 million, the second in 2004 was $15 million—a pattern of growth that repeated itself every four to five years, matching the proven returns of higher-caliber principals.

Mayor Daley took a "do-everything" approach to improving schools but understood better than anyone that leadership was the foundational pillar. Heather Y. Anichini, The Fund's director, told me that Mayor Daley never missed the school year kickoff of school administrators, delivering a passionate message of their importance in elevating schools. He also personally supported Duncan's efforts to support the other pillars of the University of Chicago's criteria, including parental involvement.

"Under Arne, parent training councils met on Saturdays. I was on the Southwest Side, running training for about twenty parents," Anichini recalled. "The mayor came in, which was a huge surprise. He stayed for twenty-five minutes and talked to every parent in the room about the importance of the work they were doing."[4]

Anichini also cited elevated standards and training for teachers as a linchpin of the district's increased success. After previously criticizing CPS for poor teacher recruitment, the Education Research Council of Southern Illinois University praised the district in a 2008 report for its increased efforts to obtain teachers with the best academic credentials and certifications, as well as for employing more than 1,200 alternatively certified instructors looking for second careers teaching science and math, subjects in which recruitment is more difficult.

"Chicago, especially, has made remarkable progress in bolstering the caliber of its teaching force and serves as a positive example for other large urban districts," the study said.[5]

• • •

While Daley and Duncan were doing everything possible to boost instructional outcomes, they also faced regular reminders of the trauma many students experienced outside the classroom, jeopardizing not only their academic futures but their personal safety. Duncan budgeted roughly $100 million annually for school security, dollars that could have bolstered learning instead. But he viewed it as a necessary evil.

"If the schools aren't safe, there's no chance for students to learn or concentrate," Duncan told me. "It was a constant worry, always on my mind. During my seven and a half years at CPS, we had a student killed in the community every two weeks on average by gun violence. I went to a lot of funerals, to the homes of parents who had lost a child. It was by far the hardest part of the job. My wife and I had two young kids at the time, and such a loss was unimaginable to me."[6]

Duncan invested in after-school programs and leaned on Maggie Daley's After School Matters project, in order to keep students in a safe school environment as many hours as possible. In time, he turned 150 schools into community centers, opening up gyms and swimming pools and arts and crafts rooms after school hours. At first, he was stymied by union contracts requiring a school engineer to be present after hours, at double time. Multiplied over the course of the year, it was a budget buster for many schools. But Duncan found a solution.

"Thank goodness, our labor attorney Jim Franczek actually read the fine print of the union contract, which dispelled the long-standing urban myth. The actual language said it had to be the school engineer *or* the principal's designee, which could be any responsible adult. That was huge," Duncan said.[7]

But a lot of principals still weren't on board, believing students would never agree to stay. They were in the habit of shooing kids out of the building as soon as the bell rang at the end of the day's classes.

"But Maggie Daley and I convinced them to try and they became believers," Duncan told me. "The whole effort was to change the institutional rules and norms that had been in place for so long, to create an extended safe space for kids."[8]

During his first term, Daley had placed two police officers in each high school and installed metal detectors at the entrances. He ordered police patrols outside schools at the beginning and end of each instructional day. Along with the expanded after-school activities and open facilities, it made a difference.[9]

"Our schools were very safe and were often the safest part of a kid's day. . . . I don't think we ever had a shooting in school. Ever. Not one," Duncan said.[10]

With safer school environments and a plethora of new initiatives, CPS academic gains continued unabated. In 2005, 83 percent of high schools improved, particularly in reading. High school juniors posted the highest gains in four years, which Daley and Duncan attributed to their steadily expanding reading initiatives.

"Once again, the key is reading," Daley emphasized. "I think reading is absolutely the foundation skill."[11]

In 2007, for the first time, a majority of CPS students (62 percent) passed the Illinois state exams in reading, math, and science. The results were tempered by changes in the exams, however, that lowered passing scores and allowed students more time to finish. Nonetheless, the 15 percent jump for CPS was twice the gain of the rest of the state. The University of Chicago's Easton said his analysis of scores found CPS students did better than their statewide peers in all but the highest achievement levels.

Proving it was no fluke, CPS continued gains in the following exam, reaching 64 percent, in a seven-year winning streak. Daley was particularly ebullient about a large jump in math scores, which he tied to a math and science initiative introduced at 180 schools several years before.

The steady academic gains continued to brighten the outlook for CPS, but the sunshine masked brewing storms ahead.

The CPS budget, expanding for years from to-the-limit property tax increases and growing state support, was being pressured by a slipping national economy, less government aid, and actuarially mandated increases to the teacher pension fund—escalating payments that would consume ever larger portions of the education pie in the years to come. The drag of underenrolled schools also pulled at the district's finances, and the slow process of closing them ensured conflict with the teachers union and parents emotionally tethered to neighborhood schools.

As early as June 2006, Duncan warned of dire financial challenges ahead. Announcing two thousand job cuts, including half in school teaching positions, Duncan forecast a $328 million deficit for the fall term and warned in a speech before business leaders that the pension crisis would soon spin out of control.

The remarkable aspect of Duncan's pension warning was that it came near the peak of a bull market in stocks. Pension fund returns were inflated. It wasn't until the Great Recession more than a year later that the actuarial calculations proved illusory. Fewer teachers supporting more retirees constituted a ticking time bomb, with rising longevity and generous state-mandated payments tied to annual cost-of-living increases.

Teacher salaries rose 50 percent during Daley's last seven years alone. Chicago teachers contributed a mere 2 percent of their paychecks to the pension fund (versus 12 percent from CPS) and were able to retire at age fifty-five with 75 percent of their salary, followed by annual, compounding 3 percent cost-of-living increases.[12] It was not surprising that when the stock market crashed and sent pension fund returns through the basement, no combination of tax increases and education cuts could, by themselves, restore long-term viability. Nonetheless, CPS was required to continue pouring more and more classroom resources into retiree pensions. Between 2002 and 2011, the district's annual expenses grew $1.7 billion, even though enrollment declined by nearly thirty-five thousand students.[13]

Duncan's pension warnings and the flashing red lights of a national economic downturn did not curtail Daley's obsession with labor peace at all costs. After another easy reelection the following year, safely ensconced for another four years, Daley nonetheless kept his political capital safely in the bank, opting for an uncontentious negotiation with the teachers union. As Labor Day 2007 approached, CPS agreed to annual 4 percent raises for the next five years, on top of the typical 3 to 4 percent seniority bumps enjoyed by most teachers.

"No one wanted a strike," Daley said, sheepishly explaining the generous terms and his failure—again—to win a longer school day and year in exchange.[14]

In December, Duncan announced he would close fifty schools over the next five years because of declining enrollment but left it to the Board of Education to approve closings annually. Enrollment at twenty-five CPS schools was below 30 percent capacity, and enrollment at another 122 fell between 30 and 50 percent. Without a sufficient mass of students and teachers, these schools could not offer normal curricula, electives, and other programs and tended to have some of the poorest teachers and outcomes. When the first eighteen closings were announced, the teachers union and community activists packed hearings with protestors and picketed at CPS headquarters.

The same dynamics played out when CPS attempted to open new schools. A Richard Day Research poll of city parents showed that 70 percent wanted more school choices. But they often ran headlong into those with a vested interest in the status quo.

"When you go to board meetings, there's the teacher's union and local school council members threatened by new school openings in their neighborhood and they're both fighting tooth and nail to keep a bad school open," said Phyllis Lockett, president of a fund that raised tens of millions for Chicago charter schools. "On the other side, you have parents and students that are desperately seeking better options. In my mind, that is an injustice."[15]

Less understood was how these conflicting agendas left a legacy of underenrolled schools producing poor outcomes for children in impoverished, depopulating neighborhoods. It was politically much easier for Daley to open a new school with the hope of change than to close an old one, even if it was dilapidated and a proven academic failure. Despite an enrollment spike in the early 2000s, Daley left office with roughly the same number of CPS students as when he entered, but with an additional sixty-four schools, a 10 percent increase that contributed to gross overcapacity. By 2018, with steadily declining enrollment, more than a hundred CPS schools were less than half full.[16]

By the beginning of Daley's sixth term, the handwriting was on the wall. The practice of opening new schools without dealing with underpopulated old ones would continue to stress CPS finances and the academic fortunes of the children left behind.

CHAPTER 28

Empire's Edge

Throughout Mayor Daley's fifth term, beginning in 2003, and throughout his next, Cook County government was a cesspool. It was also an extension of his political empire. His brother John chaired the important Finance Committee, overseeing county contracts and budgets. The board's president, John Stroger, was a powerful longtime ally controlling a vast domain of patronage jobs.

Cook County government's primary missions center on criminals (state's attorney, sheriff, courts, jails) and poor people (public hospitals and clinics, public defender, and public guardian). Unless serving on a jury or contesting a divorce or business dispute in civil court, most residents could go a lifetime without interacting with county government.

As a result, most voters had little awareness of the depth of corruption, waste, and mismanagement. A poor patient waiting for days to get care at the county hospital would notice, as would the families of patients killed through negligence, including a two-day-old baby left alone at the county's Provident Hospital. Juveniles subjected routinely to sexual abuse at the county detention center would notice. The public defender struggling under a staggering caseload would notice, as would the hapless defendant unable to receive adequate counsel. But the middle-class citizens who paid the taxes and voted were mostly unaffected.

It was no surprise, then, that county government operated largely in the shadows, as the politicians controlling it wanted. A steady flow of tax increases fueled a patronage-heavy system in which everyone got a piece; mismanagement, waste and incompetence only affected the powerless and dispossessed. Little of county government was sexy enough for the news media to devote coverage to it.

The executive—the county board president—today directly manages only the $135 million forest-preserve system. In 2003, however, the board president was also the chief executive officer for the Juvenile Temporary Detention Center, housing youths ten to sixteen years old awaiting disposition of their cases by the courts, and the vast $4 billion public health care system, consisting of three public hospitals; fifteen health clinics; five pharmacies; the CORE Center, specializing in HIV/AIDS prevention, care, and research; and the Cook County Department of Health.

The rest of county government is a hodgepodge of agencies overseen by elected officials; the county board's influence on those agencies is indirect through its control of the budget purse strings.

The first reformer on the board was Mike Quigley, elected in 1998; he was later elected to the US Congress, where he sits on the powerful Appropriations Committee. Quigley represented a liberal, well-to-do area of the city, spanning the northern lakefront. My election in 2002, and that of a handful of independent suburbanites of both parties, provided Quigley with allies for the first time.

Quigley tempered his reform rhetoric in order to maintain the collegiality necessary to pass legislation; one of his biggest wins was a landmark gay rights ordinance, a huge breakthrough at the time. By contrast, I had no desire to work from within. I drew my inspiration from the Supreme Court justice Louis Brandeis, who said, "Sunlight is said to be the best of disinfectants."[1] Only a magnified public spotlight could lay the foundation for change.

I started with the forest preserves. So much of politics is imagery, so seeing is believing. The state of the county's sixty-eight thousand acres of open space laid bare the nature of county government.

I was lucky to have recruited Doug Kucia as my chief of staff, a remarkably talented and energetic administrator. Doug was that rare combination of manager, analyst, political organizer, and media maven. He was tall, muscular, and imposing— a tough political street fighter but with a heart of gold. Doug built friendships across all gender, racial, and political lines throughout county government. Members of board president Stroger's staff would stop by to chat; Doug knew most of them from his previous campaign precinct work in Stroger's 1998 re-election and in Mayor Daley's 1999 reelection campaign.

But the most important relationships Doug cultivated were in the field. Carl Lewis, a forest preserve maintenance worker, informed Kucia that Stroger's draft budget contained pink slips for him and forty-nine other laborers to help close a sizable financial deficit. This was exhibit A in the county's misplaced priorities. The forest preserves were laying off laborers and leaving untouched the top-heavy management ranks of high-salaried patronage hires.

I introduced an amendment to restore the maintenance workers, a fight emblematic of what was to come. With Doug Kucia quarterbacking, following leads and carrying out field investigations, our office tipped off reporters to one forest preserve scandal after another. An initial *Sun-Times* story documented the vast neglect at the district's two hundred-plus facilities, including at the Ottawa Trail picnic shelter, "a mess, charred by fire and violated with spray-painted gang symbols. The fireplaces inside are crumbling, with bricks strewn about. Empty beer bottles are tossed into corners and broken glass sparkles in the sunlight. The closest privy is a shabby wooden box with a foul smell, missing toilet seats, a door that won't close properly and a sharp rusty wire poking menacingly from inside."[2]

Even the county's leader, John Stroger, wouldn't use the facilities of his own forest preserves. In an article headlined "Only Stroger's Pals Can Go in Style," the reporter Abdon Pallasch revealed that once each year, for Stroger's Eighth Ward picnic, forest preserve workers were ordered to replace the dilapidated, smelly toilets with what they derisively called the "Emperor's Thrones," five pristine outhouses kept in storage just for that one day each year.[3]

Although normally Stroger's defender, even John Daley took to the floor of the county board to acknowledge the mismanagement of the forest preserves.

"Unfortunately, this jewel is really sinking to the lowest point in years. We have known about it and we've done jack," Daley said.[4]

The forest preserve police department was making its own headlines. Two officers were arrested in a federal sting for robbing what they believed to be the cars of drug dealers. Rochelle Porter, a precinct captain in Stroger's Eighth Ward organization, was charged in a payroll kickback scheme, doctoring overtime records so that forest preserve police would take home bigger paychecks.

An employee tip led Kucia to the county's vehicle maintenance facility, where he found one hundred disabled county cars. The cars were unavailable for service because employees had stripped them for parts for sale on the black market.

With a looming financial deficit and revenue limits from tax caps, Stroger thinned the ranks of police officers to sixty-seven—to oversee 68,000 acres. He quickly regretted it, in his colorful way.

"I think we laid too many police officers off," Stroger remarked at a subsequent county board meeting. "Everybody who kills their wife or girlfriend dumps their body off in the Forest Preserves."[5]

In addition to the forest preserve police, another group was charged with watching out for girlfriend-body-dumping or other anomalies. Some sixty-five county employees occupied county-owned homes, many resembling mansions in bucolic settings. In exchange for cheap rent ranging from $225 to $450 a month, these politically connected tenants were supposed to act as watchmen. Few did. The former parks superintendent Ed Kelly's son had a house until he got eight DUIs, some in county vehicles. A forest preserve police officer, Joe Weisinger, lived in one until he was indicted for stealing $20,000 in unearned overtime pay.

With the curtain pulled back on this chronic mismanagement, I introduced a vote-of-no-confidence resolution, directed at the forest preserves chief. But it was really directed at Stroger, to force him to change course. It was purely symbolic but had a powerful political effect. Commissioners voting against it were defending the status quo, handing future opponents the ability to tag them with every news story about the district's scandals, filth, tax increases, and malfeasance. Even some of Stroger's supporters would have to defect.

With a heavy news media presence on the day of the vote, Stroger delayed the proceedings. About an hour after the normal start of the board meeting, Stroger emerged and announced that his forest preserves director had resigned. It was a big political victory but also a win for taxpayers and families.

When Stroger later named his new forest preserves leader, he ran true to form. His choice was a precinct captain from Ald. Ed Burke's organization. But this time, he had gotten it right, whether by accident or design. Steve Bylina was a professional, formerly in charge of Chicago's forestry bureau. In Daley's first term, I had worked closely with Bylina to rapidly expand the urban forest and bring back routine neighborhood tree-trimming services. Although constrained by Stroger's old-fashioned politics, in time Bylina brought much of the preserves back to life and suppressed the chicanery and blatant corruption.

But Bylina's first budget was a hard one. Stroger maxed out the legal property tax cap, handed out double-digit executive pay raises despite a 50 percent reduction in maintenance workers, and brought numerous ward heelers onto the payroll, including Palos Township Committeeman Sam Simone as an "assistant" to Superintendent Bylina at $69,000 a year ($111,000 today). Bylina already had an assistant, the Thirty-Eighth Ward committeeman Patricia Cullerton, at $90,000 a year ($145,000 today).

Under questioning at the budget hearing, Bylina struggled to explain his need for another high-priced assistant, finally offering that Simone's main job would be fixing the district's six thousand picnic tables, an explanation that elicited peals of laughter from the public audience seated behind the commissioners.

Once again, I needed a visible symbol to bring home this absurdity to citizens watching the evening news. So on a snow-blanketed January day, I invited the press to Caldwell Woods Forest Preserves on Chicago's Northwest Side, along with local mothers and their kids, sleds in hand, to focus on the giant toboggan slides there—shuttered. The children provided a great visual for the TV cameras, racing down the small hills and glancing longingly at the big slides unavailable to them.

It was a clear, understandable, and infuriating symbol of county government's disdain for its own citizens. The *Tribune* reported:

> Adrienne O'Brien has been bringing her children to sled at the Caldwell Woods Forest Preserve on Chicago's Northwest Side for six years, but snow or no snow, she's never seen the reserve's fenced-in toboggan run open.
>
> "When I moved to this neighborhood, we actually bought a toboggan so we could go on the toboggan run," O'Brien said. "Little did we know that this toboggan run would never be open."
>
> "The shuttered toboggan slide behind us is indicative of everything that is wrong with Cook County government," Claypool said as scores of children frolicked while sledding down a nearby hill, separated from the toboggan runs by a barbed wire fence.[6]

• • •

The annual property tax hikes funding county dysfunction were maddening, but only part of a larger picture of pressure on homeowners in 2003. Property values were skyrocketing and assessments along with them, leading to shocking tax bills. Residents who had purchased their homes years—or decades—before often did not have the means to keep up with the rising levies.

In researching potential solutions, I noticed an obscure county ordinance passed years earlier under authorization of the state legislature. It allowed low-income residents who had owned their homes for ten years or more to apply for a cap on increases—no more than 150 percent of the average. So if Chicago's assessments rose an average of 30 percent, and an individual's assessment rose 80 percent, the home's assessment only increased 45 percent. Most low-income homeowners were unaware of this cap, and it did nothing for the vast middle-class getting hammered by assessment spikes.

The existing ordinance gave me a simple idea. I merely struck the sentence on income limitations and the requirement of an application to the assessor. Now, every longtime homeowner in Cook County could have automatic protection from whiplash assessment increases. With a couple of strokes of the pen, I introduced the amended ordinance to the county board and held a press conference that led the news.

It set off a firestorm among the establishment—from Mayor Daley to the Illinois House speaker, Michael Madigan, to the Cook County assessor, Jim Houlihan. Madigan was blindsided, asking his staff how we had the legal authority to make such a major change to property assessments. Feeling pressure from taxpayers, Daley was caught off guard by a lowly county commissioner taking the lead. As the one setting the assessments, Houlihan had already been under attack from Mayor Daley. He scrambled to put a plan of his own together for introduction in Springfield.

John Daley grabbed me in a hallway and conveyed his brother's request that I hold off moving the ordinance to a vote, to allow the mayor time to develop his own plan. I knew Daley viewed rising property taxes as his Achilles' heel. He had worked assiduously to hold taxes down and even cut them to blunt a tax revolt during his first term. Now, the city's rising home assessments—in part a reflection of the mayor's success in revitalizing neighborhoods and schools—threatened to undercut him, even though he had no say in how they were created.

From a purely political standpoint, I should have moved ahead with a vote. My measure was too popular to be defeated, and a Stroger veto would have placed him on the wrong side of a red-hot issue. But I was aware that I had stirred up a hornet's nest, an issue with an outsize impact on my Northwest Side constituents, and I didn't want to undermine the mayor. So I stood aside. Now that I had lit the match, it was up to Daley and Houlihan to fire up permanent relief embedded in state law. (Madigan later closed the loophole that had allowed me to introduce permanent assessment caps.)

To protect his flank, and perhaps divert attention from the growing hired-trucks scandal, Mayor Daley continued to lash out at Assessor Houlihan. In his state of the city speech in February of 2004, the mayor said it was time to "blow up the property tax assessment system and start over," and blamed the assessor for shifting the tax burden from commercial properties to homeowners.

"We need to change the unfairness in the system and take the mystery out of the way the Cook County assessor's office values homes and apartments," Daley said.[7]

Houlihan was an experienced politician and an accomplished former legislator. He realized that standing by his numbers with a shrug was not going to stop the slings and arrows. His legislative answer was the "seven percent solution," an annual limit on the amount assessments could grow.

Daley sent a plan to Springfield as well, expanding the tax freeze for seniors and making home upgrades up to $75,000 exempt from taxation. This was a particular bugaboo for the mayor. During my stints as chief of staff, he would rail against the absurdity of penalizing homeowners for improving their properties. Sometimes, in fits of pique, he would order his building department to stop forwarding new home rehabilitation permits to the assessor.

Daley and Houlihan's bills traversed the usual circuitous routes—first failing in the House under objections from schools and businesses, then being resuscitated in the Senate with strong suburban support. In the end, it was Houlihan's more global approach that squeaked to a narrow victory in both the House and Senate.

In July 2004, nine months after I introduced my assessment caps county ordinance, Gov. Rod Blagojevich signed into state law a limit on assessment increases for the following three years.

• • •

With a property tax revolt in the air, Stroger wisely avoided hitting homeowners as part of his 2004 county budget. But sustaining his patronage empire required constant new infusions of revenue. His answer was a $142 million sales tax increase.

Historically, the president's budget was rubber stamped. With sixteen members on the board, it would take nine votes to defeat it. With my election the previous year and that of the Evanston Democrat Larry Suffredin, two independent Democrats had joined Quigley. Tony Peraica, an insurgent Republican attorney, had beaten a GOP stalwart. The remaining four suburban Republicans, some of whom had quietly cooperated with Stroger in the past, could be easily boxed into a "no" vote if media attention was sufficiently glaring.

We had one other weapon to ensure that no Republican strayed: the *Tribune* editorial board. The *Tribune* was the paper of choice in suburban Cook County, then heavily Republican. Suburban voters commonly looked to the *Tribune*'s endorsements as a "cheat sheet" for voting in down-ballot races such as county commissioner, and candidates plastered their mailings with the *Tribune*'s blessing.

The *Tribune*'s editorial page was led by the Pulitzer Prize-winning journalist Bruce Dold. The deputy editor was John McCormick, a former *Newsweek* correspondent who had won a series of awards for editorials on both the 9/11 attacks and the Afghanistan War. Although nonpartisan, fifty years ago both Dold and McCormick would have been described as liberal Republicans, an absurdly antiquated term in today's politics. They had increasingly shone a spotlight on the county's corrupt practices.

When major controversies came before the board, McCormick would often attend, sitting in the front row just behind the commissioners. During breaks, the Republican commissioners, one by one, would find their way over to chat, taking his temperature and making sure they were on good paper. Quigley and I would watch the kissing of the ring with amusement.

So the five Republican votes seemed secure. That made eight. We needed one more.

Joan Murphy, a white former Stroger patronage appointee and suburban Democratic organization stalwart, was in the president's pocket; John Daley obviously supported Stroger's plan. As a pioneering and powerful Black official, Stroger had the fealty of the African American members of the board. The Latino members were also solid Stroger supporters, having opportunistically put precinct captains on the county payroll, won contracts for campaign contributors, and secured administration cooperation on issues affecting their communities. It seemed a majority coalition we wouldn't be able to crack.

But one African American commissioner stood out: Earlean Collins. Representing progressive and upscale Oak Park as well as Chicago's impoverished West Side, Collins was a bit of a maverick. She had won office repeatedly without the help of power brokers, was street smart, and took pride in her independence.

Collins took seriously her duty to represent her voters, so many of whom lived in poverty. The sales taxes fell heavily on them, since every dollar went to purchase necessities. She also was outspoken on abuses at the juvenile detention center and the county jail. Nonetheless, she was reluctant to break with Stroger in such a high-profile showdown. But as long as she didn't say no, we held out hope.

The day before the vote, Collins remained uncommitted. We asked for a meeting, and she suggested we come to her house for breakfast. At 7 a.m., Quigley, Suffredin, and I dutifully showed up on her doorstep. Over coffee and rolls, we made our final pitch. She clearly was troubled by the budget's tax grab and the administration's lack of accountability for a growing host of problems. But she left us guessing as we headed downtown.

When the budget vote came, all eyes were on Collins. As each commissioner took the microphone to explain their position, Collins sat muse-like. When her turn finally came, she talked slowly and pointedly. Collins decried the division on the board, which she blamed on "egos" and "politics." She made it clear she was not part of either warring faction but was instead stepping between them to "restore sanity." Then she broke the suspense and said she would not support Stroger's budget.

Collins demanded changes that would give the board more supervisory authority. Most interesting, she fired a shot across the bows of Stroger's Eighth Ward and Daley's Eleventh Ward, insisting on a freeze in the hiring of employees "from a commissioner's district where there already exists a disproportionate number of county employees on the books."

Collins concluded, "We need to get rid of this whole concept of county government being a dumping ground for patronage and cronyism."[8]

It was a miraculous moment. The charge against the patronage abuses of the county and its unresponsive government was being led not by the board's newcomers but by a veteran commissioner who decided she'd finally had enough.

With Collins signaling her opposition as the deciding vote, Stroger pulled his budget and postponed the county board meeting to a future date.

The *Sun-Times* front-page headline was "HELL FREEZES OVER: Cook County Board Rejects Stroger's Budget." It was the first time in at least thirty years a president's budget had not been approved.

"This is like graduation day," Quigley said. "A non-vote today was the most important vote we've ever had."[9]

In explaining his defeat to the assembled press corps, Stroger unintentionally threw a political gift my way: "The media have won, along with Mr. Claypool," he remarked.[10]

In the end, Stroger was forced to make cuts to his bloated payroll. The inexorable growth of the county's political machine had come to a grinding halt.

• • •

Although the budget win was important, the most significant scandals at the county continued to fester.

In 1999, the American Civil Liberties Union (ACLU) had sued the county on behalf of detainees at the Cook County Juvenile Detention Center, alleging inadequate health care and education, arbitrary discipline, and a lack of protection against violence. A settlement required changes, including more nurses and an end to the practice of placing children in solitary confinement. But promises and plans failed to reform the facility. By late 2003, the ACLU was back in court, trying to enforce the consent decree.

In 2005, a US Justice Department report on sexual violence in prisons said Cook County's detention center led the nation in reports of sexual misconduct by staff toward its young residents.

Seven percent of the juvenile center's staff had criminal records, and a significantly higher percentage had arrest records, according to the *Tribune*. One counselor had been charged with attempted murder after witnesses testified he shot a man several times on a street corner; was arrested a second time for illegal discharge of a handgun that wounded another man; and arrested a third time for threatening a colleague. More than a fifth of the center's employees were from Stroger's Eighth Ward, including a double-dipping payroller accused of sexual harassment. The county board approved a $25,000 settlement.

In September 2005, I joined four colleagues in a resolution for an independent probe of the juvenile center. The ordinance sparked a marathon six-hour debate.

Stroger interrupted board members with a threat to cut their staff and close their district offices because "they spend all their time trying to embarrass the administration." Eventually, the Annie E. Casey Foundation performed a review documenting "multiple instances of battery or assault by staff on residents."[11]

The following month, new revelations broke about the supervisors' long-standing practice of settling disputes between residents by sending them to fight in the "Gladiator Room." The staff even handed out boxing gloves.

"Room 18—we called that the gladiator room," a former resident said. "You got problems, that door's always open. Walk in there, handle ya'll's business. Come back out, shut up and watch TV."[12]

In November, the ACLU was back in court seeking a court-appointed manager after continued reports of detainee abuses, including a juvenile whose teeth were kicked out by a supervisor. The following week, Stroger created a new leadership position at the juvenile center—for his board ally Mario Moreno's sister at $60,000 a year ($93,000 today), despite her utter lack of qualifications. (In 2014, Mario Moreno was sentenced to eleven years in federal prison for extortion, bribery, and kickback schemes while a county commissioner.)

With the ACLU begging for federal court intervention, the revelation of abuses continued—a juvenile choked by a counselor until he passed out; a young detainee beaten by a guard until his eardrum burst; thirty-six new incidents of excessive force by staff.

The Chicago Bar Association (ABA) offered to convene a blue-ribbon reform panel to look at the Juvenile Center (commonly known as the Audey Home). I responded incredulously.

"I don't need a 'blue ribbon panel' to tell me what to do," I said. "We need to fire every single manager running the Audy Home and hire professionals who will mentor and educate children instead of abuse them."[13]

County government had sunk to such depths and inflicted such torment on those it was supposed to aid and comfort that no amount of agitation by the Board of Commissioners seemed able to change its fundamental direction. I concluded that only a new chief executive could turn the page. As the next election approached, I decided to run for Cook County board president, setting up a second battle with Mayor Daley and the machine, but this one with bigger stakes.[14]

CHAPTER 29

Succession

In 2005, before I announced my challenge to county board president Stroger in the March 2006 Democratic primary, I met with Mayor Daley to let him know my intentions. It was a friendly meeting, but both of us knew he would do everything in his power to reelect his ally Stroger.

January marked the beginning of ad wars leading to the March 21 Democratic primary. Our campaign's first TV ad reminded voters of my turnaround of the Chicago Park District but quickly pivoted to attack Stroger and his $600 million in tax increases. I wasn't going to win the election on my résumé; it had to be a referendum on the incumbent.

Stroger, too, started off positive but soon ran an ad with a video of me losing my temper at a county board meeting, apparently to imply I was unstable. Another accused me of hiring friends and increasing fees when I ran the Chicago Park District, but the source in tiny print on the screen was a story headlined, "From Patronage to Professional Status."

One of Stroger's most effective ads accused me of voting against funding breast cancer research. I was a veteran of political advertising and its often-distorting prisms, but I was nonetheless astonished by the gullibility of the public. Even family and close friends asked me, "Why did you vote against breast cancer research?" I learned that a small research grant had been tucked into the multi-billion-dollar health system budget, which I had opposed because of its vast patronage waste. So technically, I had "voted against" breast cancer research.

In early January, I made my case before an audience at the City Club of Chicago. It was finally time to reform the county government built on Stroger's "friends and family" plan, I said, in which political connections replaced professional qualifications. Patient deaths at Provident Hospital, the result of gross negligence, were "unconscionable" and the riots, beatings, and sexual assaults of young people at the juvenile center were a stain on Stroger's presidency. Taxpayers paid a heavy price each year for this indifference and incompetence.

For the voters I needed to win—Northwest and Southwest Side working-class whites, lakefront liberals, and suburbanites—the only real issue was the juxtaposition of large tax increases with scandals and waste. Appropriately, our tag line was, "It's Your Money. Vote Like It."

I used Black radio and Spanish-language TV to tout my record of rebuilding parks in minority areas, expanding minority contracting, and appointing Blacks and Latinos to top positions. I didn't anticipate winning these audiences, but I needed to reduce Stroger's margins.

I won the endorsements of all the newspapers but struggled again for traction in the political class. Daley and House Speaker Michael Madigan ensured the white machine city wards remained solidly behind Stroger; one in four of the suburban and city committeemen were on the county payroll. But I did win some support.

The most significant machine defection was the Thirty-Third Ward Ald. Richard "Dick" Mell, who had a powerful Northwest Side organization. Four years before, he had played kingmaker in electing his son-in-law, Rod Blagojevich, governor. Mell loved political mischief and couldn't be satisfied with merely locking down his own ward's vote. One weekend late in the campaign, he and the Forty-Seventh Ward Ald. Eugene Schulter took their precinct captains and invaded the neighborhoods of the Twenty-Third Ward Committeeman Bill Lipinski, a powerful Southwest Side Democrat. Mell and Lipinski were friends, so Mell was tweaking Lipinski for fun. But the next week, Twenty-Third Ward captains were knocking on doors for Stroger up and down streets in Mell and Schulter's wards—tit for tat.

In late January the *Sun-Times* reported the first public poll. I was narrowly in front, by three percentage points. That convinced Congressman Rahm Emanuel to endorse me. Along with Lt. Gov. Pat Quinn and US Rep. Jan Schakowsky, Rahm was one my highest-profile endorsements. I represented the city portions of Emanuel's northwest city-suburban district, so it made political sense. On the other hand, he owed his seat to Daley, so it took guts to break with the mayor. He paid a visit to Daley beforehand so that the mayor would not be taken by surprise.

"I know it's unusual," Emanuel said at our press conference, acknowledging that he expected "blowback" from the regular organization Democrats. But "heat's the business I'm in."[1]

Mayor Daley made his endorsement of Stroger official the following month but undermined Stroger's TV attacks on my park district record by going out of his way to praise me.

"He is very honest, very dedicated" and "did a good job" as Chicago Park District Superintendent, Daley said. "Definitely the parks improved."[2]

One political heavyweight remained on the sidelines—US Sen. Barack Obama, the most popular politician in the county and already a national figure. Both Stroger and I sought his support, but Obama was torn politically. As a newly elected African American leader, the symbolism of turning his back on the most powerful elected Black official in the state would be jarring. He would also alienate state Senate President Emil Jones, his mentor and benefactor and a major Stroger backer. On the other hand, Obama's appeal as a good-government progressive crossed racial lines. The newspapers, business community, and most of the liberal parts of his base expected him to endorse me.

Obama took the path of least resistance. He did nothing, at least until near the end when it was too late: two days before the election, he casually announced he would vote for me, which only NBC reported as an endorsement. The following year, as he was preparing to run for president, the *New York Times* published a profile, "A Biracial Candidate Walks His Own Fine Line," leading the article with a recounting of the county board president primary contest and Obama's nonendorsement:

> Much of Mr. Obama's success as a politician has come from walking a fine line as an independent Democrat and a progressive in a state dominated by the party organization and the political machine, and as a biracial American whose political ambitions require that he appeal to whites while still satisfying the hopes and expectations of blacks.
>
> So Mr. Obama remained neutral. He was blasted in blogs and newspapers for hedging rather than risk alienating people he needed, though others said he had made the only shrewd choice.[3]

In a surprise, one national political heavyweight did weigh in—former president Bill Clinton. Looking to increase his political chits and solidify Black support for the upcoming presidential bid by his wife, Hillary, Clinton saturated the radio airwaves in support of Stroger.

Congressman Emanuel, a former senior aide to Clinton who helped elect him and pass some of his most significant legislation, was enraged. Here was his former boss playing in Rahm's backyard for the other team. He gave Clinton a tongue-lashing. But the ads remained.

Together, Stroger and I spent $5 million flooding the airwaves and funding precinct operations. We held multiple debates, traversing Cook County from the Indiana state line to the county lines of Lake, Will, DuPage, Kane, and McHenry Counties. Media coverage was heavy, chronicling the accusations, issues, and twists and turns.

But in the end, none of it mattered. The only thing that mattered was what happened a week before the election.

• • •

Heading into the final week, I was feeling good about our campaign, sensing momentum. At suburban events, I was receiving boisterous receptions. At a particularly enthusiastic St. Patrick's Day parade in west suburban Riverside, I was walking down the street, waving at curbside residents, when my phone rang. It was David Axelrod checking in. "How's it going?" he asked.

"We're winning the white vote," I joked.

When my pollster completed his last survey in early March, I was ahead by seven points. One out of four African American voters disapproved of Stroger's job performance. If turnout held to historic norms, I would win. But as the sagacious British statesman Benjamin Disraeli once observed: "There is no gambling like politics. Nothing in which the power of circumstance is more evident."[4]

A week before the election, I was driving back from a campaign event. The phone rang.

"Stroger has had a stroke. He's in the hospital," a staffer told me. My heart sank.

In recent joint appearances, I had noticed that Stroger didn't look well, but I attributed it to the normal fatigue at the end of a long campaign, especially for someone seventy-six years of age. I suspended my campaign and pulled TV ads criticizing Stroger. Suddenly, everything had changed.

I confided to my chief of staff, Doug Kucia, "It's over. We can't win now."

I knew a fallen Stroger would elicit a great deal of sympathy, particularly in his African American base. After twelve years and chronic problems at the county, a significant portion of the Black community had soured on Stroger. But his stroke changed the dynamic. I also knew that suburban voters, oblivious to the dynamics of city politics, would infer the stroke somehow made my election more probable and stay home, especially with no other significant race on the ballot to bring them out.

No one on the outside was certain of Stroger's condition. In truth, his condition was severe. But Stroger's personal doctor, Robert Simon, reported that Stroger was doing "outstanding, just outstanding."[5]

Stroger's allies in organized labor and the regular Democratic organization sprang into action to rally the troops. Mayor Daley seized the opportunity to score points with the Black community and show solidarity with his longtime ally. At a press conference where reporters questioned if Stroger's condition was worse than reported, Daley responded angrily for the TV cameras, accusing the press of wanting to bury Stroger prematurely. It was brilliant political theater.

In emotional exhortations, Black ministers used their Sunday pulpits to encourage parishioners to lift the wounded Stroger onto his battle shield and carry him to victory. Stroger's son Todd was greeted enthusiastically at the Salem Baptist mega church on the far South Side as he reassured the faithful.

"President Stroger will be back," he declared to thunderous applause.[6]

Meanwhile, more cynical, Machiavellian tactics were at work in the white ethnic wards on the Southwest and Northwest Sides. Ward bosses sent precinct captains door to door with a very different message: Stroger *wouldn't* be back, but if he was renominated, they—the white ward leaders—would be able to install one of their own as the replacement candidate, likely Sheriff Michael Sheahan of the Southwest Side's Nineteenth Ward. Labor bosses joined with them, deploying troops in the same neighborhoods to pass out leaflets reminding union members of my job cuts at the park district and verbally carrying the same wink-wink message as the precinct captains.

On election night, the early returns looked promising, but polling glitches had delayed vote totals in many Stroger strongholds. It took all night to sort out the ballots, but by Wednesday afternoon the outcome was obvious. Stroger had received overwhelming turnout and support in the African American community; the ward committeemen had successfully cut my margins in white city wards; and suburban turnout was too low, as I had feared.

I called Todd Stroger to congratulate his father. The *Tribune* reported:

Stuck at a margin of 52 percent to 48 percent, Claypool conceded.

"We were the victims of low turnout and, I must say just an outpouring of affection and love for John Stroger." Though voting records show Claypool thumped Stroger by as much as 4 to 1 in some lakefront and suburban areas, Claypool could only get about 60 percent of the city's vote on the Northwest and Southwest sides—places where he needed to top 70 percent.

"John Stroger is a guy who's overcome a lot in his life, holds a very powerful office, and I think that's a source of great pride in the African American community and rightly so," Claypool said. "It's obvious John Stroger has tremendous affection and respect in the African American community, and they came out strongly for him."[7]

• • •

The period after the election was one of the most bizarre in the annals of local government. Stroger's family and close political aides blocked access to the stricken president, all the while claiming he would be back soon. Week after week went by with no sightings or details of his condition.

Finally, at a May 3 county board meeting, forty-three days after the election, I spoke up about the elephant in the room.

"There's not a single person in this room who doesn't want to see President Stroger sitting back at that desk," I said. "But the truth is, we haven't heard from him in months and don't know who's running this government. Key decisions must be made. For example, there's a possible nurses' strike this weekend. I don't know if it will happen or not, but it is the job of the chief executive officer to negotiate and avert a strike.

"The health of patients in the hospitals (will be) at risk if the strike goes forward. I want someone from Stroger's staff to come forward and reassure me that he is making the decisions, and not some unelected bureaucrat filling a vacuum."[8]

James Whigham, Stroger's chief of staff, spoke up.

"President Stroger is in charge," he said. "As recently as a few days ago, I spent three hours with the president." When later asked by reporters if county business was discussed, he said it was but that "I am not going to disclose" that.[9]

But once the deadline for independent candidates to file petitions for the November ballot had passed, the Stroger camp admitted the truth. Stroger would not be back. He was completely incapacitated by the stroke.[10]

Then the board president's son, Ald. Todd Stroger, announced he wanted to be appointed to his father's place on the ballot. In the emotions of the moment, most

Black committeemen rallied around him. When white committeemen objected, their Black peers loudly pointed out their hypocrisy. Speaker Madigan had elevated his daughter to attorney general. Congressman Lipinski had arranged for his son to succeed him. The former assessor and ward boss Tom Hynes had helped slate his son for statewide office.

It was a difficult argument to challenge. The party named Todd Stroger to be the new Democratic nominee for Cook County board president. Stroger's vote percentage in the general election against Republican Commissioner Tony Peraica—53 percent—was well below the norm in Democratic Cook County, but he took his father's place at the head of county government.

• • •

Throughout the 2006 general election campaign, the problems at the juvenile center had continued to worsen. By May of 2006, with Commissioner Bobbie Steele serving as interim president, the board agreed to an ACLU proposal to share authority with a team of nationally recognized juvenile justice experts, led by the former warden and parole officer Brenda Welch. Within six weeks, Welch released her report documenting an astounding litany of continuing dysfunction:

- Asked why he never reassigned staff accused of abusing children away from direct contact with children as ordered by the court, center director Jerry Robinson told Welch it had "slipped his mind."
- Youth on suicide watch in the medical section are supposed to be checked on every 15 minutes. Instead, staff, when they are awake, check much less frequently if at all and forge cards to say they have made checks every 15 minutes, Welch wrote.
- Visiting the center at 4 a.m., when counselors are supposed to be watching the sleeping residents, Welch found eight counselors asleep, five missing and five running toward ringing phones as news of her 4 a.m. visit spread.
- A visit to the center's school found kids running and yelling in the hall. In history class, one student read his e-mail. Another played Internet spades. A third looked up the latest release of Nike gym shoes.
- A resident stood on a desk with a sheet around his neck apparently trying to commit suicide. A caseworker said he could not come up to check on the resident because he was working in the visitation room. Mental health staff could not be located.
- A girl was slicing her arm. "Numerous attempts were made to the on-call psychologist with no response," Welch wrote.
- At 2 p.m. July 6, a counselor began paging mental health for a boy talking about killing himself. The professional arrived at 3:56.[11]

By the fall, county staff were no longer cooperating with Welch, even assigning her an escort anytime she entered the facility.

A year later, after six months of inaction by the newly elected County Board president, Todd Stroger, the ACLU pleaded with federal judge John Nordberg to place the juvenile center under receivership. The following month, the state legislature passed a law transferring authority over the facility from the county board president to the chief judge of the circuit court, effective January 1, 2008. To speed the transition, the federal court appointed Earl Dunlap, head of the National Juvenile Detention Association, to serve as the juvenile center's new chief.

At last, the winds of change began to blow. Dunlap began shaking up staff, petitioning the court for private security guards, cracking down on abuse of detainees, ending employee abuses of sick and family-leave time, and setting minimum qualifications that endangered the patronage jobs of hundreds of staffers. Employees who cooperated with Dunlap had their car tires slashed and their windows smashed; a handwritten death threat against Dunlap, slipped under his office door, brought in the FBI. But in time, Dunlap began to restore a semblance of order and basic protections for juveniles.

It had taken more than ten years from the time the county first agreed to reform the juvenile center in settlement of the original ACLU lawsuit. It had taken a felled forest of newsprint exposing the systemic corruption, incompetence, and abuse. It had taken an uprising on the normally placid Cook County Board. It had taken renewed litigation in federal court, and legislation from Springfield. It took so long because the children being abused were poor and troubled, off the radar for many and viewed as insufficiently sympathetic to generate the outrage that would have shut down this hell hole in any other environment.

• • •

Like the Juvenile Detention Center, Cook County's health care system—a lifeline for the working poor—was a patronage dumping ground of incompetence and neglect. Following a six-month study, Northwestern University's Institute for Health Care Studies concluded the system was "archaic," and had "too many political workers to run properly."[12]

In an exit interview with board members and news media, the health bureau's CEO, Dr. Daniel Winship, said he had no say in the hiring of thousands of jobs. That task was "closely guarded" by Stroger and his allies, Winship said. Political patronage affected all hires, he said, including doctors.

"I couldn't do anything," Winship said.[13]

An investigation by the Illinois Department of Public Health documented the risks faced by patients:

- At Provident Hospital, on Chicago's South Side, multiple patients died after being left unattended, including a two-day-old baby.
- Supervisors were aware an employee tested positive for tuberculosis but continued to allow the staffer to work around patients for more than four months.

- Biohazardous waste containers were left in the open, unsealed. Doctors, nurses, and housekeeping staff entered a surgery area, then came out and commingled with other staff before reentering.
- Nursing aides treated an infected patient in an isolation area and then tended to others without changing or washing.
- Narcotics were left in unlocked, open cabinets.
- A security guard stomped a patient in the lobby.

"The hospital has failed to implement the most fundamental protections, by failing to ensure patient safety," the report read.[14]

FBI agents, fresh off investigations of illegal patronage hiring in the Daley administration, took notice. In 2006, the FBI raided county offices in search of employee hiring records. The raid followed a *Sun-Times* story quoting county department heads saying they had been forced to hire individuals with clout into positions for which political hiring is prohibited.

Stories of John Stroger's friends-and-family hiring were legion. *Chicago* magazine named his old friend Frank Barnes as an $81,000-a-year ghost payroller for a faith-based outreach position. He was later hired to set up prostate cancer screenings for men in Black churches but conducted only nine in three years. Another Stroger friend, ninety-one-year-old Erwin "Red" Weiner, was appointed a "maintenance supervisor" at the forest preserves for $73,000 annually, despite collecting two other government pensions totaling $115,000. Weiner resigned shortly after my deputy Doug Kucia began checking on his whereabouts. He had not been seen "supervising" any maintenance for some time.

Stroger hired his security guard as a $68,000-a-year health bureau analyst and tapped his son's thirty-four-year-old brother-in-law to lead the health department at $181,000 annually. This required a change to county ordinances, since previously a medical degree was required. Stroger's choice to lead the troubled Provident Hospital was the brother of his county public safety director. The new CEO had been charged with fraud in Houston and was fired for mismanagement in Denver. The following month, Provident's finance chief, a member of Stroger's Eighth Ward organization, was indicted in a fraud and kickback scheme.

Financial and managerial malfeasance were endemic. More than $130 million in unpaid Cook County hospital invoices were found stuffed into seventy-seven boxes. Only about $30 million could be collected; the rest were too old. The same level of incompetence plagued its pharmacies. In public hearings, frustrated patients told the board of day-long waits, only to be told their medications were not ready.

"Our pharmacy system is badly broken—as badly as I've seen it," said Dr. David Goldberg, a twenty-two-year county veteran.[15]

If qualified front-line employees serving patients were in short supply, back-office supervisors were not. At the January 2005 county budget hearing, I asked Dr. Winship, "Why does each hospital need its own bureaucratic empire?" I pointed out the fifty HR managers, eighteen PR people, and on and on. "Why not one HR department, one PR department for the Bureau of Health?"[16]

• • •

The job of county government was not to serve the people. It was to serve the politicians. That unqualified men and women could wreak such misery for so long, routinely exposing youth to beatings and sexual assaults, and patients to injury and death, is a scandal by itself. Without the sunlight brought by a vigorous and free press, nothing would have changed, in the same way nothing changes in the state-run institutions of Russia.

As with the juvenile center, the health bureau was eventually removed from the county board president's control, the culmination of years of scandals and mismanagement. It would not have happened at all but for the perseverance of the correspondents covering county government at the time.

In contrast to today's emaciated press corps, the deep newspaper talent covering county government was remarkable. During my eight years on the board, the *Sun-Times* brought an all-star lineup that included the beat reporters Abdon Pallasch, Steve Patterson, and Mark Konkol and the columnists Carol Marin and Mark Brown. The *Tribune* assigned Mickey Ciokajlo to the beat, as well as the investigative reporters Robert Becker and Hal Dardick. The *Daily Herald* covered the county with the veteran political writer Rob Olmsted; the *Daily Southtown*'s coverage was led by Jonathan Lipman. Cornelia Grumman, a Pulitzer Prize–winning editorialist, used *Tribune* commentaries to expose abuses at the juvenile center. The editorial page editors Bruce Dold and John McCormick kept a spotlight on county scandals.

Without the steady drumbeat of years of dedicated reporting, the enormous mismanagement in county government—and the tragic human suffering that resulted—likely never would have changed. The genesis for much of that reporting was the 2002 election, in which five incumbents were defeated and an independent movement on the Cook County Board was born. It illustrated once again that elections have consequences, and that through the simple act of voting, citizens can start revolutions.

Sadly, elected leaders outside the county board were largely silent, more interested in preserving patronage and the advantages of a unified Democratic organization.

Mayor Daley was not in charge of county government, although he and his brother exerted enormous influence there. He was not directly responsible for its many abuses. But as Stroger's most vocal and powerful backer and apologist, he ensured that the president and his son remained in office long after it was obvious the county was grossly mismanaged, with tragic consequences. Good politics required it. Good government did not.

CHAPTER 30

Cops on Dots

Toward the end of Police Superintendent Terry Hillard's tenure in 2003, a blip in the homicide rate and some high-profile murders, including eleven killings over Easter weekend, brought violent crime back into the public consciousness. When Daley was elected to his fifth term, instead of devoting his inaugural address to education, as had been his wont, he used the occasion to launch a full-throated attack on crime, saying "enough is enough." In his address, he previewed the controversial move he had in mind, one he and Hillard had backtracked from under pressure just four years before.

"We must target police to areas of high crime and crime hot spots so that there is both a greater police presence and more visible on-the-street crime-fighting," Daley said. The white aldermen lined up at the media microphones to protest, but minority councilmen cheered.[1]

Chicago's political system empowers each alderman as a mini lord over one-fiftieth of the city estate, controlling important decisions on zoning, liquor permits, and real estate developments. Each also acts as a watchdog, protecting their ward's share of city resources, especially the number of police assigned to patrol. So in 1998, when Hillard first broached the idea of assigning patrol officers disproportionately to areas of high crime, the white aldermen in more affluent areas erupted in protest. Daley backed off.

But this time was different. With Hillard retiring, Daley had decided on a new leader for the department, First Deputy Superintendent Phil Cline. Cline was gruff, wore a walrus mustache, and was unambiguously Caucasian, giving him more leeway than his predecessor to stiff-arm white aldermen. As the department's number two, Cline had already begun to bring a more strategic approach to resource allocation.

Daley's go-ahead meant that Cline, still the first deputy superintendent before the August baton-passing, could ramp up earlier experiments. No longer constrained by a beat approach, Cline emphasized mobility and rapid reassignments to match crime hot spots, based on information from the department's new relational data-base, Citizen Law Enforcement Analysis and Reporting (CLEAR). Cline paired the high-tech data with old-fashioned street intelligence. The changes in some ways mirrored New York's similar statistics driven CompStat system, as Cline forced officers to examine the data on crime trends and share information.[2] Chicago never became the well-oiled machine that is New York, where rigorous, data-driven com-mander accountability and aggressive street policing (including controversial "stop and frisk" policies) cut crime in half. But it quickly moved the needle in Chicago.

"Phil forced guys to share information," said Ron Huberman, the former police officer who in 2004 was appointed executive director of the Office of Emergency Management, which works closely with the police and fire departments. Not long after, Daley tapped him to be chief of staff.

"There might be eighteen shootings in an area in the last two weeks, so what's going on? It might be conflicts driven by the Four Corner Hustlers or the Gangster Disciples, or some person in charge of a little offshoot. What's the underlying conflict driving the shootings? Let's go there and stop it."[3]

Huberman noted that success also begets success.

"When the number of shootings declines dramatically, think of the additional investigative focus you can give each shooting," Huberman told me.[4]

Cline's administration was a quantum shift. Instead of the heavy emphasis on community policing, in which fixed beat patrols formed the department's backbone, the department now deployed about 20 percent of its force dynamically, assigned each day where crime hot spots dictated. The Cline strategy was called "cops on the dots" and fed off the CLEAR data.

Cline's tactics were also more aggressive, applying the principle that "the best defense is a good offense." In areas of spiking violence, the superintendent flooded the streets with officers, disrupting open-air drug markets, impounding cars, break-ing up loitering, questioning gangbangers, and otherwise displaying a muscular presence until a modicum of calm prevailed.

In his four years, Cline drove violent crime, shootings, and murders dramati-cally lower, bucking the national trend in other US cities where rates increased or reductions leveled off. By 2007, the Chicago homicide rate was the lowest in nearly forty years.

As Daley neared the close of his fifth term, he could bask in the glow of an impres-sive, steady decline in violent crime. But as is so often the case in Chicago, success on the streets took a backseat to high-profile incidents of police misconduct. Hit with fresh police brutality cases, Cline felt compelled to tender his resignation to Mayor Daley in 2007. Although no one holds the police superintendent of a giant police force responsible for every officer's behavior, Cline failed to take timely action, given the seriousness of the new offenses.

Six off-duty officers who beat four businessmen in a bar were relieved of their badges only after the incident became public. In the most serious case, the brutal beating of a female bartender by a drunken cop, the department waited a month before finally charging him and then only with a misdemeanor. The case became a worldwide sensation when video footage went public, showing the 265-pound veteran officer Anthony Abbate run behind the bar to punch, kick, and throw the 115-pound Karolina Obrycka to the floor, because she refused to continue serving him drinks.

Making matters worse, Abbate and apparently others attempted to bribe, and then threatened, Obrycka to prevent her from pressing charges. Although off duty, Abbate made more than one hundred phone calls following the beating, many to other police officers, and allegedly warned Obrycka as she lay bruised and battered that he would plant cocaine on her if she reported what happened.

Abbate was convicted of aggravated battery, sentenced to probation, and fired from the department. In the subsequent civil suit against Abbate and the city, a jury awarded Obrycka $850,000, finding that members of the police department tried to cover up her beating and minimize its severity as part of an institutionalized "blue wall of silence." It was merely the latest example of a department that, however successful in combating crime, was incapable of policing its own ranks.

In the days prior to his resignation, Cline said Abbate "tarnished our image worse than anybody else in the history of the department."[5]

Despite a long litany of previous police misconduct, Mayor Daley and the police union had resisted calls for an independent, civilian-run agency with powers to investigate officers, as in other large cities. The Abbate case forced the mayor's hand, although incrementally. Rather than a civilian-run board, a new, independent agency would report not to the police department but to Daley and would have subpoena powers along with requirements for timely investigative findings.

Given the scope of embarrassments, however, Daley felt pressure to make an additional and more radical change, in the same way his father had nearly fifty years before.

• • •

In 1960, eight officers were caught operating a burglary ring out of the Summerdale police district, stealing from legitimate businesses, creating a public crisis of confidence that the mayor could not ignore. Richard J. Daley knew an insider couldn't do what was required, so he turned to the dean of the University of California's Department of Criminology, Orlando Winfield (O. W.) Wilson. Daley replaced the incumbent superintendent and told Wilson to clean up the department. He then got out of Wilson's way.

It turned out to be a shrewd decision.

Over the next seven years, Superintendent Wilson transformed Chicago's police department. He moved its headquarters out of city hall, symbolically separating it from raw political influence. He created a strict merit promotion system; raised pay and recruited higher-caliber officers; created a nonpartisan police board; replaced politically drawn maps of police districts with operationally sound ones; targeted graft; increased discipline; and launched a series of modernization initiatives that included computer-assisted recordkeeping and communications, a state-of-the-art crime lab, squad cars in lieu of foot patrols, and faster response times to citizen calls. He recruited heavily in the African American community, promoted Black sergeants to officers, and created procedures and training to limit racial conflicts.

Perhaps with Wilson in mind, Richard M. Daley made the bold decision to go beyond his own ranks and hire FBI Agent Jody Weis to succeed Cline as superintendent.

In announcing Weis, Daley said that "because some officers have fundamentally abused their trust with the people of Chicago, public confidence in the Police Department has eroded. If we're doing all we can to lower crime in Chicago, people must have confidence that the Police Department is doing its job to 'protect and serve' them."[6]

Like Wilson before him, Weis took the mayor's order to clean up the department seriously—perhaps too seriously. Two weeks after taking office, he purged virtually its entire leadership, replacing twenty-one of twenty-five commanders, along with dozens of other top officers. The senior brass that had bucked national trends to send crime rates plummeting was now watching from the sidelines.

To many in the police department, the sudden moves created the perception of disrespect by someone outside Chicago and outside the urban police community. In his early actions and words, the *Tribune* editorialized, Weis also "clumsily telegraphed to his rank and file that he was more interested in improving community relations than in arresting bad guys."[7]

In a matter of months, violent crime spiked by double digits, reversing Cline's striking, steady success. With officers facing blistering criticism for brutality and operating under the growing perception that the new outsider superintendent didn't have their backs, officers retreated from aggressive policing. Arrests fell as a "blue flu" descended over the police force.

In a seven-hour pummeling at a public hearing of the city council, Weis took a humble approach, admitting errors, but he quickly recovered. By the following year, crime was trending down again and stabilizing. Weis accommodated officers with less onerous work schedules while tracking performance. Under his watch, the department also remained free of significant scandals, his primary mandate.

But the police department—and Daley—were still grappling with a scandal that left an ineradicable stain. In 2002 the county had authorized two special prosecutors to unravel the still unacknowledged facts around police torture in Chicago. Their report, released four years later, verified the engrained pattern of police torture over decades. But the prosecutors, Edward Egan and Robert Boyle, offered only mild criticism of Daley, leading to charges of bias from a coalition of critics led by defense attorneys, Amnesty International, and the Northwestern University Center for Wrongful Convictions.

"The record strongly suggests that the Special Prosecutors' investigation and resultant report, which cost the taxpayers of Cook County $7 million, were driven, at least in part, by pro-law-enforcement bias and conflict of interest," the coalition of critics charged, arguing the report was full of "omissions, inconsistencies, half-truths and misrepresentations. "[8]

When the special prosecutors presented their findings to the Cook County board in 2006, I sat in the hearing as a commissioner. My colleagues peppered the attorneys with questions implying that they had soft-pedaled criticism of Daley and asked why more wasn't done. Boyle defended the report but said Daley's office should have aggressively followed up then-police superintendent Richard Brzeczek's 1982 letter, which stipulated evidence of police torture of a detainee.

"Clearly, you respond. You don't fail to respond," Boyle said. "That was a complete mistake."[9]

Ultimately, Commander Jon Burge and the police in Area Two were accused of using torture to elicit confessions from more than a hundred suspects. The city paid more than $100 million in legal settlements to Burge's victims. Gov. George Ryan had previously pardoned four death-row inmates, given credible evidence that Burge had tortured them. In one of his last acts as governor, Ryan placed a moratorium on all executions, given the pall cast over capital convictions emerging from Chicago's law enforcement apparatus.

Because the statute of limitations had long passed, precluding any criminal prosecution for Burge's torture or that of his crew, the release of the special prosecutors' report was met with frustration more than relief. Only because victims continued to sue Burge for civil damages did he ultimately receive a semblance of justice.

In 2010, Burge was convicted in federal court of perjury and obstruction of justice for denying, in a civil lawsuit, that he had inflicted torture on prisoners. US Attorney Patrick Fitzgerald, who brought the charges, said "If Al Capone went down for taxes, it's better than him going down for nothing," drawing a comparison between Burge and the notorious Prohibition-era gangster who was imprisoned for tax evasion because that was the most prosecutors could prove.[10]

Burge was sentenced to four and half years in prison in January 2011 and released in October 2014. He died in 2018 at age seventy.

Why so many people in power knew or suspected torture in Area Two and failed to act is unknowable; but likely, those officials simply did not want to open Pandora's box. A small number of people tried to sound the alarm, if only briefly, before moving on.

Daley has never addressed it, but throughout his career he tried to walk a fine line between encouraging aggressive policing and combatting its sometime corollary, police brutality. Probing too deeply into Area Two's past, after Burge and two of his henchmen were fired, might have seemed dangerous, sending a message of distrust to rank-and-file officers; it also would have put a spotlight on Daley's record as state's attorney and whether he should have done more to investigate police misconduct.

Public officials were not the only ones who looked away or failed to connect the dots. The mainstream news media were also ineffectual. Only one reporter doggedly pursued the story, year after year, eventually filing twenty-three articles between

1990 and 2006. The *Chicago Reader*'s John Conroy methodically laid out facts that should have generated official investigations by the state's attorney, police, state attorney general, or US Justice Department. In fact, his initial article, "House of Screams," was cited by the city investigator Michael Goldston as the starting point of his analysis in 1991, the only comprehensive government report prior to 2006.[11]

Conroy told me that when he first published "House of Screams," he and his editor were convinced that mainstream newspapers like the *Tribune* and *Sun-Times* would take over the story.

"They were fully staffed to handle big stories and investigations, not like the skeleton crews today," Conroy said. "But they ignored the story."[12]

Conroy wrote a critically acclaimed play about Chicago police torture, *My Kind of Town,* and a book about incidents of torture in Western democracies, *Unspeakable Acts, Ordinary People.*[13] I asked him why he thought his extraordinary investigative journalism didn't ignite a broader probe or public outcry.

"I think what I learned is that there's a torturable class in every society—people beyond the pale of compassion," Conroy told me. "And in Chicago, the Burge case indicates that the class is largely, although not entirely, made up of African Americans with criminal records."[14]

To the extent the press covered news of police torture, for example after release of the Goldston report in 1992, Conroy said it was always a one- or two-day story.

"The press treated it like they would a fire," he said. "But there also wasn't a clamor from anybody else to do anything either. The university campuses didn't ignite, clergy didn't come to the fore, bar associations did nothing, and aside from Citizens Alert, a reliable but relatively small police accountability group, activists did not muster much effort. For years, not just after the first story, but well into the 2000s, there was no large-scale demonstration of outrage from any community."[15]

Conroy also said the absence of evidence on video, a more visceral medium, was a factor.

"You're dependent on people reading and being moved by what they're reading," he said.[16]

Conroy wrote a final summation shortly before the special prosecutors' report was made public, noting the stunning scale of Area Two criminality. Hundreds of police assaults qualified as felonies; numerous officers routinely committed perjury in court. All known victims were Black, some awaiting execution on death row at the time, others serving long sentences. All had made suspect confessions.

Most troubling, Conroy said, were all the people who looked away, and did nothing.

"Police superintendents were informed of the torture and knew the identities of some of the torturers. State's attorneys were informed of the torture, and no one was ever prosecuted," Conroy wrote. "Most of the accused police officers have been promoted or retired with pensions. Some of the prosecutors informed of the torture are now judges. One serves on the appellate court."

And, Conroy concluded, "One is the mayor."[17]

Sixth Term

2007–2011

CHAPTER 31

Two Systems

In September 2008, Arne Duncan took one more bow as the school system CEO, announcing yet another year of gains, although small at 1.3 percent. Duncan was particularly proud of the gain among African American students who met or exceeded state standards, to 58 percent, up from a mere 30 percent seven years before. Hispanics too gained, jumping to 74 percent, up from 34 percent when Duncan took office.

The effects of Renaissance 2010, the mayor's radical effort to shake up the moribund areas of the Chicago Public Schools (CPS), were mixed. It produced some huge successes, such as the Noble Network of Charter Schools, which leveraged Gates Foundation dollars to launch a "school district within a school district," growing to seventeen high-performing charter high schools serving a population of even more minority and poor students than the overall CPS population. Its pioneering leader, Mike Milkie, proved that a disciplined educational model without the burdens of unions and central office interference could produce outsize academic results. Noble, which today serves nearly thirteen thousand CPS students, has consistently outperformed the rest of the public school system. Freshmen are significantly more likely to earn a college degree, and its schools exceed overall CPS ratings on school quality, freshmen on track, SAT scores, graduation rates, and college enrollment.

In a mix of elementary and high schools, under the visionary leadership of financier and philanthropist Mike Koldyke, the Academy for Urban School Leadership (AUSL) transformed thirty-one failing neighborhood schools by implementing the innovative concept of teacher residencies. Koldyke's academy was the nation's first such program, recruiting and intensely training aspiring educators willing to teach in the most underserved communities. Nationally recognized, AUSL trained teachers in other school districts around the country.

In 2005, the newly elected US senator Barack Obama was touring schools and visited the Dodge Academy, long a dismal and failed elementary school. Dodge had been closed by Duncan a few years before and reopened as an AUSL academy.

"My numbers won't be exact, but it was three times better, 300 percent better, in terms of student achievement," Duncan said, remembering his Dodge School tour with Obama. "And it was just sort of—it was in the heart of the West Side, and it just sort of I think blew him away of how was this possible. . . . He wouldn't leave. He just kept asking 'How is this possible?' and 'What changed?' Because obviously it was the same neighborhood, same building, same kids, same families, same poverty, same violence, same everything, but wildly different results."[1]

What changed was the adults.

"I remember one of the teachers saying—and I think she may have been one of the only teachers who was rehired from when the school was closed before. . . . And she said that before, it was always 'those kids, those kids, those kids.' And she says, 'It's not those kids. It's our kids.'"[2]

Less than four years later, President-elect Obama chose Dodge as the location to announce his choice of Duncan to lead the US Department of Education.

But despite these successes, a 2010 *Tribune* study found that, on average, Renaissance schools failed to move the needle. Test scores at elementary schools were almost identical to citywide scores; Renaissance high schools fell below CPS averages. Given the program's "let a thousand flowers bloom" experimentation, the results are perhaps not surprising. A smarter path would have culled underperforming schools faster and channeled even more resources to the proven winners, such as Noble and AUSL.

"There has been some good and some bad in Renaissance 2010, but overall it wasn't the game changer that people thought it would be," said Barbara Radner, leader of the Center for Urban Education at DePaul University. "In some ways it has been more harmful than good because all the attention, all the funding, all the hope was directed at Ren10 to the detriment of other effective strategies CPS was developing."[3]

• • •

With Duncan off to Washington in 2009, Daley named as his successor Ron Huberman, the CEO of the Chicago Transit Authority, and a former Daley chief of staff who had also led the city's emergency management offices following a short career as a police officer. Duncan's administration used data extensively, but Huberman took it to a different level. He built a career, and turned the heads of supervisors, with his sophisticated and relentless use of data, beginning as a young patrolman assisting top brass in deploying relational databases to track suspects and make arrests.[4] In each of his subsequent roles, he deployed ever more sophisticated data to drive more effective management.

No amount of data, however, could help Huberman overcome some of his biggest battles—budget fights, union conflict, and grassroots hostility. Taking the reins as the Great Recession's toll mounted, Huberman faced a staggering $1 billion budget deficit. The one-year increase in the teachers' contract and pension obligations alone totaled $450 million. Looking to the following year, CPS owed $169 million more in higher teacher salaries and a shocking $587 million in pension payments. In just two years, CPS pension obligations doubled and would continue to grow to $700 million annually the next year. Having no other choices, Huberman laid off thousands of employees and increased class sizes. His pleas for union concessions fell on deaf ears. At the same time, he parried with protestors and the teachers union as he carried out the painful closing of nineteen schools begun under his predecessor.

As Huberman struggled with fiscal nightmares, a more personal one intruded a week before Thanksgiving in 2009. Michael Scott, the beloved sixty-year-old CPS board president, West Side activist, and real estate developer, and loyal fixture in Mayor Daley's orbit for thirty years, died by suicide. His death came just two days after he addressed the fallout of a fatal brawl at Fenger High School and a routine meeting with the teachers union. At around six in the evening on the night of his death, Scott brought a pizza to his sister at a south Loop nursing home, visiting her for less than an hour before departing. He was not seen again.

When worried family called police after Scott didn't return home, officers searched security camera footage to trace his car. Around three in the morning, they found his Cadillac at an isolated spot on the Chicago River, where it forks north and south, near an abandoned railroad drawbridge. Police found a bloody smear on a concrete bridge wall near his car and his partially submerged body on the riverbank below, along with a handgun with which he had shot himself in the temple.

Scott's death hit Daley hard. The mayor tried to think of any clues or signs he had missed in dealings with his board president and friend, but there were none.

"I'm perplexed, baffled, and extremely sad," said Scott's friend and business partner David Doig. "I can't think of a time when I saw Michael depressed or down."[5]

Despite the loss of Scott's steady leadership and increasing financial burdens, Huberman began to place his own unique imprint on Daley's education revolution in what seemed to be the beginning of a third wave of school reform.

Huberman collected reams of data about schools and what made them succeed or fail. Test scores were important, but so were other variables. One was what Huberman called a "culture of calm," in which students felt safe, suspensions and detentions were few, and teachers showed up for work consistently. He compiled numerous factors, backed by layers of data, and used them to create an internal report card for schools. Recognizing that many schools were starting from low baselines, he made the *trend* the only thing that mattered. Was the school getting better?

To drive performance improvements, Huberman looked to leadership as the most critical factor. Like Duncan, he relied heavily on the Chicago Public Education Fund's recruitment of top-notch principals. But Huberman knew he couldn't manage more than six hundred principals by himself. He inherited a system of twenty-four regional chiefs who divided oversight of the city's schools. But they had few powers and acted more as coordinators. Huberman kept twelve and replaced twelve with outsiders, some from other parts of the country. He assigned them real powers to deploy resources and manage their schools, about thirty each.

"I knew I'd never get the smartest people to come and take over thirty schools unless they were completely empowered. I told them to do what they needed to do to improve their schools and I would take the political heat," Huberman said.[6]

Huberman created a green-yellow-red system for evaluating both his regional managers and principals, setting up a war room for monthly meetings to review data. Principals with green designations, those with improving results, were exempt. Huberman put the managers and principals through their paces, examining subpar results and how his staff intended to address them.

In Huberman's CPS, principals had a limited time to turn the arrow up.

"The data was overwhelmingly clear," Huberman told me. "If the trendlines declined or remained flat in the first one to three years of a principal's tenure, then it would never reverse."[7]

Huberman turned his trove of data into school report cards, designed for internal use but ultimately leaking to the press. Without context, the headlines read of "grim" grades revealing how internal experts viewed CPS schools. The report cards gave a grade of D or worse to two-thirds of high schools and half the elementary schools; a quarter of elementary schools and 40 percent of high schools failed. Huberman responded that the data was a work in progress, had nuances, and did not consider important factors like student growth. Nonetheless, the negative publicity could not have pleased Mayor Daley.

In many ways, Huberman's data revealed a larger, more complex truth about CPS and the Daley revolution. On numerous levels, Daley's reforms were remarkably successful; on many others, they were a failure.

Daley built a choice-driven system within a public school structure, one that contributed mightily to the success of his reforms. In a choice system, the better students, teachers, and principals tend to migrate to the better schools; but that also means the lowest-performing kids, teachers, and administrators increasingly consolidate in isolated neighborhood schools, particularly those with declining populations and school attendance. Lifting those students required either the politically difficult process of consolidating underpopulated schools and incentivizing top leaders to take command, or a completely choice-based system such as vouchers, which would give every parent an alternative to the failed neighborhood public school monopoly.

"When you disaggregate the data, it's a tale of two school systems," Huberman told me. "The progress that was made was phenomenal, but you have to look at where the progress was made. It came primarily from two sets of Daley initiatives—the specialized programs and the centers of excellence at individual schools, like AUSL. They created amazing, high-performing schools. But a lot of traditional neighborhood schools did not progress. If you look at university attendance rates, for example, and back out the magnet and selective enrollment schools and the top charters like

Noble, you see flat or declining outcomes. That's why I focused on replacing bad principals faster; you couldn't just keep adding these special programs."[8]

After his first year, Huberman fired eighty principals and said another hundred were likely to be replaced the following year without swift remediation. With such glowing successes in the specialized realm of CPS, Huberman was placing a laser focus on the traditional neighborhood schools where sophisticated micromanagement and superior new leaders could potentially turn the tide.

In September 2010, however, Mayor Daley dropped a bombshell. He would not seek another term as mayor in the February elections. Huberman departed not long after.

A data-driven third surge of school reforms would have to wait.

• • •

One advantage of Daley's longevity was his ability to attack problems in waves, to learn from mistakes, and to keep a cohesive base of sophisticated support—both public and private—behind a common vision. It's likely that another term would have moved the needle further. In Huberman, he had appointed someone who seemed right for the moment, in the same way that the hard-charging Vallas and the consensus-driven Duncan were ideal for theirs. But it would fall instead to Daley's successor, Rahm Emanuel, to keep the flame of reform alive.

In August 2010, weeks before announcing he would not seek reelection, Daley inexplicably became a convert to the longer-school-day cause, announcing a program to add ninety minutes of class time at fifteen elementary schools through online courses. The teachers union objected that the mayor was subverting its contract, but Daley was dismissive.

"CPS has significantly less learning time than other large urban districts," Daley said, seemingly discovering the fact after twenty-two years in office and after negotiating four teacher contracts. "We must do more to provide additional learning time for our children."[9]

Daley's too-little, too-late initiative came after a study by the National Council on Teacher Quality documented that Chicago had the fewest school hours in the nation despite having some of the highest paid teachers. CPS students spent 270 fewer hours in school than New York students and were shortchanged by more than a year and a half of learning by the time they'd completed six grades.[10]

Despite this significant failure, Daley's reforms had unquestionably positive impacts and were accelerating on his departure. His successor, Rahm Emanuel, embraced school reform with similar zeal. At the beginning of his mayoralty he achieved what Daley could not—a longer school day. In a period encompassing Daley's last three years and Emanuel's first three, Professor Sean Reardon of Stanford University concluded that Chicago had the fastest-improving school district in the nation, with students gaining a phenomenal six years of learning in five years of instruction.[11]

Four years after Daley left office, the University of Chicago's Timothy Knowles remarked on the effect of the two mayors' reforms:

"Chicago is on track to improve high-school graduation rates by 30 points in under a decade. That's extraordinary and unparalleled. Attendance is going up for all kids, test scores are going up. . . . Literally 25,000 more kids in Chicago are in high school than there were prior to a decade ago."[12]

By 2019, the end of Emanuel's second term, the high school graduation rate had ascended to 82 percent. Nearly two-thirds of graduates enrolled immediately in two- or four-year colleges.[13]

The researcher Paul Zavitkovsky of the University of Illinois said CPS was generally outperforming school districts across the state, including the subgroups of African American, Latino, and low-income children. The University of Chicago's Elaine Allensworth, director of the Consortium on School Research, added that these academic gains were accompanied by higher student attendance, more rigorous high school curriculums, and rising graduation and college attendance rates.[14]

The reforms that began in 1995 did not turn CPS into a model of educational excellence. But given the extraordinary difficulties of an urban mega system serving poor children, with a union empowered by state law to strike and resist discipline and change, and a beginning baseline widely acknowledged to be the worst in the nation, they were immensely successful. Chicago neighborhoods were strengthened through a reverse migration of middle-class parents. More kids learned the skills they would need to lead productive lives rather than suffering "social promotions" up a ladder of failure. More kids graduated. More went to college. The fortunes of untold numbers of children ended up better because Richard M. Daley was mayor.

CHAPTER 32

Transformation

When Chicago's Plan for Transformation of its vast public housing system was at last signed in 2001, including the federal government's $1.5 billion up-front guarantee, Mayor Daley had launched his enormously ambitious ten-year program to remake entire city neighborhoods from the ground up, all at once and with unprecedented speed.

Although the Chicago Housing Authority (CHA) owned forty thousand units at the time of the city takeover, only twenty-five thousand were habitable. The mayor struck a deal with the US Department of Housing and Urban Development (HUD) to rehab or build twenty-five thousand new units but receive the equivalent funding for forty thousand, using the difference to provide an extra seventeen thousand private-market housing-choice vouchers (Section 8) to displaced tenants. Facing pressure from activists, the city also agreed to guarantee that every lease-compliant tenant had a "right to return" to a new or rehabilitated apartment.

Daley wanted to retain the eight thousand units for seniors. Because of vacancies, most seniors could be moved between buildings while contractors rehabbed apartments. It was a positive sign of good faith and anchored a strong start to the process.

Central to the massive redevelopment plan was the city's role. Daley wanted all services and capital allocations integrated into the CHA effort. Chicago police took over CHA security. The planning department ensured each new development was a complete community, with parks and schools and retail. Sometimes that meant starting over.

The twenty-eight towers of the Robert Taylor Homes sat on an island of one hundred acres, a "super block" running from 39th to 54th Streets, with no direct access to the adjacent Dan Ryan expressway. Nor did the housing project contain east-west streets connecting to the rest of the city, emblematic of its intentional isolation. Tearing down the towers and building new communities in their place required a virgin grid of city streets, each with elaborate electric work and sewer and water mains.

To his surprise, David Brint and his Brinshore Development, the suburban-based national developer of affordable housing, won the work despite competing against politically connected firms. Shortly after, he received a phone call. A woman said the mayor wanted to see him on Tuesday. "What mayor?" Brint replied.

"I didn't think it was real," Brint told me. "I thought my cousin was setting me up. He was always playing practical jokes on me, like calling the airlines and registering me for kosher meals."[1]

When they met, Brint said the mayor told him to call him personally if he needed anything important to the project.

"He's the mayor of a major city and he's calling in a developer and saying, 'You call *me*,'" Brint said.[2]

As the developer of two of the biggest teardown and replacement projects in the Plan for Transformation, Brint saw a lot of Mayor Daley, who acted much like his own planning chief, down to the smallest details.

"He would review plans and make changes," Brint told me. "He wanted brick exterior; he didn't want it to look like crap. He wanted more expensive stuff, like wrought-iron fencing to define areas. He financed those things with block grants and TIF dollars—things we couldn't have afforded otherwise."[3]

Daley also put a single person in charge of each public housing development, a one-stop shop for developer needs.

"You didn't have to go through the myriad of city departments for all the complex permits and approvals and funding and coordination between bureaucracies. The mayor's project manager facilitated everything. Without that structure, none of this ever happens," Brint said.[4]

Defying the odds, Daley had overcome tremendous political, financial, and practical hurdles, and unleashed his vision in a torrent of simultaneous motions— demolishing scores of buildings; contracting for vast new construction; laying down extensive new grids of infrastructure; constructing new parks, schools, and town squares; and overlaying a spiderweb of city services. From the Indiana state line to the western suburbs to the perimeters of Downtown's Loop, a network of vast new public works began to gradually reshape the landscape of Chicago.

• • •

The immense financial, political, and logistical challenges of the Plan for Transformation—the razing of public-housing high-rises and replacing them with mixed-income communities—are hard to overestimate. The ten years originally allocated was ambitious even before the 2008 Great Recession brought the housing market—and the economy—to a grinding halt. The eight thousand senior units were rehabbed, and although 80 percent of the promised replacement units had been delivered by 2010, it would take more than a decade of additional development to reach twenty-five thousand.

By 2015, the number of people living in CHA-owned apartments had fallen by more than thirteen thousand. Where they went has fueled controversy ever since.

Data compiled by the Better Government Association (BGA) shows that of the 16,800 families living in CHA buildings in 1999, the majority were no longer in the system fifteen years later. Deaths and evictions accounted for about 6,100 leasehold-ers, or 36 percent; the CHA was unable to trace or account for another 3,100, or 19 percent. That left one in four of the original residents still living in CHA properties, either in traditional, rehabilitated low-rise housing or in new units in mixed-income communities. A little more than one in five used vouchers to move into private housing in the suburbs and city, with the majority concentrated in ten South and West Side African American neighborhoods.[5]

The BGA had a somewhat negative view of Daley's redevelopments, asserting that the "demolition of high-rise projects like Cabrini-Green has cleared the way for rapid gentrification by wealthy whites and businesses."[6] Where the notorious Cabrini-Green projects once stood, expensive homes and upscale shops now dominated. Where the Henry Horner Homes once cast shadows near the United Center, McDonald's and Google opened new headquarters, and luxury townhomes rose.

"They're starting at $2 million apiece," said George Lemperis, owner of the Palace Grill near the old Horner homes. "Twenty-five years ago, you probably could've bought this whole neighborhood for $2 million."[7]

The BGA asserted that the Plan for Transformation sent CHA tenants to other high-poverty, high-crime neighborhoods, adding to the burden of residents and officials. Eight low-income communities, from Chatham and Grand Crossing in the south to North Lawndale and Austin in the west, gained more than nine hundred new households using CHA vouchers. The South Shore neighborhood, hard hit by foreclosures during the housing crisis, is home to the largest number of Section 8 tenants.

Ald. Leslie Hairston said her community never was given the resources to cope with the influx of people needing social services.

"I doubt that everybody who was in a housing project . . . said, 'I want to move to South Shore,'" she said. "To take people from one area to another is not a transformation."[8]

Most former tenants chose to remain near their old neighborhoods, either to stay close to friends and family or because of familiarity. Some were gangbangers. Many moved into low-income, high-crime communities with numerous buildings on the Police Department's "troubled" list, centers of drug dealing or gang activity. Most rented to voucher tenants. The *Sun-Times* cited the 2700 block of West Lexington Street in East Garfield Park, where taxpayers subsidized rents for fifty people in seventeen households, all living on the block and all in troubled buildings. A 2016 Labor Day drive-by shooting on the street left two people dead and three wounded.

Despite evidence that some CHA tenants ended up worse off, data showed that others did considerably better. At least 35 percent of families choosing Section 8 vouchers rented housing in neighborhoods close to or below the citywide average for poverty, and the homing instinct helped those in gentrifying neighborhoods. In 2016, the increasingly integrated and upscale near Northside area, where Cabrini-Green once stood, was still home to 3,200 families in CHA units or using Section 8 rent vouchers, nearly 85 percent of the number residing there sixteen years before.[9]

Many other residents looked for safer communities in the suburbs. Southern suburbs such as Burnham, Park Forest, Lansing, and Country Club Hills saw the greatest growth in Section 8 housing. Yolanda Crawford moved from the South Side's Dearborn Homes to suburban Burnham. Her housing-choice voucher covered the rent for her small home with three bedrooms and a front stoop. Her advice to mothers raising kids in high-crime city neighborhoods was to move.

"I advise any mother: Move to your suburban areas," she says. "Not taking anything from the city, [but] there's too much going on."[10]

The retiree Yvonne Patterson, who lived in the West Side's Horner Homes, eschewed vouchers and stayed. She chose a CHA four-bedroom apartment that's part of a new mixed-income development near the United Center.

"You know, we like it better—we're not stacked on top of each other," Patterson said. "To me, this is still Horner. All my friends that ain't dead, I still see."[11]

CHA tenants are also better off financially, if for no other reason than tightened eligibility and enforcement of regulations previously ignored in the lawlessness of the old high-rises. A decade after the Plan for Transformation began, the average income of a head of household had nearly doubled to $19,200. Among working age adults, a third held jobs, versus 15% the previous decade.

Until the housing collapse and the Great Recession, the Plan for Transformation had resulted in steadily rising real estate prices in the areas of demolition and redevelopment. In 2007, median home prices were up 64 percent around the Henry Horner Homes, outpacing citywide gains. Prices shot up 84 percent in Roosevelt Square, formerly the ABLA Homes, and 70 percent in Oakwood Shores, previously Ida B. Wells.[12]

Along with all neighborhoods in Chicago and nationwide, those values fell when the housing bubble burst but then gradually recovered in the following years.

By 2015, although far from complete, the mayor's plan had made a dramatic and controversial impact throughout Chicago and the region. By then, thirteen thousand CHA-owned housing units were gone, replaced by growing mixed-income communities.

• • •

Although the Plan for Transformation ultimately changed numerous neighborhoods for the better, Bronzeville epitomizes the successes, setbacks, and recoveries that occurred over two decades. It is an African American community with a rich history that has seen good times, bad times, and now an impressive upswing almost entirely orchestrated by African Americans.

Chicago's East Side Bronzeville neighborhood stretches from roughly 24th Street south to 51st Street. It was among the favorite settling places for African Americans during the Great Migration from the South that began in the 1920s. Known as the "Black Metropolis," Bronzeville was filled with Black-owned businesses, including restaurants, theaters, and clubs, such as the Checkerboard Lounge, the unofficial home of the blues great Muddy Waters. Among the other talents routinely performing in Bronzeville were Lena Horne, Miles Davis, Cab Calloway, Duke Ellington, and Count Basie.

Bronzeville was vibrant and thriving, driven by the energy of African American entrepreneurs. In 1945, the sociologists St. Clair Drake and Horace R. Clayton wrote:

> Stand in the center of the black belt—at Chicago's 47th St. and South Parkway. Around you swirls a continuous eddy of faces—black, brown, olive, yellow, and white. In the nearby drugstore colored clerks are bustling about. . . . In the offices around you, colored doctors, dentists, and lawyers go about their duties. And a brown-skinned policeman saunters along swinging his club and glaring sternly at the urchins who dodge in and out among the shoppers. . . . There is continuous and colorful movement here.[13]

Writing in *The Atlantic* in 1986, three years before Daley's election as mayor, Nicholas Lemann observed the same intersection, 47th Street and King Drive:

> It's impossible to stand at the same corner today without wondering what went wrong. The shopping strip still exists, though as a shadow of what it obviously once was, and there are heavy metal grates on virtually every storefront that has not been abandoned. Many of the landmarks of the neighborhood—the Regal Theater, the Savoy Ballroom, The Hotel Grand, the legendary blues clubs—are boarded up or gone entirely. The Michigan Boulevard Garden Apartments, a large complex that Drake and Clayton called 'a symbol of good living on a relatively high-income level,' is a housing project populated by people on welfare. Prostitutes cruise Forty-seventh Street in the late afternoon. In cold weather middle-aged men stand in knots around fires built in garbage cans.[14]

By contrast, Bronzeville today is reborn, a result of many factors, from its location not far from the lakefront and south Loop, to an improved economy, to being blessed with some of the city's most effective community organizations and leaders.

But Bronzeville's potential could not have been unlocked without the razing of public housing and the spark of new residential investments under the Plan for Transformation. Nearby, the Wells/Madden projects fell; Stateway Gardens was torn down; the sprawling Ida B. Wells projects in the North Oakland area were demolished; and most important of all, the notorious twenty-eight high-rise towers of Robert Taylor, the largest and most impoverished concentration of public housing in the nation, came tumbling down.

Rising in their place were the first wave of privately developed homes and apartments, where former public housing residents lived near middle-class and working-class families. Progress was interrupted in 2007, when Lehman Brothers went bankrupt, beginning the housing market's collapse. Without buyers and new renters, projects stalled, a lapse prolonged by the painfully slow national recovery. But after several difficult years, developers found enough new buyers and renters to fuel the next leg of redevelopments.

Among the largest is Brinshore's Legends project, twenty-four hundred homes in a mixed-income, mixed-use community rising from the ashes of the former Robert Taylor Homes. Just as important, retail and commercial development at last began to take off. In 2012, at the Bronzeville crossroads of 47th Street and Cottage Grove Avenue, a $46 million, seventy-two-unit apartment building replaced vacant lots, anchored at the bottom by a new Walmart store, and other retailers. The Local Initiatives Support Corporation (LISC) supplied housing tax credits; the city acquired the land; and the relentless, yearslong effort by the Quad Communities Development Corporation, led by Executive Director Bernita Johnson-Gabriel and Board Chairman Shirley Newsome, paid off when the duo secured two different special taxing districts to complete financing.

Not long after, Mariano's opened a fresh-food grocery store, designed by African American architects and engineers and providing jobs for hundreds of residents, including a hundred CHA tenants.

The hustle and bustle of the Black metropolis was back, as more African American businesses opened shops and stores along key corridors, such as 43rd Street's Sip and Savor coffee shop, and an earlier entrant, the Negro League Café, owned by Donald Curry.

"The good thing about what's going on is that Bronzeville doesn't appear to be headed the way Harlem went—predominately white-owned," Curry said. "You're seeing African Americans, in their mid-to-upper 30s, who have purchased condos and brownstones and businesses. It's a beautiful thing."[15]

More than twenty years after the launch of the Plan for Transformation, Bronzeville is home to a plethora of new real estate and commercial developments, including residential-retail projects such as the $100 million 43 Green, nearly one hundred residential units and five thousand square feet of retail space.[16] In 2021, sales of homes in Bronzeville outpaced sales in every other Chicago neighborhood. The median home price of $550,000 was also significantly higher than that across the city, at $318,000.[17]

If doubts remained about the bright future of Bronzeville, they were put to rest in the summer of 2021 with the announcement of a $4 billion redevelopment of one hundred acres east of King Drive and near South Lake Shore Drive, including the site of the former Michael Reese Hospital. Breaking ground in the spring of 2023, developers and city officials anticipate a massive, staged development over thirty years, starting with a $600 million life sciences and biomedical campus with a five-hundred-thousand-square-foot laboratory.[18] The first US satellite of the Israeli Sheba Medical Center will occupy part of the space; another company will operate a health innovations center for research and startups. A mixed income development will absorb the remainder, with apartments, townhomes, and hotels. In addition to Bronzeville, the project is expected to produce a steady flow of jobs benefiting neighborhoods farther south, such as Auburn-Gresham and Chatham.

• • •

Near the end of the Plan for Transformation, some CHA tenants have been displaced without support structures, trapped in high-crime neighborhoods, their fortunes worse than before. Given the plan's scope and ambition, remaking entire swaths of the nation's third largest metropolis, not every CHA tenant could be guaranteed a better life.

But in its totality, the Plan for Transformation has been an extraordinary success, removing a cancer on the city and correcting a huge historical error in public policy.

Chicago's destruction of its hellish public high-rises was, by itself, a huge boon for the city, opening development and attracting new jobs, housing, and residents. It helped fuel unprecedented growth and wealth in a short period of time, reclaiming valuable urban land for the creation of healthy communities that strengthened the entire city.

The project significantly expanded the number of public and subsidized housing choices for the poor and working poor and offered opportunities to join middle-class communities with access to jobs and job training.

Critics contend that the fall of the high-rises dispersed criminals throughout the city, instigating crime waves. In truth, crime fell. The insidious, concentrated poverty and lawlessness of the no-man's-lands ensured violence on an almost unimaginable scale, spilling into surrounding neighborhoods and holding law-abiding tenants hostage. Those tenants were often generationally locked into a cycle of poverty, dependency, and despair.

Mayor Richard M. Daley, alone among urban leaders, had the audacity, the vision, the experience, the will, the political savvy, and the clout to pull off what most thought impossible. Today, Chicago no longer bears the scar of public-housing high-rises blocking the sun, casting toxic shadows below. The poor, the working class, and middle-income aspirants to city life have more options and more opportunities. Entire communities have been reclaimed and reborn where the towers once stood, contributing inestimable value to the future of Chicago.

CHAPTER 33

Phenomenon

In early 2003, not long after I had taken my seat on the Cook County board, I attended a reception and dinner honoring the legendary Chicago philanthropist Irving Harris, a pioneer in promoting early childhood education. Harris was a generous donor to my campaign.

Like many politicians trying to manage a menagerie of events, I plotted a strategy to avoid being trapped at a dinner table for the evening. At the predinner cocktail reception, I congratulated Mr. Harris on his latest honor and then took a seat at an empty table near the ballroom's front door. From there, I could exit inconspicuously once the dinner began.

Sitting near the entrance, I watched as a Who's Who of Chicago's business, civic, and political elites began to assemble. As I waited, a young state legislator came over to chat. For the next thirty minutes, we talked about personalities and politics, family, and sports. I also thanked him for his $250 contribution to my campaign (in contrast to Mr. Harris's $25,000).

The state legislator was beginning to reconsider his choice of a career in politics. A lawyer and father of young children, he found it increasingly difficult to balance his financial and family goals with the months spent in faraway Springfield, where he was mostly a back bencher despite having passed significant legislation. More importantly, his political career had taken an apparently fatal blow the previous election. He had challenged an incumbent congressman in the Democratic primary and been blown out by more than thirty percentage points.

So as Chicago's power brokers walked just inches past our otherwise unoccupied table, they paid no attention to the obscure state legislator recently humbled in his attempt to move up or to the lowly new member of a county body responsible mostly for criminals and poor people. No one stopped to talk; no one even waved or said hello as they passed. All eyes were on the important politicians and wealthy elites further up the aisle.

Five years later, my table partner that evening was elected president of the United States.

• • •

Barack Obama's historic journey to the White House began in early 2007, about the same time Mayor Daley was elected to a sixth term. Obama's relationship with Daley was limited but respectful. The Hyde Park state senator had paid a visit to the mayor prior to his ill-fated challenge to Congressman Bobby Rush in 2000. Daley had crushed Rush in the previous year's mayoral election, winning 72 percent of the vote. Bill Daley recalled the conversation:

> I remember Rich called me and said, "Obama was just here, and he's going to run for Congress." And Rich said, "I told him, you're not going to beat Bobby Rush." I think Obama was saying to him Bobby Rush showed so poorly in that race that he's vulnerable. And Rich was like, "Don't take my election having anything to do with you taking on Bobby Rush. He is popular in that community, in that district." And I think President Obama listened to a lot of non-Black wealthy people on Lakeshore Drive who were enamored, rightfully so, with the potential in Barack Obama, and saw this as an opportunity, and were pumping him up to run. . . . So the amazing politics—the calculus of politics—Bobby Rush loses to Rich Daley big, and a year later, he beats Barack Obama easily. . . . I think at that point the president doubled down on sort of his relationships in the Black community because he was being viewed by a lot of people as spending too much time on Lakeshore Drive.[1]

If his loss to Rush caused Obama to invest more deeply in his African American base, it paid off four years later in his race for the US Senate. But Obama's rise—to a top Illinois office and then the presidency—would not have been possible but for Harold Washington's historic election in 1983 and his reelection in 1987, elevating Black voter consciousness and empowerment. Mayor Washington's nearly five years in office also calmed white fears. The sky didn't fall, and equality in hiring and contracting didn't collapse white neighborhoods. Daley's election in 1989 on a platform of racial conciliation, continuing the Washington legacy of diversity and inclusion, put overt racism and fear further into the past.

Nonetheless, when Obama's quest for the US Senate began a few years after failing to heed Mayor Daley's political advice about Bobby Rush, he seemed to face the same long odds as in his quixotic congressional campaign.

• • •

After my election to the part-time county board job in 2002, I had rejoined David Axelrod's firm. A lot had changed in the fourteen years since I left to become Daley's chief of staff. The startup had become a national media consulting and advertising powerhouse.

It was ironic that I was indirectly back on Daley's political team, given our recent rift. Daley had remained an Axelrod client, although now his reelections were mostly pro forma. Axelrod's talented partner, John Kupper, a former Capitol Hill press secretary, was integrated into Daley's day-to-day messaging discussions, so Axelrod would receive calls only when the metaphorical bile hit the fan. He became Daley's break-glass-in-case-of-emergency safety net.

My conversation with future president Barack Obama at the Harris dinner was serendipitous, because we would soon be working together. Not long after, Obama hired Axelrod to handle media and strategy in his run for the Senate. After consulting with his wife, Michelle, Obama made the race an "up or out" event. If he lost this time, he promised Michelle he would move on from politics and provide the family stability she sought.

A month before election day, it looked like Obama would be spending plenty of time with his family. He trailed three better known and better funded candidates.

But then he hit the airwaves.

Axelrod always argued that the key to a candidate's success was how his biography blended with his message, how it provided power and momentum or created a jarring dissonance. In Obama's case, it was a perfect fit. Youthful, handsome, and forceful, Obama lit up the TV screen with the story of his barrier-breaking personal journey and a positive message about the possibilities of change in Washington and America. His eloquence and optimism stood in stark contrast to the traditional negativity and drudgery of political campaigns; coming from this charismatic young African American, it was as if lighting had struck a sea of gasoline. Obama's campaign exploded, roaring to victory with an unlikely 53 percent of the vote in a seven-person field.

In retrospect, it was obvious no one else had a chance. Obama's victory crossed all lines—rural, suburban, and urban; white, Latino, Black, and Asian. He swept 49 of 50 city wards in Chicago, including its white ethnic Southwest and Northwest Sides. Twenty years before, angry protestors had hurled racial slurs at then mayoral candidate Harold Washington, driving him from the Northwest Side's St. Pascal Catholic church. It was symbolic that, on this election day, Obama carried the St. Pascal parish precinct.

After the primary, I was assigned the role of Obama's practice debate partner. But no sooner had I learned the record of the Republican nominee, Jack Ryan—another young, handsome, and eloquent newcomer—than he withdrew from the race after his unsealed divorce file revealed allegations from his ex-wife that he had pressured her to accompany him to sex clubs.

Not knowing how to counter the sudden prominence and appeal of the state's new political star, Republican leaders stumbled and bumbled in finding a replacement. When they did, it was with a strange mix of fatalism and parody. Instead of nominating an Illinois politician, they recruited Alan Keyes—a right-wing Maryland talk show host with a big evangelical following. His rhetoric focused heavily on opposing abortion and gay rights. Keyes also happened to be African American, as if this would somehow obviate Obama's advantage.

Suddenly, my job wasn't to be a stand-in for a traditional conservative white guy; it was to emulate a wildly colorful, pompous Black homophobe.

Despite Obama's overwhelming lead, Keyes got under Obama's skin with attacks on his religious sincerity, his "slaveholder mentality" (Keyes's term) on the issue of abortion, and his alleged condescension to more conservative Black churchgoers who didn't share his tolerance of gay relationships. So even our practice debates sometimes stirred Obama to outbursts of anger and frustration. He took his Christian faith seriously and struggled mightily to reconcile his support for abortion rights with religious teachings.

One of the advantages of being part of such a groundbreaking campaign is the chance to tag along and witness history up close. That was the case for me when the 2004 presidential nominee, Sen. John Kerry, tapped Obama to give the keynote address at the Democratic National Convention. Obama's "red states and blue states" speech is now famous, considered one of the greats of convention oratory. It instantly transformed him from an aspiring candidate for the United States Senate to a future contender for the presidency.

I joined Axelrod and Obama's communications director, Robert Gibbs, in Boston for the convention, handling press messaging and other logistics. When it came time for Obama to deliver his keynote speech, we walked together with him and Michelle to the Fleet Center. The sidewalk was lined on each side by metal barricades. Crowds had begun to form, watching the delegates and dignitaries file into the stadium.

In Illinois, Obama was a new political star. But he was not yet known nationwide. As we walked the long pathway, we were met mostly with silence but occasionally a whispered "That's the guy," or "It's him, the keynoter." Having seen the speech Obama had so painstakingly constructed, I knew this would be the last time he would walk with relative anonymity through a crowd of party activists.

Standing with the Illinois delegation on the floor of the convention as Obama spoke, I realized quickly that as powerful as his speech was in writing, it was even more so delivered as oratory. The arena's atmosphere crackled with electricity and gained energy and excitement with each prominent Obama line:

> The pundits like to slice and dice our country into Red States and Blue States; Red States for Republicans, Blue States for Democrats. But I've got news for them, too. We worship an awesome God in the Blue States, and we don't like federal agents poking around in our libraries in the Red States. We coach Little League in the Blue States and yes, we've got some gay friends in the Red States. There are patriots who opposed the war in Iraq and there are patriots who supported the war in Iraq. We are one people, all of us pledging allegiance to the Stars and Stripes, all of us defending the United States of America.[2]

At one point in the speech, I realized I was standing next to Illinois Senate President Emil Jones, the Chicago legislator who had taken Obama under his wing when he arrived in Springfield. He had done more to advance Obama's career than any other politician. I said to him, "You must be very proud." He turned to me, tears in his eyes. "Yes, I am," he said. "Yes, I am."

• • •

Less than four years after Barack Obama's historic speech before the Democratic convention in Boston, we stood in near zero February temperatures in Springfield, in front of the old state capitol building where Abraham Lincoln had served, as Obama announced his candidacy for president. The symbolism was powerful. Despite the cold, it was an exhilarating beginning to a historic journey.

After a marathon of presidential debates and fifty-seven primaries and caucuses (including commonwealths and US territories abroad), Obama squeaked across the finish line in May 2008, edging out a stubbornly resilient Sen. Hillary Clinton.

Obama's rise from upstart to Democratic nominee had begun nine months earlier with his victory in Iowa over Clinton, the front runner. Many things contributed to Obama's victory, but I believe the most important was his early opposition to the Iraq War.

In 2008, Hillary Clinton and the other contenders, Sen. Joe Biden and Sen. John Edwards, struggled to gain credibility on the most important issue before the voters. Each had voted to authorize the disastrous war, which was deeply unpopular across the country but even more so among the liberal activists dominating Iowa's caucuses.

Although not yet a US senator when the Iraq War began, Obama had previously delivered a speech before an antiwar rally at the Daley Center in Chicago. There, he called a possible foray into Iraq "a dumb war," unjustified by any real threat to the United States.

By following his moral compass rather than cynically bowing to the popular passions supporting the war at its outset, as Biden, Edwards, and Clinton had done, Obama looked like a leader who could be counted on to do the right thing.

As the summer unfolded, however, more than Iraq dominated the news. The worsening economy was also threatening the economic security of millions of Americans. The brewing storm was not lost on the Republican nominee, Arizona Sen. John McCain, whose surprise choice of the unknown Alaska Gov. Sarah Palin as his vice-presidential pick was widely viewed as a Hail Mary.

Reeling from the unpopular policies of his party's incumbent, President George Bush—a fiasco in Iraq and a disintegrating economy at home—McCain needed something to ignite excitement around his campaign. As a woman and quirky conservative from a remote part of America, Palin fit the bill. McCain's gambit worked for a while, sending his poll numbers upward.

When America got a closer look at the inexperienced and ill-prepared Palin, however, the sheen faded. With the collapse of Lehman Brothers in September, the final trap door sent the already reeling economy plunging. The election was over.

In November, Obama claimed victory and the presidency in Chicago's beautiful Grant Park. The evening was perfect—warm and clear. My wife and teenage daughter joined me as we boarded a campaign bus to the rally. As we looked out onto the darkened streets, the flashing red lights from dozens of escorting police cars underscored the heightened security and historic drama.

One of Chicago's own had been elected leader of the free world. Not since Lincoln and Grant had Illinois sent a president to Washington; and given those two political progenitors, it was fitting that this man would be the first African American to lead the nation. He was taking office in a time of crisis, as two wars raged, and the nation entered the deepest economic downturn since the Great Depression. Chicagoans would soon occupy key positions in the White House and the cabinet as the young president began to tackle these enormous challenges.

But that night, the world watched on TV and saw something else as well: Mayor Daley's resurgent Chicago in all its glory.

As Obama spoke, the city's dazzling skyscrapers served as the backdrop, glowing like a modern Emerald City. Under Daley, Chicago had become an international city and a magnet for talent in fast-growing industries. *Foreign Policy* magazine's list of global cities ranked Chicago eighth, rising to sixth two years later. *Fast Company*, a magazine about entrepreneurship, had just named Chicago its City of the Year. Chicago's great universities were growing; the impoverished neighborhoods that once ringed Downtown were now middle class; crime was down, and jobs were up; manicured parks bustled with people; public schools brought back middle-class families that previously had abandoned them; housing boomed; young people flocked to the city to work and partake in a robust nightlife of world-class restaurants, theaters, and music clubs. The City that Works was on the move, an example of the power of great urban centers to drive economic, technological, and cultural progress. And now, appropriately, a Chicagoan was headed to the White House.

As the year ended, Richard M. Daley had reached the zenith. He had remade Chicago into a glistening and powerful metropolis.

But it was the beginning of the end.

CHAPTER 34

Parking Meters

The excitement of Barack Obama's election was tempered by the state of the national economy, as the banking system's collapse threatened a second Great Depression.

In Chicago, the devastating effects of the downturn began to decimate tax revenues, as joblessness climbed and economic activity came to a halt. While the federal government began printing money to fight the deflationary forces, Daley had no such luxury; raising taxes and cutting expenses could only go so far in an environment where housing prices were falling and the demand for social services climbing. The mayor began searching for ways to navigate his own ship of state through the powerful storm.

His instincts led him back to where had found success before, generating one-time windfalls of cash through privatization of city assets.

Mayor Daley was a forerunner in outsourcing. He proved that private companies could carry out public functions more effectively and at less cost, from towing abandoned automobiles to delivering drug and alcohol rehabilitation services, to the management of revenue-producing civic assets such as concessions, parking garages, stadiums, and marinas.

In these instances, however, the city did not cede ownership; nor did it give up its legal authority. City project managers supervised vendors, holding them to contractual standards. Contracts were of limited duration and the municipality reserved the right to resume control or change vendors. In addition to better service, Chicago usually benefited from enhanced revenues produced by private-sector expertise and incentives.

During the 1980s, encouraged by the Reagan administration as well as investment banks seeking new assets for income-producing securities, more state and local governments began actually selling public assets. In relinquishing effective control, usually through very long-term leases, governments received enormous upfront payments. More often than not, these payments were for transportation-related assets such as bridges, tollways, and airports.

In a pioneering deal in 2005, Mayor Daley leased the Chicago Skyway, a tollway connecting the city to northwestern Indiana and the Michigan state line. The roadway was run down and the tollgates and infrastructure badly in need of upgrades. Traffic was heavy in the summer when Chicagoans escaped to the lakefront beaches and wooded tranquility of the Indiana Dunes and southwest Michigan, but otherwise it was not a major corridor.

Despite widespread skepticism about the skyway's value, Daley negotiated its ninety-nine-year lease for a whopping $1.83 billion. The contract allowed a gradual rise to market rates. It incentivized roadway modernization. A major national highway ran nearby, traversing roughly the same geography, so no motorist was forced to pay for the privilege of taking the tollway's shortcut.

It was an ideal privatization. Political blowback was unlikely, a transportation artery was upgraded, and the city received a dramatic windfall.

Building on the skyway's success, Daley eyed Grant Park's underground parking garages along Michigan Avenue as a possible lucrative long-term lease candidate, with its adjacency to shopping and cultural attractions. As parks superintendent in the 1990s, I worked closely with Standard Parking Corporation to renovate the dark and dilapidated garages. The company had invested money and expertise in making the garages safe and appealing, boosting business and sending tens of millions in new revenue into park-district coffers.

A ninety-nine-year lease of the Grant Park garages would be a hit to the park district's budget. But Daley was facing pressure from the Millennium Park bondholders, who were concerned about a default. Revenue from the underground garage was supposed to cover debt payments, but it had proved insufficient, and the reserve fund was nearly exhausted.

In late 2006, Daley moved to sell the garages to Morgan Stanley for $563 million. The proceeds wiped out Millennium Park's debt and provided $285 million in excess cash for the city, half of which Daley set aside for neighborhood park improvements.

Like the skyway deal, the sale of the parking garages was politically safe. Most customers were suburbanites; competitive pressure from other private parking operators kept prices reasonable for tourists and commuters.

Daley now had two successful privatizations under his belt. So when the Great Recession turned decades of economic assumptions on their heads, wreaking havoc on city finances and exposing shaky debt, it was no surprise Daley accelerated his quest for a third. The mayor had already begun exploring that notion in the fall of 2007, near the peak of the housing bubble.

Under the negotiated deal, to another investment consortium led by Morgan Stanley, the city leased its thirty-six thousand parking meters for seventy-five years, at the time generating a mere $22 million in annual revenue. The city had not raised rates in memory, however, and most of the hand-fed meters outside the Loop still cost a quarter an hour. For $1.15 billion, Morgan Stanley and LAZ Parking

Corporation received the right to operate and maintain the meters and set prices. The ancient street meters would be replaced with a "pay and display" system, using new boxes that accepted credit cards and provided receipts for car dashboards.

By December 2008, when the mayor presented his plan to the city council, the economy had reached its nadir. Chicago Budget Director Paul Volpe indicated that, even after the largest property tax increase in history and more than one thousand layoffs, the city's 2009 budget still faced a $500 million deficit in its $3 billion corporate budget. Without deep cuts to police and fire and more property tax increases, the budget gap could not be closed.

"The fire department is half a billion dollars at the time," Volpe recalled. "So what do you want me to do—cut the fire department?"[1]

Adding to the tax burden on homeowners was also off the table, given falling property values and rising unemployment.

"You've got foreclosures happening at record paces. You've got people just flat out abandoning their homes. In certain areas, they're abandoning their neighborhoods," Volpe said.[2]

As he would over multiple years, Daley turned to the parking meters windfall to balance the 2009 budget and forestall deep and painful cuts.

Mayor Daley dodged one bullet but put himself in the line of fire for a second.

Under the parking-meter contract, LAZ had the right to raise rates even before installing the modern equipment. Parking meters that cost a quarter now charged two dollars or more. Downtown parking rates were many multiples higher. Frustrated motorists fumbled for quarters to stuff the meters, only to find they were full. Other meters were simply broken, but stepped-up ticket writing meant expensive fines anyway.

When the company finally did roll out the new meters taking credit cards, they often ran out of paper for the display receipts, leaving enraged parkers to curse and kick the boxes. Sometimes the machine's luminous display went dark, but the failure did not relieve motorists of liability. Retail stores that depended on convenient street parking began losing business as disenchanted drivers steered clear of the minefield created by the botched rollout. In acts by vandals or vigilantes, depending on one's point of view, parking meter windows were covered in spray paint, and coin slots were stuffed with putty.

Joy Nazarian was a typical victim. She drove to downtown's Merchandise Mart to attend a fashion show. She found a parking spot and scrounged up just enough quarters to feed the machine the $3.50 required. She then hit "print" for the receipt to display on her car dashboard.

Nothing happened. No printing. No receipt.

"I didn't have my cell phone with me and I figured, gee, I don't want to get a ticket so I better leave."[3]

As is often the case in politics, it's the mundane things that surprise, taking on a significance few could predict. With residents already in an ornery mood from the depressed economy, frustrations boiled over. Had it been merely a botched rollout and higher prices, the thunder would not have heralded a storm. But Chicagoans knew that the treasure received in exchange for their parking pain largely had been spent—seventy-five years of their money gone in what seemed the blink of an eye. By 2011, only a little more than $100 million remained. Both Mayor Daley and the city council, which had compliantly approved the deal 40–5, became targets of voter anger. Aldermen scrambled for cover, holding hearings, and introducing ordinances to undo parts of the deal. It was mere performance, given their votes for a binding contract.

For two decades, Daley had ridden out political firestorms, always retaining his popularity. This time, something was different. The parking-meter debacle became a symbol of arrogant and unresponsive government, perhaps a sign Daley had stayed on too long. When shortly afterward Daley committed taxpayers to covering shortfalls from the 2016 Olympics, should Chicago win its bid, his approval rating fell to a dangerous 35 percent.[4]

As the new credit-card machines continued to malfunction, Inspector General David Hoffman issued a scathing report claiming that the city undercharged Morgan Stanley. Hoffman argued that had the city simply raised rates on its own, the present value of parking meter revenue would be at least $2.13 billion. Hoffman's assumptions were debatable, but ten years after the deal was inked, Morgan Stanley's investors had earned $500 million more than they paid the city, with another sixty-five years to go.

Almost as problematic, the contract required the city to reimburse the lessee whenever it took meters out of service for road, sewer, water, or other infrastructure repairs. In addition, investors were entitled to compensation any time a festival or other event required street closures. These additional liabilities added tens of millions in hidden costs.

The fiasco of the parking-meter rollout, with new outrages reported weekly, cut deep into Daley's public support.

Years later, the parking-meter transaction still looks like a lousy deal; but it could end up looking ironically prescient. With the emergence of Uber and Lyft ridesharing, urban parking is in decline, and driverless cars are on the horizon. In not too many years, urban street parking could be a thing of the past. The architects of the original deal pointed out that seventy-five years is a long time, and Chicago was shifting all the risk of all of those years to another party.

Time will tell.

But the possibility of future redemption was of little consolation to Mayor Daley. His public standing had taken a huge hit.

CHAPTER 35

Olympics

Mayor Daley began planning a Chicago bid for the 2016 summer Olympics as early as 2005, but in the wake of the economy's collapse in 2008, his efforts became more aggressive and took on increasing political significance. He began to see the Olympics as a path out of his political quagmire and a way to bring dollars and jobs to Chicago while the economy was stagnating.

The mayor was first asked about hosting the Olympics in 2004, as he was basking in the glow of the newly opened Millennium Park and his earlier success hosting the 1994 World Cup and the 1996 Democratic National Convention. He dismissed it out of hand, all but calling Olympic officials extortionists.

"The Olympics is a construction industry," he said. "They wanted $2 million from me just to make a proposal! They want to build everything new."[1]

A year later, reeling from the patronage and hired trucks scandals, he softened his tone.[2] Perhaps seeking a diversion, Daley began meeting with international experts and spent months studying the details of a potential bid.

By early 2006, Daley was in full cheerleader mode, touting the benefits to Chicago of hosting the summer games. The mayor harked back to the 1893 World's Columbian Exposition and the 1933 World's Fair as seminal moments in Chicago history.

"Cities always have to change. If you don't change, you live in the past, and if you live in the past, you have no future," Daley said. "When the Olympics leave, what do you have? You have housing, you have parks, you have improvements in schools, you have improvements in public transportation."[3]

The mayor sought regional support as well, holding out the possibility of high-speed rail links to Milwaukee, with its retractable dome stadium, and both the University of Illinois in Champaign and Notre Dame in nearby South Bend, Indiana, each with large stadiums.

Daley appointed an exploratory committee of civic and business leaders. To ensure public support, Daley pledged no taxpayer dollars would be used in the bidding process or in the hosting of the games. The mayor recruited the retired Aon CEO Pat Ryan to lead the city's effort.

Ryan, already a leading city philanthropist, had the unenviable job of raising $80 million in private funds required merely for the city to bid and reach the final round. Working closely with Daley and civic, community, and business leaders, Ryan helped craft a vision of how the city would host the games, officially announcing Chicago's bid.

Daley's committee conceded that to be competitive, the city would have to build its own new eighty-thousand-seat stadium, estimated at $400 million, but likely costing much more. The new stadium, the site of the opening ceremonies and track and field events, would be built in the South Side's Washington Park, as would a new aquatics center for swimming competitions. The West Side's Douglas Park would be the site of a new velodrome, an arena with banked oval tracks for cycling competitions. These two impoverished areas would arguably benefit economically during construction and retain the benefits of the arenas once the Olympics left. The Washington Park stadium, for example, was to be deconstructed and turned into a permanent ten-thousand-seat arena.

Daley proposed paying for new construction by selling public assets, including air rights over the land south of McCormick Place. The sale of broadcast rights was estimated to bring in $625 million, and corporate sponsorships $325 million. As many as 3.6 billion people—half the world's population—would tune in to some part of Chicago's Olympics. More than eight million visitors would descend on Chicago, with businesses competing for at least $7 billion in tourist spending.

Not everything would have to be new construction. McCormick Place could accommodate weightlifting and judo competitions. Soldier Field, although too small to host the main events, was a perfect venue for the soccer tournament. The United Center, the UIC Pavilion, Allstate Arena, and university stadiums were available for media and broadcast centers as well as specialized indoor sports.

But one of the most appealing aspects of Chicago's bid was the city itself. Many events would take place on the dazzling lakefront, with the backdrop of Chicago's spectacular skyline. Rowing, sailing, beach volleyball and other events would take advantage of Chicago's numerous harbors and lagoons, including Northerly Island, past which an artificial river of white-water rapids would flow. City leaders hoped these visions would encourage millions of new international tourists.

Chicago and six other cities competed for the U.S Olympic Committee's nod, but by the summer of 2006 the list had been pared to Chicago, Los Angeles, and San Francisco. In a close vote, the USOC selected Chicago over Los Angeles as the American entry. The International Olympic Committee (IOC) in turn chose Chicago, Madrid, Tokyo, and Rio de Janeiro from among a list of international applicants.

Having won the right to represent the United States, Daley moved quickly to check an important box on the IOC requirements list—labor stability. In 2007, he took the unprecedented step of negotiating a ten-year agreement with the city's major unions, or at least those that could legally strike.[4] The unions used their considerable leverage to win wage increases of 30 percent, or two and a half times the rate of inflation. But it ensured labor peace through the 2016 Olympic games.

Because Europe and Asia had hosted four of the previous five Olympics, speculation centered on a contest between Chicago and Rio de Janeiro. Rio was mountainous and divided, whereas Chicago had the advantage of compactness. Rio had a reputation for violence among drug warlords and was criticized for lawless police activity in the city's slums, areas where extrajudicial executions were common.[5] The South American city barely met the technical standards in an IOC review; Brazil's hosting of the 2014 World Cup raised questions about the nation's ability to manage both events.[6] But Rio benefited from pent-up political pressures to bring the Olympic games to South America for the first time, generating excitement among that continent's growing populations and economies.

Although Chicago faced nothing approximating Rio's levels of violence, the city and federal plan called for thirty-five thousand law enforcement officers and five thousand US military troops to join the Chicago police force, which would expand by a thousand officers. Given the density of the city, Chicago would appear much like an occupied state.

Four lanes of Lake Shore Drive and two lanes on each of the four major highways would be reserved exclusively for Olympics-related transportation, making rush hour considerably more dreadful than normal.

After reviewing Chicago's plan, the IOC sent thirteen representatives to visit the city in April 2009, part of the official tours of the four contending cities. The IOC would make its final selection in October.

With the world struggling from the aftershocks of the Great Recession, revenue was a growing IOC preoccupation. This was a double-edged sword for Chicago. Games in the United States always generate more TV revenue, but Daley's refusal to provide financial guarantees—a concession to local politics—hurt the city's position.

Many experts nonetheless felt Chicago was the front-runner, and betting odds in Las Vegas confirmed it. In the meantime, Daley was struggling to contain the city's soaring financial deficits as city revenues collapsed with the national economic downturn.

Throughout his long tenure, Daley had successfully kept property taxes reasonable and found adequate resources to fund public safety, schools, and infrastructure. Recessions in the early 1990s and 2000s had been manageable; they merely interrupted long periods of economic growth expanding city coffers. Now, however, he faced unprecedented, fearsome fiscal pressures.

In 2009, Daley had taken the politically fateful step of shoring up the city's finances by privatizing parking meters, consistent with his past success in monetizing city assets.[7] His idea was to weather the storm of the Great Recession by hunkering down with one-time revenues until calmer economic winds returned. The resulting $1.15 billion windfall accomplished Daley's budget goals, but in time led to a political firestorm unlike anything he had experienced.[8]

The mayor's popularity plunged.

As the vote of the IOC loomed, Daley was in a gambler's predicament. The odds looked favorable; another strategic move or two could put Chicago over the top. If it did, Daley's political and financial problems could be washed away in the wave of a winner's sheen and a tsunami of economic investments in the city's economy.

He decided to go for the gold.

At great political and financial risk, Mayor Daley removed his biggest remaining liability. An IOC evaluation report released in late summer highlighted Chicago's failure to sign a financial guarantee. In response, Daley broke his previous pledge, guaranteeing city revenues as insurance against cost overruns.

Despite a trail of host cities burdened with debt and little to show for it (Montreal had required thirty years to pay off its $1.6 billion debt from the 1976 games), Daley put Chicago taxpayers on the hook. Beyond the financial guarantee, the park district directed $15 million toward the aquatics center. The mayor created a new TIF to pay for the Olympic Village; the city spent $86 million to purchase the shuttered Michael Reese Hospital site as the new venue.[9]

Daley's decision was immediately unpopular, turning previous local support for the games upside down, but it cemented in the minds of many prognosticators that Chicago was the front-runner.

One final liability for the US bid Daley could do nothing about—President George Bush's poisonous legacy of the Iraq War, which was deeply unpopular among the international community. But the mayor hoped he had an antidote—the election of Sen. Barack Obama of Chicago as Bush's successor. As the nation's first African American president, Obama had captured the imagination of the world. Despite being in office only a short time, he was awarded the Nobel Peace Prize for his "extraordinary efforts to strengthen international diplomacy and cooperation between peoples."[10] Obama agreed to lend his prestige to Chicago's bid, traveling in October to Copenhagen to anchor the final presentations ahead of the IOC's voting.

Although Rio remained an emotional favorite, all the stars seemed aligned for Chicago to host the 2016 Olympic games.

On October 2, 2009, President Obama and First Lady Michelle Obama joined a large Chicago delegation that included Mayor Daley, business leaders, the celebrated TV talk show host Oprah Winfrey, the two-time Olympic gold-medal-winning gymnast Bart Connor, and the families of the famous Olympians Jesse Owens and Ralph Metcalfe. After Chicago's final presentation to the IOC voters, including a passionate speech by President Obama in support of his hometown, Daley entered his car for the trip back to the Convention Center, to watch the ballots cast in a series of elimination rounds.

In Chicago, Daley Plaza was filled with revelers awaiting a celebration. The announcement of a winner was expected to come around noon; in the meantime, spectators anticipated a morning of drama as cities were eliminated one by one.

But Mayor Daley never made it back to the Convention Center. While still in the car, he received news that Chicago had been eliminated in the first round of voting.

The outcome was as shocking as it was sudden. How could Chicago, with all its advantages, be eliminated at the starting gate? The Daley Center crowd was stunned, gradually dispersing in bewilderment. Daley redirected his car to the party being held for Chicago supporters. He addressed the deflated crowd as best he could, then steeled himself for a meeting with the press corps.

As they often do in such situations, reporters asked the drama's leading protagonist how he felt, his raw emotions in the moment. Daley responded in a restrained manner, not wishing to make the loss seem more monumental than it had been.

"Sure, you have tears, you get disappointed—you're human like anyone else," Daley said. "But you go on with your life."[11]

After Chicago's loss, Tokyo was eliminated in the second round, followed by Madrid's ouster in a lopsided third-round vote favoring Rio de Janeiro.

• • •

In the years that followed, reporters and academics debated why Chicago lost its Olympics bid to Rio de Janeiro. In the immediate aftermath, most observers argued it was simply Brazil's time. South America had never hosted the Olympics, a fact hammered incessantly by Rio in its messaging.

Brazil's president, Luiz Inácio Lula da Silva, used as a cudgel the Olympic Charter's mandate to promote international understanding, arguing that the historical absence of the games from an entire continent was unconscionable. The Olympics, he asserted, "belong to all people, all continents, all humanity."[12]

On a more practical level, some reporters cited a conflict between the United States Olympic Committee and the IOC over TV rights and revenue, a battle that had taken place below the surface almost from day one.

Explaining Chicago's first-round dismissal was more difficult, but experts insisted it was a classic trap born of quirks in the Olympic voting process, as well as cunning maneuvering by Rio and its allies. In this scenario, Rio understood that Chicago was its strongest competitor; the longer Chicago stayed in the game, the more likely its selection. So in a version of game theory, Rio conspired with the other cities and their regional allies to eliminate Chicago on the first ballot.[13]

"That's sport politics, not anything else," said the Canadian IOC member Richard Pound, speculating that Rio had indeed formed first-round alliances to remove its most significant threat. "We kind of think if you've got the best bid, the world will recognize that, and these decisions are made solely on the merits of the bid. Well, not solely."[14] Pound added that Europeans and Asians historically have proven better at outflanking their rivals than North Americans.

"All we know is that the first round is always the most dangerous," said Pat Ryan, Daley's Olympics bid chairman.[15]

In a 2012 academic paper, Professors Robert A. Baade of Lake Forest College and Allen R. Sanderson of the University of Chicago analyzed the underlying dynamics of IOC decision making, and the reasons for Chicago's loss. Among them: the US Olympic Committee, which undercut Chicago by attempting to siphon off TV revenue important to the IOC; the "Chicago Way," the city's reputation for riding roughshod over critics and providing information only on a need-to-know basis; the less than enthusiastic backing of the Chicago populace, which the authors attributed in part to the Chicago Way; and the failure of both Chicago and the USOC to sufficiently cultivate relationships with IOC delegates.[16]

Perhaps most important, the authors argued, was the city's failure to understand and embrace the values of the Olympic Charter.

"The USOC and Chicago failed to convince IOC delegates that the values espoused by the Olympic Movement in putting on the Games matched the principal motivation of the United States," their report said.

Among the lofty goals of the Olympic Charter is "to place sport at the service of the harmonious development of man, with a view to promoting a peaceful society concerned with the preservation of human dignity . . . and respect for universal fundamental ethical principles."

• • •

Years later, a decade after the stunned boosters slinked off Daley Plaza and the mayor struggled to explain Chicago's mystifying loss to his star-studded entourage and press corps, the truth finally emerged.

Professors Baade and Sanderson turned out to be right on two counts. Chicago did indeed fail to sufficiently cultivate delegates. And, yes, they were done in by the Chicago Way, although in a different way than the academics understood. But the professors were spectacularly wrong about the city's failure to uphold the values of the Olympic Charter. In fact, it was Chicago's adherence to its "fundamental ethical principles" that sealed the city's fate.

In 2017, law enforcement officials raided the home of Carlos Arthur Nuzman, the head of the Rio organizing committee, the longtime chief of Brazil's Olympic committee, and a "towering figure within the International Olympic Committee."[17] They found $155,000 in cash and a key to a Swiss vault containing sixteen gold bars.

The raid was part of a joint investigation into sports corruption by Brazilian and French authorities. Two years later, the former Rio de Janeiro state governor, Sérgio Cabral, who had presented Rio's bid before the Olympic Committee in Copenhagen, testified that nine IOC delegates had been bribed to steer the games to South America. Nuzman led the plot, financed by a Brazilian businessman, that funneled $2 million in payoffs to officials designated by Lamine Diack, the head of the world regulatory agency for track and field events.

Former governor Cabral said Nuzman had contacted him months before the vote.

"Nuzman came to me and said, 'Sergio, I want to tell you that the I.A.A.F. president, Lamine Diack, is a person that is open to undue advantages. He can secure five or six votes. In exchange he wants $1.5 million,'" Cabral said.

At a subsequent meeting, the former governor testified, he was told by Nuzman that Diack could deliver another three votes to reach nine in total, for an additional $500,000.

"I told him it would be done," Cabral said.

Cabral said the nine votes were especially critical for Rio to navigate past Chicago in the first round.[18]

At the time of his testimony, in support of the prosecution's case against Nuzman, Cabral was serving a twenty-year sentence for other corruption offenses. Nuzman was convicted and sentenced to thirty years. The eighty-seven-year-old Diack was convicted of corruption in France and sentenced to four years.

The bribery scandal added more embarrassment for the International Olympic Committee. By the time Nuzman was convicted, it had already overhauled its methods of selecting host cities following multiple other bribery accusations. The IOC also faced new revelations that it had ignored a prominent whistleblower's evidence of Nuzman's long-standing questionable conduct on the Brazilian Olympic Committee, going back more than a decade.

The IOC received only two bids for the 2026 winter Olympic Games, evidence of the deflating effect of the committee's complicity in the illicit schemes.

In addition to denying Chicago its opportunity to shine before the world, with enormous political and financial implications, the corrupt process stained Brazil's reputation, already tarnished by widespread graft in construction projects for the games. It also thrust the ill-equipped Rio into the international spotlight.

As the 2016 games began, *Chicago* magazine shared some of the headlines:

- *Rio Olympics Athletes Advised to Not Put Their Heads Under Water* (because of the high concentrations of viruses and bacteria in some of its venues)
- *Transportation Poses Ordeal for Rio Games* (the city's big transportation investment in the Games is late, over budget, just connects one rich neighborhood to another, and might not work in time)
- *The Broken Promise of the Rio Olympics* (investments and tax breaks have benefited the rich and the places they live, while tens of thousands of poor families have been evicted)
- *The Trouble With Rio's Police* (there's an increase in police killings and a likely decline in police presence in Rio's most dangerous neighborhoods during the Olympics)[19]

For Mayor Daley, ironically the leader of a city with a historic propensity for corruption, the rigged bidding had enormous implications. To win, he had played every card and pushed all his chips onto the IOC's poker table. He had done everything imaginable to meet the Olympic criteria and ensure that Chicago had an overwhelming competitive advantage.

But none of it mattered.

With the Olympics, Daley could have injected new life into the moribund Chicago economy, shaken by the Great Recession. He could have generated new tax revenues and leveraged private investments for vast new infrastructure projects benefiting the city. With weeks of television exposure to half the planet, showcasing Chicago's beauty and cultural and architectural marvels, he could have expected tourism to boom. Out of it would have come a flow of new jobs. His political standing, local as well as national and international, potentially would have soared. He would have sought—and likely won—seventh and eighth terms, taking him through the 2016 games and marking three decades in office.

All of this is informed speculation. We will never know what would have happened if the process for selecting the 2016 Olympic Games host city had been on the up and up.

But by losing his big gamble, taken to salvage an increasingly losing hand at home, Daley's political future became tenuous. His poll numbers were well below the 50 percent approval usually required to guarantee reelection. He faced a new economic landscape in which tax increases and budget cuts would predominate, with no obvious fixes to the mountainous debt and pension obligations exposed by the Great Recession.[20] He began to eye an exit from public life.

Perhaps it was because the job was no longer fun. Perhaps he feared a tough reelection battle. Perhaps he was simply tired. He was nearly sixty-nine years of age and had served as mayor for almost a quarter century. Or perhaps it was more personal.

First diagnosed in 2002, Maggie Daley's cancer was worsening. In the summer of 2010, a little more than a year before her death, Mayor Daley was speaking at an anniversary event promoting the revitalized downtown theater district. During prepared remarks, he talked about the importance of the arts in schools. His voice cracked. "Every one of these children can learn," he said, fighting back tears.[21] His wife, indelibly linked to arts education in Chicago, was clearly on his mind.

Whatever the reason, on September 7, 2010, Daley announced he would not be a candidate for reelection in the February municipal elections.

It was the end of an era.

Epilogue

In his twenty-two years in office, Mayor Richard M. Daley fundamentally reshaped Chicago. He did not end the city's historic proclivity for corruption or police misconduct; and his habit of deficit spending, even in good times, left behind inordinate debt. But on the salient issues facing all big-city mayors—crime, schools, housing, jobs, and quality of life—he left a remarkable legacy.

Nationwide and in Chicago, violent crime peaked in 1991, Daley's second year in office. In the following two decades, violent US crime fell by less than 50 percent. In Chicago, it declined by two-thirds.[1] Homicides in Chicago reached the lowest levels in more than forty years.[2]

Daley's appointments of police superintendents proved shrewd; he also shifted leadership adroitly in response to events. He never attempted to micromanage but did hold his leaders accountable. No other department chief and its senior leaders spent more time in Daley's private fifth-floor office. If senior police officials tried to sugarcoat events or withhold information, they quickly learned that Daley's bullshit meter was high.

Through multiple superintendents and shifting strategies of policing, Mayor Daley steadily made Chicago a safer place to live.

But in the same way his accomplishments elsewhere in government were tarnished by scandal, so too were his notable achievements in public safety. In 2013, the University of Illinois at Chicago released a report on the city's police corruption and brutality with reminders of the long line of scandals dating back decades. It noted that although prosecutions of police officers are unusual, 102 Chicago officers had been convicted of crimes since 2000. The authors wrote:

> The real problem is that an embarrassingly large number of police officers violate citizens' rights, engage in corruption and commit crimes while escaping detection and avoiding discipline or prosecution for many years. The "code

of silence" and "deliberate indifference" have prevented police supervisors and civilian authorities from effectively eliminating police corruption. Police superintendents and mayors typically denounce each new case as another "bad apple," and have failed to establish meaningful internal reforms or effective oversight.[3]

More than most urban leaders, Daley understood the delicate balance between aggressive policing and the potential for brutality. He maintained equilibrium for more than two decades, relying on close community relationships and lines of communication while giving his commanders the leeway to battle street gangs and other criminals. Only late in his tenure, however, did he contend with police body cameras and widespread use of mobile phone cameras.

When Daley's successor, Rahm Emanuel, was forced by court order to release video of the police murder of seventeen-year-old Laquan McDonald in November 2015, thirteen months after the shooting, it effectively ended his chances of reelection. McDonald was stopped by police after behaving erratically and carrying a small knife. Giving the lie to official police reports of justifiable self-defense, the video shows an execution. As McDonald walked away from the police, Officer Jason Van Dyke fired sixteen shots into the teenager. At public appearances, Emanuel was often heckled by protestors accusing the mayor of a cover-up, chanting, "Sixteen shots, sixteen shots!"

Emanuel was following standard city protocol at the time by not releasing evidence in a pending case before the county prosecutor; but State's Attorney Anita Alvarez sat on the videotape evidence for more than a year, acting only after the public furor following its release.[4] Besides sealing the mayor's early retirement, the scandal led to Alvarez's defeat in the following year's election.

In the wake of the McDonald murder and escalating tensions between the Black community and police, violent crime spiked higher. In 2016, the year after the video's release, homicides rose a startling 58 percent.

In late 2016, the *Tribune* published a lengthy story on the shifting urban landscape. Officers "say the anti-police furor that erupted over the vivid 2014 images continues to sink morale, hamstring officers and embolden the criminal element, contributing to a shocking jump in violence this year to levels unseen in Chicago since the late 1990s."[5]

Police Superintendent Eddie Johnson told the *Tribune* that his officers had become overly cautious, fearful of having their encounters filmed and manipulated on social media.

"I've never seen [this] level of disrespect out there on the streets," Johnson said.[6]

At traffic stops, on the street or at crime scenes, officers were being surrounded by people putting cellphones in their faces, said Dean Angelo, president of the police union.

"We have police officers who are concerned about being the next headline, the next YouTube video," he said.[7]

Official responses to the McDonald case added to police officers' perceptions that they were on their own. Responding to pressure for reforms, Emanuel signed a court-supervised agreement with the American Civil Liberties Union restricting police activity and mandating documentation of street stops, requiring about twenty minutes of paperwork each and raising questions in officers' minds of institutional second-guessing.

Street stops plunged, along with arrests. US Attorney Zachary Fardon said the new restrictions contributed to bloodshed.

"I believe there was a hit on CPD morale and a drag on officers' willingness to conduct stops," Fardon said. "Some gang members apparently felt that they could get away with more, so more bullets started flying."[8]

Emanuel's successor, Lori Lightfoot, imposed even more restrictions, including a "balancing test" for determining whether to chase a suspect on foot. It includes an assessment of the seriousness of the crime, whether a chase would put the suspect or bystanders at risk, and if the police officer believes there is "probable cause" that the person committed a crime or is about to commit one.

Lightfoot's policy also had an addendum. In making the decision, officers are not allowed to give chase "based solely on a person's response to the presence of police," including a desire to avoid being questioned. "People may avoid contact with a Department member for many reasons other than involvement in criminal activity," the new policy states.[9]

Lightfoot's policies, her decision to bypass Chicago brass in favor of choosing an out-of-state police superintendent, and rhetoric perceived hostile to the police department, spurred further discontent. Emotions reached a zenith in 2021, when two convicted felons murdered a Chicago police officer, Ella French, twenty-nine, and seriously wounded her partner. When Mayor Lightfoot visited the hospital to comfort the thirty officers holding vigil, they turned their backs on her in a united gesture of protest. The father of the wounded officer blamed Lightfoot, saying her rhetoric had encouraged antipolice sentiment and that her policies were "tying the hands" of officers, jeopardizing their safety.

In 2021, Chicago recorded nearly eight hundred murders, levels not seen in a quarter century.[10] What was more, far fewer of them were being solved.[11] Shootings, carjackings, and other violent crimes skyrocketed. Police officer retirements reached records. Investigative stops dropped nearly 60 percent. Arrests fell to two-decade lows. In 2023, Chicago led the nation in mass shootings, defined as four or more people shot in a single event, part of a pattern of steadily accelerating violence since 2013.[12]

"Loss of control and autonomy in the workplace has long been associated with lowered morale," said Arthur Lurigio, a professor of psychology and criminal justice at Loyola University in Chicago. "Fewer street stops lead to fewer arrests and decrease the visible presence of police in neighborhoods, which leaves a vacuum in authority that can embolden would-be criminals and gang members."[13]

Whether driven by technological change, public events, or political calculus, Mayor Daley's successors pursued more radical changes to how police conduct missions, abandoning Mayor Daley's longstanding balancing act, and restricting tactics and strategies that had made Chicago a national public safety leader.

• • •

Mayor Daley's steady, outsized gains in public safety created an environment that encouraged new businesses and residents to move to Chicago. His school reforms did almost as much, perhaps more, to attract middle-class parents to city life. In combination with his successor, Rahm Emanuel, Daley rebuilt dilapidated and failing public schools, considered by many the worst in the nation, and secured academic gains reflecting at least urban parity and by many measurements a position of national urban leadership. A one-size-fits-all public-school monopoly became a system of diverse choice, accompanied by rigorous accountability standards.

For a generation of children matriculating through Chicago public schools during Daley's mayoralty, the elevated quality of education will have enduring, life-changing benefits. A cascade of recent changes, however, threaten for future generations the hard-won progress of a quarter century of reforms led by two mayors, a host of educational support groups, nonprofits, philanthropies, and a united business community.

The shift from classroom to remote learning during the COVID pandemic erased more than a decade of academic gains, as students struggled to retain proficiency in home environments.[14] Resisting pressure from Mayor Lori Lightfoot and threatening a strike, the Chicago Teachers Union (CTU) kept schools closed for a year and a half, long after other schools in Illinois and the rest of the nation returned to classroom instruction.

Moreover, backpedaling on successful initiatives and a loosening of standards began to undo more progress. In 2021, Lightfoot's school board began transitioning back to CPS control thirty-one schools serving sixteen thousand students, operated by the Academy for Urban School Leadership (AUSL), a nationally recognized turnaround program deploying an innovative model of recruiting, training, and mentoring teacher residents.

"What we are voting on today is . . . the purpose of a private management company of this kind within CPS, the fact that turnaround is no longer a strategy or practice of the district, that it's a relic . . . of a previous era of school reform," said the board member Elizabeth Todd-Breland, who spearheaded the process.[15]

In 2023, the school board voted to eliminate the district's School Quality Rating Policy (SQRP) measurements, based on test scores, academic growth, closing of achievement gaps, attendance, graduation rates, and preparation for postgraduate success. In its place will be a "soft accountability" system, measuring resources provided to schools, opportunities to engage in athletics and arts, school social supports, and how students and parents feel about the school, including the extent to which students are engaged in decision making.[16]

"Part of what started this was our communities being very clear about the harm that they felt from a rating system that didn't just make them feel like it was something wrong with their schools, but something deficient with them as people, as communities, as parents," said Elizabeth Todd-Breland.[17]

Mayor Brandon Johnson's school board, in place a mere five months, announced in December 2023 a five-year plan to transition Chicago schools away from choice-based policies that "further stratification and inequity in CPS and drive student enrollment away from neighborhood schools," a policy endorsed by the new mayor, a former CTU organizer.[18]

"This plan needs to be guided and informed by the community," the board president, Jianan Shi, told the *Sun-Times*. "The goal is that we're able to change [the] current competition model so that students are not pitted against one another, schools are not pitted against one another."[19]

Parents of three-quarters of high school students and nearly half of elementary students choose schools for their children outside of their neighborhoods.[20] Because Johnson's school board did not consult these parents, or even hold a single public hearing soliciting feedback, the *Tribune* described the statement by the mayor's board president, previously an executive with the CTU-funded advocacy group Raise Your Hand,[21] as "nonsensical, self-contradictory and disingenuous blather."[22]

The former CPS CEO, Janice Jackson, an African American mother who chose to send her children to a public neighborhood elementary school and then a private high school, warned Mayor Johnson's board not to sacrifice the gains of decades of school choice on the altar of union self-interest and ideology.

"This is about politics," Jackson wrote in a *Sun-Times* commentary. "I cannot be silent when that agenda disadvantages Black and Brown kids by denying parents the same choices policymakers have made for their own children," an apparent reference to CTU President Stacy Davis Gates, who sends her son to a private school.[23]

"Shamefully, the only group of people policymakers routinely believe don't deserve their rights are poor kids of color," Jackson wrote.[24]

Thousands of impoverished Chicago students will also lose their scholarships to private schools in 2024, thanks to Gov. J. B. Pritzker and the General Assembly, which declined to renew the six-year-old tax credit allowing nearly ten thousand low-income schoolchildren access to better schools. Illinois is the first state in the nation to rescind a parental school choice program.[25]

These departures from a quarter century of reforms—changes that drove an unprecedented urban school turnaround—are harbingers of even more radical reversals. In 2024, CPS begins its transition to an elected school board, under legislation pushed through Springfield by CTU, over the vociferous objections of Mayor Lightfoot. The legislation, signed into law by Gov. J. B. Pritzker, first elected in 2018, will spawn twenty-one new politicians to steward the city's schools.

When President Bill Clinton traveled to Chicago in 1998 to proclaim, "I want what is happening in Chicago to happen all over America," he stood in front of an oversized chalkboard that read: "Standards + Accountability = Excellence." With weakening standards and oversight, accountability diffused among a committee of nearly two dozen elected school board members, a city and state rollback of parental choice, and the city's chief executive no longer responsible or accountable, Chicago's public schools face a troubling and uncertain future.

• • •

Mayor Daley's many other notable legacies stem largely from his patient, consistent focus on—and prodigious investments in—the city's infrastructure, housing stock, transportation network, and parks. To pay for them, the mayor used a combination of traditional bonds and TIF financing, requiring steady growth in city revenues. To help ensure that growth, he nurtured a business-friendly environment that drew companies large and small to Chicago. He often leveraged city funds to tip the balance for private investments that left in their wake embedded wealth and new jobs and tax revenues. He kept property tax increases modest, and used his veto pen to block onerous wage and benefit mandates on private companies. One vetoed ordinance targeted "big box" retailers in 2006, designed to prevent Wal-Mart from opening stores in impoverished neighborhoods, despite support for the corporation by African American aldermen in the affected wards.[26]

Daley's policies fueled a jobs boom in Chicago. From 1993 to the last year of his reign, the city added more jobs than Boston and Los Angeles combined.[27]

Today, Chicago's ability to invest in its future is challenged on many fronts. Nearly one in four dollars in the city's 2024 budget is earmarked for pensions, a percentage likely to grow markedly.[28] Similar pension mandates have fueled outsize property tax increases at CPS, helping to drive a 55 percent increase in its budget since 2010, despite 20 percent fewer students.[29] Decisions by the Illinois Supreme Court in 2015 and 2016 struck down pension reforms by Gov. Pat Quinn and the General Assembly. Narrow passage in 2022 of a state constitutional amendment, restricting the ability of legislators to alter collective bargaining rules, further impedes any ability to alter the fiscal trajectory. The incumbent governor, J. B. Pritzker, and new General Assembly leadership, continue to foist billions in new pension liabilities on Chicago taxpayers, even as those funds teeter on insolvency.[30]

Property tax burdens on commercial businesses in Chicago are now second only to those in Detroit among American cities and are more than double those in the largest cities in each state.[31] Under the new mayor, Brandon Johnson, elected in 2023, and the city council, private businesses are facing higher wage and benefit mandates even as they struggle with renewed inflation, increasingly brazen crimes,[32] and the impact of remote work in reducing commuter spending.

The TIF districts Daley relied on for much of his economic development have also been increasingly targeted as piggy banks for retiring budget deficits. Mayor Johnson's first budget covers 80 percent of the 2024 deficit with $434 million in onetime revenues from the LaSalle Street Reimagined TIF, leaving only $6.5 million and calling its viability into question. Designed to convert empty office buildings into residences, reflecting the postpandemic trend toward remote work, five different developments call for sixteen hundred units in the Loop, six hundred of which are affordable housing. More than $870 million in private investments are at stake.

Alderman Bill Conway warned of the shortsightedness that threatened to undercut Mayor Daley's original, successful vision—one that turned a dilapidated downtown into a potent economic engine.[33]

"This is not the day or year that we want to be draining LaSalle Street TIF. Every city in the world needs to rethink its central business district," Conway said. "It can't just be a place where people work, but a place to live and eat and shop."[34]

• • •

The years of economic growth and attendant budget flexibility during Daley's tenure had allowed him largely to fulfill his vision of a new and better Chicago. But when he retired, economic growth had come to a near standstill. The city—and the nation—were just beginning a slow and painful recovery from the greatest economic downturn since the Great Depression. The fiscal and budgetary landscape of the city was at its nadir.

Against this backdrop, in the years following his retirement, Daley received plenty of blame for the city's financial woes and pension debt, including from his successor, Rahm Emanuel, who pushed through record tax hikes.

"Had this been taken care of before," Emanuel said, "it would have been taken care of at a much cheaper price. People chose their politics over the progress of the city. They kicked the can down the road. I did not create it. But I was . . . determined to do something different, which is to fix it . . . [and stop] playing politics."[35]

Reflecting the views of many in the news media, Eric Zorn of the *Tribune* lambasted Daley for insufficiently funding pensions; paying off the Millennium Park debt by selling the Grant Park parking garages; spending tens of millions on a "feckless Olympics fantasy"; and balancing budgets with $1.1 billion in revenue from the seventy-five-year parking-meter lease rather than "cut costs or raise revenues."[36]

Criticizing Daley for spending beyond the city's means is fair game, although to some degree a benefit of hindsight, following the magnifying effects of the Great Recession on city debt.

After the tsunami of the economy's collapse, Daley could have "cut costs or raised revenues," as Zorn recommended. In fact, Daley did both. But cutting deeply or taxing heavily while facing the gale winds of an extraordinary economic downturn was impractical, as businesses closed and homeowner foreclosures mounted.

Millennium Park required taxpayer subsidies, but the rippling economic benefits have produced far more tax revenue, along with jobs and new developments. And we know now that Daley's "feckless Olympics fantasy" likely went unrealized only because of corruption on the Olympic committee.[37]

Daley deserves part of the blame for underfunded police and firefighter pensions. But in 2006, the year before the start of the financial crisis, the city's actuarial funding levels for its municipal, laborers, teachers, and park district pension funds ran well ahead of those of the state of Illinois and its five funds, which in the same year were less than 60 percent funded.[38] The real culprit was the Illinois General Assembly, which increased Chicago's pension costs with unfunded mandates, insider-driven early retirement deals, a host of pension sweeteners, and the ticking time bomb of compounding annual COLAs, passed into law long after delegates to the Illinois Constitutional Convention enshrined government pension rights in the state constitution.[39]

Mayor Rahm Emanuel argued he was "fixing" the city's pension woes with his record-shattering property tax increases, but he, too, was merely kicking the can down the road. The extraordinary tax hikes only slowed the growth of pension debt, and even then just for a time. Pension reforms, partial default, or insolvency are the only eventual outcomes. Fewer contributors supporting more retirees who are living longer, along with rising and compounding payments, guarantee an eventual reckoning. No amount of tax hikes or government service cuts can change the math. The Chicago and Illinois bills have only been delayed—again—because of the gargantuan $350 *billion* bailout of state and local governments by the Biden administration under the guise of pandemic relief.[40]

• • •

The media coverage of Mayor Daley, often fawning in his early years, turned more challenging later in his tenure. Some of that coverage was deserved, and Chicago always has been a target-rich environment for reporters investigating government corruption.

But mounting competitive pressures on local news outlets and a thinning of editorial ranks contributed to uneven—and sometimes unfair—coverage, where inference replaced fact, as struggling newspapers and broadcast stations sought audiences with eye-grabbing exposés that were sometimes less than met the eye.

A few years after Mayor Daley left office, I got a firsthand lesson in this new environment. I had spent four years as CEO of the Chicago Transit Authority, during which we rescued its finances, reformed its operations, and improved services.[41] Then I accepted an appointment as superintendent of the Chicago Public Schools (CPS). The challenges were many, but I felt then, and feel now, that we had a moral responsibility to ensure that every child in Chicago, regardless of their status or circumstances, received the foundation a strong education provides.

Central to that mission was my assessment that the state was chronically underfunding Chicago school children, 80 percent of whom were minorities and low income, relative to the aid Illinois provided to every other school district in the state. I was determined to sue the state to win justice and fair-share funding for Chicago's kids. I did not foresee that this battle would wind up costing me my public career and allow political opponents, with the help of friendly reporters, to besmirch my reputation for integrity.

Here's the short version:

I recruited the prominent law firm of Jenner & Block to handle the suit because they had an extraordinary team of litigators who were experts in civil rights cases of this kind.[42] In fact, Jenner had recently won a victory against the state under the Illinois civil rights statute, barring indiscriminate cuts to low-income schools.[43] They were, in my view, the best legal talent and gave us the best chance to win what was going to be a difficult and complex case. Randy Mehrberg, my old legal counsel from the Park District, was now a managing partner at the law firm, where I had briefly worked as a young associate almost four decades earlier.

The rub I did not anticipate came over the participation of Ronald Marmer, a retired Jenner partner and my general counsel at CPS, in overseeing the litigation from our end. Ethics rules of the Board of Education prohibit a supervisor from overseeing the work of firms in which he or she has a financial interest. This sensible requirement is designed to prevent conflicts of interest and financial self-dealing.

Marmer and I felt certain that because his retirement agreement with Jenner included fixed annual payments that were not subject to fluctuation, regardless of how much money the firm made, this rule was not applicable to him. Besides, Jenner & Block, which worked for a third of its usual billing rate for the first three months of the year-long case, and then shifted to doing it on an entirely pro bono basis, was deliberately losing money on the deal. The law firm has a well-deserved reputation for allowing its attorneys to work on cases advancing social justice, despite the hit to the business's bottom line from lost corporate billings.[44]

Yet a *Sun-Times* reporter lit on Marmer's status as a major ethics violation and wrote multiple stories, suggesting that what was a serious, good-faith effort to win fair funding for Chicago's schools was actually a sweetheart deal.

Incensed by the inference, I plowed ahead. I wanted my counsel involved in this critical legal battle and felt the ethics rule was irrelevant. No one was profiting but the children of Chicago. Yet thanks to the *Sun-Times*' persistent positioning of it as a major story, a publicity-hungry inspector general saw it as an opportunity to score points, which he did at my expense—and with my help. Without a doubt, I stubbornly cut corners I should not have cut in order to keep Marmer involved and Jenner on the case, and then I failed to take the whole matter seriously until it was too late. The story blew up, becoming a political problem for Mayor Emanuel. The school board of his appointees were poised to move against me. And so I resigned.

Looking back, I wish I had fought it out, as I was urged to do by a cadre of religious leaders who had worked with me on the civil rights case. Everything I did was in service of a cause I felt was noble and important. To have the words "ethics scandal" associated with my name after an impeccable thirty-year career of fighting for reform is an excruciating epitaph for my public career and one I believe is deeply unfair. But once the media narrative gained momentum, I was swept up in its wake. I got a taste of how, in the current environment, the vital oversight mission of journalism can go awry, and with it, any sense of proportionality.

By the end of his nearly quarter century as mayor, Daley's record was viewed at times through the same distorted lens. His substantial achievements were often lost amid an obsession with finding fault. I hope this book provides a balanced account of his record, drawing important lessons for future leaders from his distinctive achievements, without whitewashing his mistakes and less admirable policies and practices.

• • •

Nearly a decade and a half after Mayor Richard M. Daley left office, Chicago is in many ways a "city on the brink" again.

Riven by violent crime, its finances propped up only by the massive federal pandemic bailout, Chicago is struggling again to retain people and jobs. Some of its highest-profile companies, from Boeing to Caterpillar to Citadel to Tyson Foods, have moved their headquarters elsewhere. Homeless encampments are common. Graffiti mars thoroughfares. Public transit has degraded. Michigan Avenue, once the commercial heartbeat of the city, is still recovering from massive looting, unrestrained by police, following the George Floyd murder.[45] A malaise has engulfed rank-and-file police officers who feel under siege. The public schools are hemorrhaging students and families, reaching historic lows, following teacher strikes, rollbacks of reforms, and a successful union campaign for an elected school board, despite twenty-five years of steady progress under two mayors.[46]

But for all these seemingly intractable problems, Chicago remains in many ways a strong city. The embedded wealth from the growth years; the city's tourist trade; the energy and vibrancy of revived communities such as Bronzeville and Fulton Market, where tech businesses, modern condos, and restaurants have created a city within a city—all provide hope that Chicago can rebound. Chicago's airports continue to drive the regional economy. After years of investment and rising real estate values, Chicago's neighborhoods undergird a strong city foundation.

But the gains of recent decades are at risk.

Annalee Newitz, the author of *Four Lost Cities*, writes that what destroys cities "is a long period in which their leaders fail to reckon honestly with ongoing, everyday problems. . . . Unsustainable, unresponsive governance in the face of long-term challenges may not look like a world-historical problem, but it's the real threat cities face."[47]

Richard M. Daley was not a perfect mayor. Although a visionary with grand ambitions for his city, he also spent lavishly in pursuit of them, leaving considerable debt. He was a deft politician who was not above taking care of favored contractors or unions to grease the wheels of government—and his own reelections. His hubris and overreach led to twin scandals in contracting and hiring that sent many of his top operatives to prison. And although he worked hard to bridge the city's racial divides, he also failed to investigate evidence that Detective Jon Burge and his Midnight Crew had crossed the line from aggressive policing to violent and egregious violations of civil rights.

Daley's errors and misjudgments, however, should not diminish what was a momentously transformative mayoralty, one that not only reversed the fortunes of a great city but also provides a template for future urban leaders. In nearly a quarter century at the helm of the nation's third largest metropolis, Mayor Daley steered with sophisticated and effective leadership, the results unquestionable.

Daley loved Chicago. He won the hearts and minds of ordinary people in city neighborhoods, where he was a constant presence and in which he invested relentlessly. The city rallied around him in big moments. He made Chicago an international city. He shrewdly balanced competing interests while ensuring that no special interest ran roughshod over Chicago's interests. He put the city's "Beirut on the Lake" image behind it, uniting all the city's races and ethnicities.

"He inherited a divided city known for 'Council Wars.' He bequeaths a city that, while still segregated, has moved beyond race—so much so that his white successor carried every one of the city's black wards with help from a Chicagoan who went on to become the nation's first African American president," wrote the *Sun-Times* in 2011.[48]

President Obama agreed, saying Daley brought "this city together in a way that . . . a lot of people didn't imagine could be done."[49]

The former Gov. Jim Thompson said, "It's fair to say that he kept Chicago as unified as it's possible for one person to do. Part of that is due to longevity. Part of it is due to general agreement for his vision for the city and his plans to carry out those visions, and part of it is the force of his political skills."[50]

Scripture teaches that "where there is no vision, the people perish."[51] Daley had a vision of a better future for Chicago and the skill and savvy to reach for it. On his watch, Chicago moved on from its industrial past, its "hog butcher to the world" history, to become a service-driven economy and a tourist mecca showcasing theater, music, and dance; world-renowned museums; architecture; and culinary arts. Daley created a new front lawn for Chicago in the resplendent Millennium Park—for the people, but also as a cultural draw and an economic engine.

In an early show of political skills, he brokered a city-state deal that rebuilt Navy Pier into a hugely popular tourist destination. In an engineering feat, he rerouted Lake Shore Drive to unite three of Chicago's great museums—the Shedd Aquarium, the Field Museum, and the Adler Planetarium—on a campus of rolling greensward. On the same campus Daley built a new stadium for the Chicago Bears, ensuring that national broadcasts would continue to showcase Chicago's beautiful lakefront and gleaming skyline.[52]

Chicago's bourgeoning attractions encouraged more businesses, including major corporations, to move to Chicago, to draw the urban-minded knowledge workers important to today's global economy. In 1989, Chicago was competing with Minneapolis and Milwaukee for regional prominence. In 2010, *Foreign Policy* magazine ranked Chicago sixth in its list of global cities.[53]

Mayor Daley invested heavily in sustaining and expanding Chicago's transportation dominance, more than once saving O'Hare and Midway Airports from political predation. He secured Chicago's place as a trade-show and conventions leader despite fierce competition from cities in warmer climes. Although perpetually challenged by the historic urban problems of guns, gangs, and drugs, he ensured that police and neighborhood leaders worked together. His astute choices of superintendents and evolving tactics and strategies materially reduced crime and made the city safer. In a political and managerial miracle, he razed the hellish public-housing high-rises and replaced them with healthier mixed-income communities. Mayor Daley turned around a deeply troubled public school system and lifted the fortunes of hundreds of thousands of largely poor schoolchildren, while attracting middle-class families back to the city.

Known as the "green mayor," Daley made Chicago a more beautiful city, with miles of new trees and flowers and an obsessive focus on cleanliness. He used his clout and ingenuity to rehabilitate vast swaths of housing in struggling neighborhoods; and his unique economic development strategies attracted new commercial businesses to support them. He built a vast network of modern police and fire stations, libraries, schools, and colleges, leveraging their new locations to stabilize and improve communities. He expanded the city's historic park system and fostered a multitude of recreational programs for working families. Daley's relentless focus was on making Chicago a more affordable and livable city.

Remembering where Chicago was in 1989, a city on the brink; how it had traveled to international prominence by 2011; and where it stands today, fast ceding hard-won gains in public safety, education, and jobs, one might hear the faint strains of Joni Mitchell's classic song "Big Yellow Taxi," with its lament:

Don't it always seem to go, that you don't know what you got 'til it's gone?

Acknowledgments

I was fortunate to have the support of several exceptional researchers. Kenny Shaevel, a recent graduate of the University of Chicago's Harris School of Public Policy, laid a strong foundation before handing off to Doug Kucia, my former deputy in county and city government, who brought his usual prolific political and governmental insights to match his tenacity in unearthing material. My wife, Daina Lyons, used her expertise as a genealogical researcher to help me track down difficult-to-find documents; she also tutored me on web-based research tools. Dan Harper, senior archivist at the University of Illinois-Chicago, lent me his expertise in navigating the voluminous special collections of the school's Richard J. Daley Library.

I'm grateful to my former colleague David Axelrod for his unique historical perspectives and his many incisive suggestions both on content and structure, not to mention his authorship of the book's illuminating Foreword. Peter Cunningham, a senior advisor to both Mayor Daley and US Secretary of Education Arne Duncan, provided valuable contributions. More important, his revealing interviews of key actors in Daley's mayoralty for the University of Illinois-Chicago's Richard M. Daley Oral Histories project unearthed many fascinating anecdotes and observations that enrich the book.

I'd like to thank Daniel Nasset, the editor-in-chief of the University of Illinois Press, for taking my unsolicited phone call several years ago and listening to my idea for this book, and then narrowing and framing the approach to make it work. But I am especially thankful for his assignment of the editor to work with me—Martha Bayne, a gifted journalist who gave me the freedom and encouragement to write in my own voice but steered me away from unproductive tangents and ensured that I included a variety of perspectives throughout the manuscript. Her strong sense of time and place informed the book's final organization, and her many suggestions for additional, supportive content significantly enhanced the volume. I am especially grateful for Martha's early and unwavering belief in the book.

In addition, Mariah Schaefer, associate acquisitions editor at the University of Illinois Press, went the extra mile to help me time and again; she also worked closely with the university's technical experts to ensure that my less than stellar reprints of photographs and cartoons could be recreated in publishable quality.

A special thank you goes to Missy and the late Jack Higgins for authorizing publication of two of the Pulitzer Prize–winning cartoonist's works, which perfectly (and humorously) represent the bookends of Mayor Daley's remarkable mayoralty.

Finally, I'd like to acknowledge the many people who played critical roles in the dramas of Daley's long career who allowed me to interview them. Time and again, it was their unique memories and experiences that provided the most meaningful, revealing, and interesting parts of the Daley story.

Notes

Prologue

1. John O. Norquist, *The Wealth of Cities: Revitalizing the Centers of American Life* (Reading, MA: Addison-Wesley, 1998).

2. Stephan Benzkofer, "1974 Was a Deadly Year in Chicago," *Chicago Tribune*, July 8, 2012.

3. John McCarron, interview by Peter Cunningham, April 24, 2019, Richard M. Daley Oral Histories, University of Illinois-Chicago, https://collections.carli.illinois.edu/digital/collection/uic_rmdoh/id/50/rec/23.

4. R. C. Longworth, "Chicago: City on the Brink," *Chicago Tribune*, May 10–12, 1981.

5. Steve Chapman, "What Mayor Daley Left Behind: Surveying the State of Chicago," *Reason*, September 9, 2010.

6. Brad Amburn, "The 2008 Global Cities Index," *Foreign Policy*, 169 (Nov.–Dec. 2008): 68–76, https://www.jstor.org/stable/25462360.

7. Chapman, "What Mayor Daley Left Behind."

8. See epilogue.

Chapter 1. Tumult

1. Mike Royko, "Daley Embodied Chicago," *Chicago Sun-Times,* December 21, 1976.

2. David Axelrod, "The Son Also Rises," *Chicago Tribune*, September 1982.

3. Axelrod, "The Son Also Rises."

4. Evan Osnos, "The Daley Show," *New Yorker*, March 8, 2010.

5. Trevor Jensen, "Earl Bush: 1915–2006," *Chicago Tribune*, July 21, 2006.

6. Lindsey Tanner, "Chicago Pays Final Respects to Harold Washington," Associated Press, November 30, 1987.

7. Genevieve Carlton, "Inside Chicago's Chilling History of Racism, from Firebombings to KKK Rallies to Nazi Marches," All That Is Interesting, October 3, 2020, https://allthatsinteresting.com/racism-in-chicago.

8. Bruce Dold, "Edward Vrdolyak," *Chicago Tribune*, March 17, 1989.

9. For a complete and entertaining account of Madigan's career, see Ray Long, *The House that Madigan Built* (Urbana: University of Illinois Press, 2022).

10. Gary Rivlin, "City Hall: Enemies of the People," *Chicago Reader*, May 7, 1987.

11. Bruce Dold and Ann Marie Lipinski, "Making of a Mayor, Chicago-Style," *Chicago Tribune*, January 22, 2008.

Chapter 2. Alone

1. Doug Cassel, "Is Rich Daley Ready for Reform?" *Chicago Reader*, February 9, 1989.

2. Cassel, "Is Rich Daley Ready for Reform?"

3. Frank Kruesi, interview by Peter Cunningham, April 24, 2018, Richard M. Daley Oral Histories, University of Illinois-Chicago, https://collections.carli.illinois.edu/digital/collection/uic_rmdoh/id/20/rec/20.

4. David Axelrod, "Daley Calls Burke a Tool of the Mayor," *Chicago Tribune*, December 18, 1979.

5. Cassel, "Is Rich Daley Ready for Reform?"

6. Peter W. Colby and Paul Michael Green, "The Irish Game: Watch Byrne Watch Daley Watching Byrne," *Illinois Issues*, September 1980.

7. Ann Keegan, "All Were Irish till Jane Came Along," *Chicago Tribune*, March 14, 1980.

8. Mike Royko, "Machine against Daley? That's Incredible!" *Chicago Sun-Times*, October 23, 1980.

9. David Axelrod, "Byrne OKd Building Permits for Slumlord: 'Black Victim of Racism' Is White," *Chicago Tribune*, October 26, 1980.

10. David Jackson, "The Law and Richard M. Daley," *Chicago* magazine, September 1988.

11. Jackson, "The Law and Richard M. Daley."

12. "Experts See Growing Link Between Gangs, Drug Sales," *Chicago Defender*, January 10, 1989.

13. Jean Davidson and Bill Boyce, "Mourners Pay Tearful Tribute to Ben Wilson," *Chicago Tribune*, November 25, 1984.

Chapter 3. Torture

1. See chaps. 21, 32.

2. See chap. 1.

3. William Grady, "Brutality Suit Raises Concern," *Chicago Tribune*, February 15, 1989.

4. John Conroy, "House of Screams," *Chicago Reader*, January 26, 1990.

Chapter 4. Campaign

1. David Axelrod, *Believer: My Forty Years in Politics* (New York: Penguin, 2016), p. 87.

2. Ray Hanania, "Jeremiah Joyce: Remembering Chicago's Political Best," *Suburban Chicagoland*, January 7, 2013.

3. Robert Degnan, conversation with author, summer 2011.

4. Jill Cowan, "Did LBJ Really Say, 'You're Not Learning If You're Talking?'" *Dallas Morning News*, April 15, 2018.

5. In 1994, Manion steered the campaign of Pete Silvestri against Marco D'Amico, the county commissioner controlled by the powerful Thirty-Sixth Ward committeeman Bill Banks. Manion recalled Milton Rakove's classic book on Chicago precinct politics, *We Don't Want Nobody Nobody Sent*, in which D'Amico bragged about his secrets to winning votes in the precincts. "Do not go there when the woman is cleaning her home and looking her worst. . . . Do not go to homes during the daytime," D'Amico said.

"During the daytime . . . the man is not there. He is working. . . . You would rather have him there to discuss it with you, as the man of the house. Sure the woman has a right to her opinion, but you discuss this politics while the man is home." Manion flooded the district with mailers containing D'Amico's low opinion of female voters. With women leading the way, Silvestri upset D'Amico.

6. Cold calling is the solicitation of a potential donor who has had no prior interaction with the caller.

7. Joe Perticone, "Flashback: Joe Biden's First Presidential Run in 1988 Cratered amid Multiple Instances of Plagiarism," *Business Insider,* March 12, 2019.

8. David Wilhelm, interview by author, October 14, 2022.

9. Wilhelm, interview by author.

10. Edward Walsh, "In Chicago, No Daley Double," *Washington Post*, August 24, 1996.

11. Wilhelm, interview by author.

12. Wilhelm, interview by author.

13. Wilhelm, interview by author.

Chapter 5. Wins

1. *Groupthink* refers to the often dangerous tendency of homogeneous teams to reach decisions without proper vetting or debate, due to members' adherence to uniform values or opinions or a desire to avoid conflict. Disastrous historical outcomes linked to groupthink include the Bay of Pigs invasion and the Iraq War.

2. John McCarron, interview by Peter Cunningham, April 24, 2019, Richard M. Daley Oral Histories, University of Illinois-Chicago, https://collections.carli.illinois.edu/digital /collection/uic_rmdoh/id/50/rec/23

3. Better Government Association, "Mayor Daley's Name Turns Up in FBI Files on Embezzler John F. Duff Jr.," Illinois Answers Project, May 9, 2011, https://tinyurl.com /muxsjxhf.

4. See chap. 25.

5. "Navy Pier's Future," editorial, *Chicago Tribune*, May 27, 1975.

6. Steve Neal, "How Daley Put on McCormick Blitz," *Chicago Sun-Times,* July 24, 1991.

7. Over the next two decades, Daley would trek to the state capital to broker additional expansions, keeping Chicago ahead of other cities. He helped bring a thirty-three-story Hyatt Regency hotel to McCormick Place as well as new parking garages. He built a dedicated bus lane for easier access to downtown attractions. By 2006, McCormick Place shows were breaking records for attendance and exhibitors. Its seventy-five events that year had a collective impact of $3.4 billion on Chicago's economy.

Chapter 6. Quality of Life

1. Sarah Pang, interview by author, July 18, 2022.

2. Paul Toback, interview by author, June 12, 2021.

3. Adrienne Drell, "The Rat Patrol—'Only' 500,000 Left after His 23-Year Crusade," *Chicago Sun-Times,* March 2, 1995.

4. Goldman eventually served as a mayoral appointee on the boards of McPier, the Chicago Housing Authority, the Illinois Medical District, and Chicago City Colleges.

5. Rose DeWolf, "Chicago Winning War on Graffiti," *Philadelphia Daily News,* May 5, 1996.

6. Fran Spielman, "Mayor Views Shelter—Some There Welcome O'Hare Eviction," *Chicago Sun-Times,* November 20, 1990.

7. Lou Ortiz, "Fifty Protest Eviction of Homeless at O'Hare," *Chicago Sun-Times,* November 13, 1990.

8. Spielman, "Mayor Views Shelter."

9. The mayor's focus was unrelentingly granular. In an illustrative note to Daley, the Human Services director affirms fulfillment of the mayoral directive to remove huts and homeless from Clark Street and Roosevelt Road, and reports that two of six occupants had been placed in public housing, with the others declining assistance. Tim Mitchell, "Homeless Huts," April 18, 1994, University of Illinois-Chicago Library Special Collections.

10. Tom Seibel, "1,200 Abandoned Buildings Targeted as Crime Havens," *Chicago Sun-Times*, September 4, 1992.

11. David S. Broder, "Private Firms, Public Service," *Washington Post*, July 7, 1991.

12. Mark Potts, "Exxon to Quit Office Systems Business," *Washington Post*, November 28, 1984.

13. See chap. 11.

14. Michael Goldston, "Special Project Conclusion Report," Chicago Office of Professional Standards, September 28, 1990.

15. Charles Nicodemus, "Report Cites 12 years of S. Side Cop Brutality," *Chicago Sun-Times*, February 8, 1992.

16. See chap. 30 regarding the *Chicago Reader*'s John Conroy.

17. See chap. 1.

18. Fran Spielman and Zay N. Smith, "Storm of Criticism—City's Snow Efforts Hit," *Chicago Sun-Times,* February 16, 1990.

19. Fran Spielman and Zay N. Smith, "Storm of Criticism—City's Snow Efforts Hit."

20. Jessica Seigel, "Daley's Support Is Inspiration to Gay Pride Parade," *Chicago Tribune,* June 26, 1989.

21. Marj Halperin, interview by author, September 22, 2022.

22. Fran Spielman, "Daley Wary of Bills to Limit Abortions," *Chicago Sun-Times*, July 11, 1989.

23. Fran Spielman, "Daley Manages to Skirt Queries on Public Funding of Abortion," *Chicago Sun-Times*, March 6, 1992.

24. Ernest Tucker, "Access for All—Disabled Tear Down Barriers to Good Times," *Chicago Sun-Times,* July 27, 1990.

25. Henderson had a master's degree in philosophy from Oxford and was a year shy of a PhD at the University of Chicago.

26. Fran Spielman and Ray Hanania, "Confident Mayor Presides over Glitz and Crackdowns," *Chicago Sun-Times*, April 22, 1990.

Chapter 7. Downtown

1. R. C. Longworth, "Chicago: City on the Brink."

2. R. C. Longworth, "The American Millstone, Lost Jobs Leave Legacy of Despair," *Chicago Tribune*, April 29, 1985.

3. "The Decline of the City Grid," *Economist,* December 20, 2022.

4. Quoted in Steve Neal, "Daley Jumps Ship on Riverboat Casinos," *Chicago Sun-Times*, July 24, 1994.

5. In 2003, with a Democratic governor for the first time in twenty-six years, Daley made a final attempt. But when Daley went public with his casino plans, the unpredictable and opportunistic Gov. Rod Blagojevich humiliated the mayor by declaring the casino a nonstarter. Blagojevich was devoid of real beliefs; instead, he relied on extensive

polling. Expanding gambling in Illinois was unpopular, and Blagojevich calculated that standing up to Daley would make him more appealing to suburban and downstate voters, as well as to the river towns enjoying gambling monopolies.

6. In Illinois, local governments with home rule powers have unlimited taxing authority. School districts and non-home-rule units, typically small counties and municipalities, are subject to tax caps. These governments can lose revenue, but the impact is marginal unless the new development would have occurred regardless of the TIF.

7. Ben Joravsky and Mick Dumke, "The Shadow Budget," *Chicago Reader,* October 22, 2009.

8. From 2005 to 2007 alone, Daley redirected more than $1.4 billion in property taxes into TIF accounts. Ben Joravsky and Mick Dumke, "Shedding Light on the Shadow Budget," *Chicago Reader,* December 10, 2009.

9. Ben Joravsky, "University Village: The Story's Not Finished," *Chicago Reader,* May 28, 2009.

10. Sarah Pang, interview by author, July 18, 2022.

11. Columbia College Chicago, Housing Options & Information.

12. A pioneer in office-to-residential conversions, Metropolitan Properties got funding from New York's Lehman Brothers, because its projects were rejected by Chicago banks. Metropolitanproperties.com.

13. Blair Kamin and Patrick T. Reardon, "Healing Process," *Chicago Tribune,* May 15, 2003.

14. Malcolm Gladwell, "Six Degrees of Lois Weisberg," *New Yorker,* January 3, 1999.

15. Quoted in Whet Moser, "A Brief History of Block 37," *Chicago* magazine, April 11, 2012.

16. Cheryl L. Reed, "No. 1 Maggie Daley," *Chicago Sun-Times*, April 11, 2004.

17. Reed, "No. 1 Maggie Daley."

18. The introverted Eychaner is perhaps Chicago's most unsung civic hero. "Philanthropist, Business Leader, and LGBTQ Advocate, Fred Eychaner, Awarded Illinois Tech Honorary Doctorate," Illinois Institute of Technology, May 14, 2022, http://tinyurl.com/4fwtx5e9.

Chapter 8. Black Swans

1. Don Hayner and Fran Spielman, "Flood Relief-Waters Recede, Some Power Back, 'Band-Aid' Holds," *Chicago Sun-Times,* April 14, 1992.

2. Scott Sagan, thecitesite.com, https://thecitesite.com/authors/scott-sagan/.

3. Nassim Nicholas Taleb, *The Black Swan: The Impact of the Highly Improbable* (New York: Random House, 2007).

4. LaPlante joined a local engineering company. After a decent interval, his company began receiving city contracts. Unlike many ruthless politicians, Daley never tried to intentionally hurt someone's livelihood, particularly where there was no malevolence involved. The pattern repeated itself when others walked the plank in future debacles.

5. Don Hayner, "John Kenny Jr.—Fame Hasn't Faded for City's 'Flood Stud,'" *Chicago Sun-Times,* April 11, 1993.

6. Tom McNamee, "Heat Wave on the Way—And It Can Be a Killer," *Chicago Sun-Times,* July 12, 1995.

7. Mike Thomas, "Chicago's Deadly 1995 Heat Wave: An Oral History," *Chicago* magazine, June 29, 2015.

8. Flynn McRoberts and Paul de la Garza, "Daley Feeling More Heat," *Chicago Tribune,* July 19, 1995.

9. Sarah Pang, interview by Peter Cunningham, January 12, 2018, Richard M. Daley Oral Histories, University of Illinois-Chicago, https://collections.carli.illinois.edu/digital/collection/uic_rmdoh/id/86/rec/30.

10. Jonny Lupsha, "Remembering 1995 Chicago Heat Wave amid High Midwest Temps," Wondrium Daily, August 16, 2021.

11. Thomas, "Chicago's Deadly 1995 Heat Wave."

12. Terry Teele, interview by Peter Cunningham, December 7, 2017, Richard M. Daley Oral Histories, University of Illinois-Chicago, https://collections.carli.illinois.edu/digital/collection/uic_rmdoh/id/80/rec/40.

13. Thomas, "Chicago's Deadly 1995 Heat Wave."

14. Steve Neal, "Daley's Leadership Wilted in Heat Crisis," *Chicago Sun-Times*, July 25, 1995.

15. Thomas, "Chicago's Deadly 1995 Heat Wave."

Chapter 9. Airport Wars

1. Mary Wisniewski, "O'Hare Is Once Again the Nation's Busiest Airport in Terms of Total Flights," *Chicago Tribune,* February 4, 2019.

2. Avis LaVelle, interview by Peter Cunningham, December 7, 2017, Richard M. Daley Oral Histories, University of Illinois-Chicago, https://collections.carli.illinois.edu/digital/collection/uic_rmdoh/id/110/rec/21.

3. David Fremon, "Chicago's Most Endangered Neighborhood?" *Illinois Issues,* December 20, 1990.

4. In 1982, Daley threw the decisive weight of his family's powerful Eleventh Ward organization behind Lipinski's successful primary challenge to the incumbent Congressman John Fary.

5. William Lipinski, "Right from the Middle: Reagan, the Contras, and the Launch of the CTA Orange Line," *Suburban Chicagoland,* August 30, 2021.

6. Robert Heuer, "Runway Inflation," *Chicago Reader,* March 14, 2002.

7. John Kass and Rick Pearson, "GOP Moving Full Force on O'Hare, Philip Says," *Chicago Tribune,* April 8, 1995.

8. Susan Sher, interview by author, March 29, 2023.

9. Sher, interview by author, March 29, 2023.

10. Susan Sher, interview by author, September 19, 2021.

Chapter 10. Neighborhoods

1. Terry Teele, interview by author, June 9, 2022.

2. Teele, interview by author.

3. Marilyn Katz, interview by Peter Cunningham, June 9, 2018, Richard M. Daley Oral Histories, University of Illinois-Chicago, https://collections.carli.illinois.edu/digital/collection/uic_rmdoh/id/129/rec/19.

4. Teele, interview by author.

5. Teele, interview by author.

Chapter 11. Ghost Towns

1. "Make Chicago's Parks Work Again," editorial, *Chicago Tribune,* November 17, 1990.

2. John Callaway, personal conversation, fall 1993.

3. See chap. 4.

4. Malcolm Gladwell, "Six Degrees of Lois Weisberg," *New Yorker,* Jan. 3, 1999.

5. Gladwell, "Six Degrees of Lois Weisberg."

6. See chap. 1.

7. Charles Storch, "Columnist Mike Royko Joins the *Chicago Tribune*," *Chicago Tribune*, January 10, 1984.

8. Michael Sneed, "Rupert Murdoch's Brief Cloud over Chicago Newspaper World Led to One Ray of Sunshine," *Chicago Sun-Times*, September 23, 2023.

9. Mike Royko, "The Soggy Horror of Soldier Field," *Chicago Tribune*, October 12, 1994.

10. On September 29, 2003, the Chicago Bears opened a partially rehabbed, partially new $632 million Soldier Field stadium, with taxpayers covering two-thirds of the cost.

11. James Warren, "Friends in Need," *Chicago Tribune*, December 12, 1993.

Chapter 12. Broken Windows

1. Sarah Olkon, "'I See That Danny Died in Vain,'" *Chicago Tribune*, September 7, 2008.

2. Fran Spielman, "What Will Stop the Killing? Daley's Finger Points Nowhere," *Chicago Sun-Times*, October 18, 1992.

3. Thomas J. Jurkanin and Terry G. Hillard, *Chicago Police: An Inside View—The Story of Superintendent Terry G. Hillard* (Springfield, IL: Charles C. Thomas, 2006), p. 94.

4. Ron Huberman, "Richard M. Daley Oral Histories," University of Illinois-Chicago, September 22, 2017. https://collections.carli.illinois.edu/digital/collection/uic_rmdoh/id/134/rec/17.

5. Pang, "Richard M. Daley Oral Histories."

6. Jesse Smart, interview with author, October 20, 2023.

7. Smart, interview with author.

8. Smart, interview with author.

9. Smart, interview with author.

10. Smart, interview with author.

Chapter 13. Go West

1. David Schoenfield, "The 100 Worst Draft Picks Ever," April 27, 2006, Page 2, ESPN, https://www.espn.com/espn/page2/story?page=schoenfield/060427.

2. Jordan mania sometimes fueled irrational behavior. A friend relayed a story about a colleague victimized by a purse snatching. She lost cash, credit cards, and two tickets to that night's Bulls game. She got a good look at her two muggers, so a policeman accompanied her to the game, hoping to get a more detailed description of the ticket scalpers from the fans in her seats. As they walked down the aisle, the victim was astonished to see the two men who had robbed her watching the game from her seats.

3. NBC News, "Study Shows Big Economic Impact of United Center, Impact on Near West Side," July 23, 2015.

4. Daniel Walker, *Rights in Conflict, A Report Submitted by Daniel Walker to the National Commission on the Causes and Prevention of Violence* (New York: New American Library, 1968).

5. Anne Kostiner, interview by author, November 8, 2022.

6. Kostiner, interview by author.

7. Kostiner, interview by author.

8. Terry Teele, interview by author, November 10, 2022.

9. Kostiner, interview by author.

10. Kostiner, interview by author.

11. Kostiner, interview by author.

12. Teele, interview by author.

13. Teele, interview by author.

14. Steve Kloehn, "Clinton No Slacker When It Comes to Sampling Taste," *Chicago Tribune*, July 3, 1996.

15. Edward Walsh, "In Chicago, No Daley Double," *Washington Post*, August 24, 1996.

16. Jeff Bailey and Calmetta Y. Coleman, "Chicago's Strong Economy Has Led to a Renaissance," *Wall Street Journal*, August 21, 1996.

Chapter 14. Anchors

1. Terry Peterson, interview by author, June 7, 2022.

2. John Schmidt, interview by Peter Cunningham, November 1, 2017, Richard M. Daley Oral Histories," University of Illinois-Chicago, https://collections.carli.illinois.edu /digital/collection/uic_rmdoh/id/82/rec/37.

3. See chap. 21.

4. Teele, interview by author.

5. Whole Foods moved into Englewood, offering desperately needed fresh produce, but by 2023 was subleasing its space to a downscale food retailer, Save a Lot. Mariah Rush, "Englewood Residents Upset Save a Lot to Replace Whole Foods: 'We Deserve the Best,'" *Chicago Sun-Times*, January 27, 2023.

6. Led by the Englewood Community Council, including its cochairs Darlene O'Banner and Denise Dyer, in 2019 the community opened a new state-of-the-art high school to anchor neighborhood kids.

7. See chap.10.

8. Chicago, Illinois Population History, biggestuscities.com, https://www.biggestuscities .com/city/chicago-illinois.

Chapter 15. Takeover

1. See chap. 9.

2. Rick Pearson, "How Lawmakers Gave Mayors Ways to Ruin CPS Finances," *Chicago Tribune*, August 23, 2015.

3. Michael Martinez, "Schools Rate Higher Grade Better Bonds Might Save $$," *Chicago Tribune*, March 13, 1996.

4. John Kass, "Daley's Cure for Troublemakers," *Chicago Tribune*, September 16, 1995.

5. Jacqueline Heard, "School Crisis Plan Gets Unruly Welcome," *Chicago Tribune*, September 28, 1995.

6. Michael Martinez, "Schools May Get Tough on Promotions," *Chicago Tribune*, March 27, 1996.

7. Paul Vallas, interview by Peter Cunningham, April 20, 2018, Richard M. Daley Oral Histories, University of Illinois-Chicago, https://collections.carli.illinois.edu/digital /collection/uic_rmdoh/id/87/rec/41.

8. Best High Schools, 2023–2024, *U.S. News & World Report*, http://tinyurl.com /2p8bctta.

9. Vallas, interview by Cunningham.

10. Michael Martinez, "City's High Schools Take a Big Step Up on Test Scores," *Chicago Tribune*, May 1, 1997.

11. Martinez, "City's High Schools Take a Big Step Up."

12. Martinez, "City's High Schools Take a Big Step Up."

13. Rick Pearson, "Legislators Get the Message and Pass School-Fund Bill," *Chicago Tribune*, December 3, 1997.

14. The pay raises reported after teacher bargaining do not include other mandatory pay hikes built into the union contracts, which are stealth escalators. Ted Dabrowski, "Steps and Lanes: Understanding How Chicago Public School Teachers Get Multiple Pay Raises Each Year," *Illinois Policy,* February 3, 2016.

15. "Richard Daley for Mayor," editorial, *Chicago Tribune,* February 7, 1999.

16. Patrick T. Reardon, "Paul Vallas' Experiment Earns Top Marks," *Chicago Tribune,* January 4, 1998.

17. Reardon, "Paul Vallas' Experiment Earns Top Marks."

Chapter 16. Northerly Island

1. See chap. 9.

2. Gideon J. Tucker, surrogate, in an 1866 report of the final accounting in the estate of A. B.—New York Surrogate Reports, 1 Tucker (N.Y. Surr.) 249 (1866).

3. Knox Keranen, "Debate over Meigs Field Continues 15 Years Later," *Chicago Talks,* June 21, 2018.

4. Keranen, "Debate over Meigs Field Continues 15 Years Later."

5. Eric Zorn, "When the Mayor Bulldozed an Airport," *Chicago Tribune,* May 1, 2011.

6. Ryan Smith, "What's Next for Northerly Island?" *Chicago Tribune,* July 9, 2020.

7. See chap 23.

8. In his last year in office, Daley made a final attempt, announcing an award-winning design by the renowned architect Jeanne Gang, who envisioned the new park as the "Millennium Park of nature." Rising lake levels, however, and the need for infrastructure to protect the island's vulnerable shore from increasing erosion, pushed the cost of the project into the hundreds of millions of dollars, leaving the vision in limbo.

9. Blair Kamin, "Nature's Way," *Chicago Tribune,* November 1, 1996.

10. Costas Spirou and Dennis R. Judd, *Building the City of Spectacle: Mayor Richard M. Daley and the Remaking of Chicago* (Ithaca, NY: Cornell University Press, 2016), p. 99.

11. Ted Gregory, "Pastor Protests Marijuana Fest," *Chicago Tribune,* May 13, 1996.

12. Gregory, "Pastor Protests Marijuana Fest."

13. Gregory, "Pastor Protests Marijuana Fest."

Chapter 17. Legend

1. "10 Memorable Moments of Mayor Daley's Reign," CBS Chicago, May 13, 2011, https://www.cbsnews.com/chicago/news/10-highlights-of-mayor-daleys-reign/; Costas Spirou and Dennis R. Judd, *Building the City of Spectacle: Mayor Richard M. Daley and the Remaking of Chicago* (Ithaca, NY: Cornell University Press, 2016), p. 109.

2. Daniel H. Burnham and Edward H. Bennett, *Plan of Chicago* (Chicago: Commercial Club of Chicago, 1909).

3. Tranter led the influential advocacy group for thirty-three years, including during many of its battles with Ed Kelly, the imperious parks superintendent.

4. Lois Wille, *Forever Open, Clear, and Free: The Struggle for Chicago's Lakefront* (Chicago: University of Chicago Press, 1972), p. 73.

5. Wille, *Forever Open, Clear, and Free,* p. 74.

6. Wille wrote: "No one has done more for Chicago than the three men who wrote those words along the lakefront of their map of the little prairie town on the southern shores of Lake Michigan." *Forever Open, Clear, and Free,* prologue.

7. Wille, *Forever Open, Clear, and Free,* p. 79.

Chapter 18. Gangs and Guns

1. Fran Spielman, "Ramsey Favorite for Police Superintendent," *Chicago Sun-Times,* February 8, 1998.

2. Sarah Pang, interview by author, July 18, 2022.

3. Pang, interview by author.

4. Fran Spielman and Michelle Roberts, "Search for Top Cop Closing In," *Chicago Sun-Times*, December 12, 1997.

5. Thomas J. Jurkanin and Terry G. Hillard, *Chicago Police: An Inside View—The Story of Superintendent Terry G. Hillard* (Springfield, IL: Charles C. Thomas, 2006), p. 65.

6. Olivia Becker, "The Violent History of Chicago's Most Notorious Gun Shop," The Trace, June 26, 2015, https://www.thetrace.org/2015/06/the-violent-history-of-chicagos-most-notorious-gun-shop/.

7. Becker, "The Violent History of Chicago's Most Notorious Gun Shop."

8. City of Chicago and Chicago Police Department, *Gun Trace Report*, 2017, http://tinyurl.com/mr3ce6v7.

9. Vernal Coleman, "Inside the Notorious Gun Shop Linked to Hundreds of Chicago Guns," Pro Publica, December 11, 2023, http://tinyurl.com/yueucwpn.

10. In 2022, Congress passed legislation cracking down on straw purchasers, with penalties of fifteen to twenty-five years in prison (assuming enforcement by previously lenient judges). Its future impact is unknown, but it in any event came too late for Chicago police officer Ella French, twenty-nine, murdered following a routine traffic stop by a weapon purchased by a straw buyer in Hammond, Indiana, for one of the two brothers charged with the killing. *USA v. Jamel Danzy*, U.S. District Court, Northern District of Illinois, Eastern Division, August 9, 2021.

11. 5 Chicago, "The Myths and Truths About Chicago's Guns and Murder Rates," NBC News, December 11, 2018, http://tinyurl.com/6raht6dm.

12. Whet Moser, "Why Are There So Many Gang Members in Chicago," *Chicago* magazine, January 27, 2012.

13. Jurkanin and Hillard, *Chicago Police,* p. 69.

14. Jurkanin and Hillard, *Chicago Police,* p. 105.

15. Ron Huberman, interview by author, July 14, 2022.

16. Huberman, interview by author.

17. Jesse Jackson, "People of Goodwill Must Unite against New Wave of Terrorism," press release, Rainbow Push Coalition, June 8, 1999.

18. Abdon Pallasch and Fran Spielman, "An $18 Million 'Lesson for City,'" *Chicago Sun-Times,* May 9, 2001.

19. Todd Lighty and Maria Kantzavelos, "Judge Rethinks 3 Cops in Haggerty," *Chicago Tribune,* June 6, 2001.

20. Steve Mills and Todd Lighty, "Job Getting Tougher for City's Top Cop," *Chicago Tribune,* June 20, 1999.

21. Terry Hillard, interview by author, November 21, 2022.

22. Hillard, interview by author.

Chapter 19. Revolution Stalled

1. John Kass, "Vallas Stuck Neck Out for Schools, Only to Get Axed," *Chicago Tribune,* June 7, 2001.

2. Jill Blackman, "Daley: Vallas Not Pushed Out," *Chicago Tribune*, June 7, 2001.

3. Daley remained neutral in the gubernatorial race; but in the final week of the campaign, his brother John Daley, the Eleventh Ward committeeman in the mayor's home base of Bridgeport, threw the weight of the family's precinct captains behind Blagojevich. Blagojevich was elected twice but later impeached, convicted, and sentenced to fourteen years in prison for a series of crimes, including attempting to sell the Senate seat vacated by President-elect Obama in 2008.

4. Ron Huberman was an extreme example of the mayor's policy. Over a fourteen-year period, he was Daley's director of Emergency Management and Communications, the mayoral chief of staff, the CEO of the Chicago Transit Authority, and superintendent of Chicago's public schools.

5. Steve Bzomowski, interview by author, September 18, 2023.

6. Ray Quintanilla and Gary Washburn, "Surprise for Vallas Job: Obscure Deputy Was Daley's Second Choice," *Chicago Tribune,* June 27, 2001.

7. Ray Quintanilla and Michael Martinez, "It Is Back to the Basics for City Kids," *Chicago Tribune,* September 4, 2001.

8. "Richard M. Daley for Mayor," editorial, *Chicago Tribune*, February 16, 2003.

9. Diane Rado, "School Day Falls Short in Poorer Districts," *Chicago Tribune,* September 29, 2002.

10. Chris Jones, "Maggie Daley, Arts Eternally Bonded," *Chicago Tribune,* November 26, 2011.

11. Jackie Heard, interview by Peter Cunningham, May 1, 2019, Richard M. Daley Oral Histories, University of Illinois-Chicago, https://collections.carli.illinois.edu/digital /collection/uic_rmdoh/id/48/rec/13.

12. Heard, interview by Cunningham.

13. Lori Olszewski and Ana Beatriz Cholo, "Reading, Math Scores Level Off; 8th Grade Scores Best Ever," *Chicago Tribune,* June 2, 2004.

Chapter 20. Expansion

1. See chap. 9.

2. Andrew Martin and Laurie Cohen, "Politics Snarl O'Hare," *Chicago Tribune,* November 21, 2000.

3. Lester Crown, interview by Peter Cunningham, April 20, 2018, Richard M. Daley Oral Histories, University of Illinois-Chicago, https://collections.carli.illinois.edu/digital /collection/uic_rmdoh/id/35/rec/5.

4. Booz-Allen & Hamilton, Chicago Aviation Policy, November 12, 1998, p. 3, Chicagoland Chamber of Commerce, https://onlinepubs.trb.org/onlinepubs/circulars/ec032 /roper.pdf

5. Booz-Allen & Hamilton, Chicago's Aviation Policy, p. I-4.

6. Aaron Chambers, "State of the State: The Pressure's On for Illinois to Alleviate Congestion at O'Hare," NPR Illinois, July 1, 2001, http://tinyurl.com/3ep8be84.

7. Crown, interview by Cunningham.

8. Jack Lyne, "$6.6 Billion O'Hare Expansion Facing Fractious Delays before Takeoff," *Site Selection* magazine, September 1, 2003.

9. Sheila O'Grady, interview by Peter Cunningham, October 27, 2017, Richard M. Daley Oral Histories, University of Illinois-Chicago, https://collections.carli.illinois.edu/digital /collection/uic_rmdoh/id/46/rec/27.

10. Federal Aviation Administration, "Chicago's O'Hare Modernization Program," Report No. AV-2005-067, July 21, 2005, https://tinyurl.com/ckzy2z25.

11. Fergus Cole, "The Airports with the Most Direct Connections Around the World," Business Traveler, January 12, 2023, https://businesstravelerusa.com/news/find-out-which-are-the-worlds-most-connected-airports/.

Chapter 21. Razing Hell

1. In the slums cleared to build Cabrini-Green, 80 percent of families had two parents. By 1985, the percentage had fallen to 24 percent. William Mullen, "The Road to Hell for Cabrini-Green, part 1: It Was Paved with Good Intentions," *Chicago Tribune*, March 31, 1985.

2. Norquist, *The Wealth of Cities*, pp. 100–101.

3. Arnold Hirsch, *Making the Second Ghetto: Race and Housing in Chicago 1940–1960* (Chicago: University of Chicago Press, 1998).

4. Mullen, "The Road to Hell."

5. Norquist, *The Wealth of Cities*, p. 99.

6. Adam Walinsky, "What It's Like to Be in Hell," *New York Times*, December 4, 1987.

7. Kevin Klose, "Housing Authority in Chicago Faces Crisis," *Washington Post*, April 24, 1987.

8. Robert F. Wagner Jr. and Julia Vitillo-Martin, "New Hope for Old Projects, Vince Lane and the Revival of Public Housing," *City Journal*, Spring 1994.

9. Steve Johnson, "Lake Parc Place: New Look, New Tenants, New Face of CHA," *Chicago Tribune*, August 15, 1991.

10. "Vince Lane, Visionary and Fraud," *Chicago Tribune*, March 26, 2001.

11. James Warren and Patrick T. Reardon, "HUD Tired of CHA Failures," *Chicago Tribune*, May 28, 1995.

12. David Brint, interview by author, April 20, 2022.

13. Cindy Richards, "Mayor Getting Ready to Bring CHA Home," *Chicago Tribune*, August 30, 1998.

14. Stasch later served as mayoral chief of staff and president of the MacArthur Foundation, one the nation's largest philanthropies.

15. Richards, "Mayor Getting Ready."

16. Melita Marie Garza, "CHA Gives Go-Ahead to $1.5 Billion Overhaul of Public Housing," *Chicago Tribune*, January 7, 2000.

17. Robert Novak, "Infighting Stymies Housing Reform," *Chicago Sun-Times*, November 4, 1999.

18. Novak, "Infighting Stymies Housing Reform."

19. Terry Peterson, interview by author, June 7, 2022.

20. Peterson, interview by author.

21. Peterson, interview by author.

Chapter 22. Betrayal

1. See chaps. 25, 26.

2. Eric Zorn, "Daley Won't Rock the Bloat in the Race for Cook Board," *Chicago Tribune*, February 24, 2002.

3. See chap. 1.

4. John Kass, "The New Mayor Daley," *Chicago Tribune*, August 25, 1996.

5. Mark Brown, "Illinois Law Says Ex-Pols Can Keep Campaign Cash for Personal Use. One Just Pocketed $392,606," *Chicago Sun-Times*, June 25, 2021.

6. Kristen McQueary, "Blagojevich's Reasons for Distancing Mell Begin with PAC," *Daily Southtown,* January 16, 2005.

7. Lance Gough, conversation with author, March 20, 2002.

Chapter 23. Millennium Park

1. See chap. 17.

2. Andrew Martin and Laurie Cohen, "Millennium Park Flounders as Deadlines, Budgets Blown," *Chicago Tribune,* August 5, 2001.

3. Reidy proved correct. Two years after Millennium Park opened, the park's reserve fund was nearly exhausted. Facing pressure from bondholders fearing a default, Mayor Daley sold the adjacent Michigan Avenue parking garages to Morgan Stanley for $563 million, using half the proceeds to retire the debt. See chap. 34.

4. Martin and Cohen, "Millennium Park Flounders."

5. Joseph Manzi, interview by author, March 12, 2022.

6. Manzi, interview by author.

7. Donna LaPietra, interview by author, September 1, 2023.

8. LaPietra, interview by author.

9. Timothy J. Gilfoyle, *Millennium Park: Creating a Chicago Landmark* (Chicago: University of Chicago Press, 2006), p. 114.

10. Gilfoyle, *Millennium Park*, p. 120.

11. Steven R. Strahler, "Happy 90th Birthday, Lester Crown," *Crain's Chicago Business,* May 29, 2015, https://tinyurl.com/bddmsymr.

12. See chap. 20.

13. Chris Jones, "Joan and Irving Harris' Long Dance," *Chicago Tribune,* November 2, 2003.

14. Chris Jones, "At Last: The City That Makes No Small Plans Unveils Millennium Park, Its Biggest, Boldest Outdoor Cultural Project in More than a Century," *Chicago Tribune*, July 15, 2004.

15. John King, "Mayor of SF Looks Eastward for Urban Inspiration," *San Francisco Chronicle,* August 12, 2006.

16. Ed Uhlir, "The Millennium Park Effect: Creating a Cultural Venue with an Economic Impact," *Greater Philadelphia Regional Review,* Winter 2006.

Chapter 24. Deadly Silos

1. Bill Vlasic, "G.M. Inquiry Cites Years of Neglect over Fatal Defect," *New York Times,* June 5, 2014.

2. Robert Pierre, "21 Killed in Panic to Exit Chicago Club," *Washington Post,* February 18, 2003.

3. Fran Spielman and Abdon Pallasch, "New Rules for Nightclubs?" *Chicago Sun-Times,* February 20, 2003.

4. Spielman and Pallasch, "New Rules for Nightclubs?"

5. Amy E. Nevala and Rudolph Bush, "Mayor Picks 2 to Head Code-Enforcement Panel," *Chicago Sun-Times,* February 23, 2003.

6. Andrew Herrmann, "E2 panel: Clubs Should Announce How to Get Out—Daley's Probe Ends, Ducks Question of Any Role Clout Played," *Chicago Sun-Times*, July 3, 2003.

7. Kate Thayer, "E2 Owners Get Probation, Not Prison, in Resentencing after Fatal 2003 Stampede," *Chicago Tribune,* November 20, 2015.

8. Thayer, "E2 Owners Get Probation."

9. Hal Dardick, "City in New Porch Safety Push; Owners, Tenants Told to Be Wary," *Chicago Tribune,* April 16, 2004.

10. Dardick, "City in New Porch Safety Push."

11. Robert Herguth and Maureen O'Donnell, "Officials Debate Where to Lay Blame," *Chicago Sun-Times,* October 20, 2003.

12. Monica Davey, "Smoke and Panic on Stairs in Chicago High-Rise Fire," *New York Times,* October 19, 2003.

Chapter 25. Scandal

1. Milton L. Rakove, *We Don't Want Nobody Nobody Sent: An Oral History of the Daley Years* (Bloomington: Indiana University Press, 1979), p. 196.

2. Rakove, *We Don't Want Nobody Nobody Sent*, p. 318.

3. Mike Royko, *Boss: Richard J. Daley of Chicago* (New York: New American Library, 1971), p. 73.

4. See chap. 5.

5. Nathan Vardi, "Workers' Con," *Forbes,* Feb. 28, 2005.

6. Gary Washburn and Andrew Martin, "Daley to 'Look Into' Duff Family Dealings," *Chicago Tribune,* July 28, 1999.

7. Better Government Association, "Mayor Daley's Name Turns Up in FBI Files on Embezzler John F. Duff Jr.," May 9, 2011, Illinois Answers, https://tinyurl.com/muxsjxhf.

8. Welcome to Daleyland, "History Lesson—The Duff Family," welcometodaleyland .blogspot.com, July 15, 2009, https://tinyurl.com/3462rz7r.

9. Linda Lutton, "War on Independents," *Chicago Reader,* September 3, 1998.

10. Ben Joravsky, "Killing Them with Kindness," *Chicago Reader,* September 11, 2003.

11. Tim Novak and Steve Warmbir, "Paid to Do Nothing," *Chicago Sun-Times,* January 23, 2004.

12. Fran Spielman, "'I'll Take the Blame Myself'—But Mayor Hints Some Top Officials Could Lose Their Jobs over Truck Scandal," *Chicago Sun-Times,* January 31, 2004.

13. On average, over the past half century, a Chicago alderman has been convicted every sixteen months. Sun-Times Staff, "The Watchdogs: Chicago City Council Hall of Shame: Ed Burke Becomes the 38th Member Convicted in Half a Century," *Chicago Sun-Times,* December 22, 2023; Chicago Tribune Staff, "Chicago Aldermen Convicted of Corruption—and Others Facing Charges," *Chicago Tribune*, December 21, 2023; CBS Chicago, "A Look at Chicago's Corrupt Aldermen Through the Years," January 3, 2019.

Chapter 26. Hiring Fraud

1. United States v. Sorich, 06–4251 (7th Cir. 2008), April 15, 2008.

2. Carol Marin, "How Did Young Andy Finish a Four-Year Apprenticeship and Acquire Two Years of Work Experience by 19?" *Chicago Sun-Times,* September 15, 2004.

3. See chap. 24.

4. Shakman Decrees, Encyclopedia of Chicago, http://www.encyclopedia.chicagohistory .org/pages/1138.html. See also chap. 1.

5. Laurie Cohen, Todd Lighty, and Dan Mihalopoulos, "Reyes Tied to Jobs Probe," *Chicago Tribune,* December 17, 2005.

6. USA v. Sorich.

7. Natasha Korecki and Steve Warmbir, "Witness Describes City Jobs Scheme: Says He Ran Political Army, Got Patronage Chief to Reward Troops," *Chicago Sun-Times*, June 1, 2006.

8. Dan Mihalopoulos, Laurie Cohen, and Todd Lighty, "U.S. Details City Cover-Up," *Chicago Tribune,* April 11, 2006.

9. Peter Slevin, "Chicago Mayor's Popularity Dips as Associates Are Indicted," *Washington Post,* July 22, 2005.

10. Mark Brown, "New Scandal Delivers Blow to Daley's Front Door," *Chicago Sun-Times,* July 19, 2005.

11. Dan Mihalopoulos and Todd Lighty, "Feds Question Daley," *Chicago Tribune,* August 27, 2005.

12. Niccolò Machiavelli, *The Prince,* trans. George Bull (Baltimore: Penguin, 1961), p. 96.

Chapter 27. Renaissance 2010

1. Tracy Dell'Angela and Gary Washburn, "Daley Set to Remake Troubled Schools: Shut Them Down, Start Over," *Chicago Tribune,* June 25, 2004.

2. With the nation's highest child poverty rate, Mississippi has adopted similar tracking and intervention strategies and dramatically lifted the reading capabilities of its third graders. Nicholas Kristof, "Mississippi Is Offering Lessons for America on Education," *New York Times,* May 31, 2023.

3. Anthony S. Bryk, Elaine Allensworth, John Q. Easton, Penny Bender Sebring, and Stuart Luppescu, "Organizing Schools for Improvement: Lessons from Chicago," *University of Chicago Consortium on School Research,* January 2010.

4. Heather Y. Anichini, interview by author, September 29, 2022.

5. Branford R. White, Jennifer B. Presley, and Karen J. DeAngelis, *Leveling Up: Narrowing the Teacher Academic Capital Gap in Illinois,* Illinois Education Research Council, June 2008, https://files.eric.ed.gov/fulltext/ED502243.pdf.

6. Arne Duncan, interview by author, October 16, 2023.

7. Duncan, interview by author.

8. Duncan, interview by author.

9. Under Mayor Brandon Johnson, the Board of Education has served notice that it intends to remove police officers from public schools. In his 2023 campaign, Johnson said that "armed officers have no place in schools, in communities already struggling with over-incarceration, criminalization, profiling and mistrust." Sarah Karp, "Chicago Board of Ed Wants Cops Out of Public Schools This Fall, Principals Told," *Chicago Sun-Times,* January 2, 2024.

10. Arne Duncan, interview by Peter Cunningham, January 23, 2018, Richard M. Daley Oral Histories, University of Illinois-Chicago, https://collections.carli.illinois.edu/digital/collection/uic_rmdoh/id/105/rec/10.

11. Ana Beatriz Cholo, "Reading Efforts Pay Off; 83% of City High Schools Post Better Numbers," *Chicago Tribune,* August 4, 2005.

12. Jason Grotto and Alex Richards, "CPS Finances Tell a Grim Tale: Years of Labor Peace Exacting a Price as Fiscal Outlook Worsens," *Chicago Tribune,* September 16, 2012.

13. Grotto and Richards, "CPS Finances Tell a Grim Tale."

14. Carlos Sadovi and Gary Washburn, "Deal Reached with City Teachers; 4 Percent Raises Okd Sources Say," *Chicago Tribune,* August 30, 2007.

15. Noreen S. Ahmed-Ullah, "CPS Heads for Charter Showdown," *Chicago Tribune,* January 26, 2011.

16. Sarah Karp and Becky Vevea, "Will Chicago Close Another 50 Schools?" WBEZ Chicago, November 25, 2017, http://tinyurl.com/mptyb728.

Chapter 28. Empire's Edge

1. Louis Brandeis, "What Publicity Can Do," *Harper's Weekly,* December 20, 1913.
2. Abdon Pallasch, "Welcome to Your Cook County Forest Preserves," *Chicago Sun-Times,* July 6, 2003.
3. Abdon Pallasch, "Only Stroger's Pals Can Go in Style," *Chicago Sun-Times,* September 8, 2003.
4. Steve Neal, "Stroger's Obstinance Keeps FP in Squalid State," *Chicago Sun-Times,* Aug. 29, 2003.
5. Abdon Pallasch and Carlos Sadovi, "Forest Preserve Worker Held in Payroll Kickback Scheme." *Chicago Sun-Times*, October 10, 2003.
6. Alex P. Kellogg, "Official, Residents Say County to Blame in Toboggan Runs' Ruin," *Chicago Tribune,* January 7, 2005.
7. Gary Washburn and Dan Mihalopoulos, "Daley Tags Assessor for Mounting Taxes," *Chicago Tribune,* February 11, 2004.
8. Abdon Pallasch, "Crushing Defeat for Stroger," *Chicago Sun-Times,* December 10, 2003.
9. Pallasch, "Crushing Defeat for Stroger."
10. Pallasch, "Crushing Defeat for Stroger."
11. Ofelia Casillas, Todd Lightly, and Mickey Ciokajlo, "FBI Targets Youth Facility," *Chicago Tribune,* April 7, 2006.
12. Annie Sweeney and Abdon Pallasch, "Teens: Fights Allowed, Encouraged," *Chicago Sun-Times,* October 5, 2005.
13. Annie Sweeney and Abdon Pallasch, "Juvenile Home Riots Reported: ACLU: Suit Filed," *Chicago Sun-Times*, December 30, 2005.
14. Steve Patterson, "Commissioner Takes on the Powerful—Again," *Chicago Sun-Times,* March 6, 2006.

Chapter 29. Succession

1. Steve Patterson, "Emanuel Breaks from Party, Picks Claypool over Stroger," *Chicago Sun-Times,* February 7, 2006.
2. Fran Spielman, "Daley Backing Stroger, But Praises Claypool," *Chicago Sun-Times,* March 1, 2006.
3. Janny Scott, "A Biracial Candidate Walks His Own Fine Line," *New York Times,* December 29, 2007.
4. Benjamin Disraeli, *Endymion.*
5. Simon was later appointed head of the Cook County health care system by Todd Stroger, who was installed by ward committeemen to replace his stricken father on the ballot. Steve Patterson and Abdon Pallasch, "Stroger Improving, Top Aide Says," *Chicago Sun-Times,* March 16, 2006.
6. Scott Fornek, "Stroger's Son Declares Dad Will Return," *Chicago Sun-Times,* March 20, 2006.
7. Steve Patterson, Abdon Pallasch, and Mark Konkel, "Claypool Concedes to Stroger: Cites 'Affection and Love' for Ill President," *Chicago Sun-Times,* March 23, 2006.
8. Victoria Ozokwelu, "Claypool Wants To Know Who's in Charge," *Daily Herald,* May 4, 2006.
9. Ozokwelu, "Claypool Wants to Know Who's in Charge."
10. John Stroger never appeared in public again. He died on Jan. 18, 2008.
11. Abdon Pallasch, "Juvenile Center Reports Falsified, Memo Says," *Chicago Sun-Times,* July 30, 2006.

12. Steve Patterson, "Study: Patronage Bad for County's Health," *Chicago Sun-Times,* Aug. 8, 2006.

13. Steve Patterson and Fran Spielman, "Even Docs Needed Clout, Says Ousted Chief of County Hospitals," *Chicago Sun-Times,* November 3, 2006.

14. Steve Patterson, "State: Patients at S. Side Hospital Face Serious Risk," *Chicago Sun-Times,* July 25, 2005.

15. Steve Patterson, "Pharmaceutical System 'Really Messed Up' County Told," *Chicago Sun-Times,* June 29, 2005.

16. Steve Patterson, "Claypool Hits 'Bureaucratic Empire' in County Hospitals," *Chicago Sun-Times,* January 13, 2005.

Chapter 30. Cops on Dots

1. Gary Washburn and David Heinzmann, "Daley Hints Police Will Go to Hot Spots," *Chicago Tribune,* May 6, 2003.

2. Rich McHugh, Evan Stulberger, and Jonathan Dienst, "An Inside Look at the System That Cut Crime in New York by 75 Percent," *NBC News,* April 16, 2016, http://tinyurl.com/75sfrjww.

3. Ron Huberman, interview with author.

4. Ron Huberman, interview with author.

5. Associated Press, "Top Cop Retires," *Chicago Tribune,* April 3, 2007.

6. Gary Washburn and Todd Lighty, "New Top Cop Seeks to Fix Broken Trust," *Chicago Tribune,* November 30, 2007.

7. "Crime's Up. Why?" Editorial, *Chicago Tribune,* July 17, 2008.

8. Ron Barth Jr.,"Police Torture Probe Was a Sham: Groups," *Chicago Sun-Times,* April 23, 2007.

9. David Heinzmann, "Prosecutors Defend Burge Report," *Chicago Tribune,* August 1, 2006.

10. Steve Mills and Jeff Coen, "Feds Catch Up with Burge: Notorious ex-Chicago Commander Charged with Lying About Torture," *Chicago Tribune,* October 22, 2008.

11. See chap. 6.

12. John Conroy, interview by author, March 15, 2023.

13. Conroy is also the author of *Belfast Diary: War As a Way of Life* (New York: Random House, 1988), about life in Northern Ireland during the Troubles.

14. John Conroy, interview by author.

15. Conroy, interview by author.

16. Conroy, interview by author.

17. John Conroy, "The Police Torture Scandals: A Who's Who," *Chicago Reader,* June 15, 2006.

Chapter 31. Two Systems

1. Duncan, interview by Cunningham.

2. Duncan, interview by Cunningham.

3. Stephanie Banchero, "Daley School Plan Fails to Make Grade: Renaissance 2010 Officials Defend Efforts to Upgrade Education over Last 6 Years," *Chicago Tribune,* January 17, 2010.

4. See chap. 18.

5. Ahmed Azam, Annie Sweeney, and Todd Lighty, "Chicago Grapples with Scott Suicide," *Chicago Tribune,* November 17, 2009.

6. Ron Huberman, interview by author, November 4, 2022.

7. Huberman, interview by author.

8. Huberman, interview by author.

9. Ahmed Azam, "Daley Outlines Plan for Longer School Day: 90-Minute Pilot Program Will Require Infrastructure Upgrades," *Chicago Tribune,* August 25, 2010.

10. "Kids Knock Off Early," editorial, *Chicago Tribune,* June 6, 2009.

11. Peter Cunningham, "What's Driving Chicago's School Turnaround Success? Lessons from 30 Years of Ed Reforms," *The 74,* January 16, 2018.

12. Emma Green, "Rahm Emanuel: 'I Am Not an Education Reformer,'" *The Atlantic,* July 3, 2015.

13. Karin Chenoweth, "In Chicago, Public Schools Are Often Called a Mess. Truth Is, They've Improved—a Lot," *Washington Post,* August 26, 2021.

14. Cunningham, "What's Driving Chicago's School Turnaround Success?"

Chapter 32. Transformation

1. David Brint, interview by author.

2. Brint, interview by author.

3. Brint, interview by author.

4. Brint, interview by author.

5. Mick Dumke, Tim Novak, Chris Fusco, and Brett Chase, "Daley's CHA Plan Jolted Region," Illinois Answers Project, June 25, 2016, https://illinoisanswers.org/2016/06/25/daleys-cha-plan-jolted-region/.

6. Dumke et al., "Daley's CHA Plan."

7. Dumke et al., "Daley's CHA Plan."

8.-Dumke et al., "Daley's CHA Plan."

9. Brett Chase, Chris Fusco, Tim Novak, and Mick Dumke, "CHA's Transformation Reshaped a City," Illinois Answers Project, June 25, 2016, https://illinoisanswers.org/2016/06/25/chas-transformation-reshaped-a-city/.

10. Chris Fusco, Tim Novak, Mick Dumke, and Brett Chase, "Public Housing Families Flee to Suburbs," Illinois Answers Project, June 25, 2016, https://illinoisanswers.org/2016/06/25/public-housing-families-flee-to-suburbs/.

11. Dumke et al., "Daley's CHA Plan."

12. "Mixed Income Developments: Creating the Foundation for Improved Communities and Lives," RW Ventures, March 28, 2007.

13. Horace R. Cayton and St. Clair Drake, *Black Metropolis* (London: Jonathan Cape, 1946), p. 379.

14. Nicholas Lemann, "The Origins of the Underclass," *The Atlantic,* June 1986.

15. John McCarron, "At Last, Bronzeville's 'Alleluia,'" *Chicago Tribune,* July 17, 2012.

16. Lukas Kugler, "Crane Permit Issued for 43 Green Phase 2," *Urbanize Chicago,* August 14, 2023.

17. "Chicago Betting Bronzeville Revival Here to Stay," *The Real Deal,* February 16, 2022.

18. "Officials Break Ground on Multi-Billion Dollar Development Project at Former Michael Reese Hospital Site," NBC 5 Chicago, March 29, 2023.

Chapter 33. Phenomenon

1. William Daley, interview by Peter Cunningham, February 21, 2018, Richard M. Daley Oral Histories, University of Illinois-Chicago, https://collections.carli.illinois.edu/digital/collection/uic_rmdoh/id/101/rec/8.

2. Barack Obama, 2004 Democratic National Convention Keynote Address, July 27, 2004, https://www.youtube.com/watch?v=eWynt87PaJ0.

Chapter 34. Parking Meters

1. Paul Volpe, interview by Peter Cunningham, November 1, 2017, Richard M. Daley Oral Histories, University of Illinois-Chicago, https://collections.carli.illinois.edu/digital/collection/uic_rmdoh/id/18/rec/43.

2. Volpe, interview by Cunningham.

3. Kathy Bergen and Philip Hersh, "Small Loss to Chicago Parking Meter Is a Big Deal to Driver," *Chicago Tribune*, December 15, 2009.

4. See chap. 35.

Chapter 35. Olympics

1. Gary Washburn, "Daley Considering Bid to Get 2016 Olympics," *Chicago Tribune*, July 27, 2005.

2. See chaps. 25 and 26.

3. Gary Washburn, "Mayor Expands Olympic Dream," *Chicago Tribune*, January 5, 2006.

4. One exception was the police union, which under state law cannot strike. To embarrass the mayor, officers picketed city hall during the 2009 IOC visit.

5. John Ahni Schertow, "Violence, Evictions, and Extrajudicial Killings Lead in the Pan Am Games 07," *Intercontinental Cry*, July 5, 2007.

6. Sam Cholke and Tanveer Ali, "Chicago's 2016 Olympics: What It Meant and Why It Didn't Happen," *DNA Info*, August 3, 2016.

7. See chap. 34 for a discussion of Daley's sale of the Chicago Skyway and Grant Park garages.

8. See chap. 34.

9. The Michael Reese site became a white elephant, sitting dormant until a 2022 real estate development.

10. The Nobel Peace Prize, 2009, Nobel Foundation, https://www.nobelprize.org/prizes/peace/2009/obama/facts/.

11. Kathy Bergen and Philip Hersh, "Flameout: Not Even the Bronze: Chicago's Shocking 1st-Round Exit in Vote for 2016 Olympics Is Rio's Dream Realized," *Chicago Tribune*, October 3, 2009.

12. Bergen and Hersh, "Flameout."

13. Adam Hayes, Game Theory, Investopedia, https://www.investopedia.com/terms/g/gametheory.asp

14. Bergen and Hersh, "Flameout."

15. Bergen and Hersh, "Flameout."

16. Robert A. Baade and Allen R. Sanderson, An Analysis of the Political Economy of Bidding for the Summer Olympic Games: Lessons from the Chicago 2016 Bid, University of Chicago, http://tinyurl.com/5e3s7urx.

17. Tariq Panja, "Olympic Official Who Delivered Rio Games Sentenced to 30 Years for Bribery," *New York Times*, November 26, 2021.

18. Tariq Panja, "Former Rio Governor Describes Extensive Bribery in Bid for 2016 Olympics," *New York Times*, July 5, 2019.

19. Whet Moser, "An Olympics in Chicago Would Have Been a Bad Idea," *Chicago* magazine, August 4, 2016.

20. In some ways, Daley's position was like that of the four-term New York governor Nelson Rockefeller as he watched Governor-elect Hugh Carey prepare to take over the state. In a story passed around among politicos over the years, Rockefeller purportedly

confided to a friend, "Hugh thinks it's going to be fun to be governor. But it's only fun if you have money. And I spent it all."

21. Jones, "Maggie Daley, Arts Eternally Bonded."

Epilogue

1. Ames Grawert, Matthew Friedman, and James Cullen, "Crime Trends: 1990–2016," Brennan Center for Justice, New York University School of Law, April 18, 2017, https://www.brennancenter.org/our-work/research-reports/crime-trends-1990-2016.

2. Andrew V. Papachristos, "48 Years of Crime in Chicago: A Descriptive Analysis of Serious Crime Trends from 1965 to 2013," Institution for Social and Policy Studies, Yale University, December 9, 2013, http://tinyurl.com/48n78bkh.

3. John Hagedorn, Bart Kmiecik, Dick Simpson, Thomas J. Gradel, Melissa Mouritsen Zmuda, David Sterret, et al., "Crime, Corruption and Cover-Ups in the Chicago Police Department," Anti-Corruption Report No. 7, University of Illinois-Chicago, January 17, 2013, https://pols.uic.edu/wp-content/uploads/sites/273/2018/10/ac_police corruptionb6e6.pdf. The report put more blame on the war on drugs, of which Daley had been an integral part since 1980. "Today, the major source of police corruption is the war on drugs. . . . [T]he strong demand for drugs means that many people will risk the dangers of trafficking. Violence will continue as a way to settle disputes. The large amounts of money involved mean that police corruption will remain endemic as long as current policies continue."

4. In 2019, Van Dyke was convicted of second-degree murder and sentenced to six years, nine months in prison.

5. Jeremy Gorner, "Morale, Policing Suffering in Hostile Climate, Cops Say," *Chicago Tribune,* November 27, 2016.

6. Gorner, "Morale, Policing Suffering."

7. Gorner, "Morale, Policing Suffering."

8. Gorner, "Morale, Policing Suffering."

9. Jeremy Gorner, "New Policy on Foot Pursuits Announced," *Chicago Tribune,* May 27, 2021.

10. Annie Sweeney, "Chicago Reached at Least 800 Homicides in 2021, a Level Not Seen in 25 Years," *Chicago Tribune,* January 3, 2022.

11. John M. Hagedorn, Robert Aspholm, Teresa Cordova, Andrew V. Papachristos, and Lance Williams, "Chicago's Gangs Have Changed. Our Violence Intervention Strategies Should Too," *Chicago Reporter,* April 16, 2019. The authors write: "Over the last ten years, the Chicago Police Department cleared the fewest homicides per capita than any other major city in the U.S."

12. Claire Malon and Sam Charles, "Wave of Violence a Grim Reminder: Illinois and Chicago Routinely Rank among Nation's Worst for Mass Shootings," *Chicago Tribune,* January 28, 2024. The authors note: "At a rate of one mass shooting every 11 days, no other city in the country even comes close. The next three cities combined didn't have as many in the same period. In fact, if Chicago were a state, it would rank only behind California in total mass events across the decade."

13. Gorner, "Morale, Policing Suffering."

14. Sarah Karp, "The COVID-19 Pandemic Thwarts Years of Academic Improvement for Chicago Students," WBEZ Chicago, October 24, 2022, http://tinyurl.com/mppk6xwa.

15. Hannah Leone, "CPS to Take Back 'Turnaround' Schools: Controversial Program That Saw Schools Shift to Private Operators and Teachers Fired Is Being Dismantled," *Chicago Tribune,* May 28, 2021.

16. Sarah Karp, "Chicago Drops Public School Ratings in Favor of a Less Punitive System for Assessing Schools," *Chicago Sun-Times*, April 26, 2023.

17. Karp, "Chicago Drops Public School Ratings."

18. Sarah Macaraeg, "Chicago Board of Ed Votes to Shift Priorities from School Choice to Neighborhood Schools," *Chicago Tribune*, December 14, 2023. Of the more than fifty-four thousand children attending public charter schools, 96 percent are Black and Latino, and 86 percent are from low-income households. Of the more than twelve thousand students attending magnet schools, more than 70 percent are Black and Latino, and a majority are from low-income families. Paul Vallas, "Opinion: The Battle over School Choice Reveals Racism at Work—But Not in the Way Most Might Think," *Crain's Chicago Business*, December 20, 2023.

19. Sarah Karp, "Brandon Johnson's Board of Ed Looks to Move Away from School Choice, Toward Neighborhood Schools," *Chicago Sun-Times*, December 12, 2023.

20. Macaraeg, "Chicago Board of Ed Votes to Shift Priorities."

21. *Sun-Times* Staff, "THE WATCHDOGS: CTU Allies Benefit from Newly Enriched Union Foundation," June 24, 2016.

22. "Be Very Afraid for Chicago's Stellar Selective-Enrollment Schools," editorial, *Chicago Tribune*, December 13, 2023. The *Tribune* wrote: "If you genuinely desire community input to guide and inform you, then you present the issue to the community without bias and solicit views. You don't state the policy and try to get it passed in spirit by a governing body *first*. And then see what 'the community' wants to do. And then act *surprised and shocked* if 'the community' aligns with the goals of the Chicago Teachers Union. Even some former Soviet apparatchiks would have blushed at that brazen tactic."

23. Sarah Karp, "Chicago Teachers Union President Defends Sending Her Son to Private School," *Chicago Sun-Times*, September 7, 2023.

24. Janice Jackson, "Gutting school choice in Chicago would be terrible for Black, Brown students," *Chicago Sun-Times*, Dec. 18, 2023.

25. Samantha Smylie and Cara Fitzpatrick, "Many States Are Moving toward Private School Choice. Illinois Is Letting Its Program Lapse," *Chalkbeat Chicago*, November 14, 2023.

26. "Daley Still Upset at Wal-Mart Resistance," CBS News Chicago, March 17, 2011.

27. Evan Osnos, "The Daley Show," *New Yorker*, March 8, 2010.

28. "Chicago Pension Debt Rises to $35 Billion as Mayor Hunts for Fix," *Crain's Chicago Business*, July 3, 2023.

29. Hannah Schmid, "Chicago Public Schools Spends 55% More on 20% Fewer Students Since 2010," *Illinois Policy*, January 10, 2023, http://tinyurl.com/yuv7xmyf.

30. Pritzker signed two bills, one sweetening benefits for firefighters in 2022, and another for police in 2023, increasing Chicago pension liabilities by $3.85 billion. A. D. Quig, "Pritzker Deals Another Blow to Lightfoot with Signing of Firefighter Pension Bill," *Crain's Chicago Business*, April 5, 2021; Adam Schuster, "Bill to Boost Chicago Police Pensions Would Cost Taxpayers $3 Billion," *Illinois Policy*, March 9, 2022. Chicago firefighter and police pensions are funded at 19 percent and 23 percent, respectively. City Council Office of Financial Analysis, "Overview of the Firemen's Annuity and Benefit Fund & The Policemen's Annuity and Benefit Fund of Chicago," May 13, 2022.

31. Justin Carlson, "Chicago Has Second Highest Commercial Property Taxes in U.S.," *Illinois Policy*, July 7, 2023, http://tinyurl.com/2t98ssst.

32. Alysa Guffey, "Shop Owners Targeted by Smash-and-Grab Burglars Want Solutions: 'We Just Got to Hope That Our City Can Do Better,'" *Chicago Tribune*, December 30, 2023.

33. See chap. 7.

34. Fran Spielman, "LaSalle Street Revamp Threatened by Johnson's Plan to Declare Record $434M TIF Surplus, City Council Members Say," *Chicago Sun-Times,* October 18, 2023.

35. Eric Zorn, "Deal's Off! Time for Emanuel to Name and Shame Daley," *Chicago Tribune*, May 3, 2018.

36. Zorn, "Deal's Off!"

37. See chap. 35.

38. Civic Federation, The State of Illinois Retirement Systems: Funding History and Reform Proposals, October 26, 2006, https://www.civicfed.org/sites/default/files /civicfed_220.pdf. In 2006, the Chicago municipal, laborers, teachers, and park district pension funds were approximately 65, 90, 79, and 75 percent funded, respectively. Civic Federation, Status of Local Pension Funding 2009: An Evaluation of Ten Local Government Employee Pension Funds in Cook County, February 10, 2011, http://tinyurl .com/37xuwufx.

39. Insider deals also affected state pension funds. In one particularly egregious early retirement deal for state employees, Gov. George Ryan's plan was so generous that 11,372 employees participated, exceeding the anticipated new pension fund liabilities by hundreds of millions of dollars. Ray Long, *The House That Madigan Built*, p. 107–8.

40. Ironically, the inflation unleashed by Biden's $1.9 *trillion* stimulus could help "solve" the pension crisis by inflating government revenue and devaluing dollars paid to retirees.

41. "The Turnaround Pro," editorial, *Chicago Tribune,* July 17, 2015.

42. The Jenner & Block team included two former US Supreme Court clerks. David Debruin had clerked for Justice John Paul Stevens and Matt Price for Justice Stephen Breyer.

43. Chicago Urban League vs. Illinois State Board of Education, Settlement Agreement, Circuit Court of Cook County, February 17, 2017.

44. Jenner & Block provided more than a million dollars in free legal services during the case.

45. Jeremy Gorner, "With Chicago Slipping toward Chaos amid George Floyd Protests, Report Outlines How Police and City Leaders Missed Signs Unrest Was Escalating and Botched Response," *Chicago Tribune,* February 20, 2021.

46. Chenoweth, "In Chicago, Public Schools Are Often Called a Mess."

47. Annalee Newitz, "Americans Don't Know What Urban Collapse Really Looks Like," *The Atlantic,* January 31, 2021.

48. Fran Spielman, "A Legacy Secured," *Chicago Sun-Times,* May 15, 2011.

49. Spielman, "A Legacy Secured."

50. Spielman, "A Legacy Secured."

51. Proverbs 29:18.

52. In September 2021, the Chicago Bears purchased a 326-acre former racetrack site in suburban Arlington Heights from Churchill Downs Corporation for $197 million to build a new stadium, a development made possible by the unsophisticated leadership of Chicago's then mayor, Lori Lightfoot. Mayors Daley and Emanuel, with their Rolodexes of powerful business leaders and financiers, would never have allowed such a unique property to fall into the hands of the cash-constrained team's owners, the McCaskey family.

53. Rebecca Frankel, "The Global Cities Index," *Foreign Policy,* September/October 2010, pp. 124–25, https://foreignpolicy.com/2010/08/11/the-global-cities-index-2010/.

Index

Connor, Bart, 281
Conroy, John, 251
Consortium on Chicago School Research, 223–24
Contract with America, 80
Conway, Bill, 293
Cook County Juvenile Detention Center, 235–36, 242–43
Corcoran, Ed, 46
Corcoran, Jerry, 46
Cosa Nostra, 40
Coughlin, John, 140
Council Wars, 9–13, 32, 297
Cousins, William, 202
Coventry, Dale, 23
COVID pandemic, 290
Crain's Chicago Business, 79, 188
Crawford, Bob, 32
crime, 49–50, 122, 296; broken windows theory and, 100–103; Citizen Law Enforcement Analysis and Reporting (CLEAR) and, 145–46, 247; gangs, 90, 99–104, 142–49; organized, 39–40, 142; public housing and, 165–67, 263–64
Crist, Peter D., 119
Crown, Lester, 160–61, 188
Csontos, Sally, 92
Cullerton, Patricia, 175, 231
Cunningham, Peter, 37
Cuomo, Andrew, 169–71
Curry, Donald, 266

Daily Herald, 245
Daily Southtown, 245
Daley, Bill, 4, 27–28, 32, 35, 77, 79, 155, 269
Daley, John, 42, 175, 181, 209, 213–14, 219; Cook County government, 228, 230, 232
Daley, Kevin, 15, 19
Daley, Maggie, 15, 27–28, 35, 65–66, *106, 194,* 285; After School Matters (ASM) program and, 157–58, 225
Daley, Michael, 62
Daley, Richard J., 3, 5, 10, *105,* 143, 206–7, 208; career ladder, 14; death of, 15; Hamburg Athletic Club and, 21; pier renovation under, 41; violent incidents against African Americans near home of, 21–22
Daley, Richard M., *105–9, 191–95;* blamed for Washington's ascent, 10; changes in media coverage of, 294; Chicago police

abuses and, 23–24; Council Wars and, 9–13, 32, 297; election loss to Harold Washington, 10, 27; first administration of (*see* Daley administration, first term); focus on drugs and violent crime as state's attorney, 18–20, 99; Great Recession and, 275–77; legacy of, 287–98; McPier and, 40–42, 44; personal traumas of, 15; persona of, 3–4; reelection campaign for state attorney, 3–4; second campaign for mayor, 4–5 (*see also* Daley mayoral campaign, 1989); support for abortion rights, 53–54; unique leadership of, xiv, xiv-xv; as visionary, 296–98
Daley, Sis, 65
Daley administration, fifth term: city truck scandal during, 211–13; Cook County government corruption and, 228–36; Cook County health care system during, 243–45; Cook County Juvenile Detention Center and, 235–36, 242–43; county office building fire during, 203–5; crime and policing during, 246–51; E2 nightclub disaster during, 201–2; forest preserves and, 229–31; hired truck contracts scandal during, 213–15; hiring fraud and, 216–22; Hispanic Democratic Organization (HDO) scandal and, 209–11, 214, 215, 219; Lincoln Park apartment collapse during, 202–3; police reforms during, 248–51; political tools used in, 220–22; popularity and power of Daley during, 206; property taxes and values during, 231–33; Renaissance 2010 during, 223–27; Windy City Maintenance scandal in, 208–9
Daley administration, first term: agenda of, 40–42; casinos and, 58–60; crime and, 49–50; Feb 14 blizzard and, 50–51; Forrest Claypool in, 44–49; homelessness addressed in, 47–49; independent agencies during, 37; Inquiry and Information agency during, 45; majority-minority cabinet of, 37–38; neighborhood cleanliness addressed in, 45–47; offices of, 38–39; playing to the margins in, 51–54; statewide job-creating projects and, 40–41; tax-increment financing districts (TIFs) and, 60–67; team assembled for, 36–37, 44

Daley administration, fourth term: aviation issues during, 159–62; Claypool's involvement in politics during, 172–82; education reforms during, 155–57; final city council meeting of, *195*; Millennium Park and, 183–90; popularity and power of Daley during, 172–73; public housing reforms during, 163–71; test score issues and, 153–55

Daley administration, second term: Community Alternative Policing Strategy (CAPS) and, 101–4; gang and drug problems during, 90, 99–104; Gary, Indiana airport agreement and, 80–82; heat wave of 1995 as black swan in, 71–74; neighborhood planning during, 83–87; 1992 flood as black swan in, 68–71; O'Hare Airport and, 75–82; parks and recreation areas during, 88–98; Third Airport planning in, 75–78

Daley administration, sixth term: announced as Daley's last term, 259; election of Barack Obama as president during, 269–77; public housing development during, 261–67; school reforms during, 256–59; 2016 summer Olympics and, 278–85

Daley administration, third term: Auburn Gresham neighborhood during, 120–21; Chicago Loop during, 113; Democratic National Committee convention during, 114, 117–19; gangs and gun crimes and, 142–49; Illinois Institute of Technology and, 121–22; marijuana legalization and, 136–37; Michael Jordan and, 113–14; Millennium Park projects during, 138–41; Northerly Island and, 132–37; real estate development during, 114–17; school reforms during, 124–31

Daley mayoral campaign, 1989, 22, 28–35; business community and, 30; Daley's advertising in, 32; Daley's hesitancy to enter, 27–28; Daley's key advisers in, 28–30; Daley's victory in, 35; door to door campaigning in, 34–35; Eugene Sawyer and, 12, 27, 32–35; fundraising by Daley in, 30–31; media coverage of, 32–34; Press Secretary Marj Halperin and, 33–34; racial themes in, 34; Rahm Emanuel and, 30–31; state of Chicago in 1989 and, xiii, 32

Daniels, Lee, 125
Daniels, Serena, 147–48
D'Arco, John, 16
Dardick, Hal, 245
Davis, Danny, 54
Davis, Dantrell, 99
Davis, Wallace, 12
DeAngelis, Aldo, 76, 78–80
Degnan, Francis, 29
Degnan, Robert, 29
Degnan, Tim, 29–30, 35–37, 40, 42; Chicago Parks and, 89, 97; scandals and, 210, 211, 215, 221–22
Dellimore, Craig, 32
del Valle, Miguel, 126
Democratic National Convention, 1968, 6
Democratic National Convention, 1996, 114, 117–19, *191*, 278
Demuzio, Vince, 42
DeNard, Ron, 96
Dennis, Richard, 30, 173
Devine, Richard, 89, 203–4
Diack, Lamine, 283
Disraeli, Benjamin, 240
Dixon, Alan, 45
Dodge Academy, 255–56
Doerr, John, 179
Dold, Bruce, 233–34, 245
Donoghue. Edmund, 73–74
Doria, Helen, 91
Downtown flood, 1992, 68–71
Drake, St. Clair, 265
Duchossis, Craig, 121–22
Dudycz, Walter, 43
Duff, Jack, Jr., 39–40, 208–9
Duff, James, 208
Duff, Patricia Green, 39–40
Duncan, Arne, 155–56, 223–27, 255–56
Duncan, Karen, 155
Dunlap, Earl, 243
Dunn, Tom, 42
Durbin, Dick, 30

Easton, John, 223, 226
Education Research Council of SIU, 224
Egan, Edward, 249
Edgar, Jim, 43, 58–59, 77–79, 124, 130, 134
education. *See* Chicago Public Schools (CPS)
Edwards, John, 272

Obama, Barack, 3, 177, *194,* 222, 238–39, 281; Bobby Rush and, 269; Claypool's work with, 270–71; David Axelrod and, 270; Dodge Academy and, 255–56; elected president, 273; Great Recession and, 274–77; on the Iraq War, 272; on legacy of Richard M. Daley, 297; speech to the Democratic National Convention in Boston, 271–72
Obama, Michelle, *194,* 270–71, 281
O'Brien, Adrienne, 231
Obrycka, Karolina, 248
Ociepka, Frank, 70
Ogden, William, 206
O'Grady, Sheila, 162, 171
O'Hare Airport, 75–82; capacity at, 75; Congressional interest in, 161; corporate interest in expanding, 160–61; as major hub, 75, 159; Modernization Program (OMP), 161–62; proposal for third Chicago airport to alleviate traffic at, 76–79; Republican control of state government and, 80–81; studies of, 76
Olajuwon, Hakeem, 113
Olmsted, Fredrick Law, 88
Olmsted, Rob, 245
Olympics, 2016 summer, 278–85, 293
Operation Greylord, 18–19
Operation PUSH, 12, 20
organized crime, 39–40, 142
Outliers, 91
Owens, Jesse, 281

Palestine Liberation Organization (PLO), 30
Palin, Sarah, 272
Pallasch, Abdon, 230, 245
Pang, Sarah, 45, 62–63, 72–74, 101, 118, 143
parking meter equipment, 275–77
Park Kids program, 92
Patterson, Steve, 245
Patton, George, 122
Patton, Steve, 202
Peña, Michi, 211
Penn, Robert, 88–89, 97
Peotone, 78–79
Peraica, Tony, 233, 242
Percy, Charles, 3
Peters, Tom, 49
Peterson, Terry, 120–21, 171
Pfleger, Michael, 120, 137
Phelan, Dick, 53

Philip, James "Pate," 42–43, 59–60, 78, 124
Piano, Renzo, 189
Plan for Transformation, 168–71, 261–67
Plensa, Jaume, 188, *193*
police, Chicago, 22–24, 50; broken windows theory and, 100–101; Citizen Law Enforcement Analysis and Reporting (CLEAR) and, 145–46, 247; Community Alternative Policing Strategy (CAPS), 101–4; Daley's legacy regarding, 293–94; gang problem and, 142–49; Orlando Wilson and reform of, 248–51; Phil Cline and, 246–47; Ramsey and Hillard and, 142–49, 246; recent reforms to, 288–90; scandals involving, 247–48; shooting of Laquon McDonald by, 288
Porter, Rachelle, 230
Powell, Colin, 103
Pritzker, Cindy, 187
Pritzker, J. B., 291–92
Pritzker, Robert, 122
property values and taxes, 231–33, 294
Provident Hospital, 228, 237, 243–44
public health, 243–45
public housing/Chicago Housing Authority (CHA), 7, 122, *193;* Bronzeville neighborhood, 264–67; drop in number of people living in, 263; effects of the Great Recession on, 262, 264; Plan for Transformation in, 168–71, 261–67; post-war expansion of, 163–66; safety of, 165–67, 263–64; successes in, 267
public schools. *See* Chicago Public Schools

Quad Communities Development Corporation, 266
Quigley, Mike, 229, 233–35
Quinn, Patrick, 89, 238, 292

Raba, John, 22
racial divisions in Chicago politics, 5–12, 240–41
Radner, Barbara, 256
Raica, Robert, 43
Ramsey, Charles, 100, 142–43
Ranney, George, 140
Ranney, Vicky, 140
Reagan, Ronald, 17, 18, 19, 60, 79, 124, 274
Reardon, Sean, 259
Recktenwald, William, 88
Reidy, Bridget, 136, 171, 184
Rein, Irving, 4

FORREST CLAYPOOL has served as the Chief Executive Officer of the Chicago Park District (1993–1998), the Chicago Transit Authority (2011–2015), and the Chicago Public Schools (2015–2017). He was the chief of staff to Mayor Richard M. Daley in his first and third terms.

The University of Illinois Press is a founding member of the Association of University Presses.

———————————————

Composed in 11.5/13 Garamond Premier Pro
with Gotham display
by Kirsten Dennison
at the University of Illinois Press
Manufactured by Sheridan Books, Inc.

University of Illinois Press
1325 South Oak Street
Champaign, IL 61820-6903
www.press.uillinois.edu